LANGUAGE, LINGUISTICS
AND MIDDLE ENGLISH LITERATURE

LANGUAGE, LINGUISTICS AND MIDDLE ENGLISH LITERATURE

ESSAYS IN HONOR OF KARLA TAYLOR

Edited by
Elizabeth Allen and Catherine Sanok

D. S. BREWER

© Contributors 2025

All Rights Reserved. Except as permitted under current legislation
no part of this work may be photocopied, stored in a retrieval system,
published, performed in public, adapted, broadcast,
transmitted, recorded or reproduced in any form or by any means,
without the prior permission of the copyright owner

First published 2025
D. S. Brewer, Cambridge

ISBN 978 1 84384 739 7

D. S. Brewer is an imprint of Boydell & Brewer Ltd
PO Box 9, Woodbridge, Suffolk IP12 3DF, UK
and of Boydell & Brewer Inc.
668 Mt Hope Avenue, Rochester, NY 14620–2731, USA
website: www.boydellandbrewer.com

A CIP catalogue record for this book is available
from the British Library

The publisher has no responsibility for the continued existence or accuracy
of URLs for external or third-party internet websites referred to in this book,
and does not guarantee that any content on such websites is, or will remain,
accurate or appropriate

CONTENTS

    List of Illustrations   vii
    List of Contributors   viii
    Acknowledgements   xi
    List of Abbreviations   xii

I: INTRODUCTION: LANGUAGE MATTERS

1   Karla Taylor's Philology   3
    Elizabeth Allen

2   Recent Methods and the Persistence of Philology   18
    Catherine Sanok

II: THE SPECIAL AFFORDANCES OF LITERARY TEXTS FOR THE HISTORY OF ENGLISH

3   Borrowed Suffixes in Late Middle English Poetry: Multilingualism, Decomposability, and End-Rhyme Architecture   41
    Chris C. Palmer

4   *Congregation* or *Coven*: Talking about Civic Assembly in Middle English   73
    Colette Moore

III: THE LEXIS OF MIDDLE ENGLISH LITERATURE

5   Overcome by Words: Supplementarity and Advisory Ethics in the Tale of *Melibee*   95
    David Lavinsky

vi CONTENTS

6 Buddha and the Grail: Speaking of the Unstable World in *Barlam and Iosaphat* and Malory's *Le Morte Darthur*   117
  Kenneth Hodges

IV: THE AESTHETICS OF LANGUAGE IN MIDDLE ENGLISH LITERATURE

7 Facing the Reeve: Reason, Resonance, and the Tragedy of the Local in the *Canterbury Tales*   143
  Stephanie L. Batkie

8 "Borne to Blisse": Souls in Flight and (In)Authentic Vision in Chaucer's *Canterbury Tales*   170
  Ashby Kinch

V: LANGUAGE BETWEEN TEXTS: INTERTEXTUALITY ON THE LEVEL OF LANGUAGE

9 Treason and the Royal Person: Chaucer to John Lane   193
  Andreea Boboc

10 Tears of Survival: Myrrha and Criseyde   216
  Elizabeth Allen

Karla Taylor's Published Writing   243

Index   245

Tabula Gratulatoria   258

ILLUSTRATIONS

3. Borrowed Suffixes in Late Middle English Poetry: Multilingualism, Decomposability, and End-Rhyme Architecture, *Chris C. Palmer*

Fig. 3.1: Occurrences of tokens of each suffix for every 10,000 words	54
Fig. 3.2: Lexical density scores, measured as number of suffix types per 10,000 words	56
Table 3.1: Absolute frequencies of suffix types for each poet, with numbers normalized to occurrences per 10,000 words in parentheses	53
Table 3.2: Total number of types for each poet	55
Table 3.3: Examples of *-cion* lexemes from different lexical fields	58
Table 3.4a: End-rhyme percentages for Chaucer	61
Table 3.4b: End-rhyme percentages for Gower	62
Table 3.4c: End-rhyme percentages for Hoccleve	62
Table 3.4d: End-rhyme percentages for Lydgate	62

4. *Congregation* or *Coven*: Talking about Civic Assembly in Middle English, *Colette Moore*

Fig. 4.1: Semantic field of GATHERING, ASSEMBLY	80
Table 4.1: Words in the ME semantic field of GATHERING, ASSEMBLY	78
Table 4.2: Occurrences of GATHERING, ASSEMBLY words in *MED*, *CMEPV*	79

CONTRIBUTORS

Elizabeth Allen is Professor of English at the University of California, Irvine. She is the author of *False Fables and Exemplary Truth* (2005) and *Uncertain Refuge: Sanctuary in Medieval English Literature* (2021). Her most recent essays are "Emaré/Egaré: Sanctuary, Exile, and Romance" (*Social Research*, 2024) and "Medieval Sanctuary, Gothic Entrapment, and the Fugitive Self in Colson Whitehead's *The Underground Railroad*" (*postmedieval*, 2023). She is co-editor of a 2023 special issue of *Exemplaria* on "Spaces and Times of Crisis," and her work on Chaucer, Gower, romance, and sanctuary appears in *JMEMS*, *New Medieval Literatures*, *Speculum*, *Studies in the Age of Chaucer*, and elsewhere.

Stephanie L. Batkie is a Teaching Professor of English and the Director of Writing Across the Curriculum at the University of the South. Her research focuses on the relationship between political aesthetics and poetic forms of the later Middle Ages, with a particular focus on the role Anglo-Latin texts played in shaping political subjectivity in the medieval period and beyond. Her work has appeared recently in *The Southern Atlantic Review*, *The Yearbook of Langland Studies*, the *Chaucer Review*, and in a number of edited collections. She is also a co-editor of *A New Companion to Critical Thinking on Chaucer* (2021).

Andreea Boboc is a fiction writer and Associate Professor of medieval literature at the University of the Pacific in Stockton, California. She is the author of "Work and the Legal Person in Thomas More's *Utopia*" (*University of the Pacific Law Review*, 2016) and the editor of *Theorizing Legal Personhood in Late Medieval England* (2015).

Kenneth Hodges, Professor of English at Virginia Tech, specializes in literature of King Arthur. He has published two books, *Forging Chivalric Communities in Malory's Morte Darthur* (2005) and *Mapping Malory: Regional Identities and National Geographies in Le Morte Darthur* (co-author Dorsey Armstrong,

2014), and he is finishing *How Spenser Reformed Malory*. Recent articles include "How Galahad Regained his Virginity: Nineteenth-Century Responses to Malory's Catholic Grail" (*Arthurian Literature*, 2023) and "Spenser, Malory, and Regionalism in Arthurian Literature" (*The Arthurian World*, ed. Victoria Coldham-Fussell, Renée Ward, and Miriam Edlich-Muth, 2022).

Ashby Kinch is Vice Provost and Dean of the Graduate School at the University of New Hampshire. He is the author of a book-length study of the late medieval art and literature of dying, *Imago Mortis: Mediating Images of Death in late Medieval Culture* (2013). He edited the medieval volume (800–1450) in the Bloomsbury series *A Cultural History of Death* (2024). He has published several articles on the European influence of Alain Chartier along with an edited collection, *Chartier in Europe* (2008), and articles on Chaucer and visual culture.

David Lavinsky is Associate Professor of English at Yeshiva University in New York City. His research explores late medieval contexts for vernacular religious writing, biblical translation, and the history of the book, with a focus on the cultural production of John Wyclif and the Lollards. He is the author of *The Material Text in Wycliffite Biblical Scholarship: Inscription and Sacred Truth* (2017). His current project is a book-length study of Middle English devotional writing and communities of practice in fifteenth-century London.

Colette Moore is Associate Professor of English at the University of Washington. She teaches and writes about the English language and its history, particularly in the fields of historical pragmatics, historical sociolinguistics, historical stylistics, and the history of standardization. Her books include *Quoting Speech in Early English* (2011) and a co-edited teaching volume, *Teaching the History of the English Language* (co-editor Chris C. Palmer, 2019). Her recent publications have focused on information structure and information design in Middle English manuscripts, and she is working on a project about the history of standardizing processes in English.

Chris C. Palmer is Professor of English at Kennesaw State University. He has written multiple articles on historical English morphology including "Measuring productivity diachronically: Nominal suffixes in English letters, 1400–1600" (*English Language and Linguistics*, 2015) and "The History of -eer in English: Suffix Competition or Symbiosis?" (co-author Zachary Dukic, *Languages*, 2024). His recent books include *Teaching the History of the English Language* (co-editor Colette Moore, 2019), *Teaching Language Variation in the Classroom* (co-editor Michelle D. Devereaux, 2019), and *Teaching English Language Variation in the Global Classroom* (co-editor Michelle D. Devereaux, 2021).

Catherine Sanok is a Professor of English and (by courtesy) Women and Gender Studies at the University of Michigan. Her research explores premodern concepts and experiences of history, temporality, and community. She is the author of *Her Life Historical: Exemplarity and Saints' Lives in Late Medieval England* (2007) and *New Legends of England: Forms of Community in the Late Middle Ages* (2018), and co-editor of *The Medieval Literary: Beyond Form* (2018). She is currently working on a book about the solar day as a geosocial temporality in late medieval literature.

ACKNOWLEDGEMENTS

Exemplary teacher, meticulous scholar, generous mentor and colleague, Karla Taylor devoted her career to showing how close attention to language, in ordinary and artful use, clarifies complex relationships between persons, institutions, and political structures, and how it can illuminate the role and potential of imaginative literature as a forum for social change. Her former students gather in this volume as tribute to Karla and demonstration of the ongoing influence of her work.

This gathering took its first form as a panel at the 57th International Congress of Medieval Studies in May, 2022. We thank the participants – who included Anne Curzan and Susan Nakley as well as the contributors to this volume – for the contribution their research made to our understanding of Karla's methodological commitment to the intersection of linguistics and literary scholarship. Our thanks also to the audience, including Karla herself, for a vigorous discussion of how language matters. We are also grateful to the University of Michigan's Department of English Language and Literature, who supported in-person conviviality and celebration of Karla's career to complement the virtual panel.

Caroline Palmer offered early support for this volume and expert guidance in seeing it to press. We are grateful for helpful feedback from the press's two readers, especially for suggestions concerning the structure of the two introductory essays. Kelly Rafferty's timely and professional editorial assistance is also greatly appreciated.

With all the contributors to this volume, we honor Karla Taylor for her forceful and lapidary written oeuvre and for her rigorous, playful, and committed teaching.

ABBREVIATIONS

ME   Middle English

CMEPV   *Corpus of Middle English Prose and Verse*. Online in *Middle English Compendium*, ed. Frances McSparran et al. (Ann Arbor: University of Michigan Library, 2000–18), http://quod.lib.umich.edu/m/middle-english-dictionary/

MED   *Middle English Dictionary*, ed. Robert E. Lewis et al. (Ann Arbor: University of Michigan Press, 1952–2001). Online edition in *Middle English Compendium*, ed. Frances McSparran et al. (Ann Arbor: University of Michigan Library, 2000–18), http://quod.lib.umich.edu/m/middle-english-dictionary/

OED   *Oxford English Dictionary*, ed. Herbert Coleridge et al. (Oxford: Oxford University Press, 1858–2013), ed. Michael Proffitt et al., 3rd ed. (Oxford: Oxford University Press, 2013–), https://www.oed.com

PMLA   *Publications of the Modern Language Association*

PART I

INTRODUCTION: LANGUAGE MATTERS

1

Karla Taylor's Philology

ELIZABETH ALLEN

This book is about matters of language and about how language matters. Karla Taylor has taught her students to appreciate the *matter* of language: the ways language is materially apprehended, the sheer intricacy of linguistic patterning, and the relation between language's literal meanings and its literary, social, and historical figurations. With characteristic intensity, she has also taught us that such study of language *matters*. She has always articulated a varied and deeply ethical sense of its value and purpose for students and, indeed, for any readers.

We bring together some of Taylor's former students both to recognize her influence on the field of Middle English studies through her graduate teaching and mentorship and to explore the current intersection of two disciplines that Taylor's pedagogy brings together: literary study and linguistics. The work of Taylor's students is gathered in this volume to illuminate the utility of imaginative literature for historical linguistics and the provocation that the etymological, semantic, and phonological capacities of literary lexicons offer a critical understanding of Middle English literature and its social significance. The volume's project suggests the currency of Taylor's approach in our disciplinary moment. As Catherine Sanok proposes in the second chapter of this book, current methods in both fields lay the groundwork for a newly productive relationship between socio-linguistics and literary analysis because they share an interest in how language matters, both to a text's avowed projects and as evidence of its reciprocal relation to the social worlds in which it is produced and received.

If Karla Taylor works at the intersection of literature and linguistics, the name that she has often given their combination is "philology" – a method that she has stubbornly or apologetically announced as hers regardless of fashion, explicitly in her teaching and implicitly in her written oeuvre. Etymologically the "love of language" or "love of words," philology is reflexively assumed to have been long superseded by psychoanalytic, historicist, and other methods. Yet if Taylor has always understood declaring herself a philologist to be slightly perverse, her insistence now seems prescient: not only generative, but current. As Sanok points out, more recent discussions about language-forward literary methods like "surface reading" versus the "hermeneutics of suspicion" have (re)turned to the value of affective and immediate responses, advocating practices of description and attendance to the linguistic surfaces of literary texts as opposed to reading language as a set of symptoms that express hidden psychic or ideological content. Sanok argues that such methods bear a significant resemblance to Karla Taylor's philology: to her scholarly practices of description, accounts of readerly desire, and attention to linguistic surfaces. Taylor's work provides an occasion to think afresh about the storied term "philology" in ways that acknowledge its methodological staying power and help us see its relevance to new literary and linguistic approaches like those collected in this volume.

To survey Karla Taylor's work is to encounter her incisive powers of observation, her focus on linguistic details, and her capacity to track down the logic of the way language shapes both authorial and readerly desire. In *Chaucer Reads 'The Divine Comedy'*, her germinal book on Chaucer's response to Dante, observations about point of view and verb tense ground a complex analysis of the ways in which each author differently authenticates the world he creates.[1] In a series of dense and lapidary essays written over the course of her career, she almost always begins with a linguistic detail. In one essay, the use of doublets and puns creates contrasting social aesthetics, while in another, verbs of perception identify subjectivity, and in others, rhyme words play with cultural presupposition and appropriation. Such expansive attention to different linguistic features and their social effects recognizes the contingencies of language in use: not only are different literary texts occupied with different linguistic operations by virtue of their discursive and social concerns, but the very function of literary language – as much as ordinary language – depends on linguistic qualities, geographical locus, and political situation.

Taylor's study of linguistics begins with the work of historical linguist Émile Benveniste, whose approach to problems of narration and subjectivity grounds her analysis of the connections between certain linguistic forms (pronouns, or adverbs of place and time like "here" and "now") and the relative intimacy or distance among author, character, narrator, and reader.[2] Taylor's thinking about what we might call the "mismatch" or failure of absolute correspondence between intention and effect (author and reader, event

---

[1] Karla Taylor, *Chaucer Reads 'The Divine Comedy'* (Palo Alto: Stanford University Press, 1989).

[2] Émile Benveniste, *Problèmes de linguistique générale* (Paris: Gallimard, 1966). See also Taylor, "Introduction," in *Chaucer Reads*, 3–19 (at 5–6).

and story) later drew on the work of the Prague linguistic circle, including Roman Jakobson, Jan Mukařovský for the social dimension of art, and the Russian semioticist Sergei Karcevskij for a linguistic account of the inevitable sonic as well as semantic ingredients of linguistic miscommunication. Her intellectual kinship with this group of thinkers should come as no surprise, since the Prague School included scholars of both linguistics and literature who claimed a broad, shared interest in philology, albeit today we associate them more with either linguistics as a discipline or literary theory.[3] Like Prague School scholars, Taylor practices a philology primarily interested in historical languages that extends well beyond etymological determinism: her work demonstrates that describing the linguistic features of historical texts has ethical, affective, and socio-political entailments – particularly around gender and social status – and that philological methods can exhibit not just historical sensitivity, but also ideological flexibility and a capacity for self-critique.

Taylor's interest in linguistic systems and the ordinary communicative function of language continued and deepened throughout her career. That said, her work is focused on specifically literary texts: indeed, her writing on Dante and Chaucer illuminates a fundamental argument between the two poets about the spiritual versus temporal purview of poetry *per se*. In later work, Taylor shows that this argument hinges on a linguistic disagreement that is inflected by the status of literary tradition in English versus Italian languages.[4] Often, she makes her analysis accessible by invoking ordinary language functions; for instance, she describes an error in conventional presupposition

---

[3] Jan Mukařovský, *Aesthetic Function, Norm and Value as Social Facts*, trans. Mark E. Suino (Ann Arbor: University of Michigan Press, 1970); cited in Karla Taylor, "Social Aesthetics and the Emergence of Civic Discourse from the *Shipman's Tale* to *Melibee*," *Chaucer Review* 39.3 (2005), 298–322 (at 300). Sergei Karcevskij, "Du dualisme asymétrique du signe linguistique," *Travaux du Cercle linguistique de Prague* 1 (1929), 88–92; translated by Wendy Steiner as "The Asymmetric Dualism of the Linguistic Sign," in *The Prague School: Selected Writings, 1929–1946*, ed. Peter Steiner (Austin: University of Texas Press, 1982), 47–54; cited in Karla Taylor, "Chaucer's Volumes: Toward a New Model of Literary History in the *Canterbury Tales*," *Studies in the Age of Chaucer* 29 (2007), 43–85 (at 81), and in "The Motives of Reeds: The Wife of Bath's Midas and Literary Tradition," in *Later Middle English Literature, Materiality, and Culture: Essays in Honor of James M. Dean*, ed. Brian Gastle and Erick Kelemen (Newark: University of Delaware Press, 2018), 25–41 (at 33).

[4] See Karla Taylor, "Chaucer's Uncommon Voice: Some Contexts for Influence," in *Boccaccio and the "Canterbury Tales": New Essays on an Old Question*, ed. Leonard M. Koff and Brenda Deen Schildgen (Madison: Fairleigh Dickinson University Press, 2000), 47–82; "Writers of the Italian Renaissance," in *Oxford History of Literary Translation in English, Volume 1 (to 1550)*, ed. Roger Ellis (Oxford: Oxford University Press, 2008), 390–406.

6   ELIZABETH ALLEN

through the example of an imagined American college teacher who says to her students, "You remember, of course, that Lombardy was associated with tyranny in the late fourteenth century." The example applies to the storytelling of Chaucer's Merchant, who likewise invokes "a hierarchy of knowledge in which [the audience] is subordinate."[5] Ultimately, Taylor seeks to apply her linguistic observations to poetry's heightened aspiration to stability, that is, its fundamentally literary effort to transcend the inevitable effects of time and change on readerly understanding. Her early work details Chaucer's defining refusal to accept Dante's account of the capacity for language to refer reliably to a stable reality. Later, her work on Chaucer and Gower finds a similar disagreement in another key, contrasting Gower's hope of transparent, stable reference with Chaucer's acknowledgment of linguistic unpredictability. Throughout her career, Taylor sought to account for both the power of language to create reality and the power of readers to use, mistake, resist, and reconstrue that reality.

This interest in communicative gaps or failures derives from linguistic detail, accreted and contextualized through historical and literary knowledge. Despite its density, Taylor's work does not advocate a hermeneutics of suspicion or reading against the grain, nor does it take ideological critique as its initial purpose. Rather, like "surface reading," her work prioritizes observation and description of the text's intricate verbal material, starting often with its most literal meanings. *Chaucer Reads 'The Divine Comedy'*, for example, locates its exploration of poetic world-making in the details of verbal allusion. But Taylor does far more than trace sources and influences: her nuanced observations tease out the ties between words and their literary situations. For example, Dante authenticates his world by using the past tense (Italian "passo remoto"). To lay claim to the authority and objectivity of his vision, he portrays himself as a formerly unknowing pilgrim. In that context, in *Inferno* V he can sympathetically depict the soul of the damned Francesca, who was inspired by a book to betray her husband – even as he reveals as misplaced his own former pity for her. If Taylor's philology begins on the surface, that surface gradually accrues figurative, historical, even ideological significance.

Verbal allusion can revolve around the arrangement of a single highly charged word. Taylor notices in *Troilus and Criseyde*, Chaucer's most ambitious response to Dante, a network of allusions to Francesca's anaphora on love: "Love, which is quickly kindled in a gentle heart, seized this one … Love, which absolves no loved one from loving, seized me … Love brought us

---

[5]   Karla Taylor, "Chaucer's Reticent Merchant," in *The Idea of Medieval Literature: New Essays on Chaucer and Medieval Culture in Honor of Donald R. Howard*, ed. James M. Dean and Christian K. Zacher (Newark: University of Delaware Press, 1992), 189–205 (at 193–4).

to one death."[6] Instead of setting off Francesca's speech in one voice, however, Chaucer distributes her phrases among Troilus, Pandarus, and the narrator, across the first three books of the poem, echoing Francesca's elevation of love but calling into question Dante's moral condemnation. By fragmenting Dante's compressed account, Chaucer emphasizes Criseyde's hesitation in the face of Pandarus's efforts at persuasion and, even as he exalts love as the binding force of the universe, also makes us aware that love's demise awaits.[7] From Taylor's description of this allusive language – based in anaphora, but reframed as spoken from different points of view, in present-tense dialogue that locates the story in temporal history rather than in the afterlife – derives a more extensive Chaucerian engagement with Dante than previous scholars had observed. More important, she shows how Chaucer re-situates love as varied earthly experience rather than moral failure; she finds that he authenticates a mutable world based not on divinely inspired speech but on human language use in time; and she argues that Chaucer's linguistic changes to Dante exemplify readerly resistance – a fundamental problem of linguistic transfer to which Taylor's work returns time and again over her career. In the pagan Troilus, and in the narrator of the poem, "Chaucer offers a model of ... an unconverted reader"[8] – a portrayal of love that inhibits Dante's moral judgment and spiritual authority in favor of a more earthbound, historically embedded, and unfinished process of human life and love. To observe such disagreement is to observe the affective and ethical entailments of each author's project. Taylor's criticism evinces an ethical stance that gives both Dante and Chaucer their due, albeit she finds that her own orientation toward variety and instability in communication repeatedly places her in Chaucer's camp.

That is, Taylor finds herself agreeing with the Chaucerian critique of Dantean truth-claims precisely because of the linguistic mutability that occupies her. If philology has sometimes been construed as overly reliant on the fixed origins of words as explanations for their current meanings, Taylor's body of work instead approaches philology as an account of linguistic change, and in turn as a critique of poetic – and readerly, not to say scholarly – desires for stability. In *Chaucer Reads 'The Divine Comedy'*, language's mutability spurs Chaucer's quarrel with Dante's spiritual authority. Whereas Dante's figurative language instantiates his role as "scriba Dei," Chaucer's consciousness of linguistic change is especially salient at the conclusion of *Troilus and Criseyde*, when the narrator urges his "litel bok" out into the world, but continues anxiously

---

6 "Amor, ch'al cor gentil ratto s'apprende, / prese costui ... / Amor, ch'a nullo amato amar perdona, / mi prese ... / Amor condusse noi ad una morte" (*Inf.* V, 100–6). Quotations from Dante are from Charles S. Singleton, ed. and trans., *The Divine Comedy*, 3 vols (Princeton: Princeton University Press, 1970–5).

7 Taylor, *Chaucer Reads*, 66–72.

8 Taylor, *Chaucer Reads*, 76.

8 ELIZABETH ALLEN

that, since "ther is so greet diversitee / In English and in wryting of our tonge, / So preye I God that noon miswryte thee, / Ne thee mismetre for defaute of tonge."[9] Taylor's comments on this passage describe Chaucer's combination of desire for stable signification and admission of its impossibility: "exact transmission and order of a poetic text are crucial to its meaning, but the act of making such a plea implies a recognition that change and instability in language are likely."[10] To admit that language depends on both convention and variation – on stability and change – critiques Dante's essential claim that his figurative language derives from and instantiates divine truth. As we will see, this admission also entails a critique of Dantean sexual morality.

Taylor insists on Chaucer's consciousness of the circumstantial uses of language. In Chapter 4 of *Chaucer Reads*, "Figuring the World," she details Chaucer's use of proverbs, which appear to be among the most traditional and therefore stable forms of language but, in Chaucer's hands, turn out to mean various things in various contexts. Conventional love language, similarly, aspires to an ideal stability, especially in the mouth of Troilus, who truly believes stock metaphors like love-as-hunt and love-as-heaven. After Criseyde has been traded to the Greeks and Diomede courts her, he uses the same metaphors as Troilus, to very different effect. Taylor argues that Chaucer thus confronts us with the impossibility of Troilus's idealist treatment of language:

> The words of love are conventions which mean only what we can agree that they mean. Just as with proverbs, their significance is relative to context – speaker, listener, the worsening political circumstances in Troy – and their fixed form derives not so much from semantic stability as from our desire for such an absolute relationship to reality.[11]

Far from simply confirming "semantic stability," Taylor's work acknowledges how the human desire for meaning drives authors' efforts to create a stable relationship between reality and the language that represents it. Yet language cannot finally firm up a stable relation to events: if the conventional topoi of courtly eros do not equate to love but rather allow for the reformulation of love according to radically different circumstances, then we might say the same of any traditional language, from ordinary proverbs to classical literary topoi. Taylor acknowledges linguistic change at several levels – in the act of translation from Italian to English, in the mutation of love language from one scene to another and one poem to another, in the failure of linguistic stability that leads to miswriting and mis-metering. This mutability conditions

---

9   *Troilus and Criseyde*, V.1793–6. All quotations from Chaucer are from Larry D. Benson, ed., *The Riverside Chaucer*, 3rd ed. (Boston: Houghton Mifflin, 1987).

10   Taylor, *Chaucer Reads*, 163.

11   Taylor, *Chaucer Reads*, 170.

Chaucer's relation to Dante, inasmuch as Dantean transcendence cannot be fulfilled in the world of time and change portrayed in *Troilus and Criseyde*.[12]

More than this: for Taylor, Chaucer's failure to "secure stability through traditional language" is both a linguistic inevitability and a poetic strategy, and it points to an understanding of the affordances of philology that remains fresh almost forty years later.[13] Philological method can take as its object both ordinary language and poetry, the self-conscious and artificial use of language designed to invite analytical curiosity.[14] In fact, the study of proverbs, in Taylor's hands, illuminates ways in which authors repeat and change literary topoi, so that the proverb "Better the reed that bends than the rod that breaks" informs Chaucer's complex treatment of tree similes in the *Troilus*, echoing the *Aeneid* and *Metamorphoses* as well as *The Divine Comedy*. Finding patterns of syntax and figuration is both linguistic and literary, here using the former to inform the latter. In the process, the method is also both synchronically precise and attentive to diachronic variation. The objects of Taylor's philological method are transregional and transhistorical, as she crosses among Italian, French, and English poetic traditions, interested in cultural transfer and change that resist the reification of national or colonial projects.[15]

---

[12] Taylor's claims about Chaucer's resistance are distinct from those of previous scholars, principally Winthrop Wetherbee, who finds in Troilus an authoritative Dantean reader in *Chaucer and the Poets: An Essay on "Troilus and Criseyde"* (Ithaca: Cornell University Press, 1984). Her work initiated a line of criticism that explored Chaucer's complex responses to Italian predecessors, for example the work of David Wallace, whose primary interest is in Chaucer's use of Italian political ideas, often understood through his experiments with women's political power; see *Chaucerian Polity: Absolutist Lineages and Associational Forms in England and Italy* (Palo Alto: Stanford University Press, 1997). See also Warren Ginsburg, who argues that Dante and other Italian poets authorize Chaucer's increasing metropolitanism in *Chaucer's Italian Tradition* (Ann Arbor: University of Michigan Press, 2002).

[13] Taylor, *Chaucer Reads*, 162.

[14] It is through linguistic analysis and dictionary work that Taylor finds access to uses of language that exceed the literary. Taylor remarks on the capacity for the *MED* to provide far more than word origins and definitions; its quotations provide a corpus that can indicate discourses, ideologies, and social functions of words. The *MED*, she writes, "can contribute, that is, to the study of culture." See Karla Taylor, "Language in Use," in *Chaucer: Contemporary Approaches*, ed. Susanna Fein and David Raybin (University Park: Pennsylvania State University Press, 2010), 99–115 (at 102).

[15] This cosmopolitanism is evident in "Chaucer's Uncommon Voice"; "The French Tradition," in *Approaches to Teaching* Troilus and Criseyde *and the Minor Poems*, ed. Tison Pugh and Angela Weisl (New York: Modern Language Association, 2007), 33–8; and "Writers of the Italian Renaissance." See also, co-edited with Susan Nakley, "What We Think of When We Think of the *Prioress's Tale*," a special issue of the *Chaucer Review* 59.3 (2024).

Taylor's inductive attention to linguistic observation and description proves particularly attuned to gender and social class. Her work explores problematics of reference ranging from Criseyde's subjectivity to the Wife of Bath's appropriative language, and from the tyrannical narration of the Merchant to the dubious royal judgment advised in Gower's *Confessio Amantis*. To locate power and oppression in the mechanisms of point of view, rhyme, and linguistic translation applies philological methods to problems of historical hierarchy, oppression, and dissent that have been at the forefront of medieval literary study at least since Paul Strohm's *Social Chaucer*.[16] Taylor's brand of historicism registers political and social entailments of language's history: that is, her historicism is philological, which does not mean it is confined to lexical and semantic – or even stylistic – observation. As Taylor writes in the field-surveying essay "Language in Use" (2010), "Because language is an essentially social phenomenon, it offers literary historians an unusually direct means of access to the social dimensions of literature."[17]

In medieval texts, these "social dimensions" involve dynamics that are historically unfamiliar to present day readers – different gender assumptions, monarchical political systems, historically specific status categories, and historically different religious institutions. Philology, rather than obscure or deflect these differences, can make them visible. As Taylor writes, "A fine-grained attention to language in use can put flesh on the cultural conditions within which utterances, including Chaucerian texts, take and shape their meanings."[18] Indeed, in her hands, philology (and its step-sibling Linguistics) can expose such categories to complex scrutiny, forcing us to be aware of, say, the marginalization of the Reeve with his northern dialect ("Language in Use"), or a class nostalgia suggested in the word "serement," which links magic and aristocratic fantasy ("Uncommon Voice"), or an uncomfortable similarity between discourses of heresy and absolutist rhetoric ("Inside Out").[19] Such explorations resist simply attributing to the past socially regressive forms of misogyny, rigid class hierarchy, absolute sovereignty, or univocal Christianity. Moreover, Taylor accounts for social oppression within the

---

[16] Paul Strohm, *Social Chaucer* (Cambridge, MA: Harvard University Press, 1994). Taylor's work, in its insistence that language study *is* historical, is responsive to but distinct from the historicisms of the late 1980s through the early 2000s. For useful critique of historicism's dominance in the field, see Elizabeth Scala and Sylvia Federico, eds., *The Post-Historical Middle Ages* (London and New York: Palgrave Macmillan, 2009).

[17] Taylor, "Language in Use," 100.

[18] Taylor, "Language in Use," 105.

[19] Karla Taylor, "Inside Out in Gower's Republic of Letters," in *John Gower, Trilingual Poet: Language, Translation and Tradition*, ed. Elisabeth Dutton with John Hines and R.F. Yeager (Cambridge: D.S. Brewer, 2010), 169–81.

context of linguistic mutability and human communicative failure, complicating any view of the past in which medieval oppression is encompassed in a broader teleology, as either innocent precursor to or guilty origin of later imperial designs. Her work, that is, resists scholarly approaches that would render inevitable the national and colonial projects that were incipient, or yet to come, in the varied social conflicts that occupy medieval texts.

Taylor's approach to gender is a case in point. She does not overtly seek to authorize feminine voices afresh, as in the work of many feminist medievalist literary critics over the last forty years, such as (among others) Jill Mann and, more recently, Nancy Bradley Warren and Holly Crocker, who are interested in reclaiming experiences or qualities sometimes dismissively associated with the feminine – passivity, bodily perception, emotional fortitude, endurance – in order to redefine a medieval gendered subjectivity.[20] In a scholarship whose feminist claims are implicit but pervasive, Taylor typically begins with a grammatical or lexical choice in a poetic text, and seeks to show how the choice instantiates a structural linguistic problem *and* how the choice involves historical, often institutional discourses (courtly love, alchemy, theories of political resistance). In her analysis of Criseyde in "Inferno 5 and *Troilus and Criseyde* Revisited," Taylor explores how the structural capacity for courtly language to represent subjectivity becomes especially problematic for women.[21] Though Criseyde is often the subject of verbs in Books 2–3, her pronoun usage deflects agency when she bemoans women's hatred of her: "They wol seyn, in as muche as in me is, / I have hem don dishonour, weylawey!" (5.1065–6). Taylor points out that the objectification of Criseyde, her self-identification as exemplary in the phrase "in me," is often how courtly language treats its women characters (including Dante's Francesca). She argues that *Troilus and Criseyde* includes "the story of Criseyde's diminishing subjectivity, and her growing complicity with the pressures that shape her experience."[22] What such pronoun usage affords, in her view, cannot circumvent gender oppression, though it can point out the problem: "By focusing on the difficulties of representing [the possibilities of female subjectivity], with tools forged by the tradition out of which he writes, Chaucer can at least gesture toward the

---

[20] Jill Mann, *Feminizing Chaucer* (Cambridge: D.S. Brewer, 2002); Nancy Bradley Warren, *The Embodied Word: Female Spiritualities, Contested Orthodoxies, and English Religious Cultures, 1350–1700* (Notre Dame: University of Notre Dame Press, 2010); Holly Crocker, *The Matter of Virtue: Women's Ethical Action from Chaucer to Shakespeare* (Philadelphia: University of Pennsylvania Press, 2019).

[21] Karla Taylor, "Inferno 5 and *Troilus and Criseyde* Revisited," in *Chaucer's Troilus: "Subgit be to alle poesye": Essays in Criticism*, ed. R.A. Shoaf (Binghamton: SUNY Press, 1992), 239–56.

[22] Taylor, "Inferno 5," 255–6.

voices that tradition excludes."[23] Limited by indirection, Chaucer's gesture toward alternative formulations of feminine subjectivity calls upon readers to exceed authorial capacities in a potentially positive direction, so that readers' mismatch with authorial intent might have the socially beneficial consequence of imagining something outside the discursive limits of the poem.

Something perhaps closer to the reclamation model of feminist scholarship seems to undergird Taylor's later treatments of the Wife of Bath as avatar of productive misreading. In her 2007 tour de force "Chaucer's Volumes: Toward a New Model of Literary History in the *Canterbury Tales*," she argues that Chaucer's appropriation of a Dantean lexical pair, the rhyme words *volume/custume*, generates a wide-ranging argument about poetic authority and literary history.[24] In *Paradiso* XXXIII, Dante figures the unity of the created universe and its creator in the culminating metaphor of a book (*volume*) whose bound leaves fuse the relations (*custume*) between substances and accidents. The Wife of Bath appropriates the rhyme – "volume" is new to English in the 1380s and "still rare" by the time Chaucer uses it – to describe the polemical book of Jankyn, where misogynist writings are all "bounded in o volume. / And every nyght and day was his custume / ... To reden on this book of wikked wyves" (III.680–5). Initially, this seems as neat a refusal of Dantean idealism as one could wish for. But in Taylor's hands, the Wife of Bath's resistance becomes something far more complex because her allusive method is not simply destructive but is also accommodating, linked by another use of the word "volume" to the Clerk's simultaneous obedience to the host and resistance to the work of "Chaucer."

For Taylor, the Wife of Bath reclaims women among all wayward readers, and she shows that Chaucer's engagement with his sources is not merely rivalrous. He is introducing an Italian and Latin tradition into English by rehearsing his predecessors. Still, lacking the authority of Italian literary tradition including its continuity with Latin, Chaucer instead emphasizes the multiplicity and dispersal of sources. Taylor argues that Chaucer inscribes readers who collect and accommodate sources, rehearse and amalgamate their achievements, and push against them: it is this broader method that affords an understanding of the Wife of Bath's fullest authority. She becomes the "model of literary tradition forged from misreadings and bad judgment" involving "defects of the ear."[25] When the Wife misappropriates Ovid's story of Midas's ass-ears as a model of female garrulity (instead of a male barber's garrulity), she allows a refiguration of authorship as an ongoing process: through her, Chaucer's text does not support one authority superseding another, but a series of readers juxtaposing varying accounts. The Wife's idiosyncratic reading of

---

23   Taylor, "Inferno 5," 256.
24   The argument continues in Taylor, "The Motives of Reeds," 25–41.
25   Taylor, "The Motives of Reeds," 36.

the story of Midas's ears is fed by social hierarchy and oppression, which constrain and shape her account, but which nonetheless provide the framework within which an alternative model of authority can emerge, an authority arising not from a battle between literary giants but from the variability of interpretation and the waywardness of readers.

Reading Taylor's body of work, then, suggests that philology has the capacity to reveal possible avenues for female authority, and further, that a woman reader provides a model for a literary authority based in collection, accretion, and amalgamation rather than rivalry. To observe a single rhyme is to start with a surface observation, to which contextualizing language gradually accrues, slowly enriching the verbal and socio-political situation and zooming out to regard Chaucer's poetics as a process of collection that Taylor associates with magpies – a bird's-eye view. This kind of philology might not only afford us ethical insight into past cultural oppression but also unlock a history of new readers that authorizes reading methods currently called for in some language-forward methods such as surface reading or slow reading. In particular, Taylor's philological thought on the failures of communication that inhere in language authorizes not only women but any readers who approach medieval literature freshly or askew, as students, enthusiasts, or fans, or with an otherwise non-professional attention to surfaces or the slower pace of amateurs.[26] Taylor's philology is a linguistically attuned, inductive method, irreducible to word histories but certainly attentive to the varied uses of words in historical situations, a method that amalgamates or accretes sources and attends to social difference: it is a philology not unlike the hermeneutics of the Wife of Bath that she describes. To accept and even embrace the mismatch between author and reader acknowledges the authority of non-specialist readers without dismissing the value of historical curiosity or conceptualization.

Taylor's linguistic approach can be more synthetic as well, even dovetailing with distant reading, since the context she gathers relies on comprehensive tools like the *Middle English Dictionary*, *The Linguistic Atlas of Late Medieval English* (1986), and the online *Corpus of Middle English Prose and Verse*, as well as sociolinguistic histories of the function of English generally.[27] With the enormously increased availability of online dictionaries, manuscripts, and

---

[26] On amateurs reading medieval texts, see Carolyn Dinshaw, *How Soon Is Now? Medieval Texts, Amateur Readers, and the Queerness of Time* (Durham: Duke University Press, 2012). In her well-known salvo in the surface-reading debates, *The Uses of Literature* (Oxford: Blackwell Publishing, 2008), Rita Felski calls for literary scholars to "engage seriously with ordinary motives for reading – such as the desire for knowledge or the longing for escape – that are either overlooked or undervalued" (at 14).

[27] Taylor, "Language in Use," *passim.*

corpuses, readers amateur and academic have at their disposal new tools that enable searching and collection of verbal instances, and that give access to large amounts of information quickly. A key image Taylor uses in one essay, the traditional woven rugs made in Iran, Turkey, and elsewhere, makes vivid the surface-patterning of language that occupies her. A break in any woven pattern points to its social significance by reminding us of the artifice, the "acts of perception and memory" involved in both making and seeing the work of art.[28] The image suggests the importance of accreting detail and gathering data in order to regard both the pattern and the flaw from a perspective further away. Taylor's philology anticipates recent approaches that resist skepticism and depth hermeneutics in favor of attention to surfaces and distant, larger-scale understandings of linguistic use. To be sure, in Taylor's hands, such data collection typically serves the description of a given text or textual relation; but her focus on linguistic function also requires panning out to a bird's-eye view.

Linguistic research is especially crucial for understanding a past literature obscured by time and change. Certain historical moments create especially charged linguistic situations, especially with shifts in the public terms of political power. This is true recently, for instance, with the emergence of a newly loaded usage of words related to truth and mendacity, for example the buzz phrase "fake news" and the closely related phrase "election fraud" – phrases whose manipulation has had not only ideological but materially violent repercussions. In the late fourteenth century in England, increasing political conflict, including the fifteen-year lead-up to Richard II's deposition, produced a similarly charged linguistic situation.

In "Social Aesthetics" (2005), Taylor contends that Chaucer's response to that charged historical situation is at once social and semantic: the *Shipman's Tale* hinges on cross-linguistic puns, which are socially divisive, while the *Melibee* hinges on doublets – one Latin word translated into multiple English ones – which are socially inclusive, "generating a new lexicon for civic life in English" (312). Puns, Taylor points out, say many things with the same word, and, together with jargon and in-group knowledge, they block sociality. By contrast, the *Melibee*'s doublets seek to reconcile conflicting elements of civil society, supporting a monolingual audience by reciprocally glossing one another: *Melibee* mends social bonds by replacing expressive economy with plenitude. Taylor's argument here attends to the classed nature of social conflict by surveying the semantic choices that govern the tale. The French-speaking in-group of the cross-linguistic pun versus the monolingual English speaker who benefits from doublets: these are classed categories, and class exclusion heightens the charge on socially exclusive language.

---

[28] I am slightly redirecting Taylor's image here, which she uses to assert the mutual dependency of pattern and flaw, analogized to the mutual dependency of form and the social. See Taylor, "Social Aesthetics," 300–1.

In her later essays on Gower and Chaucer, she continues to approach the problem of political integrity philologically, again in ways that anticipate the language of the Trump era in American politics. Gower uses the rhyme "corage/visage" to indicate that a king should put a good face on things, as it were, opening a problematic fissure between intention and appearance that is more than a problem of aesthetic representation: it opens into the question of royal truth. Does a king's heart (*corage*) show in his face (*visage*)? The rhyme complicates Gower's typical fantasy of referential transparency, what we might call honesty – "a linguistic version of ethics."[29] To what extent does the king's control over what shows in his face amount to monarchical subterfuge? When does the king's hiding his "corage" open the way to tyranny? Chaucer refers to Gowerian integrity in framing the Clerk's tale, but he associates that framework with Walter's tyrannical duplicity, exposing the "ethical slippages" that Gower's advice to princes allows. As Taylor sees it, Gower's allowance of a Walterian disjunction between "corage" and "visage" slides in the direction of support for Richard II's tyranny, and Chaucer's portrayal of Walter issues "a sharp warning about the pitfalls that threaten to swallow up Gower's own efforts to correct the king through poetry."[30] The problem of linguistic referentiality brings into focus poetry's capacity to register in language the tension between referential integrity and the mechanisms of social change.

The claim goes even further: Taylor argues that Chaucer's semantic experiments *seek* social change. In "Social Aesthetics," she ascribes to him the hope that "the inclusive linguistic bonds created by [*Melibee*'s] doublets might change social and civic bonds as well."[31] Language in use relies on a certain stability in meaning in order to be understood at all. But it is also bound up in sociopolitical shifts, so that the study of language can track avenues of change, from class mobility to regime change. This capacity for language to rely upon, yet exceed, conventional usage remains the fascinating core of Taylor's linguistics-based literary criticism. Philology, in this sense, points from past to future, from synchronic function toward sociopolitical change over time. Diachronic linguistic change can be valued either positively, as when it is associated with social expansion or inclusivity; or negatively, as when it is associated with political or intimate betrayal, the failure of intentions or expectations, or the consolidation of colonial power.

---

[29] Karla Taylor, "What Lies Beneath," in *John Gower in Manuscripts and Early Printed Books*, ed. Martha Driver, Derek Pearsall, and Robert F. Yeager (Cambridge: D.S. Brewer, 2020), 71–88 (at 78–9).

[30] Karla Taylor, "Reading Faces in Gower and Chaucer," in *John Gower: Others and the Self*, ed. Russell A. Peck and R.F. Yeager (Cambridge: D.S. Brewer, 2017), 73–90 (at 83).

[31] Taylor, "Social Aesthetics," 316.

For Taylor the valuation of linguistic change is not coldly analytical but has a distinct affective dimension. That is, her philology is prompted by and conscious of feeling, especially salient in her accounts of readerly desire: for example in the Merchant's manipulation of audience expectations through narrative pacing, and in the narration of Criseyde's betrayal of Troilus and the loss in love and war that she is made to embody. Taylor's account of Criseyde is part of a history of affective engagements with Criseyde as a character.[32] But for her, such affect remains grounded in the analysis of linguistic strategies of attachment, the verbal and perspectival shifts that play with distance and intimacy. The reader's sense of betrayal when Criseyde leaves Troilus is essentially a problem of reference: it is what happens "if we begin to believe literally that love is the same thing as conventional love language"[33] – that is, the affective response hinges on and derives from a linguistic fantasy of stable and transparent referentiality that can never be fulfilled because of the inherently mutable nature of language itself, a mutability that belongs, as well, to human beings, especially a woman subject to wartime shifts in her situation. Taylor's philology is an analytical method designed to account for affective response: inasmuch as she describes both the aspiration to, and the limits of, language's ability to achieve stable reference, she also uses reading experience – "our desire" – as the starting point for tracing the reader's attachment to a character, and the subsequent loss of affective intimacy.

Change, in language as in human life, entails both desire and loss: because of this, Taylor's understanding of linguistic communication includes affect, and in this sense, her philological method anticipates the readerly absorption that interests proponents of surface reading. I referred earlier to the "teaching moment" she imagines in one of her early essays, "Chaucer's Reticent Merchant" (1992). This piece indicates why audience resistance to authorial intention has remained ethically and affectively important to Taylor throughout her career – it is because ethically, she values the freedom of readers to refuse authorial control. She calls the Merchant a tyrannical storyteller, describing his "habitual refusal to tell us what we need to know in order to follow his bewildering shifts among genres, tones, directions of sympathy and antipathy, and to follow also his pyrotechnic display of an allusiveness so brilliant that it seems designed to go right over any audience's head."[34] When an author withholds his own knowledge – his presuppositions – from his audience, he pulls rank by labeling the ground between them as *not* common. In the

---

[32] The classic reflection on this history is Carolyn Dinshaw, *Chaucer's Sexual Poetics* (Madison: University of Wisconsin Press, 1989), 28–64.

[33] Karla Taylor, "Proverbs and the Authentication of Convention in *Troilus and Criseyde*," in *Chaucer's 'Troilus': Essays in Criticism*, ed. Stephen A. Barney (Hamden: Archon, 1980), 277–96 (at 289).

[34] Taylor, "Chaucer's Reticent Merchant," 191.

Merchant's Tale, a long digression that delays the conclusion of the wedding feast makes readers *desire* the consummation between old January and young May; when January's skin is finally, intimately described as disgusting, we and our curiosity are "the true targets of the savagery."[35] When May and Damyan have sex in the tree, similarly, the Merchant encourages us to desire their consummation, then implicates us in an act that turns out to be unceremonious and cruel. The Merchant, in her reading, is a tyrannical narrator, playing tricks with our desires.

Karla Taylor's work traces a philology whose lineaments suggest a methodological continuity between language history and linguistics: open to all levels of readership, attentive to surfaces, and interested in readerly absorption. Observation and description – a precise attention to language – can not only encourage but account for the ethical, affective, and social responses of readers. Such a philology is concrete, flexible, attentive to desire, and socially and politically aware. And it makes available a form of methodological self-critique: Taylor's philology demands articulation of literary and linguistic capacities and an attention to both the power and the limits of language's capacity to shape readers and the world.

Throughout her teaching career, Karla Taylor conveyed to the students whose work appears here the importance of language's fundamental social purposes, and in teaching both linguistic and literary scholarship – in teaching a historically and socially conscious philology – she helped us identify the problems of social cohesion and conflict registered in the medieval literature we studied with her. Taylor's work expresses a conviction about the centrality of the primary text as an object of study, the validity of historical methods based in observation of linguistic functions and collection of discursive patterns, and the capacity for attention to language to matter, affectively and ethically. Her work has always been conscious of the gap between linguistic reference and social effect: she has been particularly attuned to the myriad indirections that characterize language in use, including the resistances and misunderstandings that are endemic to any effort of communication. The gaps between reader and writer, writer and audience, teacher and student may be uncomfortable or poignant; but they leave space for interpretive difference and freedom for diversity of thought.

---

[35] Taylor, "Chaucer's Reticent Merchant," 199.

2

Recent Methods and the Persistence of Philology

CATHERINE SANOK

Karla Taylor's philology, as Elizabeth Allen describes it in the previous essay, has what may at first seem an uncanny resonance with recent methods of literary study that orient critical reading toward greater attention to the linguistic "surface" of a text. From a different disciplinary vector, it may also open a question about the relationship between literary studies and sociolinguistics, which has recently made space for research on self-consciously literary texts. Beyond celebrating Taylor's contributions to Middle English studies as a scholar and a teacher, this volume launches from the example of her scholarship to pursue a disciplinary question and an interdisciplinary one: first, why have the methodological similarities between philology and some recent critical practices not been recognized and, second, how might we rethink the relationship between literary studies and linguistics through their shared methodological interest in the linguistic "surface" of literary texts. The rubric of "philology" as claimed by Karla Taylor, that is, may encourage us to attend to the histories and affordances of current language-oriented approaches to literature.

Several recent methods of literary study orient critical reading toward a more descriptive account of a text or a greater focus on readerly affect.[1] These methods include several varieties of "new formalism" that prioritize verbal structure, patterning, and repetition;[2] "surface reading," a catch-all for

---

[1] Elaine Auyoung makes an even broader claim that, in academic literary study, "what we mean by reading" is essentially the recognition or invention of textual patterns, and that claims made regarding these patterns are valued largely according to the scholarly pleasure they produce. See Elaine Auyoung, "What We Mean By Reading," *New Literary History* 51.1 (2020), 93–114.

[2] The variousness of recent formalist approaches makes it impractical to identify a representative sampling. For a recent account of some of them that also identifies

approaches that attend to the material or linguistic features of a text rather than seeking to uncover an occluded significance;[3] "post-critique," which moves away readings that aim to expose a text's or genre's covert ideological projects;[4] and the valorization of amateur or "uncritical" reading practices, which celebrate patient, recursive attention to the text, as well as openness to ahistorical or "anachronistic" interpretations and uses of a text that are licensed by changes to how the language, genre, or referents of a text are understood across time.[5] These critical approaches often emphasize an affective orientation toward the text as well as (or in lieu of) an analytical one, and they sometimes focus on readerly pleasure in particular. They advocate or license reading with, rather than against, the "grain," developing a sympathetic or "reparative" rather than suspicious account of a text, and prioritizing meanings made available to readers through the text's own sense-making capacity rather than attributed to any absent cause. That is to say, these current critical modes – despite their different projects and commitments – advocate a shared critical practice that can be broadly defined as close attention to a text's language, a conviction that its language matters.

The current reckoning in literary study with the evidentiary value of a text's language also creates an opportunity for recognizing cross-disciplinary projects it may share with sociolinguistics, the field of linguistics that attends to language as a social phenomenon that contributes to and reflects how social and institutional power is created and sustained. Sociolinguistics increasingly recognizes the value of taking imaginative literature as an object of inquiry.[6] Imaginative and self-consciously literary texts, once avoided by linguists because they do not reflect everyday language use, offer special purchase on some aspects of the social life of language precisely because such texts create

---

some of the context, stakes, and capacities of new formalisms, see Jonathan Kramnick and Anahid Nersessian, "Form and Explanation," *Critical Inquiry* 43.3 (2017), 650–69.

[3] Stephen Best and Sharon Marcus, "Surface Reading: An Introduction," *Representations* 108.1 (2009), 1–21.

[4] Rita Felski, *The Limits of Critique* (Chicago: Chicago University Press, 2015); Eve Sedgwick, *Touching Feeling: Affect, Pedagogy, Performativity* (Durham: Duke University Press, 2003), Chapter 4.

[5] Caroline Dinshaw, *How Soon is Now? Medieval Texts, Amateur Readers, and the Queerness of Time* (Durham: Duke University Press, 2012); Brian Glavey, "Having a Coke with You is Even More Fun Than Ideology Critique," *PMLA* 134.5 (2019), 996–1011; Michael Warner, "Uncritical Reading," in *Polemic: Critical or Uncritical*, ed. Jane Gallop (London and New York: Routledge, 2004), 13–38.

[6] For the field of Middle English, see for example Tim William Machan, *English in the Middle Ages* (Oxford: Oxford University Press, 2003). For an account of socio-linguistics as a field, see Robert Bayley, Richard Cameron, and Ceil Lucas, "The Study of Language and Society," in *The Oxford Handbook of Sociolinguistics*, ed. Robert Bayley, Richard Cameron, and Ceil Lucas (Oxford: Oxford University Press, 2013).

and reflect cultural systems of value, license a playful use of language, and self-consciously explore the potential significance of non-semantic features of language such as phonology. This volume proposes that current methods in both fields lay the ground for a newly productive relationship between sociolinguistics and literary analysis because they share an interest in how language matters both to a text's avowed projects and as evidence of its reciprocal relation to the social worlds in which it is produced and received. As Taylor states in a programmatic essay, "Because language is an essentially social phenomenon, it offers literary historians an unusually direct means of access to the social dimensions of literature as well."[7] So too, as her own interest in sociolinguistics attests, because literature is an essentially social phenomenon, it offers sociolinguists a distinctively valuable means of access to some of the social dimensions of language.

That surface reading and sociolinguistics take up core facets of philology, however, is not generally acknowledged in either field. The currency of philology, in the form of these two different analytical approaches to literary texts, is obscured by debates about the value or danger of philology's "return," itself a perennial trope in the history of literary criticism.[8] For literary studies, this occlusion is perhaps most tellingly indexed by the proximity of one of the most visible recent indictments of philology and its threatened return, Geoffrey Galt Harpham's "Roots, Races, and the Return of Philology" (published in the May 2009 issue of *Representations*), to Stephen Best and Sharon Marcus's influential essay heralding a large-scale reorientation of literary scholarship from "depth" hermeneutics to "surface" reading (published in the November 2009 issue of the same journal).[9] This essay thus first addresses how philology

---

[7] Karla Taylor, "Language in Use," in *Chaucer: Contemporary Approaches*, ed. Susanna Fine and David Raybin (University Park: Penn State University Press, 2010), 99. This essay identifies sociolinguistics as an essential "pole" of language-focused approaches to Chaucer.

[8] On "the perpetual need for 'return' that has always characterized philology," see Michelle Warren, "Shimmering Philology," *postmedieval* 5.4 (2014), 389. See also Andrew Hui, "Review: The Many Returns of Philology," *Journal of the History of Ideas* 78.1 (2017), 137–56, and Merve Emre, "The Return to Philology," *PMLA* 138 (2023), 171–7. The trope of return is signaled by titles of essays including Jonathan Culler, "The Return to Philology," *Journal of Aesthetic Education* 36.3 (2002), 12–16; Paul de Man, "Return of Philology," in *Resistance to Theory* (Minneapolis: University of Minnesota Press, 1986; repr. 2002), 21–6; Lee Patterson, "Return of Philology," in *Past and Future of Medieval Studies*, ed. John van Engen (Notre Dame: University of Notre Dame Press, 1994), 231–44; Edward Said, *Humanism and Democratic Criticism* (New York: Columbia University Press, 2004), Chapter 3, "The Return of Philology," 57–84.

[9] Geoffrey Galt Harpham, "Roots, Races, and the Return of Philology," *Representations* 106.1 (2009), 34–62.

is conceptualized through efforts to parry its "return," before considering how attention to some of its signature methods might help to clarify the goals, intervention, and status of recent modes of reading that have been presented as corrective, complementary, or endemic to professional criticism. Our goal is not a normative definition of philology as a method (what kinds of evidence and which practices constitute it) or as a discipline (what projects and goals define it); much less is it to prescribe or pronounce upon current practices of surface reading, post-critical reading, or readerly attachment. Instead, we hope this discussion prompts further reflection on the disciplinary histories of these practices, on the forms of attention that might advance them, and on the contributions to literary study that they do and might make.

We then address how linguistics, defining itself against philology at its own institutional origin, now takes up some of the core projects of philology in the subdiscipline of sociolinguistics. We suggest that philology's "return" in a different discipline has the potential to shape the way that literary scholars, too, undertake those projects. Cutting-edge work in sociolinguistics that takes imaginative and formally-invested texts as its object of inquiry may have much to offer "surface reading" methods in particular. Finally, we offer a survey of the volume's chapters within the frame of these current disciplinary possibilities.

Philology's Returns

Etymologically, the "love of language" or "love of literature," *philology* names a sustained and wide-ranging practice of attention to language. Michelle Warren – whose recurrent interest has perhaps done the most to keep the term in play in the field of Middle English studies – observes that, identified by its etymology as a form of love, *philology* may designate "a potentially infinite array of activities."[10] Although often associated with highly technical modes of knowledge production, philology can really only be defined by the evidentiary priority it gives to language, and in practice, it encompasses a wide range of methods and projects. Rooted in written documents, philology can refer to the methods for creating a textual edition. As a form of cultural analysis, it both relies on and contributes to an understanding of the culture

---

[10] Michelle Warren, "Post-Philology," in *Postcolonial Moves: Medieval Through Modern*, ed. Patricia Clare Ingham and Michelle Warren (London and New York: Palgrave Macmillan, 2003), 19–45 (at 20). Warren's meditations on philology also include "Relating Philology, Practicing Humanism," the introduction to "Philology Matters," a special issue of *PMLA* 125.2 (2010), 283–8; *Creole Medievalism: Colonial France and Joseph Bedier's Middle Ages* (Minneapolis: University of Minnesota Press, 2010), Chapter 4, "Island Philology"; "Shimmering Philology," cited above; and "Philology in Ruins," *Florilegium* 32 (2015), 59–76.

in which a document is produced; it may, as an extension of this sense, have a narrow address to texts perceived as "literary" (where that designation primarily marks received cultural value). As a kind of linguistics, philology approaches documents as historical witnesses to language use; used in this sense, "philology" may be used pejoratively, as a generic term for outdated methods not used in current linguistic scholarship, or for a pedantic fascination with etymology and language "trivia," or for suspiciously teleological genealogies of language "families."

Partly because it cannot be characterized by a restricted set of analytical practices, philology cannot be defined by a single intellectual or ideological project. In Warren's pithy formulation, it "creates and dismantles coherence, stabilizes and undermines tradition, multiplies and singularizes, wanders and roots" (286).[11] To some scholars, philology is a positivist project that seeks to resolve textual cruces, while to others it is a critical endeavor that challenges the monumentalization of texts as authorizing "foundations," both at the level of individual works[12] and at the level of epistemological orientation.[13] Philology may insist on a rigorously historical understanding of a text, via detailed study of the linguistic landscape contemporary to its first audience, or it may gain analytical traction through attention to its constitutive "anachrony," the diachronic difference between the text and its reader.[14] Indeed, defined at the level of method, philology can be recognized – as Sheldon Pollock, Benjamin Elman, and Ku-ming Kevin Chang argue – as a global project of knowledge production that stretches back to the first millennium BCE and that has been employed in myriad cultural projects, variously oriented toward different ideological ends.[15]

[11] Warren, "Relating," 286. See, e.g., Carissa Harris's philological study of "wench" within a Black feminist analytical framework in the interest of reproductive justice: Harris, "Chaucer's Wenches," *Studies in the Age of Chaucer* 45 (2023), 35–72.

[12] Philology defined in this way harks back to Joseph Scaliger's philological approach to the Bible.

[13] An example of this familiar to medievalists is the value accorded to textual variants over critical editions by the so-called "New Philology" announced in a 1990 special issue of *Speculum* curated by Stephen Nichols: see Nichols, "Introduction: Philology in a Manuscript Culture," *Speculum* 65.1 (1990), 1–10. Now see John Frow, "Philology: On Reading Slowly in a Digital World," *Journal of Language, Literature and Culture* 65.2 (2018), 81–6.

[14] Sean Gurd, ed., *Philology and Its Histories* (Columbus: Ohio State University Press, 2010), 10.

[15] Sheldon Pollock, Benjamin Elman, and Ku-ming Kevin Chang, eds., *World Philology* (Cambridge, MA: Harvard University Press, 2015). Compare Jerome McGann's call for a "new kind of philology, online and therefore global at an entirely new level": McGann, *New Republic of Letters: Memory and Scholarship in the Age of Digital Reproduction* (Cambridge, MA: Harvard University Press, 2014), x.

This long history of philology as a method, and the variety of practices and projects that it has supported, however, are often obscured by the fact that "philology" also names the early disciplinary formation of literary study in the Western academy, and as such can be identified with the specific research and ideological projects of nineteenth-century professional scholarship. In particular, philology is sometimes understood to be irremediably structured by the racist, nationalist, and imperialist agendas it was used to advance when it also served as the disciplinary name for Anglo-European literary scholarship and established itself as the core humanistic research project in the modern university.[16] Pollock, Elman, and Chang's recognition of philology as a global endeavor across a long history not only provincializes the discipline of nineteenth-century Western philology – that is, identifies a particular disciplinary formation as a contingent and local instance of a broader phenomenon rather than its necessary, universal, or paradigmatic form – but also establishes a historical frame for understanding why scholars have for so long disagreed about its disciplinary status. Philology is sometimes identified by its disciplinarity, as per its familiar academic reputation, which identifies philology with hyper-specialization and rigid modes of knowledge-production,[17] but it is also credited for its anti-disciplinarity, as per Sophus Helle, who insists on its cross-disciplinary reach and anti-foundational orientation.[18] It may be seen as pre-disciplinary, as in James Turner's account of its role as impetus to or origin of many academic disciplines,[19] or as sub-disciplinary, to riff on Jerome McGann's term for the assumption that philology names the preliminary linguistic and textual scholarship that makes literary works available to more professionally valued cultural analysis.[20]

Put simply, there is confusion about whether philology is a methodology, defined by its epistemological orientation and wide array of corresponding methods, or a scholarly discipline, defined by its research projects and

[16] See, e.g., Harpham, "Roots, Races, and the Return of Philology." See also John Guillory, *Professing Criticism: Essays on the Organization of Literary Study* (Chicago: University of Chicago Press, 2022), 181–7, and Marc Nichanian, "Philology from the Point of View of its Victims," *boundary 2* 48.1 (2021), 177–206.

[17] See, for example, Wendy Steiner, "Ce Vice Impuni," *Journal of Aesthetic Education* 36.3 (2002), 30–4. Steiner asserts that nineteenth-century philology made "the study of literature more disciplinary in nature than the approaches that came later" (30).

[18] Sophus Helle, "What is Philology?: From Crises of Reading to Comparative Reflections," *Poetics Today* 43.4 (2022), 611–37. See also Jonathan Culler, "Anti-foundational Philology," *Comparative Literature Studies* 27.1 (1990), 49–52.

[19] James Turner, *Philology: The Forgotten Origin of the Modern Humanities* (Princeton: Princeton University Press, 2015).

[20] McGann, *New Republic of Letters*, 19. See also Matthew Giancarlo, "Mark Twain and the Critique of Philology," *ELH* 78.1 (2011), 213–37.

institution building – that is, whether it is a critical orientation that prioritizes language or a discipline that prioritized a narrow canon of Western literature. This confusion is partly a function of the recurrent debate about philology's "return." Harpham's unwitting prologue to Best and Marcus's codification of surface reading is a case in point. Harpham's essay identifies philology as a discipline, rehearsing an institutional history of nineteenth-century literary study and exposing its racializing projects. The essay specifically rejects an understanding of philology as a critical orientation or set of methods: its account of philology is derived from "actual historical practice" in philology's early institutional history rather than putative "essential or authentic" episte-mological categories and relations by which it might be defined as a method, abstracted from that history (38). In characterizing philology in terms of the disciplinary agenda to which it was put in the nineteenth century, Harpham emphasizes, in particular, its early project of finding the origins of literary texts, including determining the dates and compositional process for ancient texts and attempting to reconstruct the original forms they were imagined to have had. This focus underwrites Harpham's claim that philology's first and ongoing legacy in contemporary literary scholarship is a "conviction" that "things are explained when their origins have been identified" (54). As Harpham shows, this conviction was often motivated by, and contributed to, racist, nationalist and colonialist projects in the period in which "philology" was the disciplinary name for literary study. Defined by its desire for origins, its myth of national literatures, and its supremacist claims for the universal value of English and European literature, the discipline of philology stands in Harpham's account as antecedent to contemporary literary studies, the discipline superseded by the modern field, as well as a latent ideological possibility that threatens to return.

The stakes of identifying philology as a discipline rather than a method are thus clear, if implicit, in Harpham's argument: the trope of philology's return distinguishes it categorically from contemporary literary study. Philology, understood as a prior and separate discipline absorbs responsibility for the ideological projects undertaken by academic study of language and literature in the nineteenth and early twentieth centuries, and modern literary study is made innocent of its harms, provided that it continually performs this distance by thwarting philology's "return." Philology – as the name for a disavowed disci-plinary alternative – can only threaten to "return," after all, if it is presently absent. Modern academic literary study is, in turn, defined implicitly not by its methods (which might resemble philology's), but above all by its *distinction from* the field's erstwhile projects, a mythical rupture by which literary study is separated from its disciplinary past, even as it continues to occupy the same institutional locations.

This framing of philology – that is, as an institutional discourse defined by its projects rather than methods – has another, and more curious, effect in

Harpham's essay: it allows the facultative adoption (return?) of some of philology's signature methods, unrecognized as such. Indeed, the essay's avowed methodological principle, on which the very argument for identifying philology in terms of its disciplinary projects is grounded, is itself closely aligned with the defining epistemological orientation of philology as a method: focusing on actual use rather than abstract paradigm.[21] If there is some irony in the way that the essay also adopts the "conviction" that something is explained by its origin (the epistemological signature and legacy of philology as a discipline, as Harpham defines it), more genuinely philological is the methodological priority it gives to historical instantiations rather than abstract categories.

On its surface, the most striking parallel with philological methods is the evidentiary value that Harpham affords to language, and especially to current language use – namely, his interest in the use of the term "philology" in the titles of the journals *Modern Philology* and the *Journal of English and Germanic Philology*. As it happens, this is also the main forum in which Harpham takes up the question of whether philology should be understood as a methodology or a discipline. Noting the "loose eclecticism" of essays published in these journals, Harpham rejects an understanding of philology as a methodology since, in these venues, it does not delimit an identifiable or consistent analytical approach; he argues that the journal titles witness instead a "dream or myth of origins" (54). While his attention to language here seems at first to affiliate Harpham's approach with philology, the claim derived from that evidence ultimately ignores language use (the evidence provided by the essays, as well as key aspects of the term's persistence in the journal titles, as I suggest below) in favor of a transhistorical abstraction: this dream or myth inheres only in the term "philology" itself, assumed to be locked into its disciplinary past.

How might the ongoing use of "philology" in these titles be read philologically? As a method that necessarily attends to the historically dynamic quality of language and literature, philology's signature orientation is diachronic: it is attentive to difference and change across time, even – or especially – when its objective is to learn something about an earlier, or even an "originary" version of a text. Philology teaches, above all, that language is subject to ongoing use. Against a fantasy of language's ahistorical transparency, philology attends both to the histories that exert pressure on later iterations of language and to the counter-pressure that later use exerts on prior forms and meanings. Philology recognizes both the prior histories and current historicity of a word's semantic range, as well as the salience of the local social and inscriptional

---

[21] This methodological premise may take the form of a broader epistemological commitment as well, as in the "counter-philology" that James Porter identifies in Auerbach's work: Porter, "Erich Auerbach's Earthly (Counter-) Philology," *Digital Philology* 2.2 (2013), 243–65 (at 259).

contexts in which it is found. This is one way that philology understands language to matter: the past meanings and current uses of any word exist in complex and dynamic relation that requires careful attention to a range of social, institutional, and historical factors. In this case, a philological approach might take into account how academic journals are archived and accessed and what current institutional and material norms or structures shape or even supersede the referentiality of their titles. It might attend, more locally, to how a current penchant for abbreviation – as in *JEGP* for the *Journal of English and Germanic Philology* – obscures prior disciplinary histories and makes space for new methods. That is, a philological reading of the use of "philology" in the title of these journals would recognize how the use of the term is informed by current institutional practices as well as associations the term still carries from prior use.[22]

At the same time, read philologically, "philology" – in the title of a journal begun in 1897[23] – troubles the logic of return, the implied discontinuity between nineteenth-century philology and contemporary academic literary study, by registering the ongoing effects of the discipline's history on its current formation. Like the P in the Library of Congress Classification, which also originally abbreviated "philology," the P in *JEGP* persists not as a dream of origins but rather as an index of the term's history as a name for the discipline of literary study. That is, it points to the history of our discipline, a history in which there is no total rupture, no alternative origin, that can mark contemporary academic literary study as fully separate from its past. The persistence of "philology" in the titles of these journals, that is, constitutes a trace of ongoing structural legacies of the earlier disciplinary formation of literary study, which was called philology, in the constitution of modern academic disciplines. Perhaps trivial itself, the term's persistence in the title of these journals and in academic archives indexes far more salient legacies: the organization of the discipline by national literatures as witnessed by their institutional division into different departments; the myths of monolingual literary cultures which inform what is included, optional, and excluded in those departments; the schemes of periodization that derive from English and European political, social, and intellectual histories; and the systems of value that prioritize written expressive cultures over oral ones. These all constitute forms of path dependency through which modern literary study follows the furrows set down at an earlier point in the discipline's history, which are obscured by the trope of philology's (perennially threatened but not achieved)

---

22 In this way, such an analysis would allow for a distinction to be made between *JEGP* and, say, *Digital Philology: A Journal of Medieval Cultures*, founded in 2012.

23 The *Journal of English and Germanic Philology* was originally the *Journal of Germanic Philology*, the title under which its first four volumes were published; its new title dates from volume 5 (1903/5).

"return" from some mythic interval in which it does not continue to shape the discipline. The recognition of philology as a methodology, rather than an evacuated discipline that preceded our own, requires literary scholars, and especially those in English departments, to reckon with the ongoing effects of the discipline's inaugural projects, which are obscured when the specter of philology's "return" identifies modern literary study as a separate discipline whose rejection of philology witnesses its own innocence of the ideological projects through which it was founded.

Philology as a method can, moreover, provide a model for a critical regard on the disciplinary origins of literary study. Jonathan Culler follows his brisk account of how assumptions about, or claims made for, philology as a descriptive foundation of literary study, prior to putatively secondary interpretive frames, disguise its reliance on particular historical, ideological, and disciplinary suppositions, but he also acknowledges that "in principle as well as in practice," philology supplies the tools for challenging these same assumptions and claims. Philology, in his account, both enables the reconstruction of texts or textual cultures at risk of fragmentation and loss *and* directs attention to "the aesthetic and ideological assumptions about the meaning of texts on which reconstructive projects depend" (52).[24] Philology learns from its approach to texts a crucial form of self-critique: as Andrew Hui remarks, its reflex is to be "self conscious and self critical of its own purposes and limitations."[25]

Philology as the Pre-history of Post-Critique

The erasure of philology as method, exemplified by but not unique to Harpham's essay, also voids the comparandum it might otherwise provide for some of the interpretative protocols of surface reading or post-critique. Understood as a mode of inquiry that attends to language in terms of its social use as well as its dynamic history as manifest in its written form, philology may be understood, as Helle argues, as "a systematic engagement with crises of reading."[26] This definition echoes Barbara Johnson's declaration, some thirty years ago, that "what is at stake" in philology is "the question of the nature of the act of reading," whether "close or distant."[27] This question is also at the heart of recent scholarly churn about academic and extra-academic modes of reading "now."

[24] Culler, "Anti-foundational Philology," 52.
[25] Hui, "Review: The Many Returns of Philology," 144.
[26] Helle, "What is Philology?" 611.
[27] Barbara Johnson, "Philology: What's at Stake?" *Comparative Literature Studies* 27.1 (1990), 26–30 (at 30).

Indeed, the implications of Harpham's essay appear very different when approached retrospectively, from the vantage of Stephen Best and Sharon Marcus's programmatic, field-hailing "Surface Reading: An Introduction," which opened an issue of *Representations* devoted to "The Way We Read Now," that was published just a few months after Harpham's critique of philology.[28] Best and Marcus influentially conceptualized "surface reading" as a constellation of new methods that attend especially to the linguistic "surface" of a text, which they define as that which "insists on being looked at" rather than that which one endeavors to "see through" (9). In a posture that also fairly represents the critical orientation of post-critique and "reparative" reading, these methods are presented as a departure from "symptomatic" reading: the various "hermeneutics of suspicion," in Ricoeur's influential phrase, that seek to identify the "*non-dit*" or "political unconscious" or otherwise occluded projects or investments of a text. In contrast to the interpretive protocols of such "depth" hermeneutics, they argue that it is not necessary to "read against the grain" of a text, to approach it with suspicion or paranoia, or to look beneath its "surface" for a hidden depth in order to see how literary texts – that is, fictional and/or formally-interested texts – reflect, resist, and reimagine the social worlds in which they circulate.

Best and Marcus identify both a positively-valenced affective orientation to the text and a method rooted in observation and description as "nascent practices in the text-based disciplines" (3). But the phenomena to which surface reading attends parallel those of philology: e.g., the "intricate verbal structure of literary language" (10) and "patterns that exist within and across texts" (11), as well as the text's "literal meaning" (12). So too does its primary modality: a "practice of critical description" (11). Most resonant are the similarities in critical orientation and in its effects: surface reading, like philology, is characterized by "an affective and ethical stance," namely, one committed to elucidating the text's own meanings rather than supplementing, or replacing, them with the critic's own (10). The surface-reading scholar, like the philologist, "assembles" rather than merely "debunks" (19). Literary scholarship in this mode, that is, includes acts of recreating, of recreation, in both senses: oriented by the pleasure they take in a text, the surface-reading critic reconstitutes the work in the very act of engagement with it.

Though advocates of surface reading and post-critique rarely avow it, that is, the practices they advocate adopt epistemological values and interpretive practices of philology. Philology anticipates the acknowledgement, and valuing, of the affective impetus behind scholarly practices; it shares with recent methods a focus on careful attention to, and description of, a text's avowed projects and particular language; and it recognizes the evidentiary value

---

[28] Stephen Best and Sharon Marcus, "Surface Reading: An Introduction," *Representations* 108.1 (2009), 1–21.

of readerly use, response, attachment, and absorption. Harpham's review of philology itself provides resonant formulations, such as the notion of philology as a practice of "responsiveness and imagination" he attributes to Said (38), or the idea, advanced by some nineteenth-century scholars, that philology invited creative engagement with a text that gave it new currency (41). We can recognize the affinity between philology and "post-critical" reading especially in five core shared practices: (1) attention to a text's surface and interpretations that rely on semantic frames rather than ideology critique;[29] (2) an emphasis on description rather than interpretation;[30] (3) readerly affects that might be fairly identified by philology's etymon, "philo" (love, pleasure, immersion, attachment, devotion);[31] (4) idiosyncratic curiosities and textual observations as prompts to inquiry;[32] and (5) an open, reflective approach that might, with Sean Gurd or Michelle Boulous Walker, be called "slow reading."[33]

Claims for the novelty of surface reading are perhaps most credible when they rely not only on the positive affect which orients the reader to the text – as Deirdre Lynch reminds us, scholars have long been assumed or enjoined to "love" literature[34] – but also on the recent celebration of non-professional readers as the model for this orientation, or the way that attention to readerly pleasure blurs the ostensible divide between professional academic protocols of reading and non-professional ones. Given the long-standing association of philology with (excessive, even risible) erudition, surface reading or post-critical reading can most readily be seen as "new" if it arises from non-academic reading cultures, or from any extra-institutional ones. Nevertheless, this too is thin grounds for distinguishing between surface reading and the resurfacing of philology, and not only because the rubrics "surface reading" and "post-critical reading" are proper to professional academic study. While philology's epistemological orientation often takes the form of highly specialized methods, the patient, recursive attention to language that philology values is also paralleled by the devoted, iterative practices that Michael Warner calls

---

[29] E.g., Glavey, and Timothy Bewes, "Reading with the Grain: A New World in Literary Criticism," *differences* 21.3 (2010), 1–33.

[30] E.g., Heather Love, "Close but not Deep: Literary Ethics and the Descriptive Turn," *New Literary History* 41.2 (2010), 371–91. Paul de Man, in an essay that remains a vexed touchstone for understanding the disciplinary history of philology, defines it and rhetoric as "descriptive sciences" that are "allied with but distinct from" literary study: de Man, "Return to Philology," 21.

[31] E.g., Rita Felski, *Hooked: Art and Attachment* (Chicago: University of Chicago Press, 2020). See also Glavey, Sedgwick, Warner, and Deirdre Lynch, *Loving Literature: A Cultural History* (Chicago: University of Chicago Press, 2014).

[32] E.g., Dinshaw, *How Soon is Now?*.

[33] Gurd, *Philology and Its Histories*, 10; Michelle Boulous Walker, *Slow Philosophy: Reading Against the Institution* (London: Bloomsbury, 2016).

[34] Lynch, *Loving Literature*.

"uncritical reading," or the "amateur" engagements celebrated by Carolyn Dinshaw.[35]

Indeed, philology has itself long been an arena occupied by both professionals and amateurs, as Dinshaw's discussion of Hope Emily Allen reminds us. In her discussion of the affective intensities of studying medieval literature, Dinshaw links Allen's status as an "amateur" at once to her immersive philological attention to the *Book of Margery Kempe*, her animating attachment to Kempe, and her dilated ("slow") engagement with the text.[36] Allen embodies the amateur as philologist: engaged in patient, devoted attention to the text, in a project that ramifies precisely because it is conducted outside of the institutional demand for a final, authoritative presentation of findings and readings.

How, then, might recent enthusiasm for post-critical or surface reading help us understand the status of philology, as a method, in the field of literary study? And how might surface reading, as a method, be conceptualized more fully through comparison with philology? Three core questions surface: the first centers on their shared affective orientation, to and by some form of "love." How might remembering that literary study has a name for reading practices rooted in pleasure, attachment, or immersion advance our understanding of the intellectual, social, and institutional value of such practices, and of their potential limitations and exclusions? Thinking about some modes of "surface reading" in relation to philology might, in particular, help us specify better how feelings about a text shape analytical approaches to it. The second key question is about the status of description. Observation, pattern tracing, "close but not deep" reading: these have all been offered as alternatives to the putatively exhausted methods of depth hermeneutics. And yet the "surfaces" of contemporary surface reading are not different from the evidence of language on which philology has always depended. Philology recognizes some categories of evidence – a text's lexis, individual words that seem eccentric to a text, words understood in relation to a large corpus – that are also valued in recent reading practices. Thinking with philology, we may also be better able to account for what recent formalisms seek to "explain" by distinguishing between those that attend closely to language and those that train attention on supra-linguistic phenomena.[37]

---

[35] Warner, "Uncritical Reading." For a historical perspective on the relation between amateur readers and philologists as foundational to the discipline of literature, see Michael Warner, "Professionalization and the Rewards of Literature," *Criticism* 27.1 (1985), 1–28.

[36] Dinshaw recounts ways that Allen and her correspondents refer to Kempe and other medieval mystics as though they were living persons with whom they have affective and social entanglements: Dinshaw, *How Soon is Now?*, 120. For Dinshaw's most extensive reflections on the relation between philology and amateurism, see 97–9.

[37] Kramnick and Nersessian, "Form and Explanation."

Third, and more broadly, how might philology enrich the baseline assumption of surface and postcritical reading: that language matters. Philology explores how specific features of a text's language – its lexis, its morphology, its phonology, its syntax and rhymes and verbal echoes – anchor it in a material social world: language isn't only the basic unit of textual patterns, it also substantiates historical and social relations, meanings produced in relation to extra-textual phenomena, and readerly engagement or interpretation. In this attention to the many ways that language matters, philological approaches can, as Barbara Johnson once mused, "open up irresolvable difficulties, resistances to meaning, or other, unexpected meanings within the text" (28), a methodological objective it shares with surface reading.[38]

Philology also insists that language goes on mattering: the language in a text continues, beyond the moment of its composition, to exert concrete force on the extra-textual world, and it continues to change in response to that world. Language roots a text in the past, in the meanings and associations established by earlier uses and affiliations, especially those whose preservation in written form makes them accessible across time. Language also, of course, roots a text in the social context in which it is read, informed by and informing contemporary modes of relation. It is perhaps less frequently acknowledged that language roots a text in an unknown future, when its meanings will be reshaped by the dynamic quality of language, which changes continuously through users' invention and their experience of new historical exigencies and accidents. To the extent that some forms of post-critical reading are oriented toward "reparative" rather than "paranoid" ends, toward literature's capacity to create new forms of community or imagine possibilities beyond the status quo, philology may also provide resources for understanding how language goes on mattering.

Philology, Socio-Linguistics, and the Evidence of Literature

The philological principle that language matters also marks a potentially productive intersection between literary scholarship and linguistics. In addition

---

[38] In its commitment to the evidentiary value of language and its methodological demand to attend to language as a historical phenomenon, philology may remedy the sort of epistemological failures that Elaine Auyoung ascribes to the field of literary study: Auyoung, "What We Mean By Reading," 93–114. Claiming that "our discipline lacks a metadiscourse for assessing the inferences we make" (110), Auyoung asserts that the criterion for the value of a critical reading, such as it is, is the pleasure to be found in pattern recognition (107). Philology may, however, supply criteria that Auyoung finds lacking, as her own turn to philological evidence (e.g., contemporary written witness to an idea as evidence for the currency of Wordsworth's conceptualization of friendship) suggests (106).

32 CATHERINE SANOK

to philology's intradisciplinary relation to post-critical reading, this volume seems to limn recent productive cross-disciplinary relationships between literary study and sociolinguistics. As a name for the contact zone for analytical approaches to the evidentiary status of literary language, philology can at once suggest to literary scholars the value of sociolinguistics and, in turn, help to conceptualize the value of self-consciously literary texts for active research questions in sociolinguistics. If, with Erich Auerbach, we define philology as systematic attention to language "in particular with works of art composed in language,"[39] then sociolinguists' current interest in literary evidence creates a new opportunity for thinking about the disciplinary configuration of linguistics and literary study.

As a field defined against philology, linguistics was founded in a rejection of this configuration: indeed, a key dividing line between linguistics and philology was attention to literary works and the phenomena which define them as such, including the use of a special literary lexis or formal features such as rhyme. The putative antagonism between philology and linguistics helped to create the latter's disciplinary boundaries from at least the inaugural issue of *Language*, the flagship journal of the Linguistic Society of America, founded in 1925. Leonard Bloomfield, in the prolegomenon justifying the establishment of the society, identified linguistics as the "science of language" whose project is to identify universal qualities of language and particular instantiations of these qualities.[40] In a footnote, Bloomfield defines philology, in contrast, as the "study of national culture" (4, n. 1), but the more telling phrase is in the essay's main text, where he defensively remarks that a "student of language" is perceived "a kind of crow-baited student of literature" (4). "Crow-baited," as a philologist might be inclined to explain, is a term used of horses that are so worn out as to make them easy targets for nuisance scavengers. To escape this fate, the new "science" of linguistics should not be "placed in any close connection with the study of fine arts, of which literary history and criticism form a part" (4).

Bloomfield's invocation of a broad disciplinary difference between science and arts is interesting primarily for the anxiety it betrays about the priority, vigor, and efficacy of language study, which he imagines strikingly as enervated, spent by age or over-work, even in this inaugural moment of the field as such. The impetus to separate linguistics from philology, Bloomfield's

---

[39] Erich Auerbach, *Introduction aux études de philologie romane* (Frankfurt: V. Klostermann, 1949), 9; quoted in the English translation by Suzanne Fleishman, "Medieval Vernaculars and the Myth of Monoglossia: A Conspiracy of Linguistics and Philology," in *Literary History and the Challenge of Philology*, ed. Seth Lerer (Palo Alto: Stanford University Press, 1996), 91–2; cited in Seth Lerer, "Philology and Criticism at Yale," *Journal of Aesthetic Education* 36.3 (2002), 19.

[40] Leonard Bloomfield, "Why a Linguistic Society?" *Language* 1.1 (1925), 1–5.

metaphor suggests, is less a matter of developing "scientific" protocols for studying language than a claim to novelty in response to representations of philology – and perhaps the humanities in general – as moribund. That novelty lies less in developing either a more theoretical or more empirical discipline, as Bloomfield's identification of linguistics as a "science" might at first imply, than in the rejection of "literature" as the object of inquiry.

As Margaret Winters and Geoffrey Nathan explain in "First He Called Her a Philologist and Then She Insulted Him," the relation between linguistics and philology was hashed out in fuller and more complex terms in short order.[41] The two disciplines were sometimes seen as complementary, as the study of the general phenomena of language (linguistics) and its local instantiations (philology), and they were sometimes seen as categorically different. Part of the problem, as George Melville Bolling noted in his 1929 essay, "Philology and Linguistics," was the variety of practices identified as philology, some of which he thought proper to linguistics, some to philology, and some not really proper to either.[42] That is, philology's broad range of methods made it impossible for linguistics to distinguish itself clearly on the grounds of analytical categories and procedures. Instead, as a kind of science, rather than a form of "love," linguistics was more readily codified in this early moment of disciplinary formation by its rejection of literature as its object of study.

Linguistics as a field remained shy of literary evidence well beyond its inaugural self-definition as a discipline, and despite the eclipse of philology in literary scholarship, because qualities that identify literature as such – e.g., the degree of formal patterning they exhibit and/or the fictionality that untethers them from certain forms of reference – make it eccentric to ordinary language use. For this reason, as Christopher Palmer remarks in his essay in this volume, literary texts have been understood to provide uncertain evidence for linguistic research. As Palmer notes, however, imaginative or self-consciously literary texts also provide special purchase on the relations between "language, culture, and thought," perhaps especially for early periods, given that both their historical distance and the vagaries and politics of archival preservation limit our capacity to access the thought worlds of past cultures. At the same time, recent work in sociolinguistics – including Palmer's essay and that of Colette Moore, the volume's first case studies – can bear on the disciplinary contours of literary study by modeling the field's potential to address key lines of shared inquiry, including those concerning multilingualism, vernacularization,

---

[41] Margaret Winters and Geoffrey Nathan, "First He Called Her a Philologist and Then She Insulted Him," in *The Joy of Grammar: A Festschrift in Honor of James D. McCawley*, ed. Gary Larson, Lynn MacLeod, and Diane Brentari (Amsterdam: John Benjamins, 1992), 351–67.

[42] Winters and Nathan, "First He Called," 353.

political community, the affordances of poetic form, and the political work of narrative fiction.[43]

So, for example, Palmer proposes that the "reservoir" of linguistic possibilities in the multilingual environment of late medieval English literature facilitated the development of a formal "architecture" of end rhyme because it provided an expanded range of possible word endings. He argues for the value of examining derivational suffixes (e.g., the *-age* in *marriage* or the *-cion* in *corrupcioun*) in rhyme position in order to illuminate how the use of end rhymes might have facilitated the decomposability of endings: that is, the independent legibility of suffixes, which in this case allows them to be productive across languages. He then argues that this phenomenon indexes the degree to which endings registered distinctions – or their absence – between the languages of late medieval England for their users. Surveying evidence from works of Chaucer, Gower, Hoccleve, and Lydgate, Palmer presents quantitative and qualitative evidence regarding the degree to which vernacular audiences could navigate and even understand the component parts of words. This evidence has implications for whether the multilingual environment of late medieval England should be understood through the analytical frame of code-switching or, as Palmer ultimately argues, translanguaging. Where code-switching assumes a significant linguistic and social distinction between languages understood as discrete from each other, translanguaging refuses *a priori* distinctions between languages on the grounds that language users themselves do not necessarily assign some words or word parts to different languages.

In tracing the relay between prosodic and morphological form to advance our understanding of the relationship between England's several languages, Palmer's study demonstrates that literary texts offer specific kinds of linguistic evidence by virtue of the very features that distinguish them from quotidian, non-marked language use, which is usually preferred in sociolinguistic research. Colette Moore's essay, with which Palmer's is paired in the volume's first section, demonstrates another way that imaginative literature may hold special evidentiary value for sociolinguistic approaches. In particular, she shows that literary texts could be an important arena for re-valuing topically freighted terms – in this case, the lexicon of civic assembly, as it was coded and re-coded in the wake of 1381, as political movements and expressions of social unrest made certain ideas of collectivity suspect or threatening to those

---

[43] A notable arena of shared inquiry is language history, such as Mark Amsler, *The Medieval Life of Language: Grammar and Pragmatics from Bacon to Kempe* (Amsterdam: Amsterdam University Press, 2021); Kathy Cawsey, *Images of Language in Middle English Vernacular Writings* (Cambridge: D.S. Brewer, 2020); and Eric Weiskott, *Meter and Modernity in English Verse, 1350–1650* (Philadelphia: University of Pennsylvania Press, 2021).

invested in current social hierarchies and institutions. Moore offers what a literary scholar might call a "reparative" reading: she uses linguistics methods to identify how imaginative literature created positive representations of civic assembly against the derogative associations they acquired in conservative discourses. Removed from actual events by its fictionality, and drawing on the relay of significance within the boundaries of a story, imaginative literature in Moore's account serves as a forum for recognizing modes of affiliation and sociality that are elsewhere delegitimized in the service of the status quo.

In this way, her essay provides one example of how forms of "surface reading" explored in recent methodological discussions might be conceptualized at the level of lexis: it asks how literary works re-code terms and concepts in the context of the negative connotations or even ideological exclusion they may suffer in other discourses. Such attention to literature's role in expanding or revising the connotations of a lexico-conceptual category has an exciting resonance with the project of "surface" reading: further, it provides a methodological model for how to track surface collocations that matter, as well as an exemplary case study for the kind of socio-political inquiry to which this method can contribute. Demonstrating the distinctive capacities that literary texts have for developing, shifting, or making concrete a set of connotations, Moore's approach at once justifies the potential value of literature for linguistic research and demonstrates the potential value of such research for our understanding of the political potentials of imaginative literature.

Finally, we note, more generally, that the combination of qualitative and quantitative analysis that Moore and Palmer both pursue may have special promise in regard to some recent meditations on the methods of literary study. Their work points the way for literary scholarship that may want to study texts at scale, as they do, in reciprocal relation to local attention to textual detail. Linguistics, that is, provides some useful ways to think about the relationship between the quantitative approaches of "distant" reading, the attention to language patterns of "surface" reading, and the cultural work of literature valued by reparative readings.

We offer this set of essays, headed by Palmer and Moore's contributions, then, to show that current attention to how "language matters" produces a fertile potential for cross-disciplinary encounter. Essential to this is an attention shared by sociolinguists and literary scholars to the social and political stakes of literary language. Together the essays that constitute the volume provide overlapping or methodologically proximate models for investigating how language both registers and participates in socio-economic power and political brutality, as well various reparative projects for valuing civic community, imagining the possibility of evading the world, or seeking transcendence and stability. The work collected here – which explores an expanding Middle English lexicon, the literary affordances of phonological and morphological features of Middle English, and the ways in which Middle English literary texts take up multilingual sources on the level of language – demonstrates that even local linguistic details of imaginative literature have social and existential repercussions. Understanding them fully, we suggest, requires attention to distinctive features of language that are the disciplinary domain of linguistics, such as phonology, morphology, and semantics, and the distinctive features that are the traditional disciplinary domain of literary scholarship, such as form and genre. This is because some of the most salient ways that imaginative literature mirrors, molds, and mitigates social hierarchies are co-constituted by modes of language use that are the domain of sociolinguists and features of literary texts that are the domain of literary interpretation.

The book proceeds in four sections, gathered in a rough chiastic structure: the first two sections ask what medieval literary texts can reveal about the history and function of language; the second two sections invert the question, asking what linguistic observations might reveal about literary texts. The domains of discourse range across social and political themes, from civic to spiritual discourses and from verbal echoes to visual traditions.

The first section comprises the essays by Palmer and Moore, which together exemplify the particular value that literary texts have for research on the history of English. The volume's second section continues Moore's attention to lexical range, but does so through literary rather than linguistic methods. David Lavinsky, like Moore, takes up the "socio-semantic" dimensions of literary works concerned with civic practices. He builds on lexicographic evidence that Karla Taylor surveyed in her influential reading of Chaucer's *Tale of Melibee* to argue that its "florilegial form" identifies the local effects of language, not the text's sweeping but notional allegory, as the primary arena for its social vision and prudential ethics. Such features also implicitly claim new forms of cultural capital for prose, which has a plasticity that invites "supplementary" dilation of advisory language that registers the situated nature of social interactions. Kenneth Hodges likewise explores how literary language points beyond individual ethics to a pragmatic view of social life. Hodges identifies a surprising overlap in the language linking chivalry to asceticism in *Barlam and Iosaphat*, a fifteenth-century Middle English translation of a saint's life that began as a life of Buddha, and Malory's Quest for the Holy Grail. This lateral relation, across the divide of religious and secular narrative, points to shared identification of the "unstable" world, rather than personal virtue, as the warrant for ethical practices of self-denial.

The third section traces the functions of language by observing aesthetic effects, grounded in the sensory particularity of language: Stephanie Batkie's essay explores what words can do sonically, and Ashby Kinch's piece asks how a verbal tradition is distinct from its visual corollary. Batkie's piece on Chaucer's *Reeve's Tale* begins with a pun that points to sound – *resoun/ resounen* – but finds the Reeve to be tragically entrapped within the logic of reason instead of resonance. Despite the cleverness of his puns and repetitions and his sly use of rhythm, he fails to see the way his own linguistic resonances offer potential for escape from the strictures of service that define him. Batkie argues that, even as we register the Reeve's complicity in his own social constraint, Chaucer also uses him to suggest the hope of release. Kinch similarly explores linguistic manipulation in his essay on Chaucer's appropriations of the visual image of the soul in flight, which occur in the *Summoner's*, *Merchant's*, and *Second Nun's Tales*. Kinch shows that Chaucer deploys this affect-laden visual discourse – one that inspires hope in the bereaved – not so much to confirm as to complicate the seductive potential of images themselves. For Kinch, Chaucer's skeptical use of the image of the soul in flight suggests a wariness about the spiritual and communal power of the image tradition, which promises spiritual comfort but can also threaten to mislead. Chaucer's exposure of tension between spiritual vision and poetic appropriation, Kinch contends, opens the possibility of readerly decision and suggests the ethical potential of aesthetic forms.

The final section of the book centers on intertextuality and allusion, the building blocks of so much of Karla Taylor's work. Andreea Boboc explores a continuation of Chaucer's *Squire's Tale* written in 1615/30 by the poet John Lane, who explores and extends the Squire's story of the offspring of Cambuskan (Gengis Khan) as they compete among themselves for honor and land, using black and white magic to wage civil war and eventually make peace. Boboc argues that Lane's poem harks to the *Squire's Tale* and to Prudence in the *Melibee*, associating them with the now dead Queen Elizabeth I. To link Elizabeth nostalgically with Chaucerian discourses of prudence, Boboc argues, calls to account the Stuart connection between witchcraft and treason. A more local allusion – to Ovid's Myrrha, whose illicit desire for her own father resulted in her being turned into a myrrh tree – provides the focus for Elizabeth Allen's essay. Allen finds that incest confuses forms of communal obligation, raising the question whether community is founded in shared feeling or differentiated roles, whether it relies on lateral affective bonds or hierarchical obligations. The stanza's language prompts her to argue that Criseyde's survival is a communal duty, but one that dismantles the poem's fantasy of compassion based on fellow-feeling.

As this brief summary suggests, a core theme linking the essays across the volume is language in community, whether the community be civic gatherings (Moore), provincial manors (Batkie), the geographically extended community of Buddhist and Christian asceticisms (Hodges), or the temporally enlarged community of post-medieval readers (Boboc). Several essays show that, while communities are constituted in and through language, their relations are neither stable nor transparent since they remain subject to the flux of language in use. Imperfect communication happens at the level of morphology in the problem of translinguistic word formations (Palmer) or at the level of lexis in the excesses of translation (Lavinsky). It happens in the differential forms of authentication in a visual tradition rendered potentially deceptive in its verbal instantiation in Chaucer (Kinch) and in the tension between line and syntax in an Ovidian incest narrative alluded to in a moment of political crisis in Chaucer's *Troilus* (Allen). The various scales at which Taylor's students have applied her mode of thought is a testament to the portability of her philological methods and the power of her conviction that language matters, then and now.

PART II

THE SPECIAL AFFORDANCES OF LITERARY TEXTS FOR THE HISTORY OF ENGLISH

3

Borrowed Suffixes in Late Middle English Poetry: Multilingualism, Decomposability, and End-Rhyme Architecture

CHRIS C. PALMER

Poetry is rarely a first choice for linguists investigating language phenomena. The genre can certainly be indispensable in studies of sound, including metrics and phonology.[1] But because of its highly structured and sometimes atypical diction and grammar, it is often treated as a highly marked register. In my early studies as a graduate student, a linguist once recommended to me that, if at all possible, poetry be excluded from historical studies since it presents grammatically "weird" constructions that are unlikely to reflect everyday language use. When I discussed this comment with Karla Taylor, we agreed that part of why we study medieval poetry is *because* it's weird – but also because it has important things to tell us about language, culture, and thought in earlier historical periods.

We can of course acknowledge the idiosyncrasies of poetic discourse while avoiding assumptions about its general representativeness of typical linguistic behavior. In fact, poetry should not be dismissed so readily. As the following chapter will illustrate, end-rhymed poetry from the late medieval period turns out to inform interesting questions about the history of borrowed derivational morphology in English: what sorts of discourses (e.g., legal, religious, economic) were poets primarily drawing upon when using different borrowed nominal suffixes such as *-age* (e.g., mariage), *-ite* (e.g., auctorite), and *-cion* (e.g., imaginacioun)? How does a descriptive account of a poetic use of suffixes help us better understand their productivity (frequency and

---

[1] Consider the LINGUIST List discussion of the pronunciation of "thou" in the seventeenth century and beyond, which relies in part on evidence from poetry: http://www.linguistlist.org/issues/7/7-1473.html.

diversity of use in different words) and decomposability (their transparency as independent, word-making endings within larger words) in Middle English (ME)? And in light of contemporary debates about phenomena such as code-switching and translanguaging, how might an analysis of borrowed suffixes in ME poetry make us consider whether multilingual writers perceived Latin, French, and English as distinct language channels, or instead as a single multilingual reservoir for imaginative literature?

To explore these questions, this chapter will first provide some contexts for studying derivational suffixes in late ME poetry and clarify key concepts such as decomposability, productivity, naturalization, code-switching, and translanguaging and their relevance to language use in this period. It will then provide a brief overview of previous studies of borrowed derivatives in poetry and justification of the texts selected and methods of analysis used in this particular study. The chapter next offers a case study of the use of four suffixes (native *-ness*, as in "goodness," and borrowed *-ite*, *-age*, *-cion*) in a corpus of late ME rhymed poetry (Chaucer's *Canterbury Tales*, Gower's *Confessio Amantis*, Hoccleve's *Regement of Princes*, and Lydgate's *Reson and Sensuallyte*). To compare the morphological status of these endings in the corpus, I apply some measures of productivity that are generally applicable to analyses of suffixation within any register. These measures depend on assessments of various frequencies. The analysis first focuses on token counts: absolute frequencies (i.e., total counts of uses of each suffix in the corpus) provide general evidence about usage patterns of words containing the suffixes, but do not necessarily impact the transparency of suffixes themselves. To assess the potential productivity of suffixes, the analysis also considers factors such as the diversity of derivative types used. Lexical fields (i.e., sets of semantically related words) are also explored in order to provide a more nuanced understanding of the lexeme groups most likely to contribute to the use of each suffix as well as to identify several discursive motivations for incorporating different sorts of borrowings in verse.

While analyzing this morphological data, the chapter argues that there are specific facts about the development of these suffixes in Middle English that are particular to the genre of poetry. For example, an examination of positional occurrence – i.e., whether or not lexemes occur line-finally – provides potentially revealing information about both the relative "naturalization" of different borrowed suffixes, in David Burnley's terms,[2] and the aesthetic motivations for using words with these endings in the first place. And an analysis of the use of borrowed derivatives in rhymed couplets demonstrates the effects of poetic structure on the salience and transparency of suffixes. Because several

---

[2] David Burnley, "Lexis and Semantics," in *The Cambridge History of the English Language, Vol. II: 1066–1476*, ed. Norman Blake (Cambridge: Cambridge University Press, 1992), 409–99.

ME poets use such diverse ranges of borrowed derivatives in their writing, I explore ME poets' varied motivations for using frequent numbers of them in their verse, as well as the potential impact on the analyzability of borrowed suffixes in English when poetic audiences are exposed to frequent numbers of derivatives in salient poetic patterns.

Ultimately, this study aims to show some of the ways in which the study of medieval literature can inform the study of language and vice versa. By looking to form, both poetic and morphological, the chapter illustrates the significant role some borrowed suffixes played in helping Middle English poets build an architecture based on end rhyme. And it suggests that the varied and frequent use of these suffixes contributed to their decomposability and perceived productivity in English – at least within communities that would have been exposed to these poems (most likely upper- and upper-middle-class readers and listeners). This analysis also demonstrates how poets frequently leaned on borrowed derivatives to create a variety of poetic discourses (including legal, religious, and scientific), which in turn reveals different motivations for borrowing and expanding the English lexicon. The chapter concludes by considering how such studies of borrowing in medieval language and literature might be productively put into conversation with contemporary debates about multilingualism, code-switching, and translanguaging.

Some Contexts and Concepts for Studying Borrowed Suffixes in Middle English Poetry

Formal and Discursive Motivations for Using Borrowed Derivatives

Two canonical fourteenth-century poets, Chaucer and Gower, were interested in Continental poetic forms and used a relatively high number of words borrowed from Latin and French.[3] And two of their successors in the early fifteenth century, Hoccleve and Lydgate, continued and extended Chaucerian poetic practices. All four of these poets were motivated to use borrowed derivatives (such as "possessioun," a noun derived from the verb "possessen" "to possess" + -cioun) for a variety of reasons: the semantics of the lexemes, their prosodic qualities, their usefulness as words signaling an aureate or high style in the vernacular, and their capacity to signal non-literary discourses (such as law). The utility of borrowed derivatives was partly a result of these poets' interest in verse forms that emphasized end rhyme rather than alliteration as

---

[3] Here I simply mean that many of the words in their English works have etymons in Latin and/or French. The use of these words may have been a result of direct borrowing from the source language – e.g., *sublimation* borrowed from Latin. Others, especially those in Anglo-French (e.g., *brocage*), may have been available to Chaucer and Gower in their spoken language since these poets were multilingual.

the primary rhyming device. Borrowings with endings such as *-able*, *-ite*, and *-cion* provided vernacular poets with a new stock of multisyllabic words all ending in the same sonic sequences. Some of these forms allowed for double (i.e., disyllabic or so-called "feminine") rhymes, where the last syllable would be unstressed (*-able*); some allowed for single (i.e., monosyllabic or so-called "masculine") rhymes, with stress on the final syllable (*-ite, -cion*).

Although the derivatives were chosen by these poets for their phonological and semantic properties, this word choice had morphological consequences. The most obvious effect is an increase in the absolute frequencies of different morphological types used by a specific set of English writers – i.e., those producing courtly poetic discourse in the vernacular in the late medieval period. This increase in the use of borrowed derivations was part of a larger trend in the late fourteenth century.[4] I have shown elsewhere that a number of emerging English vernacular prose genres in the fourteenth and fifteenth centuries – such as guild records;[5] medical writing and Wycliffite Biblical prose;[6] and personal correspondence[7] – also began to use significant frequencies of derivatives from French and Latin. Even though this was a general trend in the period, writers likely had motivations for using borrowed derivations that were particular to each genre. One of the particular motivations for poets, for example, may have arisen from aesthetic and formal concerns; borrowed derivatives made for useful end-rhyming devices. Another motivation for writers of imaginative literature was likely the utility of borrowed derivatives to signal other "non-literary" discourses. Because there has been scant investigation into these specific derivatives and the discourses from which they emerge within ME poetry, the case study offered later in this chapter provides a fuller descriptive account.

---

[4] For accounts of the rise of borrowed derivatives in the history of English in the fourteenth and other centuries, see Christiane Dalton-Puffer, *The French Influence on Middle English Morphology: A Corpus-based Study of Derivation* (Berlin: De Gruyter, 1996), as well as Karen Anderson, "Productivity in English Nominal and Adjectival Derivation, 1100–2000" (Ph.D. thesis, University of Western Australia, 2000).

[5] Chris C. Palmer, "Borrowed derivational morphology in Late Middle English: A study of the records of the London Grocers and Goldsmiths," in *Studies in the History of the English Language IV: Empirical and Analytical Advances in the Study of English Language Change*, ed. Susan M. Fitzmaurice and Donka Minkova (Berlin: De Gruyter, 2008), 231–64.

[6] Chris C. Palmer, "Base and suffix paradigms: Qualitative evidence of emergent borrowed suffixes in multiple Late Middle and Early Modern English registers," *Inozemna Philologia* 116 (2011), 45–52.

[7] Chris C. Palmer, "Measuring productivity diachronically: Nominal suffixes in English letters, 1400–1600," *English Language and Linguistics* 19.1 (2015), 107–29.

Decomposability and Productivity

In contrast to prose, end-rhymed poetry makes its formal structure transparent visually (through lineation when in lineated manuscripts) and audibly (through metrical patterns and rhyme schemes). Because poetry used borrowed derivatives frequently as end rhymes, these borrowings receive a type of foregrounding that is particular to this genre. And the potential effects of the use of derivatives in these specific poetic contexts on poetic audiences deserve further investigation.

Visually and audibly, derivatives receive more salience and emphasis when they manifest in poetic contexts, particularly in end-rhyme position, as observed in the following excerpt from the beginning of Chaucer's *Friar's Tale*:

> (1)   Whilom ther was dwellynge in my contree
> An Erchedekene a man of heigh degree
> That boldely dide <u>execucioun</u>
> In punysshynge of <u>fornicacioun</u>
> Of wicchecraft and eek of bawderye
> Of <u>diffamacioun</u> and Auowtrye
> *Canterbury Tales* (my emphasis)[8]

This example illustrates one way in which poetry may uniquely provide potential evidence of the decomposability of a derivative into its component parts. Decomposability can be defined as the ability for a language user to see both a base (e.g., execute) and a suffix (e.g., *-cioun*) as transparent, independent parts of a complex word, rather than perceiving that word as a single unit (e.g., execucioun rather than *execut-* + *-cioun*). Dalton-Puffer[9] reminds us that linguists cannot assume complex words in Middle English are necessarily decomposable: words using French or Latinate material for both base and ending, such as "execucioun," could either be a whole-word borrowing from French or Latin, or a derivative composed of a borrowed base (execute) and a productive suffix (*-cion*) in English. But the poetic form of example (1) makes the decomposability of *-cion* derivatives more likely because the rhyme in the couplet "execucioun/fornicacioun" makes the attachment of *-cioun* to two different stems quite salient for readers and listeners. In other words, the couplet performs a visual juxtaposition of similar word-formation, highlighting that the ending *-cioun* can be used to create two meaningfully different nouns. The attachability of *-cioun* is then further foregrounded by the use of "diffamacioun" two lines later, showing a third possible derivative it can generate.

---

[8]   All poetry citations in this chapter come from the *Corpus of Middle English Prose and Verse*, http://quod.lib.umich.edu/m/middle-english-dictionary/ (accessed 6 January 2023).

[9]   Dalton-Puffer, *The French Influence*, 219.

Decomposability thus suggests that a suffix is more analyzable (as one part of a complex word) and more transparent for language users. And both analyzability and transparency, along with frequency of different types of derivatives, are key characteristics that make a suffix productive in a language, meaning that it can be used to create a variety of words, including neologisms.[10] Thus, by looking at the positional placement of borrowed suffixes within the poetic line and their frequency of use in different types of derivatives, this study aims to locate additional evidence of the decomposability and productivity of selected borrowed suffixes in Middle English.

Naturalization, Code-Switching, and Translanguaging

The use of borrowed derivatives in example (1) above also speaks to the question of *naturalization*, a process in which linguistic constructions borrowed from another language come to be seen as less "foreign." Assumptions about the naturalization, or lack thereof, of borrowings has informed certain linguistic studies of literature. James Wimsatt, for example, has argued that ME poets were more likely to place borrowings, such as "execucioun" and "fornicacioun" in example (1), in end-rhyme position since poets need the range of consonant and vowel combinations available in borrowed words to effectively construct a reliable and aesthetically appealing rhyme scheme.[11] Drawing on evidence primarily from *Pearl*, he speculates that end-rhyming is harder to achieve with native English (Germanic) word stock alone, so it is more natural to place non-borrowed words in non-end-rhyme positions. Because this claim about the varying naturalization of words needs to be tested on a broader range of ME poetry, with consideration of the role of suffixes, it will be one point of consideration later in this chapter.

Moreover, decomposability seems to be a necessary step in the naturalization of borrowed suffixes in English. According to Burnley, affixes on borrowed derivatives may become productive after "analysis of the word structure" begins to occur; after such decomposability, the affix may still be seen as foreign and may productively attach to borrowed bases; and if it becomes very frequent in coinages, the affix may "cease to be considered exotic" and become fully naturalized, attaching to "bases of any origin."[12]

---

[10] Christiane Dalton-Puffer, "Productive or not productive? The Romance element in Middle English derivation," in *English Historical Linguistics 1992*, ed. Francisco Fernández, Miguel Fuster, and Juan Jose Calvo (Amsterdam and Philadelphia: John Benjamins, 1994), 248–9.

[11] James Wimsatt, "Rhyme, the Icons of Sound, and the Middle English *Pearl*," *Style* 30.2 (1996), 189–219.

[12] Burnley, "Lexis and Semantics," 445–6.

Wimsatt's and Burnley's ideas on the naturalization of borrowings in Middle English, while useful considerations for this study, also need to be put into conversation with contemporary linguistic debates over multilingual phenomena such as code-switching and translanguaging. Michelle Devereaux and I have noted that in current scholarship on Global Englishes, models of code-switching tend to assume that speakers cognitively and practically keep languages in separate "boxes," switching between them for rhetorical or other situational purposes. Translanguaging models, by contrast, tend to assume that multilinguals don't keep languages in separate boxes but rather freely traverse languages as needed in all communicative contexts.[13] Thus, under a translanguaging model, the boundaries between languages are real only in an ideological sense – i.e., because we name them separately and claim them separately for national, social, or other reasons.

It would seem that code-switching models can be well aligned with models of naturalization and share some assumptions about language use: namely, that languages for both monolingual and multilingual speakers are seen as having clear and distinct boundaries. Thus, the act of borrowing a derivative such as "execucioun" in Middle English assumes that language has been taken from the domain of French, Anglo-Norman, and/or Latin, and imported into a separate and distinct domain of (Middle) English, when the writer needs to rhetorically signal a specific sort of religious or legal demand or decree. Naturalization perhaps collapses some of those boundaries in its ultimate stages, but in Burnley's model there is still an assumption that a borrowed suffix like *-cion* would shift away from a perceived state of being "foreign" or "exotic" if it were fully naturalized. In other words, naturalization still assumes the boundaries between native and foreign languages are intact even as a borrowed suffix transforms from an "exotic" one to a "naturalized" one.

Even though there have been substantial scholarly treatments of code-switching among speakers of earlier Englishes,[14] there has been far less engagement with translanguaging approaches in medieval English scholarship. This is somewhat surprising, as one of the earliest and most highly cited translanguaging pieces on present-day multilingualism singles out Chaucer's Middle English (the first four lines of the *Canterbury Tales*, specifically) as

---

[13] Michelle D. Devereaux and Chris C. Palmer, *Teaching English Language Variation in the Global Classroom: Models and Lessons from Around the World* (New York: Routledge, 2022), xviii–xx.

[14] For good overviews of code-switching in the early centuries of English, see *Code-switching in Early English*, ed. Herbert Schendel and Laura Wright (Berlin: De Gruyter, 2011), as well as *Multilingual Practices in Language History: English and Beyond*, ed. Päivi Pahta, Janne Skaffari, and Laura Wright (Berlin, Boston: De Gruyter, 2017).

an example of why translanguaging may be quite relevant to the context of ME poetry:

> Now what can we say about these four lines? Are they an example of mixing English and French, of code switching? Or are they an example of what philologists today call Middle English? As we have insisted, this question has no linguistic answer (no answer based on lexicon and structure), for it assumes societal judgments regarding the features that a named language should or should not contain. At the level of the individual English poet, we can say that Chaucer's idiolect contained both words brought to England by the Anglo-Saxons and words brought by the Normans; and he used them all with no apparent consideration of their history, just as Ricardo and Ofelia [the authors] freely use all the words they know at home. Whether Chaucer is code switching or writing in what is called by some philologists Middle English is a question about how he and his poem are perceived by others; it is not really a question about either Chaucer himself – his idiolect – or his poetry. This distinction between what societies view as language and what individuals do with their lexical and structural features leads us to the further elaboration of the notion translanguaging ...[15]

While it seems unlikely that Chaucer had "no apparent consideration" of the history of the words he used, these scholars' larger point here is that there are differences in how we (speakers, linguists, medievalists, and so on) perceive and name languages (e.g., whether Chaucer is code-switching between English and French, or writing in an English that exhibits many elements borrowed from French, or some other possibility). And then there are differences between these naming practices and how individuals use language(s) in practice. An additional implication here is that translanguaging might be a more useful model for explaining at least some phenomena in the Middle English period than has currently been considered.

The following study of borrowed suffixes in late Middle English poetry will explore, when relevant, some of these ideas regarding naturalization, code-switching, and translanguaging, resisting the temptation to claim that any one framework can fully or singly explain all the data under analysis. Indeed, certain sections below will test some of Burnley's and Wimsatt's ideas on how much late ME poetry might be able to tell us regarding the naturalization of foreign suffixes in English verse. But theories of translanguaging remind us that the relationship between languages in late medieval England for multilingual poets may not have depended on an a priori sense

---

[15] Ricardo Otheguy, Ofelia García, and Wallis Reid, "Clarifying Translanguaging and Deconstructing Named Languages: A Perspective from Linguistics," *Applied Linguistics Review* 6.3 (2015), 295–6.

of linguistic differences – a perspective that will affect how we interpret some of this morphological data.

Previous Studies and Text Selection

To date, there have been few comprehensive studies of poetry and borrowed derivational morphology in the history of English. Fisiak provides one chapter on derivational morphology in Chaucer, offering a catalogue of affixes with a brief feature analysis.[16] Donner has explored Chaucer's wordplay, with derivational morphology only a small part of the analysis.[17] The studies most relevant to the questions posed in this chapter have been lexicographic, almost singularly focused on the vocabulary of Chaucer.

Mersand provides an early statistical analysis of the use of Romance lexemes in Chaucer.[18] He estimates that 60% of nouns in the *Canterbury Tales* are of Romance origin,[19] and that in most of Chaucer's works, the percentage of Romance words used as rhymes ranges from approximately 30% to 55%.[20] He also discovers some specific poetic effects on Chaucer's lexicon: (a) Chaucer tended to use a higher percentage of Romance lexemes when translating from Latin than from French;[21] and (b) he used higher percentages of Romance loans when writing tales than when writing allegories.[22] Mersand's study is helpful primarily because it identifies various features that affected the use of borrowings in Chaucer's verse and lays out a range of expected Romance usage. But his study cannot necessarily be extrapolated to Middle English poetry more generally, and he does not provide specific statistical counts of Romance derivations.[23]

Christopher Cannon and R. Carter Hailey each present lexicographic studies of Chaucerian language.[24] Hailey proposes that Chaucer had an effect on the

---

[16]   Jacek Fisiak, *Morphemic Structure of Chaucer's English* (Tuscaloosa: University of Alabama Press, 1965).

[17]   Morton Donner, "Derived Words in Chaucer's Language," *Chaucer Review* 13 (1978), 1–15.

[18]   Joseph E. Mersand, *Chaucer's Romance Vocabulary* (New York: Comet, 1939).

[19]   Mersand, *Chaucer's Romance Vocabulary*, 117.

[20]   Mersand, *Chaucer's Romance Vocabulary*, 87–8.

[21]   Mersand, *Chaucer's Romance Vocabulary*, 97.

[22]   Mersand, *Chaucer's Romance Vocabulary*, 99.

[23]   He does provide an appendix of Romance words appearing in any works by Chaucer, yet he does not provide counts for any words occurring more than four times.

[24]   Christopher Cannon, *The Making of Chaucer's Language: A Study of Words* (Cambridge: Cambridge University Press, 1998); R. Carter Hailey, "To 'Finde Wordes Newe': Chaucer, Lexical Growth, and *MED* First Citations," in *Words and Dictionaries from the British Isles in Historical Perspective*, ed. John P. Considine and Giovanni Iamartino (Newcastle-upon-Tyne: Cambridge Scholars, 2007), 14–24.

lexical diffusion of a number of new terms in Middle English, many of them borrowed derivatives. He tracks lexemes which have first attestations in the *MED* in either the *Cursor mundi* or the *Ayenbite of Inwit* and second or third attestations in Chaucer, noting that the senses of the terms originated by Chaucer frequently appear as the primary definitions in the *MED* and are cited often by subsequent authors. Hailey attributes this lexicographic phenomenon to the fact that Chaucer was one of the most widely read writers in the period, whose vocabulary had an impact on later writers. Combing through his list of terms that were taken up by Chaucer and diffused into other texts, I found two *-ite* lexemes (quantite, magnanimite) and many *-cion* derivatives (abusion, dissencioun, generacioun, extorcioun, satisfaccioun, significacioun, corrupcioun, possessioun, imaginacioun, detraccioun, conversacion, complexioun, compassioun, porcioun). There were also words with other borrowed affixes, including *-aunce* (e.g., aboundaunce, distemperaunce), *-ous* (e.g., riotous, suspecious), and *-ify* (e.g., fructifien, glorifien). Altogether, a significant portion of Chaucer's innovations and early adoptions – at least 13% (or 45 out of 330) in Hailey's survey – consists of borrowed derivatives.

Like Chaucer, Gower also used a significant number of borrowed derivatives in his English verse. Yonekura provides a comprehensive list of first attestations from the *OED* attributed to Gower's *Confessio Amantis*.[25] Appearing in Yonekura's list of 459 words, which include first attestations of new senses of older words in the language, are derivatives ending in *-age* (gaignage, pilage, herbage, visage), *-ite* (adversite, auctorite, congruite, fraternite, nativite, unite, virginite), and *-cion* (approbacion, calculacion, congelacion, deificacion, deputacion, distallacion, incantacioun, prolificacion, revolucion, subfumigacioun, sublimacion, substitucion, supplantacion, commendacion, conclusion, constitucion, demonstracion, descencion, disposicion, division, generacion, impression, interpretacion, invocacion, meditacion, operacion, prolacion, proporcion, question, supplicacioun). Yonekura's study suggests that a range of relatively new borrowed derivations in English appear in Gower's vernacular verse.

Because they were two of the more widely distributed texts in the medieval period, Chaucer's *Canterbury Tales* and Gower's *Confessio Amantis* were both selected for this study's corpus. To reduce the effects of poetic idiosyncrasies and make broader generalizations about rhymed ME poetry possible, I have also added Hoccleve's *Regement of Princes* and Lydgate's *Reson and Sensuallyte*. These early fifteenth-century poets are commonly considered the successor generation to Chaucer and Gower. Fisher argues that Hoccleve

---

[25] Hiroshi Yonekura, "Gower's Contribution to the English Vocabulary," *Kotoba no kozo to rekishi. Structural and Historical Studies on Languages: Essays Presented to Dr. Kazuo Araki on the Occasion of his Seventieth Birthday*, ed. Hirozo Nakano and Kazuo Araki (Tokyo: Eichosa, 1991), 503–24.

and Lydgate were both instrumental in the "initiation of a plan to cultivate English as the official and prestige language of the nation," which led to the Chancery's shift to English.[26] This plan depended on both poets' closeness to the Lancastrian court, their interest in promoting and circulating Chaucer's vernacular work, and their commitment to writing original verse in English.[27]

Methods: General Considerations

To approach these texts from a quantitative and qualitative perspective, editions were chosen from the Compendium of Middle English's *Corpus of Middle English Prose and Verse* (CMEPV). While digitized versions of several different manuscripts of the *Canterbury Tales* are available in the CMEPV, the Ellesmere was chosen because it is often seen as one of the most complete and definitive versions. The prose sections of the *Canterbury Tales* – namely, the *Tale of Melibee* and the *Parson's Tale* – were not considered.

Four suffixes were chosen for this study: three are from borrowed derivations (*-age*, *-ity*, *-cion*) and one from native (i.e., non-borrowed) formations (*-ness*). The quantitative and qualitative accounts of *-ness* serve as a basis for comparisons in usage patterns between one native and several non-native forms. Orthographic variation and plural forms of each affix were factored into the total counts for each ending. If a token included a suffix followed by other inflectional and derivational suffixes, it was not retrieved in searches (e.g., charitable was not counted for *-ite*).

Token Counts: Absolute Frequencies

Absolute token frequencies (i.e., the total number of occurrences of words ending in a particular affix) are not typically used as direct measures of morphological productivity in scholarly accounts. Baayen's numerous studies find that productive processes tend to be characterized as having low frequencies of a broader range of derivative types (e.g., a wide range of derivatives ending in *-ness* or *-age* appearing only once or at most a few times each in a corpus).[28]

---

[26] John Fisher, "A Language Policy for Lancastrian England," *PMLA* 107 (1992), 1178.

[27] Fisher, "A Language Policy," 1178.

[28] For Harald Baayen's conclusions about frequency and productivity, see *A Corpus-based Approach to Morphological Productivity: Statistical Analysis and Psycho-linguistic Interpretation* (Amsterdam: Vrije Universiteit, 1989); "Quantitative Aspects of Morphological Productivity," in *Yearbook of Morphology 1991*, ed. Geert Booij and Jaap van Marle (Dordrecht: Kluwer, 1992), 109–49; and "On Frequency, Transparency and Productivity," in *Yearbook of Morphology 1992*, ed. Geert Booij and Jaap van Marle (Dordrecht: Kluwer, 1993), 181–208. For a helpful summary

In contrast, unproductive processes tend to exhibit higher frequencies of fewer types (e.g., unproductive suffixes such as *-th* or *-dom* appearing in only a few types of derivatives, such as "depth" or "kingdom," even if those few derivatives are quite commonly used). Cognitive Grammar and frequency-based theories of morphology suggest that morphologically complex words are more likely to be stored and retrieved by speakers as whole words as their frequency of use increases.[29]

Even so, it is not immediately clear that these conclusions about token frequencies and morphology are entirely relevant to the linguistic situation of borrowed derivational morphology in Middle English. Most studies of present-day English productivity approach suffixes as already established linguistic units in the mind – either part of a rule or a schema. While some ME speakers (e.g., those who were multilingual and translanguaged among French, English, and Latin) may have stored such representations of borrowed suffixes, many were likely encountering a number of these derivatives with these endings for the first time. As will be seen in later sections, many derivatives in *-cion*, for example, came from highly learned discourses such as science and law (e.g., sublimacion, calcinacion, jurisdiccion) that would not have been widely known. In other words, many of these derivatives were in a stage of vocabulary acquisition for Middle English speakers. Encountering texts that frequently used these derivatives likely helped some readers or listeners who were less familiar with these terms recognize, even on an unconscious level, the deriva-tives' endings as potentially productive suffixes in Middle English. In this sense, repeated exposure to derivatives using *-ite*, *-age*, and *-cion* in texts such as poetry likely helped to produce the very rules or schemas that eventually allowed language users to perceive the derivatives' endings as independent units that could attach to different bases.

Language acquisition studies have found that type frequency (i.e., the total number of different words ending in the same suffix) impacts learners' ability to analyze derivations into roots and affixes.[30] Donna Lardiere posits that frequency affects second language learners' ability to recognize derivationally

---

of these views, see also Laurie Bauer, "Productivity: Theories," in *Handbook of Word-Formation*, ed. Pavol Stekauer and Rochelle Lieber (Dordrecht: Springer, 2005), 315–34.

[29] For Cognitive Grammar approaches, see David Tuggy, "Cognitive Approach to Word-formation," in *Handbook of Word-Formation*, ed. Pavol Stekauer and Rochelle Lieber (Dordrecht: Springer, 2005), 233–65. For frequency-based theories of morphology, see Joan Bybee, *Frequency of Use and the Organization of Language* (Oxford: Oxford University Press, 2007).

[30] Eve Clark, *The Lexicon in Acquisition* (Cambridge: Cambridge University Press, 1993).

related words and their use in different syntactic contexts.[31] Linda Jarmulowicz has discovered that token frequencies of *-cion* and *-ity* affect children's abilities to learn prosodic rules associated particularly with those affixes; she speculates that "rule development" of derivational morphemes is "based on frequency of exposure" – i.e., higher frequencies enable stronger or faster development – both in terms of tokens and types.[32]

In light of these studies, I assume that token frequency matters in accounts of borrowed derivational morphology, at least in a limited sense. For speakers to learn a new morphological rule, a certain level of derivatives must exist in usage so that those forms can be analogized. It is thus important to provide a general descriptive account of the texts and authors who were more or less likely to use different borrowed derivatives. Such an account provides a rough picture of patterns of diffusion and distribution within the corpus, helping to answer the "who is using what and why?" question central to corpus linguistic inquiry.

Table 3.1 below provides the total token counts for each poet in the corpus; normalized counts appear in parentheses. Figure 3.1 represents a side-by-side comparison of normalized word-counts:[33]

Table 3.1: Absolute frequencies of suffix types for each poet, with numbers normalized to occurrences per 10,000 words in parentheses.

	Chaucer	**Gower**	**Hoccleve**	**Lydgate**
-ness	216 (10.5)	197 (9.5)	177 (39.9)	203 (50.0)
-ite	210 (10.2)	128 (6.2)	98 (22.1)	60 (14.8)
-age	208 (10.1)	272 (13.1)	52 (11.7)	76 (18.7)
-cion	331 (16.1)	372 (17.9)	129 (29.1)	176 (43.4)

The graph demonstrates that Chaucer and Gower tended to trend together in their rates of use of all four affixes, while Lydgate and Hoccleve were typically more likely to use much higher rates of derivatives. There are statistically

---

[31] Donna Lardiere, "Knowledge of Derivational Morphology in a Second Language Idiolect," *Proceedings of the 8th Generative Approaches to Second Language Acquisition Conference (GASLA 2006)*, ed. Mary Grantham O'Brien, Christine Shea, and John Archibald (Somerville, MA: Cascadilla Proceedings Project, 2006), 72–9.

[32] Linda Jarmulowicz, "English Derivational Suffix Frequency and Children's Stress Judgments," *Brain and Language* 81 (2002), 192–204.

[33] The total word counts for each text are as follows: Chaucer's *Canterbury Tales* (205,703), Gower's *Confessio* (207,378), Hoccleve's *Regement* (44,354), and Lydgate's *Reson* (40,600).

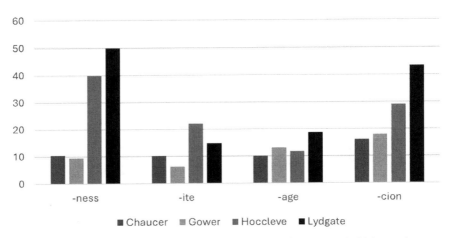

Fig. 3.1: Occurrences of tokens of each suffix for every 10,000 words.

significant differences[34] between Chaucer's and Gower's rates of -*ity* and -*age*, but for the most part these differences are slight compared to differences between these two poets and Hoccleve/Lydgate. The only exception to this general pattern concerns the suffix -*age*, which Chaucer, Gower, and Hoccleve employ at rates similar to one another and significantly less than Lydgate.

Some scholars might speculate that the general differences between the earlier (Chaucer, Gower) and later (Hoccleve, Lydgate) generations are attributable to their differing commitments to "aureate style." Denton Fox explains this possibility as follows: "the theory is that Chaucer studied, and followed, the rules recommending ornate diction which were laid down in most of the medieval treatises on poetry, and that the fifteenth-century poets imitated and exaggerated his practice."[35] While Fox rightly doubts that the fifteenth-century poets' diction was necessarily dependent on Chaucer's own practice, the data above suggest that Hoccleve and Lydgate did employ substantially higher rates of borrowed derivatives in their poetry than did Chaucer or Gower. But the data also demonstrate that the fifteenth-century poets also used remarkably higher rates of -*ness* derivatives. An interesting possibility here is that the high style developed by Hoccleve and Lydgate might have depended not on

---

[34] Chi-square tests show significance between Chaucer's and Gower's use of -*ity* ($p = 0.000$) and -*age* ($p = 0.003$).

[35] Denton Fox, "Chaucer's Influence on Fifteenth-Century Poetry," in *Companion to Chaucer Studies*, ed. Beryl Rowland (Toronto: Oxford University Press, 1968), 385–402.

Latinisms solely, but on polysyllabic and morphologically complex lexemes more generally, including words that were not borrowed.

The graph also shows that, among the borrowed derivatives, *-cion* was consistently the most frequently used borrowed derivative type for all four poets. It was even more frequent than *-ness* in Chaucer and Gower. As will be seen later in this chapter, the relatively high frequency of *-cion* may have been due to both its attractiveness as a useful end-rhyming device and the variety of lexical fields from which its derivatives could be drawn.

Suffix Types: Frequencies and Semantics

The following sections provide a quantitative and qualitative examination of the diversity of lexemes under investigation. The first section develops the notion of lexical density in order to account for similarities and differences in the use of these suffixes among the four poets of this study. The final subsection provides a qualitative, semantic analysis of the various types in order to determine the most prominent semantic motivations for using each suffix.

Type Frequencies and Lexical Density

The total number of distinct types of each suffix for each poet appears in Table 3.2 below:

Table 3.2: Total number of types for each poet.

	Chaucer	**Gower**	**Hoccleve**	**Lydgate**
-ness	61	34	62	48
-ite	36	28	30	23
-age	29	28	16	19
-cion	115	105	66	59

It is possible to assume that a greater number of types implies a higher likelihood that a suffix will be transparent and decomposable for language users associated with each text (i.e., the poet and his readers/listeners). If so, then an initial glance at the chart suggests that derivatives with these affixes may have seemed most decomposable in Chaucer, and that high lexical diversity contributed to *-cion*'s transparency more than for the other affixes. However, total word count must also impact the effects of such diversity. For example, compare Gower's use of 28 *-ite* types to Hoccleve's 30 types. Intuitively, even though the number of types used is roughly the same for each poet, it would seem that a reader would be more likely to recognize analogous

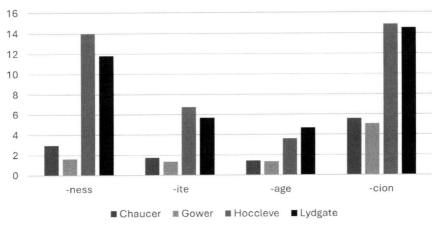

Fig. 3.2: Lexical density scores, measured as number of suffix types per 10,000 words.

-*ite* forms in Hoccleve than in Gower because of differences in overall word count. Specifically, a reader would encounter, on average, approximately 7 different -*ite* derivatives for every 10,000 words of Hoccleve compared to only 1 different -*ite* derivative for every 10,000 words of Gower. In other words, based on type frequency exposure alone, -*ite* would be more likely to be seen as transparent and productive in Hoccleve than in Gower, despite the fact that both poets use a similar number of -*ite* types overall. To examine this factor for all suffixes in all poets' works, consider Figure 3.2 above, which presents the normalized counts of types for each poet and suffix.

Each value can be considered a lexical density score, the proportion of total types adjusted to 10,000 words of text by each poet. Because type frequency has been found to correlate with productivity in present-day studies of frequency and morphology, I hypothesize the following: a higher lexical density score correlates with an increased likelihood of perceived decomposability, while lower scores may suggest a decreased likelihood that type diversity impacts the transparency of a suffix (i.e., that it is an independent morpheme that can attach to multiple bases).

According to these scores, it is clear that Chaucer and Gower trend together in their rates of use of different types of these suffixes. The only statistically significant difference between them concerns -*ness*; a chi-square test between these poets' use of this suffix yields a p-value of .005. While type frequency is not typically considered a criterion for evaluating stylistic similarity, it is interesting to consider the possibility that these poets – who are sometimes described as stylistically similar – may have used derivational suffix types in comparable amounts. Similarly, Hoccleve and Lydgate trend together.

Chi-square tests show no statistically significant differences between these two poets' lexical density scores for any of the four suffixes.

The most evident difference in the graph is the consistently higher scores for Lydgate and Hoccleve compared to Gower and Chaucer. Hoccleve and Lydgate exhibit higher rates of diverse usage of these suffixes, so to speak. This disparity may be a result of differences in word count more than any other factor. Even so, the effects on transparency in these texts might be significantly different. If morphological transparency is a function of lexical diversity of types, then Hoccleve and Lydgate may have been even more likely to prompt readers to see these derivatives as decomposable than Chaucer and Gower were. According to these data, then, -*cion* and -*ness* may have been generally more likely to have increased transparency than -*ity* and -*age* due to the effects of lexical density alone, at least within the poetic corpus assembled for the present study.

Lexical Diversity and Semantic Motivations: Building Poetic Discourses

To complement the preceding quantitative analyses of type frequencies, this section provides a qualitative analysis of the different suffix types employed by the four poets. The analysis finds that many of the derivatives of each suffix inhabit particular lexical fields, and that the use of derivatives from specific discourses suggests some of the semantic motivations for the poets' use of these particular derivatives. In addition to serving as a descriptive overview of the semantic classes of the derivatives appearing in these poetic works, the section also establishes for each suffix the lexical fields which contributed most to its usage in this type of poetry.

Perhaps unsurprisingly, Christian terminology supplies a substantial number of derivatives, both native and borrowed, in the corpus. Many -*ness* words in all four texts, for example, have religious valences; they are typically nominalizations of adjectives connoting virtues or vices. Examples include unkindnesse, wikkidnesse, drunkennesse, ydelnesse, lustynesse, Hethenesse, unbuxomnesse, unclennesse, clennesse, goodnesse, ryhtwisnesse, holsum-nesse, meknesse, holinesse, sobrenesse. But Chaucer's derivations include some more innovative forms that do not signify religion, such as newfangel-nesse and mazednesse. Other than a single example with -*age*, all other hybrids formations (i.e., lexemes that mix stems and affixes from different languages) found in this study were formed with -*ness*, including buxomnesse (Gower, Hoccleve), pitousnesse (Gower), mazednesse (Chaucer), likerous-nesse (Chaucer), doubleness (Lydgate, Chaucer).

Derivatives with -*ite* are also typically taken from religious discourse (charite, virginite, Trinitee, nativite, prodegalite, humylitee, Cristyenytee, benyngnite). But they also include traits and general characteristics without solely religious denotations (diversite, femynynytee, prolixitee, notabilitee, curiosite, sensibilite, quantyte).

Lexemes with *-age* come from a variety of discourses, many of which are broadly legal, often denoting social order and obligations. Some signify taxes and other monetary matters (costage, taillage, arrerage). Others describe various dwellings (herbergage, messuage), or words associated with travel by water (rivage, lodemenage). Many denote collectives, either related to family (cousinage, heritage, marriage) or feudalism (baronage, vassellage, servage, truage). There is one hybrid form, lodemenage, but all other *-age* lexemes are based on borrowed word stock.

Lexemes in *-cion* are far more varied than lexemes with the other endings, with between two to three times as many different *-cion* derivatives as there are *-ite* or *-age* types for all four poets. Part of this rich lexical diversity must have been due to the number of discourses from which *-cion* formations were drawn. Some observable lexical sets in the data are listed in Table 3.3 below:

Table 3.3: Examples of *-cion* lexemes from different lexical fields.

	Chaucer	**Gower**	**Hoccleve**	**Lydgate**
Religious terms	savacioun absolucion redempcion persecucion dampnacion	justificacion salvacion devocion absolution contricioun	savacioun dampnacioun fornicacioun dileccioun resurreccioun	perfeccion devocioun
Legal terms	cavillacion jurisdiccion	deputacion substitucion constitucion excusacioun	probacioun abusion excusacioun	iurisdiccion accusasion collusion
Scholarly/ clerical terms	deliberacioun meditacioun	consideracion meditacioun enformacion	significacion contradiccioun	demonstracion interpretacion
Scientific terms	declynacion calcinacion albificacion citrinacion	sublimacion calcinacion fixacion	n/a	calculacion computacion

These lexical fields do overlap, of course. "Deliberacioun" has legal valences, "meditacioun" has religious meanings, and so on. From a morpho-semantic point of view, a word ending in *-cion* is particularly useful for a poet because it is a nominalization of an action, resulting in one word of a few syllables. By using *-cion* derivatives, poets can convey processes and actions compactly and synthetically when needed, rather than relying on longer paraphrases. Some examples of such poetic motivations will be qualitatively explored later in this chapter.

To identify the borrowed derivatives that all four poets were motivated to use, we can consider the following list, which itemizes those lexemes for each suffix type which occurred in each poet's work at least once:

- ***-ity***: adversite, auctorite, chastite, dignite, diversite, equite, felicite, humilite, nativite, prosperite, superfluite, virginite
- ***-age***: avantage, corage, heritage, langage, lynage, servage, viage
- ***-cion***: affeccion, conclusion, condicion, confusion, corrupcion, destruccion, devocion, discrecion, disposicion, eleccion, entencion, mencion, occupacion, perfeccion, possession, presumpcioun, question, subieccion

Unsurprisingly, many of the words ending in *-ite* and *-cion* come from religious lexical fields. This may indicate nothing more than the fact that all four medieval poems treated religious themes in great detail. But note that the majority of the most broadly disseminated *-cion* derivatives are terms denoting cognitive processes, including reasoning (conclusion, confusion, discrecion, entencion, question) and affect (affeccion, disposicion). Legal and scientific terms do not appear to be the most distributed types of *-cion* derivatives within the corpus. These usage patterns likely reflect the fact that all four poets relied on meditative and rhetorically aware language when treating a variety of themes – religious or otherwise.

Another notable finding is that the most commonly distributed *-age* derivatives in this corpus do not come from economic discourse. Suzanne Fleischman has suggested that *-age* derivatives in this period were primarily employed to denote either economic transactions (such as fees listed in the ledgers of the Grocers' records) or feudal relationships.[36] In this poetry corpus, the primary semantic field for *-age* is terminology that defines social rank and relationships (avantage, heritage, lynage, servage). There is likely a register-specific explanation here, in that these poems often dealt with feudal themes and/or social rank explicitly (e.g., Chaucer's myriad of pilgrims from different estates). It is reasonable to speculate that different registers in the late ME period contributed to the development of *-age* in distinct ways: account books were most likely to reflect and impact the productivity of *-age* via the use of words for fees and duties, while poems may have been more likely to impact the suffix's perceived transparency via lexemes denoting social rank.

Ultimately, by considering the lexical fields of derivatives, it is possible to determine which semantic categories were contributing most to the use and spread of derivations in registers such as ME poetry: for *-ite*, it was religious

---

[36] Suzanne Fleischman, *Cultural and Linguistic Factors in Word Formation: An Integrated Approach to the Development of the Suffix -age* (Berkeley: University of California Press, 1977). For discussion of borrowed suffixes in the Grocers records, see Palmer, "Borrowed Derivational Morphology in Late Middle English," 231–64.

terminology expressing virtues and vices; for -*age*, terms denoting social rank and relationships; and for -*cion*, lexemes signifying cognitive processes and, to a lesser extent, religious actions. For literary scholars, this analysis reveals the significant role that borrowed suffixes played in helping poets to develop and expand diverse types of vernacular discourses in their poetry. And it also illuminates for historical linguists a number of discursive motivations for borrowing so many of these derivatives into English usage. The naturalization framework might interpret this data as evidence that some of these French and Latinate discourses were becoming more "Anglified" over time, particularly for jargon repeated in multiple texts across the two generations of poets. And while there could be an argument that these poets were code-switching into and out of Latin or French as they invoked these discourses, it is equally plausible that these poets were simply translanguaging among discourses as needed without much regard for the source languages of the derivatives. And perhaps translanguaging is a more apt model for explaining hybrid forms in which borrowed and native morphemes were mixed, such as "unbuxomnesse" and "lodemenage": it might seem more reasonable to analyze these examples as free mixing of linguistic elements rather than rhetorically motivated shifts between languages in the middle of words.

Borrowed Derivatives as End Rhymes

The preceding sections have presented a quantitative and qualitative analysis of tokens and types – including frequency measures and lexical field analysis in order to assess patterns in the use of borrowed suffixes and to identify potential motivations for the spread of different types of borrowed derivatives in late ME poetry. While these measures could be applied to any text type, the remainder of this chapter turns to features specific to poetic texts. These features, such as positional distributions within the poetic line and couplet structures, provide valuable information about morphological processes. By analyzing these genre-specific qualities, I locate further evidence of motivations for the use of different suffixes in poetry.

Positional Distributions

While not the first poets to rely primarily on end rhyme, Chaucer and Gower were certainly two of the most influential figures in popularizing rhymed verse forms in the late fourteenth century, with Hoccleve and Lydgate maintaining this practice into the following century. Chaucer experimented with different rhyme schemes in the *Canterbury Tales*, from couplets to rhyme royal. Hoccleve too preferred rhyme royal for the *Regement*, while Gower in the *Confessio* and Lydgate in *Reason* relied strictly on couplets. In his studies of "Pearl," which mixes alliteration and end rhyme, Wimsatt discovers that the poetic skill required to produce end-rhymed verse has a direct effect on the poet's use of borrowings from other languages:

> [A]s the requirements of the prosody increase, so does the proportion of words of non-English etymology increase. We may hypothesize that the stressed words in Pearl that involve no rhyme, neither alliteration nor end-rhyme, represent the most natural word choice of the poet. Alliteration (initial rhyme), involving a single sound, requires a somewhat larger exertion of artistry. And end-rhyme, consisting of a sequence of vowels and consonants, requires still more. Consequently, the use of both French and Norse words increases as the artistic requirements increase.[37]

Wimsatt stresses the fact that by using end rhyme, Middle English poets are compelled to reach into borrowed word stock. They must find enough varied vowel and consonant sequences to secure both the sound and sense of the versification.

Similarly, the present study finds that when borrowed derivatives are employed in Middle English rhymed verse, they appear primarily in the end-rhyme structures of the poem. In other words, while these Latinate and French derivatives certainly have important semantic and thematic functions, they primarily serve as building blocks within the poetic architecture of the poems themselves.

To study this phenomenon, I conducted a count of the positional occurrences of *-ness*, *-ite*, *-age*, and *-cion* in the poetry corpus. Position was considered a binary variable: derivatives were classified as either "end-rhyme" or "non-end-rhyme." Derivatives were counted within each individual poetic work to establish ranges for the percentages of derivatives of each suffix type occurring as end-rhymes. Separation of poets also helped to ensure that no single poet was too idiosyncratic in his derivational usage. Tables 3.4a–4d below provide the total token counts and percentages of tokens in end-rhyme positions for each suffix type within each poetic work:

Table 3.4a: End-rhyme percentages for Chaucer.

Chaucer	Total # Tokens	Total # Tokens in End-Rhyme Position	Percentage of Use in End-Rhyme Position
-ness	216	148	68.5%
-ite	210	177	84.3%
-age	208	149	71.6%
-cion	331	286	86.4%

[37] Wimsatt, "Rhyme," 199.

Table 3.4b: End-rhyme percentages for Gower.

Gower	Total # Tokens	Total # Tokens in End-Rhyme Position	Percentage of Use in End-Rhyme Position
-ness	197	135	68.5%
-ite	128	97	75.8%
-age	272	210	77.2%
-cion	372	335	90.1%

Table 3.4c: End-rhyme percentages for Hoccleve.

Hoccleve	Total # Tokens	Total # Tokens in End-Rhyme Position	Percentage of Use in End-Rhyme Position
-ness	177	128	72.3%
-ite	98	62	63.3%
-age	52	35	67.3%
-cion	129	109	84.5%

Table 3.4d: End-rhyme percentages for Lydgate.

Lydgate	Total # Tokens	Total # Tokens in End-Rhyme Position	Percentage of Use in End-Rhyme Position
-ness	203	159	78.3%
-ite	60	56	93.3%
-age	76	69	90.8%
-cion	176	172	97.7%

Interestingly, there are no statistically significant differences[38] in the four poets' use of *-ness* as an end rhyme. The suffix is used as an end rhyme in percentages ranging from 68.5% to 78.3% of the time. The lack of significant variation may occur because this was a native derivation type that would have been less marked for the sorts of aesthetic considerations discovered in Wimsatt's study

---

[38] To test for statistically significant differences between two poets' positional use of the same suffix and between two different suffixes used by the same poet, I ran these numbers through a binary logistic regression.

of borrowings. If so, then it is possible that this is a normal distribution range for the use of naturalized, open-class, morphologically complex words as end rhymes, though further research would be needed to confirm this hypothesis. For purposes of comparison between native and borrowed lexis in the present study, this range for *-ness* can be tentatively assumed to represent positional distributions of unmarked derivatives.

Among the four poets, only Lydgate's use of *-age* is significantly different. He employs derivatives with this affix over 90% of the time as end rhymes, while the other poets do so between 67.3% and 77.2% of the time. Thus, in most of the corpus *-age* is distributed similarly to *-ness*, with the exception of Lydgate, who uses *-age* significantly more often as an end rhyme. The results for *-ite* are similarly mixed. Chaucer and Lydgate employ *-ite* a significantly high number of times as an end rhyme (84.3% and 93.3%, respectively), while Gower and Hoccleve use it within the same range as *-ness*.

The suffix most evidently marked for use as an end rhyme in this study is *-cion*, which all four poets used in percentages ranging from 84.5% (Hoccleve) to as high as 97.7% (Lydgate). In general, *-cion* is far more likely to occur as an end rhyme than *-ness*. In contrast, there is no significant difference between the use of *-age* and *-ness* as an end rhyme for any of the poets; a naturalization framework would thus suggest that *-age* is as naturalized as *-ness*. The suffix *-ite* is used significantly more than *-ness* in only Chaucer (though the difference in Lydgate almost shows statistical significance as well). In comparing the three borrowed affixes with one another, *-ite* and *-age* are used similarly as end rhymes in all poets but Chaucer, who uses *-ite* almost 13% more often than *-age* at the end of poetic lines. For all poets, *-cion* is consistently used more often than *-age* and *-ite* as an end rhyme, even when percentages for *-age* and *-ite* are already significantly high. Wimsatt's framework would hold that among these suffixes, *-cion* is clearly the least naturalized.

While there are likely several factors that could explain these high percentages of end-rhyme occurrence for all four suffixes, the overall numbers confirm Wimsatt's supposition that borrowed linguistic elements are more likely than not to occur as end rhymes. Even so, such an analysis also demonstrates that levels of naturalization as determined by position within the poetic line differ for different suffixes, since *-cion* is by far the suffix most likely to occur line-finally.

Motivations for Suffixes as End Rhymes

So what factors were driving the decision to use derivatives predominantly as end rhymes? The ending *-cion* deserves particular attention since it is the most frequently occurring end-rhyming derivative in this study. Some individual cases may be due to imitation or translation of texts from Latinate and Romance sources; Karla Taylor, for example, has shown that end rhymes

64 CHRIS C. PALMER

in languages other than English are sometimes borrowed by poets like Chaucer when translating or alluding to poets writing in other languages.[39] Part of the motivation may be prosodic, since *-cion* derivatives are all at least trisyllabic (and most of four or more syllables) and could be placed at the end of lines to create a sequence of iambs. Both *-cion* and *-ite* may have been particularly convenient for poets since they guaranteed final-syllable stress; any time poets wanted to create a single/monosyllabic rhyme, they had a well of lexemes from which to draw. But this is also true of *-ness* forms with odd numbers of syllables (e.g., bitternesse, worthiness).

While translation and prosody were likely factors, there must have been other motivations driving the high use of *-cion* in final positions. One possibility is that *-cion* (and to a lesser extent *-ite*) may have signaled a "Latinate" sound in Middle English, particularly when it is accentuated at the ends of verse lines. For example, Lydgate's frequent use of *-cion* derivatives – 97% of which occurred as end rhymes – may have helped him communicate an aureate style to his readers. Lydgate's rhyme scheme would have given even more salience to *-cion* derivatives, in turn emphasizing the Latinate sonicity of the suffix. From this perspective, the positional placement of borrowed derivatives can be considered an additional feature of poetic style in this period.

In some cases, the reader can witness the process of borrowing overtly Latinate derivatives into the vernacular of the poem. In Book 1 of the *Confessio*, for example, Gower first introduces the concept of presumption, as a specific form of the sin of pride, in one of his Latin insertions:

(2) Omnia scire putat, set se <u>Presumpcio</u> nescit,
     Nec sibi consimilem quem putat esse parem
     Qui magis astutus reputat se vincere bellum,
     In laqueos Veneris forcius ipse cadit.
     Sepe Cupido virum sibi qui <u>presumit</u> amantem
     Fallit, et in vacuas spes redit ipsa vias
     (Book 1, b/w ll. 1882 and 1883, my emphasis in underlining)

As signaled in this insertion, presumption will become a primary theme in this section. Gower first translates the Latinate concept of presumption into the noun "surquiderie" in most of the subsequent vernacular verses. But when he comes to the exemplum of Capaneus one hundred lines after this Latin insertion, he brings the vice of presumption into the rhyme scheme itself:

(3) And upon such presumpcioun
     He hield this proude opinioun

[39] Karla Taylor, "Chaucer's Volumes: Toward a New Model of Literary History in the *Canterbury Tales*," *Studies in the Age of Chaucer* 29 (2007), 44.

By using "presumpcioun" in his vernacular, Gower has made a direct textual link between the Latin and English language portions of his poem, perhaps providing the clearest example of code-switching between languages in this study and illustrating how a Latinate borrowing can get naturalized in English discourses. He increases the Latinity of the poetic structure since "presumpcioun" has immediately recognizable Latinate valences: it was dragged from Latinate text, adapted, and embedded into an English rhyme scheme soon after. At the same time, he makes the borrowing more accessible by pairing it with the rhymed and alliterated gloss "proude opinioun," which consists of a common English adjective preceding a noun likely more familiar to readers and listeners.

As this example suggests, Gower may have been motivated to use a high percentage of *-cion* forms as end rhymes for thematic, etymological, and sonic reasons. Indeed, throughout the *Confessio*, Gower draws attention to the Latinity of his poem through lexical means, emphasizing the connectedness of his poetic narrative to many of his classical sources (e.g., Ovid). It may be possible that his and the other poets' lexical choices attempted to manage the risks of using the vernacular; the salience of Latinate end rhymes was intended to maintain the prestige of the poems and to remind readers of the poems' classical resonances and commitment to high-minded Christian themes such as the embrace of virtues and the avoidance of vices.

Another possibility, which was detailed in the previous section on lexical diversity and type frequencies, is that *-cion* forms offered a variety of semantic choices for the Middle English poet since they came from a number of semantic fields (including legal, religious, and scientific discourses). Indeed, there is qualitative evidence that all three borrowed derivatives in this study were used as end rhymes to emphasize certain topics. Since a line break and a rhyme draw emphasis to the final word of a poetic line, poets may have wanted to highlight many of these lexemes for thematic reasons. For example, Chaucer relies on rhymed *-ite* derivatives with Christian valences to emphasize the Wife of Bath's rejection of idealized notions of feminine sexuality:

> (4) And many a seint sith the world bigan
>   Yet lyued they euere in perfit <u>chastitee</u>
>   I nyl nat enuye no <u>virginitee</u>
>   Lat hem be breed of pured whete seed

Similarly, the verse of her prologue and tale employs many *-age* derivatives as end rhymes signifying social relationships and, in particular, marriage: mariage, costage, parage, heritage, lynage. These terms were particularly important to emphasize, since one of the primary themes of the prologue and tale is women's sovereignty over their sexuality and relationships.

Borrowed derivatives were often used to establish antonymic relationships between lexemes:

(5) Prydë þe noght for no <u>prosperitee</u>,
Ne heuye þe for non <u>aduersite</u>.
(Hoccleve)

(6) Whan he withstandeth oure <u>temptacioun</u>
It is cause of his <u>sauacioun</u>
(Chaucer)

(7) Ther scholde no corrupcioun
Engendre upon that <u>unite</u>:
Bot for ther is <u>diversite</u>
Withinne himself, he may noght laste
(Gower)

(8) The hihe almyhti <u>Trinite</u>,
Which is o god in <u>unite</u>
(Gower)

Examples (5) and (7) contrast almost exact antonyms, while (6) and (8) showcase near antonyms. In fact, (8) sets up the seeming contrast trinite/unite in order to foreground the paradoxical quality of Christian theism – that the trinity is only "o god." Such antonymic contrasts occurred most often with *-ite* derivatives in the corpus. Indeed, by foregrounding *-ite* lexemes as end rhymes in examples (7) and (8), Gower demonstrates his interest in the struggle between unity and division, which is seen throughout the *Confessio*.

Synonymic relationships between borrowed derivatives were also occasionally foregrounded in end-rhyme position:

(9) I put al the surplusage
In thyn ovne <u>eleccion</u>
After thy <u>discrecion</u>,
To chese or leve, sith thow art free
(Lydgate)

(10) And if thou were of such <u>lignage</u>,
That thou to me were of <u>parage</u>
(Gower)

And sometimes an end-rhymed derivative was preceded by a synonym that was likely more familiar to readers/listeners than the borrowing:

BORROWED SUFFIXES IN LATE MIDDLE ENGLISH POETRY   67

> (11)   ffirst, he seith, it is better seek to be,
>   Of a <u>sekenesse</u> or <u>infirmite</u>
>
>   (Hoccleve)

> (12)   Vnder the yok of honeste,
>   In <u>clennesse</u> and <u>chastite</u>
>
>   (Chaucer)

In examples (11) and (12), the poet likely chose to place the borrowing at the end of the line because it was a convenient rhyme that matched the ending desired in the preceding line. Each borrowing was then paired intralinearly with a near synonym, perhaps because the synonym was a native, less "hard" form. This phenomenon was not frequent in the corpus. But when it did occur, it typically involved *-ite* and *-ness* derivatives.

The analysis of examples in this section illustrates that derivatives were borrowed into vernacular verse primarily for poetic-structural purposes; they were deliberately placed into end rhymes for prosodic, etymological, and semantic/thematic reasons. Of course, the most general explanation for the usefulness of all of these derivatives is practical in nature: the lexemes provide numerous possibilities for creating rhymes – with native words, with other borrowings, or even with each other. Some morphological consequences of these different types of rhymes will be discussed in the following section.

Salience, Analyzability, and Morphology

In this section, I argue that the decision to place borrowed derivatives primarily in end-rhyme positions in Middle English had morphological consequences. Specifically, it increased the salience of these derivatives. And when multiple derivatives were rhymed together, readers and listeners were more easily able to analyze these forms as morphologically complex words with potentially separable suffixes. More specifically, I speculate that proximate or even adjacent uses of derivatives, observed most easily in the couplet – when a derivative with the same ending appears in two consecutive lines of poetry – increase the transparency of affixes. Below I describe how the salience and analyzability of borrowed suffixes were encouraged by these patterns of rhyme in Middle English. Consider the examples below:

> (13)   He spak touchende of <u>Mariage</u>.
>   The king knowende his hih <u>lignage</u>
>
>   (Gower)

> (14)   Tak Avarice and tak also
>   The vice of <u>Prodegalite</u>;

Betwen hem <u>Liberalite</u>,
Which is the vertu of Largesse

(Gower)

(15)   Virginitee is greet <u>perfeccion</u>
And continence eek with <u>deuocion</u>

(Chaucer)

In all of these examples, derivatives of the same ending from the same lexical fields are juxtaposed with one another in the rhyme scheme. In (13), Gower pairs two terms denoting familial relations, "Mariage" and "lignage." From a visual perspective, the proximity of derivatives in this couplet gives them more salience as a connected pair of words. And from an oral perspective, the rhyme creates a sonic link between the two. The semantic, sonic, and visual connections between these words all help to create a moment of potential morphological reanalysis: specifically, that -*age* may be a detachable part of "Mariage" and "lignage." Moreover, the availability and textual occurrences of bases mari and lyn in this poem (and in the period at large) likely aided such analysis of mariage into [mari[-*age*]] and lignage into [lin[-*age*]]. Similarly in examples (14) and (15), "Prodegalite/Liberalite" and "perfeccion/deuocion" are placed into highly salient positions in the poem. In the former case, -*ite* is potentially analyzable as a suffix attached to stems Prodegal- and Liberal-, whereas -*cion* may be seen as attached to stems perfec- and devo(c)-. Even though stems such as "devote" or "prodigal" are not attested in the *OED* until the sixteenth century, the analysis in these examples may have been facilitated by the availability of liberal and perfect in the Middle English lexicon. In fact, the use of "prodegalite" and "deuocion" in such salient contexts in the fifteenth century and beyond – i.e., whenever they co-occurred with analogous analyzable derivations in poetry, prose, or formal oral contexts – may have eventually helped encourage the use of those stems as regular words in the language via back-formation.

As demonstrated in the preceding examples, end-rhymed derivatives in a single couplet are in a highly salient context that potentially encourages the increased morphological transparency of the endings. A more extreme example of this effect can be found in Gower's scientific borrowings of words ending in -*cion*:

(16)   Ferst of the <u>distillacion</u>,
Forth with the <u>congelacion</u>,
<u>Solucion</u>, <u>descencion</u>,
And kepe in his <u>entencion</u>
The point of <u>sublimacion</u>,
And forth with <u>calcinacion</u>
Of veray <u>approbacion</u>
Do that ther be <u>fixacion</u>

(Gower)

This passage is unusual for Gower, in that he rarely repeats the same rhyme in contiguous couplets. He presents this as a set-piece of mostly alchemical terms with the exact same termination, rhyming them with non-scientifically technical lexemes with the same ending (entencion, approbacion). And he even folds in a line-medial rhyme with solucion. The saturation of *-cion* derivatives strongly compels the reader or listener to perceive the ending as a suffix that can attach to a number of different verbal stems, many of which would have been lesser known to non-alchemists (e.g., sublime, calcine), but some of which may have been more familiar (e.g., entend, aprove).

The effect of rhymed couplets on perceived decomposability likely depends on their overall frequency in verse. Among the borrowed derivatives in the corpus, *-cion* exhibits the highest frequency with 294 total couplets. The suffix *-age* has the next highest number with 126. And there are only 25 total couplets with *-ite*. Thus, if the salience of end-rhymed couplets does impact decomposability of derivatives, the effect would be greatest for *-cion* and the least for *-ite*.

The analysis in this section has demonstrated the following: while end rhymes increase the salience of all derivatives placed at the ends of poetic lines, derivatives that rhyme with one another become potentially more morphologically transparent in that context. It is possible that couplets, which visually and/or aurally juxtapose two different types of derivatives in the same suffix in highly salient and proximate positions, would have increased the transparency of that suffix more than other rhyming patterns, though further study of this question would be needed. Based on frequency of occurrence in the corpus, this "proximity effect" (and perhaps a more specific "adjacency" or "couplet effect") would have likely been greatest for *-cion* and weakest for *-ite*. Furthermore, suffixal analyzability in these rhymed derivatives is reinforced whenever the possible bases of the derivatives are extant in the language. Because the majority of borrowed derivatives were used in end-rhyme positions, it is possible that rhymed verse in Middle English contributed – at least in small part – to the decomposability of borrowed derivatives and the emergent productivities of suffixes such as *-age*, *-ite*, and *-cion* in the history of English.

Conclusions and Considerations: Suffixes, Middle English Poetry, and Multilingualism

Presenting a case study of the use of selected nominal suffixes in a sample of Middle English verse, this chapter develops a framework for character-izing the use of borrowed derivatives and the perceived productivities of their morphemes in late medieval rhymed poetry. Token frequencies reveal general patterns of use. They do not indicate levels of productivity, but they help identify the texts which were most likely to use different derivative types, as well as the suffix types most likely to be exposed to readers and listeners encountering these texts. Lexical density scores, which measure the frequencies of a varied number of derivative types standardized to a particular word count, allow for comparisons between texts and between suffix types. Lower lexical density scores suggest forms that are more likely to be opaque for readers of a particular text. Higher scores suggest the possibility of the increased decomposability of lexemes that are newly encountered or reinforce representations of decomposable derivatives that are already mentally stored by language users. The salience and potential decomposability of derivatives are also impacted by their frequent placement as end rhymes, particularly when the same suffix type is juxtaposed in rhyming couplets.

In applying this framework, the following conclusions can be drawn regarding each of the borrowed suffixes represented in this study:
(a) In terms of overall tokens, *-cion* is by far the most frequently used borrowed suffix in the work of all four poets. In Chaucer and Gower, it is even more frequently used than native suffix *-ness*. Moreover, it exhibits the broadest range of types among all suffixes for all poets in the study. Its highly frequent use in rhymed couplets might have increased its salience and decomposability in poetic contexts. (b) *-age* is used much less frequently than *-cion*, and it has the lowest lexical density scores (i.e., the narrowest range of unique derivatives) out of all suffixes in the study. (c) The suffix *-ite* has a much narrower range of types than *-cion*, but slightly more than *-age*. The effect of couplets on its salience and decomposability was likely very small, since it appeared in only 25 couplets (compared to 126 for *-age* and 294 for *-cion*).

Many poetic motivations for using derivatives were identified. A pivotal argument of this chapter is that Middle English poets were driven to employ borrowed derivatives, at least in part, by their recognition that the suffixes made for useful end rhymes.[40] This fact is unequivocally true for *-cion*, which is used as an end rhyme in high (and in some cases, extremely high) percentages. The suffix *-age* is used in less noteworthy percentages overall. Other than Lydgate, it inhabits the same range of percentages as *-ness*, though it must be acknowledged that it is consistently used as an end rhyme more than two-thirds of the time (and in Lydgate's case, over 90% of the time). In general, *-ite* had percentages of end rhyme similar to or significantly more than *-age*, but always less than *-cion*.

Poets were not only motivated to use borrowed derivatives for their distinct prosodic qualities, but they were also attracted to them for semantic reasons.

---

[40] This is not to say that there were not other motivations, as there likely were varied reasons for using these suffixes in the prose writings of these and other Middle English (ME) authors. This chapter makes no claims about relative frequencies in prose versus poetry; it does not answer whether ME prose or poetry is more likely to use a borrowed derivative. But this study's data illustrates end rhyme utility as a particular motivation for this sample of ME poets.

To establish certain characters or themes, poets drew upon these derivatives because they inhabited lexical fields that were useful for poetic diction. The handiest -*ite* derivatives came from religious discourse; -*age*, from terminology signifying social rank and relationships; and -*cion*, from lexical fields concerning Christianity and cognitive processes.

While this study has identified both prosodic and semantic motivations for the use of borrowed suffixes in Middle English, one limitation is that it only assesses selected nominal suffix use in poetry, and even more narrowly court poetry (with only four selected poets). It remains to be seen if the patterns observed here are generalizable to a wider range of suffixes or to a wider range of Middle English poetry. It is also unclear whether the rates of usage of derivatives would differ in the prose versus the poetry of this period. Future studies could in fact conduct a contrastive analysis of the prose versus poetic output of writers such as Chaucer. Even so, the value of the present study is its identification of genre-specific motivations – namely, the demonstration that positional occurrence within the poetic line was a driving factor for ME poets' use of borrowed morphemes. In theory, these poets could have positioned words with these suffixes anywhere within the line. But the overwhelming evidence is that they very much saw these suffixes as elements to frequently use line-finally, as convenient devices for constructing rhyme and rhythmic patterns and for foregrounding various discourses and themes in their narratives.

And there is also the matter of what this study of borrowed ME suffixes offers for larger debates about naturalization, code-switching, and translanguaging in historical linguistics and historical literary and cultural studies. If we apply the framework of translanguaging, we complicate the ideas of Wimsatt and Burnley that borrowing is a process of using foreign, non-native (i.e. French and Latin) lexical material in an English domain and that borrowed suffixes "naturalize" into English over time.[41] From a translanguaging point of view, multilingual poets like Chaucer, Gower, Hoccleve, and Lydgate are not code-switching or borrowing between separate language domains in their poetry as much as they are combining all sorts of grammatical and lexical material, regardless of how that material is named. Suresh Canagarajah distinguishes this as multilingual competence: "Multilinguals do not have separate competences for separately labeled languages (as traditional linguistics assumes) but an integrated competence that is different in kind (not just degree) from monolingual competence."[42]

---

[41] Burnley, "Lexis and Semantics," and Wimsatt, "Rhyme."

[42] A. Suresh Canagarajah, "World Englishes as Code-meshing," in *Code-meshing as World English: Pedagogy, Policy, Performance*, ed. Vershawn Ashanti Young and Aja Y. Martínez (Urbana: National Council of Teachers of English, 2011), 274.

It strikes me that translanguaging might be quite useful in explaining some linguistic phenomena, such as lexical hybrids, as when Chaucer uses "lodemenage" (navigation) (Old English ladmann + French *-age*). It could seem to a present-day linguist that he is code-switching or borrowing or mixing separately named language domains – e.g., adding an English base to a suffix borrowed from French – but it is less clear that he or his readers would have processed this word or labeled and conceived of its parts in this way. This contrasts with examples of self-conscious code-switching, as discussed in examples (2) and (3) above. There Gower alternates between (what I perceive as) clearly-intending-to-be-Latin and clearly-intending-to-be-English passages, using the Latinate "presumpcio" in a section of Latin as a precursor to the derivative "presumpcioun" in vernacular English verse. So perhaps different models (borrowing, code-switching, translanguaging) might be useful for explaining different sorts of linguistic phenomena in Middle English poetry – and in Middle English more generally. In any case, more engagement with ideas from translanguaging studies would benefit studies of ME language and poetry; it is important to always complicate questions such as "What does and doesn't get to count as 'English' or 'native' or 'natural' speech and writing in this text?"

Beyond its relevance to contemporary studies of multilingualism, perhaps the most broadly applicable contribution of this chapter is its insistence that analysis of poetry has much to offer diachronic analyses of morphology and vice versa. Quite typically in historical studies, poetic texts are actively sought out only for phonological evidence (e.g., prosodic patterns), or only if there are insufficient prose sources available in a particular period. This study demonstrates that poetry should not be so begrudged. While ME poetry may not have influenced the spread of borrowed derivations among speakers on a massive scale, it certainly reflected a more general trend in the late ME vernacular in its use of a frequent number and range of lexemes ending in *-ite*, *-cion*, and *-age*. The audience of this poetry may have been already familiar with many of these words (especially those from religious discourse), but they may have been less familiar with a significant number of derivatives (those from scientific and legal discourses, those first attested in the poetry of this period, etc.). But no matter how familiar they were with these lexemes, the poets' use of these derivatives increased the audience's exposure to a range of these words. And the effects of such increased exposure on the transparency of the derivatives and the analyzability of their suffixes should be studied in this Middle English register as much as any other.

4

Congregation or *Coven*: Talking about Civic Assembly in Middle English

COLETTE MOORE

You shall know a word by the company that it keeps.[1]

How do the meanings of words serve as a clue to cultural perceptions in late medieval England? Methods in semantics and in literary scholarship help to give us a perspective on how lexical usage both reflects and shapes collective ideologies. This small study considers how the connotative resonance of words about social gathering indicate mixed attitudes to civic assembly and suspicions about particular groups in the late fourteenth century.

It is generally understood that words in our language acquire *connotation*: the affective meaning that indicates the emotive and associational aspects of a term.[2] *Connotation* is conceived in opposition to *denotation*, the dictionary or referential sense for the word. Lexical connotations may be personal or shared by a group, and they both reflect and influence how we perceive concepts. As such, they can be a touchstone for the study of changing culture and can influence wider social ideology.

In 2005, Karla Taylor examined how words about civic gathering acquired connotations of suspicion in the 1380s in the wake of late fourteenth-century social fragmentation around political and economic tensions which came to a head in events such as the Peasants' Revolt, and how Chaucer's *Tale of Melibee* worked to fashion a nonpejorative vocabulary for its depiction of

---

[1] J.R. Firth, "A synopsis of linguistic theory 1930–1955," in *Studies in Linguistic Analysis*, ed. J.R. Firth (Oxford: Blackwell, 1957), 11.

[2] See "Connotation," in *The Oxford Companion to the English Language*, ed. Tom McArthur, Jacqueline Lam-McArthur, and Lise Fontaine, 2nd ed. (Oxford: Oxford University Press, 2018).

civic community. The semantic field of civic assembly can indicate cultural anxiety about togetherness in times of social unrest: to what extent do lexical items for social gathering indicate this anxiety and to what extent can poetry reconstruct affirmative connotations for the words? Here is Taylor's description of the point in the *Chaucer Review*:

> In the *Melibee*, then, Chaucer aims to create a civil society by means of language – not just to represent one, but genuinely to make one. One must always be wary of moving too easily from implied textual readers to real people, capable of historical agency. Nonetheless, if the *Melibee* can change the way people talk about civil society – and the lexicographical evidence suggests that it did – then the inclusive linguistic bonds created by its doublets might change social and civic bonds as well.[3]

In other words, the doublets in the *Tale of Melibee* create new connotations for words of civic gathering, and these effect a cultural and semantic change to soften the connotative suspicion of people assembling. The present investigation follows up on Taylor's analysis by applying the data analytic tools that have emerged in the twenty years following its publication.

I will use the expanded databases of Middle English (ME) texts, the Historical Thesaurus of English, and data visualization applications to examine the words that share the sense of a gathering or assembly and to consider their usage in late medieval English. The second section (following) provides a brief history of methods in lexical semantics, the third section provides a description of the semantic field of words about GATHERING, the fourth section describes the methodologies of examining lexical connotation in Middle English, the fifth section provides a qualitative examination of the hits for the semantic field of GATHERING in the ME databases, the sixth section discusses these words in the context of the *Tale of Melibee*, and the final section offers some concluding remarks. The stories of words, we find, are the stories of their users, and they illuminate and co-create one another.

Examining word meaning

Examining patterns of related words in texts is an interpretative process that builds upon methods in literary and linguistic studies, one which can draw upon both qualitative and quantitative analysis for insight. This section unfolds how word meaning has been studied. It builds upon models of lexical semantics for examining meaning, particularly the connotative senses for words and the ways that words cluster in groups of related senses.

---

[3] Karla Taylor, "Social Aesthetics and the Emergence of Civic Discourse from the *Shipman's Tale* to *Melibee*," *Chaucer Review* 39.3 (2005), 316.

Connotation as a term is a medieval conception; the word and several of its meanings appear to derive from William of Ockham's 1320 *Summa logicae*.[4] The distinction between *denotation* and *connotation* was first formulated by John Stuart Mill in his *System of Logic*,[5] which distinguished between the different kinds of sense meanings. Notions of connotative meanings are then taken up by early linguists: Leonard Bloomfield linked connotation to the concept of a speech community,[6] and Louis Hjelmslev developed a list of connotators.[7] Following Hjelmslev, whose articulation of connotation was linked to literary analysis, the conceptual and ideological implications of connotation led twentieth-century critical theorists in the wake of Roland Barthes to develop the connotation/denotation dichotomy into a semiotic system for cultural analysis. The connection between cultural and discursive practice became a cornerstone for theoretical perspectives, following Michel Foucault's influential formulation of discourse as participating in a historically-contingent social system of material conditions that make statements meaningful. Literary theorists, therefore, have taken language analytic tools and adapted them to focus not solely on the language itself, but on the social systems that simultaneously produced and were fashioned by the lexical and discursive elements of language. The analysis of connotation illustrates the shifting currents of twentieth-century linguistic-literary theory; it has continued to develop through twenty-first-century modes of data-driven analysis, as well.

In examining how words share meaning, semanticists have discussed notions of *synonymy*, words that may be substituted for one another,[8] and *overlapping terms*, perhaps a better description of the way that similar words are not really perfectly substitutable, but overlap in meaning.[9] Shared meaning can be conceived, therefore, in groupings of words: semantic fields, also called lexical fields or semantic domains, are clusters of words that refer to a particular area of experience or a related concept.

---

[4] Beatriz Garza-Cuarón, *Connotation and Meaning*, trans. Charlotte Broad (Berlin: De Gruyter, 1991), 15.

[5] John Stuart Mill, *A System of Logic, Ratiocinative and Inductive, Being a Connected View of the Principles of Evidence, and Methods of Scientific Investigation, Vol. 1* (London: John W. Parker, 1943), 190. Available online: https://www.google.com/books/edition/A_System_of_Logic_Ratiocinative_and_Indu/y4MEAAAAQAAJ?hl=en&gbpv=0&kptab=morebyauthor.

[6] Leonard Bloomfield, *Language* (New York: Holt, Rinehart, and Winston, 1961 [1933]), 151–2.

[7] Louis Hjelmslev, *Prolegomena to a Theory of Language*, trans. Francis J. Whitfield (Madison: University of Wisconsin Press, 1969 [1943]).

[8] D.A. Cruse, *Lexical Semantics* (Cambridge: Cambridge University Press, 1986); M. Lynne Murphy, *Semantic Relations and the Lexicon* (Cambridge: Cambridge University Press, 2003).

[9] Eugene Nida, *Componential Analysis of Meaning* (The Hague: De Gruyter, 1975).

The field of lexical semantics offers several frameworks and approaches which have been prevalent in different periods, described by Dirk Geeraerts as historical-philological semantics, structuralist semantics, generativist semantics, neostructuralist semantics, and cognitive semantics.[10] These frameworks were based on different approaches and evidence, and, to some extent, considered different questions. The notion of semantic fields, for example – a grouping of words of similar meaning – characterized structuralist approaches to sense and reference, and opened up new directions for research on word meaning, first in Germany in the 1930s[11] and then in the US in the 1970s;[12] it assumed relatively fixed components of meaning.[13] Research using semantic fields took a number of turns in the twentieth century,[14] and began to move beyond a more static sense of a field as an amorphous conceptual mass and towards a more contingent and interconnected understanding.

The model of semantic frames emerged in later decades to include some aspects of semantic fields, but to widen the focus.[15] Semantic frames are conceived more cognitively, though: focusing on how a speaker using a word builds upon a conceptual schema and on how the words relate to the conceptual schema that divides the frame. Owing to the nature of our evidence of Middle English, approaching ME semantic relations from the direction of speaker intuition and underlying conceptual relationships would involve more conjecture than approaching late medieval lexical semantics through a bottom-up way of examining word usage in the extant texts.

---

[10] Dirk Geeraerts, *Theories of Lexical Semantics* (Oxford: Oxford University Press, 2010), xiii–xiv.

[11] Leo Weisgerber, "Die Bedeutungslehre: Ein Irrweg der Sprachwissenschaft?" *Germanisch-Romanische Monatsschrift* 15 (1927), 161–83; Jost Trier, *Der Deutsche Wortschatz im Sinnbezirk des Verstandes: Die Geschichte eines sprachlichen Feldes, Band I: Von den Anfängen bis zum Beginn des 13. Jahrhunderts* (Heidelberg: C. Winter, 1931).

[12] E.g., Leon Vassilyev, "The theory of semantic fields," *Linguistics* 137 (1974), 79–93.

[13] Elizabeth Closs Traugott, "Semantics and lexicon," *English Historical Linguistics: An International Handbook. Volume 1: English Historical Linguistics*, ed. Alexander Bergs and Laurel J. Brinton (Berlin: De Gruyter, 2012), 165.

[14] See summary in Brigitte Nerlich and David D. Clarke, "Semantic fields and frames: Historical explorations of the interface between language, action, and cognition," *Journal of Pragmatics* 32.2 (2000), 125–50, https://doi.org/10.1016/S0378-2166(99)00042-9.

[15] Charles J. Fillmore, "An alternative to checklist theories of meaning," *Proceedings of the Annual Meetings of the Berkeley Linguistics Society* 1 (1975), 123–31; Roman Kalisz, "Frame semantics and its validity for linguistic description," *Linguistica et Anglica Gedaniensia* 2 (1981), 83–95; Jef Verschueren, "Problems of lexical semantics," *Lingua* 53 (1981), 317–51.

In other words, ME textual evidence is less suited to recent cognitive methods in lexical semantics; it is in many ways a better fit for the historical-philological approaches that Geeraerts described: "Because linguistic semantics is a historical discipline, its primary material consists of texts from dead languages or from previous stages in the development of a living language. Its basic methodological procedure is therefore the interpretation of those texts."[16] Analyzing a field of related words in texts is a hermeneutic pursuit, therefore, one that draws upon literary and linguistic interpretative methods, but one that can be aided by corpus and computational methods.[17]

Investigating semantic relationships from centuries ago can be problematic, of course, owing to the paucity of evidence and the absence of speaker intuition as a resource.[18] But the drawbacks of studying words from the past are offset by at least some attending advantages, since we have evidence for how the words went on to evolve in meaning. The ensuing question, though, of whether related words might shift semantically in the same direction (which would reflect shared cultural perceptions of the wider concept) or shift in different directions (if the words were becoming more distinct from one another to differentiate different shades of meaning) is an interesting one. Both options seem possible. We can observe that related words often narrow over time to become more distinctive; famous examples include doublets in which words borrowed from other languages take on a slightly different meaning in English (in, for example, the widely-taught set of English/French-derived doublets of Middle English in which the French word for the animal is borrowed into English and then narrows into the word for the cooked meat, creating a pair of words: *cow/beef, sheep/mutton, pig/pork*, etc.). Conversely, we can also observe that groups of words referring to stigmatized groups of people can behave collectively (in, for example, words about women or about lower-class men that, reflecting cultural prejudice, pejorize in similar directions over time to indicate purported immorality: *hussy, harlot, churl, villain*). So words that overlap in meaning can potentially affect one another: sometimes by encouraging the development of distinct senses or meanings in contradistinction to the other words in a semantic field, and sometimes by sharing a connotative shift reflecting ideologies of the broader culture. Investigating words in the context of their semantic fields and in the context of the connotative senses that are assigned to them offers a lens on the ME speech communities that produced our extant texts.

[16] Geeraerts, *Theories of Lexical Semantics*, 14.

[17] Susan Fitzmaurice, "Semantic and Pragmatic Change," *The Cambridge Handbook of English Historical Linguistics*, ed. Merja Kytö and Päivi Pahta (Cambridge: Cambridge University Press, 2016), 265–9.

[18] Christian Kay and Kathryn Allan, *English Historical Semantics* (Edinburgh: Edinburgh University Press, 2015).

Semantic field of GATHERING, ASSEMBLY

This section investigates the semantic field or set of words about GATHERING and ASSEMBLY by using digital tools to produce a list of Middle English words related to social collection and to generate a data sample of the different usages of the words. This permits us to map out different related words and to speculate on their connotative senses.

First, I began by making a quick survey of the nouns in the late medieval semantic field of GATHERING, ASSEMBLY. The *Middle English Dictionary*'s advanced search function allows a search of the definitions of *MED* words, permitting users to plumb the dictionary's definition field in order to collect synonyms and related words. To this list, I added words gleaned from the *Historical Thesaurus of English*'s cluster for AN ASSEMBLAGE/ COLLECTION, taking from *HTE*'s cluster the nouns that had some evidence of usage in the late ME period (1350–1500).[19] This created a list of nouns which were connected in meaning to GATHERING, ASSEMBLY. I focused on nouns rather than related verbs like *gather* in order to simplify the syntactic environments and use the *HTE*'s clusters.

Table 4.1: Words in the ME semantic field of GATHERING, ASSEMBLY.

> as(s)emble
> commocioun
> congregacioun
> conventicle
> covine
> gaderinge
> meting(e)
> quilet
> samning(e)
> semble

This list omits related words like *throng*, *rout*, or *compaignie* since those refer more directly to the group of people itself rather than the event of the gathering. *Parlement* was also omitted, since it seemed to be used in ME primarily in reference to a governing body (usually the governing body of England) or to a discourse/parley produced by the group rather than to the gathering itself.

In order to explore the semantic field, I took the list of words from Table 4.1 and searched for them and their variant spellings in the *Middle English*

---

[19] Christian Kay, Marc Alexander, Fraser Dallachy, Jane Roberts, Michael Samuels, and Irené Wotherspoon, eds., *The Historical Thesaurus of English*, 2nd ed., version 5.0 (Glasgow, 2022), https://ht.ac.uk/ (accessed May 2022).

Dictionary (*MED*) quotations and the *Corpus of Middle English Prose and Verse* (*CMEPV*) to generate a rough list of frequencies. This is an imprecise method, of course – such a search cannot produce an estimate for the frequency of usage of these words in spoken Middle English, which contained a different and inaccessible set of genres, settings, and constraints, but rather, it presents the frequency of usage of these words in the *MED* and the *CMEPV*. It presents, in other words, a rough view of the relative usage of these words in major surviving ME texts rather than in the language itself. Further, even as a depiction of written Middle English, the sources have limitations. The *CMEPV*, for instance, is a database rather than a curated corpus, so it includes multiple manuscripts of the same texts (particularly Chaucer MSS), so that a simple count risks overrepresenting hits from those texts. In my tallies, I eliminated repeat instances from different witnesses of the same text where it was possible to tell that the instances were repeated. Those databases are also, for practical reasons, constructed of editions that are out of copyright, meaning that their editorial and textual practices are often not in keeping with present-day methods. It is true, of course, that the words of the text are less subject to emendation than other aspects, so it seems not unreasonable to draw upon them for lexical research, with the caveat that the databases are only as good as their sources would be for addressing particular questions. In being composed of early editions, for example, *CMEPV* data comes from the texts that earlier editors chose to edit, overrepresenting, for example, poetry over municipal documents. They are not representative across regions or dialect areas of Middle English, either, and thus represent the semantic fields within surviving written ME, rather than representing ME in all of its dialectal range. Even given the caveats, the results, set out in Table 4.2, are interesting.

Table 4.2: Occurrences of GATHERING, ASSEMBLY words in *MED*, *CMEPV* (see full table with variant spellings in Appendix 1).

Word (lemmatized form)	Total hits
as(s)emble	77
commocioun	17
congregacioun	4
conventicle	17
covine	22
gaderinge	53
meting(e)	111
quilet	9
samning(e)	17
semble	122

Fig. 4.1: Semantic field of GATHERING, ASSEMBLY.

Table 4.2 presents the number of occurrences of each of the identified words in the *MED* and the *CMEPV*. The appendix gives the full list of the words as they appear in the corpora with a breakdown of the frequencies for the spelling variations for each lemmatized form. As seen in the appendix data, the most frequent usage in the databases is the variant *semble*, an aphetic shortening of *assembly* (*OED*, "sembly," n.); it has 122 hits.

Constructing a word cloud as a data visualization of the semantic field gives a general sense for the different variant lexical forms with their relative proportions as part of the set (see Fig. 4.1). The image depicts lexical patterns in discussing the social ways that people come together, and graphically represents a semantic field as a collective concept, drawn upon in cultural imagination or in textual practice as options for variable expressions of a concept or idiom. Comparing frequency, of course, does not provide a sense for the connotations of usage. For that, we need to look towards other methods.

Connotation and literary methods

If, following J.R. Firth's sentiment quoted at the onset of this article, we know a word by the company that it keeps, the question is how, methodologically, to assess that company. How can we describe lexical contexts – the environments for word usage – and assess patterns in those contexts? This section will discuss methods to investigate the semantic sense of words through their contextual environments, describing newer quantitative tools and their drawbacks for ME applications.

Among the new computational methods emerging for semantic analysis, collocational analysis has emerged as a tool for examining patterns in the contexts of words. To investigate a word's collocates is to look systematically at the words that tend to occur near it in text; a word's collocates occur more often than would be predicted by chance.[20] The notion of collocation goes back to early twentieth-century teaching of the phraseology of English: the phrases and connections between words were seen by some linguists as helpful to teaching English to multilingual language learners.[21] More recently, collocational analysis has grown out of corpus linguistics: corpora can use concordancing tools to focus on keywords in context (KWIC) to sort and align the contexts for searched words,[22] and then to analyze the collocations of words in the surrounding contexts. Machine learning presents new potential directions for concordancing and collocational applications: AI can be trained to process the collocation of the words with other concepts and plot a semantic network.[23]

Another computational tool is sentiment analysis, a Natural Language Processing (NLP) technique that assesses the positive or negative connotations of a usage. Sentiment analysis builds upon a large collection of data to evaluate passages of texts and tally affect scores for lexical items. Given the scale of data collection for NLP methods, however, sentiment analysis would not work very well for Middle English data. The sheer volume of present-day English written information makes possible large-scale computational analysis of patterns; it takes a very large amount of data in order for any advantages of the technological tools to begin to outweigh the circumstantial contingence of meaning assessment in any given text. For sentiment analysis, too, the assessments depend on present-day semantic connections which can come down to speaker intuitions, evidence which would flatten differences between past and present usage. Even for present-day data, sentiment analysts are realizing just how much their methods depend on textual domain and time period.[24] One could imagine a small version of ME sentiment analysis for a study like this: surveying each hit in the sample and categorizing it as positive, negative, or neutral to attempt to collect an impressionistic sense for the connotation. Continued examination of the sample, however, established that this would not provide very good data: first, most of the hits are not marked very apparently

---

[20] Sonja Poulson, *Collocations as a Language Resource: A Functional and Cognitive Study in English Phraseology* (Amsterdam: John Benjamins, 2022), 4.

[21] Harold Edward Palmer, *A Second Interim Report on English Collocations* (Tokyo: Kaitakusha, 1933).

[22] Chris Manning and Hirich Schütze, *Foundations of Statistical Natural Language Processing* (Cambridge: MIT Press, 1999), 35; Paul Baker, *Using Corpora in Discourse Analysis* (London: Bloomsbury Academic, 2006), 95–120.

[23] John Sowa, "Semantic Networks," *Encyclopedia of Artificial Intelligence*, ed. Stuart C. Shapiro (New York: Wiley, 1987), 1011–24.

[24] William L. Hamilton, Kevin Clark, Jure Lesovec, Dan Jurafsky, "Inducing Domain-Specific Sentiment Lexicons from Unlabeled Corpora" (2016), https://doi.org/10.48550/arXiv.1606.02820.

for affect, and second, this technique would weight all texts as being equally reflective of the connotation of the word, when some texts obviously had a more limited circulation, were more restricted by the constraints of their production and audience, or were using a word in a more recherché or less generalizable manner.

Reflecting on the limitations of computational methodologies demonstrates the extent to which the holistic historical and textual methods of the humanities provide essential tools for approaching semantic and cultural analysis of the present – and even more particularly of the past. If single words rely upon their neighbors to stabilize their meanings,[25] then chunks of words rely upon discourse, upon discourse communities, and upon culture. Literary methods and the qualitative examination of word usage show the connotative clashes more clearly than quantitative examination. This study will follow Taylor's examination by pursuing the database sample qualitatively in the following sections.

What we talk about when we talk about GATHERING

One kind of evidence for historical word meanings is contemporaneous metadiscursive commentary. When historical commentary on the senses of words can be found, it provides direct description of the usage. The sample of hits for the words about gathering offers only a few metadiscursive comments about the words, however, and likely about the ones that were less familiar. So, for example, the *MED* cites the *Promptorium Parvulorum*, the first English-Latin dictionary, with an entry for the word *semly* (an uncommon spelling of assembly/semble):

(1) (1440) PParv.(Hrl 221)452 : Semly, gaderynge to-gedyr of men: Congregacio. (*MED*, semble)[26]

This entry glosses *semly* (usually a variant of *seemly* rather than, as here, *assembly*) as a gathering together of men and offers the Latin *congregacio* as its translation.

Searching the *MED* quotations also offers an example of *semble* being glossed:

(2) a1425 *York MGame [OD col.] (Dgb 182)xxxii : The semble [Vsp: assemble], þat men clepeth gaderynge, shulde be maked in þis manere. (*MED*, semble)

---

[25] Gill Philip, *Colouring Meaning: Collocation and Connotation in Figurative Language* (Amsterdam: John Benjamins, 2011), 3.

[26] Throughout, I have added emphasis to the words of gathering in the examples.

In this citation from *The Master of Game by Edward, Second Duke of York*, the word *semble* is glossed by the clause "þat men clepeth gaderynge" to make clear what the sense of the word is. The fact that (1) and (2) use *gaderynge* as the gloss suggests that *gaderynge* might be more widely-known in the vernacular as a category term, even though versions of *assembly* have more attestations in written texts. Not having a range of vernacular dictionaries and metalinguistic works, Middle English does not provide a lot of commentary about word meaning, however.

Determining the resonance of words, then, must depend on more qualitative examination of the instances in the sample and considerations of their circulation and influence. The ME civic discourse of assembly has influential examples like a 1384 proclamation by London mayor Nicholas Brembre forbidding unsanctioned community gatherings:

> (3) The Mair, Shirreues, and Aldermen, and alle othere wyse wyth hem, that habbeth the gouernaille of the Citee, under oure lige Lord the Kyng, by vertue of the Chartre of oure franchise, comaundeth on the Kynges bihalf, and on hire owene also, that <u>noman make none congregaciouns, conuenticules, ne assembles of poeple,</u> in priue nen apert, ne no more than other men, with oute leue of the Mair; ne ouer more <u>in none manere ne make alliances, confederacies, conspiracies, ne obligaciouns, forto bynde men to gidre,</u> forto susteyne eny quereles in lyuingge and deyengge to gidre; upon peyne of enpresonement, vche man that is yfounde in swych defaute, and his bodi at the Kyngges will, and forfaiture of al that he may forfaite a yens oure Lord the Kyng, as wel in tenementz as in catel.[27]
>
> [The Mayor, Sheriffs, and Aldermen and all other wise with them, that have the governance of the city under our liege Lord the King, by virtue of the charter of our franchise, commands on the King's behalf, and on their own also, that <u>no man make congregations, conventicles, nor assemblies of people,</u> in private or apart, not more than other men, without leave of the Mayor, no ever more <u>in no manner to make alliances, confederacies, conspiracies, or obligations, for to bind men together,</u> for to sustain any quarrels in living and dying together, upon pain of imprisonment, each man that is found in such default, and his body at the King's will and forfeiture of all that he may forfeit against our Lord the King, as well in tenements as in cattle.]

We see here the civic suspicion of unauthorized assemblies: people may not come together in congregations, conventicles, etc. without permission from

---

[27] 1384 Procl.Brembre, in *A Book of London English, 1384–1425*, ed. R.W. Chambers and M. Daunt (Oxford: Clarendon Press, 1931), 31–3.

the mayor. The genre of interdictory proclamation and the legalistic language contributes to the sense of wrongdoings against the public good, creating a mistrust which extends to the words chosen: the activities sound transgressive because of the words attached to them. Thus, the connotations of marked words like *confederacies* and *conspiracies* color the words that might have been neutral, such as *assemblies*. While we do not presume that every gathering was a source of mistrust, the implication of nefarious purpose in a text like this infects surrounding words, and if the neutral words occur often in these contexts then the increased frequency of such usages might color the connotation for the word.

When we look at the full collection of examples from the databases, we see both negative and positive contexts for the set of assembly words. Some contexts establish positive resonance, for example with adjectives like *joyfull* or *mery*:

(4) A joyfull <u>metyng</u> was þer þore,

[*a joyful meeting was there there*]

(The Romance of Emaré, from *CMEPV*)

In (4), the modifying adjective clarifies the positive affect. Other usages employ modifiers to clarify negative implications:

(5) it shall gefe grett boldnesse to them and alle oder mysdoeres to make <u>congregacyouns</u> and <u>conuenticles</u> riottously, on-abille to be seysed, to the subuersyon and finall distruccyon of your ...

[it shall give great boldness to them and all other misdoers to make <u>congregations</u> and <u>conventicles</u> riotously, unable to be stopped, to the subversion and final destruction of your ...]

(Paston Letters, from *CMEPV*)

The context and subsequent adverb makes clear the negative connotations; the misdoers are making congregations and conventicles *riotously*. In (6), the postmodifying prepositional phrase for the assembly confirms its negative overtones:

(6) þay allegged þat þay myȝte not wiþ oute plegges and ostage come ne goo to þe <u>semble</u> of deceyvable peple

[they alleged that they might not without pledges and hostages come nor go to the <u>assembly</u> of deceitful people]

(*Polychronicon*, from *CMEPV*)

TALKING ABOUT CIVIC ASSEMBLY IN MIDDLE ENGLISH 85

The word *semble* does not necessarily project any negative sense in (6) by itself, though we are then told that the assembly being spoken of is constituted of deceitful or treasonous people. Negative examples in the sample often seem to focus around groups that are a perceived threat to the civic order – here is from a well-known letter from Henry VI on the suppression of the Lollards:

(7) and also of soweris of cedicious, disclaundrours, or trubulos langage, or talys. Oũ yis nat sufferyng pryue <u>gaderynges</u>, or <u>conuenticles</u> to be had or made, be nyght, or be day …[28]

[and also of sowers of seditious, slanderous, or troublesome language or tales. Or is not suffering private <u>gatherings</u> or <u>conventicles</u> to be had or made by night or by day …]

The context clarifies the negative connotations for the words: that the *gaderynges* and *conuenticles* go along with the sedition, slander, and trouble. The perceived dangers of Lollards assembling is apparent in the language.

The danger attached to *conventicles* does not refer only to the perceived transgressive threat of Lollards, though. Interestingly, and conversely, the word *conuenticlis* also appears in this Wycliffite text worrying about evil gatherings:

(8) wan men schuld tent to preyers and to Goddis seruys ; and þat in silk tyme men tent not to idil talis, foul spechis, harlotries, bakbityngis, or <u>conuenticlis</u>, purposing iuel, as þeft, or manslawt, or swilk oþer ; so no synnis were vsid in þe kirk ; þat þe house of God be not maade a den of þefis.[29]

[… when men should tend to prayers and to God's service, and that in such time men tend not to idle tales, foul speeches, harlotries, backbitings, or <u>conventicles</u>, purposing evil, as theft, or manslaughter or such other; so no sins were used in the church, that the house of God be not made a den of thieves.]

The iniquitous intent of *conuenticlis* is established in conjunction with the elements grouped with it – *idle tales, foul speeches, harlotries, backbitings* – as

---

[28] "Letters from King Henry VI to the Abbot of St. Edmondsbury, and to the Alderman and Bailiffs of the town, for the suppression of the Lollards: Communicated by John Gage, Esq. F.R.S., Director, to Henry Ellis, Esq. F.R.S., Secretary, &c.," in *Archaeologia: or Miscellaneous Tracts relating to Antiquity*, vol. 23 (London: Society of Antiquaries of London, 1831), 343.

[29] James Henthorn Todd, ed., *An Apology for Lollard Doctrines, Attributed to Wicliffe. Now first printed from a manuscript in the library of Trinity College, Dublin* (London: Camden Society, 1842), 50.

86 COLETTE MOORE

well as with the modifying clause "purposing evil." In this case, the perceived danger is not a threat to the civic community, but to the religious one.

The *MED* describes a sense of the word *conventicle* that is, "used disparagingly of a religious house or church" (*MED*, *conventicle*, 1c). This sense is illustrated by quotations from three Wycliffite texts warning of threats, particularly those of clerical abuses of power:

> (9) ?a1425(a1415) Wycl.Lantern (Hrl 2324)60/29 : In þe fendis chirche.. foolis fynden <u>conventiclis</u> þat haasten hem to helle.
>
> [In the fiend's church ... the foolish find <u>conventicles</u> that hasten them to hell.]

In the assessment of the *MED* lexicographers, then, *conventicle* has a defined sense that is pejorized. In later supplemental materials, however, the *MED* added the following addition:

> (10) a1500?Scrope Ribot First Monks (Lamb 192)129/36 : Thys hows is named..'Sem[ni]on'..Sem[ni]on in Grew is as meche to seyn in Latyn, aftyr transposed in to Englysch, a <u>conuentycle</u> of honest folk.
>
> Note: ?New sense or modify gloss of sense (c) 'used disparagingly of a religious house or a church'. There seems to be no negative connotation to 'conuentycle' as used here.

This addendum notes that although there are usages of *conventicle* with a marked negative connotation, the senses of the word include some with a more neutral or positive valence as well. This affect is clear from the surrounding context in (10): that the conventicle is of "honest folk."

As described, one approach for an examination of connotation is to consider the positive and negative valence of nearby words, and the kinds of influence that these have. In (11), for example, the assembly house is surrounded by negative words: *horrible*, *sin*, *simony*, *forswearing*.

> (11) a1450(a1397) WBible(2) GProl.(Hrl 1666)p.51 : Loke now wher Oxunford is in thre orrible synnes..The iij orrible synne is symonie and forswering in the <u>semble</u> hous.
>
> [Look now where Oxford is in three horrible sins ... The third horrible sin is simony and vowing falsely in the <u>assembly</u> house.] (Wycliffite Bible, from *MED*)

This passage as a whole has a negative resonance because of the collection of words of negative affect. None of these words of moral condemnation are modifying the *assembly*, however, or are directly attached to it; indeed, the third sin seems to be horrible precisely because the simony and forswearing is happening in the assembly house, suggesting that the virtue and integrity of the assembly house enhances the violation of the moral corruption. Being in an environment of negative words, therefore, does not entail that a word is also negative – the word in question could have a neutral sense and be surrounded by other words such that the effect of the whole is negative. A sentiment analysis, of course, would not be able to distinguish this difference, and would note merely the environment of negative words and consider that the word in question had a negative affect. Indeed, a word which is continually used in a context of negative words might acquire a negative connotation associatively in this way, and it can be difficult to tell sometimes when a word crosses the line between neutral and negative in connotation. A robust methodology, therefore, must be able to consider the local context (i.e. when do "leaky" negative words infect surrounding neutral words?) and also the effects of frequency or repetition for the cultural perceptions of the word's connotation (i.e. when does the frequency of negative contexts in local word usages pass a tipping point in collective usage such that these infect the cultural sense of the word?).

In discussing people coming together, we see, the texts often infuse a word for assembly with affective meaning which incorporates a stance about the gathering. Sometimes the words evolve in different directions; there is an obvious difference between a word like *parlement* and a word like *rout*. *Parlement* had acquired by the Middle English period connotations of order-liness and the rule of law, even when it did not refer to the governing body of the land, and *rout* had overtones of lawlessness and mob rule. Sometimes, too, words in a semantic field evolve in the same direction, for example when a wider cultural perception or ideology affects the whole field.

Over the course of Middle and Modern English, some of these GATHERING, ASSEMBLY words narrowed in meaning, such that *congregation* mostly goes with church gatherings (a sense that seems to become primary in the sixteenth century; *OED*, *congregation*, n.), and *coven* ultimately goes with witches (the first citation for this sense in the *OED* is from the seventeenth century; *OED*, *coven*, n.). It is not apparent, though, the extent to which the words of assembly gain a negative sense themselves versus the extent to which they are used neutrally (as in example 11 above), with a negative sense created by a surrounding context.

Congregacioun in the *Tale of Melibee*

Returning, finally, to the *Tale of Melibee*, we can reflect on Chaucer's two uses of the word *congregacioun*, the word that he chooses for gathering people together. In the first instance, Melibee assembles a group of advisors:

88 COLETTE MOORE

(12) by the conseil of his wyf Prudence, this Melibeus leet callen a greet
<u>congregacion</u> of folk, / as surgiens, phisiciens, olde folk and yonge,
and somme of his olde enemys reconsiled as by hir semblaunt to his
love and into his grace; / and therwithal ther coomen somme of his
neighebores that diden hym reverence moore for drede than for love,
as it happeth ofte. / Ther coomen also ful many subtille flatereres and
wise advocatz lerned in the lawe. (*Tale of Melibee*, ll. 1004–7)

[by the counsel of his wife Prudence, this Melibeus had called a great
<u>congregation</u> of folk: surgeons, doctors, old folk and young, and some
of his old enemies reconciled as it seemed to his love and into his grace,
and therewith came some of his neighbors who did him reverence more
from fear than love, as often happens. There came also many subtle
flatterers and wise advocates learned in the law.]

And in the second usage, his prudent wife Prudence comments on their advice:

(13) And sith ye woot wel that men shal alwey fynde a gretter nombre
of fooles than of wise men, / and therfore the conseils that been at
<u>congregaciouns</u> and multitudes of folk, there as men take moore reward
to the nombre than to the sapience of persones, / ye se wel that in
swiche conseillynges fooles han the maistrie. (*Tale of Melibee*, ll.
1258–60)

[And since you know well that men shall always find a greater number
of fools than of wise men, and therefore the councils that are at <u>congre-
gations</u> and multitudes of folk, where men value more the number than
the wisdom of persons, you see well that in such councils fools have
the mastery.]

Although the word *congregacioun* does not appear to presume a negative
connotation in these two instances, both of these references to gatherings are
treated with wariness: the congregations are said to be composed partly of
flatterers in (12) and foolish men in (13). The contexts of the word, therefore,
depicts a hesitation about both the motives and wisdom of the collective body.
Taylor's reading of the tale points us to an interpretative overlap, however,
with the lexical field of JUDGMENT: words such as *deliberacion, juggement,
arbitracioun*.[30] The linking of these groups of words suggests that it is through
the inner and outer rule of law, through deliberate discernment, that the advice
of a congregation can be sought and tempered. Through these collocational

---

30 Taylor, "Social Aesthetics."

connections, Prudence teaches that the advice of a council can be heard and then processed and filtered through perceptive judiciousness.

I would add, further, that this same dynamic is mirrored in the way that the tale itself is constructed partly by practices of textual and discursive "congregation" – as a compilation of the folk wisdom of proverbs and aphorisms.[31] The tale is a proverb collection and characterized by passages of strung-together adages: a kind of crowd-sourced sagacity. The text itself is a kind of congregation in this case, a gathering of phrases of collective wisdom expressed in proverbial *sententiae*. By extension, then, we might read Prudence's advice as meant for the reader of the tale as well as for Melibee: that listening to the proverbial expressions of collective wisdom is helpful, but that they must be interpreted and applied with discernment to particular personal contexts. The words of *deliberacion, juggement, arbitracioun*, therefore, begin to describe the interpretative role of a reader in search of wisdom on leading a good life. Thus does an observation about cooccurring lexical fields in a text extend from a semantic point about language choice to an interpretative reading of the tale's catalog of proverbs.

Linguistic and literary methods together help us to approach ME texts with our own *deliberacion*. Concordance tools and text-mining applications help us to see words as part of a lexical network, and qualitative methods for examining collocation and connotation help us to see the resonances of words in their lexical contexts. These insights equip us, then, to read literary texts better. Conversely, literary attention to patterns of imagery in interpretation helps us to understand more clearly the semantic networks of language.

Conclusion

The category "Middle English" (to the extent that the phrase can pick out a unified phenomenon) most directly refers to the language of a body of texts that we believe to have been produced during a particular span of time in a particular language. To read these texts as a collected group is to project that the people who produced them shared, in some sense, a cultural space. To do that, we move from the words of the texts into imagined lexical relationships – we make hypotheses about the implications and connotations of the words.

We know, certainly, that the words do not represent fixed meanings and that their denotative senses and – even more so – their connotative senses

---

[31] Betsy Bowden, "Ubiquitous Format? What Ubiquitous Format? Chaucer's *Tale of Melibee* as a Proverb Collection," *Oral Tradition* 17.2 (2002), 169–207; Nancy Mason Bradbury, "The Proverb as Embedded Microgenre in Chaucer and *The Dialogue of Solomon and Marcolf*," *Exemplaria* 27 (2015), 55–72; Christopher Cannon, "Proverbs and the Wisdom of Literature: *The Proverbs of Alfred* and Chaucer's *Tale of Melibee*," *Textual Practice* 24.3 (2010), 407–34.

are shifting in response to the speech communities and the culture that draw upon them and reproduce them. To study connotation, therefore, is to aim at a moving target. Yet to read the texts of the past is to engage with those sociocultural levels of meaning and to revive the contexts of words and texts.

Taylor's examination of the doublets in the *Tale of Melibee* raises questions about the words of civic assembly and how to contextualize them. Extending her insights into the corpora lets us use text-mining tools to examine the semantic field of words about GATHERING/ASSEMBLY. We see that to speak about civic assembly in the years of the Peasants' Revolt and the Lollard movement is to use words which had been influentially employed to describe suspicious or threatening practice. While we cannot describe the cognitive response of late fourteenth-century speakers, we can notice that a disproportionate number of references to assemblies occur in negative contexts, and we can note how certain words such as *conventicle* developed markedly negative senses. We can also note that the focus of fear of assemblies falls upon groups that are perceived to pose a threat, either to the economic, political, or clerical establishment, or, in the case of the Wycliffite text, to the religious community.

And, therefore, we come back to Taylor's point that one role for art is to reshape and recast the words. The cultural milieu of suspicion about civic assembly is not merely a fourteenth-century phenomenon, of course; we can see analogues in later periods, most recently in the culture of suspicion around peaceful protest that emerged in 2020: the Black Lives Matter protests that responded to police killing of African-Americans. Many of the 2020 media discourses around urban social assembly echoed Nicholas Brembre's suspicion of congregating in 1384, even if the words were not the same.

Poetry, in the ways that it conjoins words, connects ideas, and constructs community, creates collocations that invite us to recast our cultural suppositions. Present-day poetry (and its cousin, popular song lyrics) can help us see common ground and might attempt to show us ways to broach cultural chasms. In times of division, in other words, art can help to show us lexical ways back together.

Appendix 1: Occurrences of GATHERING, ASSEMBLY words in the *Middle English Dictionary* **and the** *Corpus of Middle English Prose and Verse*

as(s)emble	**77 (total)**
assembly	9
assemble	61
asemble	7
commocioun	**17 (total)**
commocioun	17
congregacioun	**4 (total)**
congregacion	4
conventicle	**17 (total)**
conuenticle	17
covine	**22 (total)**
covine	17
couyne	3
coueyne	1
covyne	1
gaderinge	**53 (total)**
gadering	12
gadring	15
gaderyng	26
meting(e)	**111 (total)**
meetyng	1
Meeting	1
metyng	76
meting	33
quilet	**9 (total)**
quelet	1
quylet	2
quylete	1
quelecte	1
coillet	1
coylthe	1
coilett	1
coylett	1

samning(e)	17 (total)
samninge	3
samnyng	5
samnung	1
samenyng	6
samyng	1
sampninge	1
semble	**122 (total)**
semble	122

PART III

THE LEXIS OF MIDDLE ENGLISH LITERATURE

5

Overcome by Words: Supplementarity and Advisory Ethics in the Tale of *Melibee*

DAVID LAVINSKY

Melibee is framed in complex ways by its inclusion in fragment VII of the *Canterbury Tales*, where the formal limits of reading and storytelling are overtly thematized, even strictly policed.[1] Showing a concern for proportion and narrative scale, Chaucer tells us to expect something suitably manageable in size, yet goes on to deliver a lengthy prose treatise, held together – just barely, some would say – by numerous proverbial sayings and quotations from the *auctores*. Drawn mostly from familiar classical and biblical sources, these authoritative references share the concentrated moral force and self-enclosed singularity of medieval *proverbia* more generally, and their function in *Melibee* is comparable to that of learned sayings and quotations in a wide range of compilatory texts from the period, including Chaucer's immediate source, Renaud de Louens's *Livre de Melibée et de Dame Prudence*, a French version of Albertanus of Brescia's *Liber consolationis et consilii*.[2] At the

---

[1] *Sir Thopas* and the *Monk's Tale* are brought to premature conclusions – stinted, according to the rubrics – by audience members who object to the tales on aesthetic grounds. Glenn Burger notes "the fragment's emphasis on 'little things' rather than on wholes": Burger, "Mapping a History of Sexuality in *Melibee*," in *Chaucer and Language: Essays in Honour of Douglas Wurtele*, ed. Robert Myles and David Williams (Montreal: McGill-Queen's University Press, 2001), 61–70 (at 69). I leave aside here speculation about the early date of *Melibee* and whether Chaucer intended a sequence of tales different from the one reflected in most modern critical editions. For more, see *The Riverside Chaucer*, ed. Larry D. Benson, 3rd ed. (Boston: Houghton Mifflin, 1987), 862–3, as well as 1120–1. All quotations of Chaucer's work are from this edition.

[2] Although Albertanus "drew on familiar sources for his works, among them Seneca, Cicero, Justinian, Cato, Godfrey of Winchester, and the Bible," he also,

96   DAVID LAVINSKY

same time, the tale also signals how its prose departs in this respect from stylistic precursors. Apologizing in advance if his version might "varie" from those already familiar to his listeners, the pilgrim Chaucer defines the story as one that has "somwhat moore / Of proverbes than ye han herd bifoore" (VII 954–6).

As the basic narrative structure of a dialogue between husband and wife recedes from view, we might puzzle over Chaucer's initial presentation of his tale, since it considerably understates what follows.[3] Such variations in shape and substance, he has just informed us, should not really matter, any more than local differences in "speche" or wording do between his tale and its source text; meaning resides instead in an irreducible *sentence*, as disclosed by the normative literary practices such a concept authorizes, especially allegorical interpretation (VII 954, 961).[4] Indeed, "[i]f the rhyme of *Sir Thopas* bothered Harry," Lee Patterson memorably wrote in reference to these lines, "the prose of *Melibee* will be utterly transparent."[5] The sense that *Melibee* escapes formal visibility relative to its textual counterparts undoubtedly has much to do with

---

according to Angus Graham, appears "to be the first writer to make use of the work of the Spanish convert from Judaism, Peter Alfonsi, and may well be the first scholar to have assembled all twelve books of Cassiodorus's *Variae*. In this sense we can regard Albertanus as a precursor of the Renaissance book collector": Graham, "Albertanus of Brescia," in *Medieval Italy: An Encyclopedia*, ed. Christopher Kleinhenz, vol. 1 (New York: Routledge, 2004), 9–11 (at 10). On the nature of proverbs, see Roman Jakobson, who likens them to riddles "in their pungent brevity and verbal skill": Jakobson, *Language in Literature*, ed. Krystyna Pomorska and Stephen Rudy (Cambridge, MA: Harvard University Press, 1987), 257.

   [3]   James Powell notes that the *Liber consolationis et consilii* was unique among Albertanus's works in using the conventions of dialogue form. James M. Powell, *Albertanus of Brescia: The Pursuit of Happiness in the Early Thirteenth Century* (Philadelphia: University of Pennsylvania Press, 1992), 77. Relevant here as well, of course, is the moment slightly earlier in the prologue when Chaucer describes his tale as "a litel thyng in prose" (VII 937).

   [4]   The parallel is drawn to the Gospels; despite outward variations among the four accounts, "doutelees hir sentence is al oon" (VII 952). The Robertsonian appropriation of *Melibee* on behalf of Christian allegorical instruction has its basis in these passages. D.W. Robertson, *A Preface to Chaucer: Studies in Medieval Perspectives* (Princeton: Princeton University Press, 1962), 369. Noting the derivation of "proverbes" from Latin *proverbium*, a term associated in biblical and exegetical contexts with Greek *parabola*, Thomas Hill similarly suggests that these lines (VII 954–7) privilege the tale's figurative meaning as "an allegorical rather than an historical or even quasi-historical narrative": Hill, "Chaucer's Parabolic Narrative: The Prologue to the *Tale of Melibee*, Lines 953–58," *Chaucer Review* 46.3 (2012), 365–70 (at 370).

   [5]   Lee Patterson, "'What Man Artow?': Authorial Self-Definition in *The Tale of Sir Thopas* and *The Tale of Melibee*," *Studies in the Age of Chaucer* 11 (1989), 117–75 (at 153).

its status as a close translation; while other fragment VII tales self-consciously foreground the contingent material features of literary style and textual design – the Monk, for instance, proffers a saintly *vita* only to settle abruptly on *de casibus* writing – the same choices in *Melibee* are presumably determined by its derivative relationship to Chaucer's French "original."[6] Moreover, the restrictive aesthetic conditions under which "prose" is invoked – "I wol yow telle a litel thyng in prose" – cast the tale's amplification of form and ethical scope in a problematic light (VII 937).

But if all this decenters formalist concerns, the prologue also attests to a text reshaped by authorial intention, and reminds us that form influences how vernacular audiences apply received wisdom to the points at issue in the tale's representation of violence and its aftermath. Taking its cue from Karla Taylor's now classic account of the socio-semantic contexts created by Chaucer's doublets, this essay explores the question of *Melibee*'s formal supplementarity.[7] It aims to show how the florilegial textures and layered formal effects of *Melibee*'s language shape its advisory ethical functions as a prose treatise.[8] Though seen as inimical to good poetry in fragment VII, surplus and textual accretion are essential to good counsel, and generate narrative structures that counter the various instances of abrupt or arbitrary judgement Prudence laments. We hear about those unwise advisors who eschew deliberation and instead act "sodeynly" (VII 1028) or in "haste" (VII 1054), who would "breken" the tale (VII 1043) and "abregge" (VII 1043) the words of those more knowledgeable than themselves, and who prefer reckless expediency over discernment. Like sin, anger, and covetousness, "hastifnesse" is an affliction of what Prudence calls "sodeyn thought," and should be driven

---

[6] For Frederic Jameson, even cases where "content" is determined by the "projection of form," form also speaks "of its own coming into being," so that all literary texts "emit a kind of lateral message about their own process of formation": Jameson, *The Prison-House of Language: A Critical Account of Structuralism and Russian Formalism* (Princeton: Princeton University Press, 1972), 89. Compare the discussion of *Melibee* in the *Riverside Chaucer*: "The prose here and in The Parson's Tale is workmanlike but uninspired, perhaps because in both cases Chaucer was translating" (17). For more sustained discussion, see Dominick Grace, "Telling Differences: Chaucer's *Tale of Melibee* and Renaud de Louens' *Book of Melibee and Prudence*," *Philological Quarterly* 82.4 (2003), 367–400, and Dolores Palomo, "What Chaucer Really Did to *Le Livre de Mellibee*," *Philological Quarterly* 53.3 (1974), 304–20.

[7] Karla Taylor, "Social Aesthetics and the Emergence of Civic Discourse from the *Shipman's Tale* to *Melibee*," *Chaucer Review* 39.3 (2005), 298–322. I am much indebted to this important essay, which also exemplifies qualities I was fortunate enough to experience firsthand with Karla as my dissertation advisor: deep learning deployed with generosity and rhetorical flair.

[8] For comparable points, see Colette Moore's examination of Chaucer's shaping of the contemporary lexicon of social gathering in this volume.

out of one's heart (VII 1133, 1134). In *Melibee*, these prudential imperatives are actively rescripted for a discursive context in which the work of form comes under intense scrutiny.[9]

Reimagining florilegial form

Rather like Pandarus, that "walking encyclopedia of *sententiae*" who "always has an appropriate saying for any situation," Prudence deploys authoritative references at every turn.[10] Even more relevant than the sheer number of quotations in *Melibee* is their distributed effect within the tale's different strata of proverbial meaning. Though their origins were not always obscure, proverbs were experienced by most medieval audiences as decontextualized bits of wisdom or advice.[11] Glossed commentaries and compilations made provisions for their use as such, enabling readers to extract units of sentential reasoning discontinuously, and to apply them (often working from memory) in allegorical contexts; this arrangement is evident, for instance, in manuscript copies of Chaucer's ultimate Latin source for the tale, the *Liber consolationis et consilii*. Discussing its significant European transmission, Angus Graham has suggested that Albertanus's treatise, like his other major works, was widely valued for its properties as a kind of *florilegium*.[12] Copies of Albertanus's writings make such an affiliation explicit. In Bodley MS Add. C. 12, an anthology produced

---

[9]   For discussion of form relevant to the questions raised here, see *Chaucer and the Subversion of Form*, ed. Thomas Prendergast and Jessica Rosenfeld (Cambridge: Cambridge University Press, 2018); *The Medieval Literary: Beyond Form*, ed. Robert Meyer-Lee and Catherine Sanok (Cambridge: D.S. Brewer, 2018); and Marion Turner, "The Form of the *Canterbury Tales*," in *The Cambridge Companion to the Canterbury Tales*, ed. F. Grady (Cambridge: Cambridge University Press, 2020), 1–20.

[10]   Karla Taylor, "A Text and its Afterlife: Dante and Chaucer," *Comparative Literature* 35.1 (1983), 1–20 (at 12). On proverbs in *Troilus and Criseyde*, see Taylor, "Proverbs and the Authentication of Convention in Troilus and Criseyde," in *Chaucer's 'Troilus': Essays in Criticism*, ed. Stephen A. Barney (Hamden: Archon Books, 1980), 277–96, as well Douglas Gray, "'Lat be thyne old ensaumples': Chaucer and Proverbs," in *Interstices: Studies in Middle English and Anglo-Latin Texts in Honour of A.G. Rigg*, ed. Richard F. Green and Linne R. Mooney (Toronto: University of Toronto Press, 2004), 122–36; cited in Hill, "Chaucer's Parabolic Narrative," 367, n. 6.

[11]   Chaucer's description of his tale as a "litel thyng in prose" might just as readily stand for the transferability and atomistic signifying power of individual proverbs themselves (VII 937). Susan Deskis, drawing on the sociolinguist Einar Haugen, refers to the discursive "language ecology" of medieval proverbs: Deskis, *Alliterative Proverbs in Medieval England: Language Choice and Literary Meaning* (Columbus: Ohio State University Press, 2016), 5–18.

[12]   Angus Graham, "A Supplementary Census of Latin Manuscripts," *Studi Medievali* 41 (2000), 429–45 (at 430). On the content and structure of *florilegia*, see

SUPPLEMENTARITY AND ADVISORY ETHICS IN THE TALE OF *MELIBEE*   99

in Italy during the first half of the fifteenth century, material from Albertanus, including the *Liber consolationis*, is bound with a lengthy sequence of *flores* and florilegial extracts from authorities such as Cassiodorus, Socrates, Seneca, and Cicero (to name only a few).[13] An opening *tabula* listing each collection of "flores" by its putative author's name reinforces Albertanus's own standing as *auctor*, and suggests that his moral treatises might be read for the same reasons, and with the same concern for referential selectivity, as these other compendia of authoritative quotations.

The reception of proverbial writing, such examples show, depended on its transposition into specific material settings governed by established conventions of manuscript apparatus and design.[14] *Tabulae, ordinatio*, and the inclusion of different but related materials in the same volume were all crucial elements for making sense of the *Liber consolationis* as a didactic text. Textual classification and authorial intent are no less concerns in *Melibee*, as suggested by the prologue's shifting terms for defining what kind of story we can expect to hear, and its resemblance to the one on which it is based; such ambiguities are bound up with Chaucer's choice to adapt an established genre, the prose treatise, on his own terms. But while precursors for later attempts at fashioning an English "tretys" along the lines of what Chaucer means in his opening description of *Melibee* could be found in encyclopedic works and didactic treatises, including the *Liber consolationis* itself, the disposition of proverbial content in *Melibee* subtends functions specific to its formal qualities as discursive prose in the vernacular. Rather than the selective moral application of any single proverb, then, what matters is its function within the verbal structure of the tale itself.

This pattern is evident in the way Chaucer uses proverbs for interpretive framing and expository paraphrase.[15] Having assembled a "greet congreg-

---

Mary A. Rouse and Robert H. Rouse, *Authentic Witnesses: Approaches to Medieval Texts and Manuscripts* (Notre Dame: University of Notre Dame Press, 1991), 101–88.

[13] The copy of *Liber consolationis* in this manuscript comprises fols. 44r–63v, and the various collections of *flores* take up fols. 121v–157v, though several leaves have been lost in this section.

[14] Such conventions are discussed at length in Robert H. Rouse and Mary A. Rouse, *Preachers, Florilegia and Sermons: Studies on the "Manipulus Florum" of Thomas of Ireland* (Toronto: Pontifical Institute of Mediaeval Studies, 1979). More recently, see Vincent Gillespie on the study of classical authors in *The Cambridge History of Literary Criticism, Vol. 2: The Middle Ages*, ed. Alistair Minnis and Ian Johnson (Cambridge: Cambridge University Press, 2005), 178–80.

[15] On "expository paraphrase" in homiletic writing and legal commentaries, see Fiona Somerset, "How Canon Lawyers Read the Bible: Hilton's *Scale II* and the *Wordes of Poule*," in *Manuscript Culture and Medieval Devotional Traditions: Essays in Honour of Michael G. Sargent*, ed. Jennifer N. Brown and Nicole R. Rice (York: York Medieval Press, 2021), 222–39 (see references at 233, 234).

acion" of folk, Melibee solicits their advice about how to proceed, clearly favoring revenge for the attack on his wife and daughter (VII 1004). "And by the manere of his speche," we read, "it semed that in herte he baar a crueel ire, redy to doon vengeaunce upon his foes, and sodeynly desired that the werre [war] sholde bigynne" (VII 1009). His "olde wise" counsellors argue against acting "sodeynly," a word repeated often in this section (VII 1037; VII 1009, 1028, 1033); what they desire instead is "leyser and espace to have deliberacion in this cas to deme" (VII 1029). Here Albertanus cites a maxim from the *sententiae* of Publilius Syrus, a first century Latin writer and a frequently quoted *auctor* in the *Liber consolationis*: "Ad poenitendum properat, qui cito judicat."[16] Rendered in the French text as "Qui tost juge tost se repent," Chaucer's translation of this line – "He that soone deemeth, soone shal repente" (VII 1030) – follows Renaud's wording while at the same time adopting a distinctive sentential style to go with his use of the vernacular "hastifnesse," rashness or impetuosity; this term, the *OED* notes, was "[f] ormed within English, by derivation," and is thus distinguishable in Middle English contexts from "hastivess," a borrowing from French and the more direct translation for Renaud's "hastiveté."[17] Prose translation reinforces the intended ethical idea by embedding proverbs in the textual space of the tale. At the same time, the semantic and referential field produced as a result of this nested structure shapes our perceptions of *Melibee* as a vernacular work. Linking sound judgment to the prolonged interval of time ("leyser and espace") needed for deliberation is not only an appeal for patience from Melibee's wiser counsellors; it also mandates, on ethical grounds, the dialogic amplification of content that follows, and recasts textual space in material terms, suggesting a meaning for the word "espace" outside of that typically reserved for it in Middle English doublets, where it signifies temporal extension.[18] Here "espace" implies a supplementarity adequate to the tale's ambitious

---

[16] Albertanus of Brescia, *Albertani Brixiensis Liber consolationis et consilii*, ed. T. Sundby (London: N. Teubner & Company, 1883), 39, ll. 10–11.

[17] For the French text, see the edition in William Askins, "The Tale of Melibee," in *Sources and Analogues of the Canterbury Tales*, ed. Robert M. Correale with Mary Hamel, 2 vols (Cambridge: D.S. Brewer, 2002–5), vol. 1, 321–408 (at 336; for "hastiveté," see 349, 352). The *OED* notes that the origins of "hastivess" are as a "borrowing from French," modifying the French etymon hastivesce.

[18] *MED*, "espace," n., 5a–b, citing this example: "(a) Time in which to do something, leisure; opportunity to do something; pl. proper times, appropriate season; with 'of' phrase: time for (sth.); also, freq. with inf.: time (to do sth.); (b) in phrases: ~ and time, time and ~; leiser (lif) and ~; might (wille, wit) and ~; etc." This paragraph also extends the implied signification of the term "deliberacion" in Taylor's remarks on the same passage. She describes it as a linguistic "fence-sitter: it refers both to the inner mental act and a public, collective version thereof": Taylor, "Social Aesthetics," 315.

SUPPLEMENTARITY AND ADVISORY ETHICS IN THE TALE OF *MELIBEE*   101

compilation of translated *sententiae*; for the same reason, it explains form from the vantage point of adaptation and authorial craft: "Chaucer's" English prose treatise.

By refusing to reproduce the discursive fiction of transparency and authorial self-effacement that characterize the *compilatio* tradition, *Melibee* insists on its formal visibility as text and translation.[19] Language and vernacular form inscribe Chaucerian author functions in other ways as well. In the passage just discussed, Chaucer presents Publilius's maxim on the perils of rash decision making as a "commune proverbe," and in the next sentence glosses it using proverbial language not found in *Melibee*'s Latin ancestor (VII 1030). We can track this pattern when the relevant sequence in Albertanus is set alongside Chaucer's adaptation from the French:

> De facto autem vindictae atque guerrae faciendae dubium maximum videmus, quare, quid melius sit, adhuc judicare non possumus, unde spatium deliberandi causa postulamus; non enim subito vel celeriter est judicandum, "omnia enim subita probantur incauta," et "in judicando criminosa est celeritas," et "ad poenitendum properat qui cito judicat," quare dici consuevit: Optimum judicem existimo, qui cito intelligit et tarde judicat; nam licet mora omnis odio sit, non tamen in judicando mora competens est reprobanda …[20]

> Mais de mouvoir guerre ou de toy venger tantost, nous n'en povons pas bien juger en si pou de temps lequel vault mieux. Si demandons espace d'avoir deliberation, car on dit communément: Qui tost juge tost se repent. Et dit on aussi que le juges est tres bons qui tost entend et tart juge. Car ja soit ce que toute demeure soit ennuyeuse, toutevoie elle ne fait pas a reprendre en jugement et en vengence quant elle est souffisant et raisonnable.[21]

> But certes, for to moeve werre, ne sodeynly for to doon vengeaunce, we may nat demen in so litel tyme that it were profitable. / Wherfore we axen leyser and espace to have deliberacion in this cas to deme. / For the commune proverbe seith thus: "He that soone deemeth, soone shal repente." / And eek men seyn that thilke juge is wys that soone understondeth a matiere and juggeth by leyser; / for al be it so that alle tariyng be anoyful, algates

---

[19] "Insofar as he offers his own material," Ralph Hanna writes, "the compiler translates into platitudinous moral statement the more elaborate rhetoric of his *auctores*; rather than an individual, he becomes a subdued voice of cosmic statement, one unembarrassed by the banality of his own language." However, the Wife of Bath's prologue reveals that "the depersonalization of the *compilator* is a rhetorical fiction": Hanna, *Pursuing History: Middle English Manuscripts and their Texts* (Palo Alto: Stanford University Press, 1996), 251–2.

[20] *Liber consolationis et consilii*, ed. Sundby, 8, l. 17–9, l. 4.

[21] *Sources and Analogues*, ed. Correale, 336.

102   DAVID LAVINSKY

it is nat to repreve in yevynge of juggement ne in vengeance takyng, whan it is sufficeant and resonable. (VII 1028–32)

In the *Liber consolationis*, the quote from Publilius's *sententiae* ("ad poenitendum properat qui cito judicat") is followed by commentary extolling patient judges ("nam licet mora omnis odio sit, non tamen in judicando mora competens est reprobanda").[22] Since Chaucer relied on a heavily revised French version of the Latin text, the various departures from Albertanus apparent in the passages above should not surprise us.[23] At the same time, the foundational status of *Melibee*'s French source comes under some pressure here with the introduction of a phrase whose stylistic origins lie in English proverbial language: "for al be it so that alle tariyng be anoyful," a version of which is recorded in Whiting's catalogue as "In long tarrying is noys."[24] The passage goes on to specify how this fragment of proverbial speech might be applied to the ordered civic polity imagined by Albertanus no less than that associated with Melibee's own putative audience of late medieval "new men": to delay in acting is "anoyful" except when time is required to judge or to deliberate about the proper dispensation of justice, in which case it is both "sufficeant and resonable." Here ethical discernment is also enacted semantically, by means of a clausal qualifier that modifies "anoyful" using elevated legalisms ("sufficeant and resonable"). Stylistic idiom foregrounds the act of textual *assemblage*, and therefore Chaucer's aesthetic choices as compiler and storyteller; those

[22] Although the side-by-side presentation of passages enables certain comparisons, it must not be assumed that Renaud "worked with a text of the *Liber consolationis et consilii* which resembled the edition of Thor Sundby": *Sources and Analogues*, ed. Correale, 324.

[23] Powell describes Renaud's translation as "more a paraphrase and a somewhat shortened version, suppressing some sections of the original and abridging others": Powell, *Albertanus of Brescia*, 124. David Wallace stresses that Chaucer had "dozens of opportunities" to consult the Latin manuscripts of Albertanus's work given their wide European dissemination, and that he "would have recognized Albertano's *Liber consolationis et consilii* (even through vernacular intermediaries) as a work of counsel authored not by a magnate but by someone (much like himself) confecting a social and authorial identity from divergent bases of authority: a 'new man'": Wallace, *Chaucerian Polity: Absolutist Lineages and Associational Forms in England and Italy* (Palo Alto: Stanford University Press, 1997), 215, 220.

[24] Bartlett Jere Whiting, with Helen Wescott Whiting, *Proverbs, Sentences, and Proverbial Phrases from English Writings Mainly before 1500* (Cambridge, MA: Harvard University Press, 1968), 576 (T44) (as cited in *Riverside Chaucer* explanatory notes for l. 1032). This self-consciously vernacular contextualization of the word "(a)noiful," which Chaucer uses for *ennuyeuse*, is enhanced by its association with English translations attributed to Trevisa and the Wycliffites. *MED*, "noiful," adj., 1b: "bothersome, annoying; boring, tiresome, tedious."

same choices are crucial to the proper ethical contextualization of a significant Latin maxim derived from Albertanus.

The textual effects produced by the amalgamation of different formal elements in this passage define the key functions of the English prose treatise as Chaucer seems to have understood them, which center on "clarity of exposition," but in the particular ethical sense enabled by a translational mode that embeds *sententiae* in the verbal substance of Prudence's discourse.[25] The productive mediating role of form can be seen from a slightly different angle in the tale's treatment of *sententiae* from Petrus Alphonsus and, later in the discussion, the Decretals. The first occurs as Prudence nears the end of her disquisition on good counsel, instructing Melibee to consider "if thou mayst parfourne it and maken of it a good ende" (VII 1212). This is no simple matter; as the conditional language here suggests, it involves evaluating probability and future contingents, and demands a certain forward-looking moral acuity on the part of all those who exercise power in the world. The quote Prudence then extracts from the *Disciplina Clericalis* encapsulates these complex instrumental and ethical considerations, despite its flat moralizing tone: "And Piers Alphonce seith: 'If thou hast myght to doon a thyng of which thou most repente, it is bettre 'nay' than 'ye.'" "This is to seyn," she continues, glossing the *sentence* from Petrus, "that thee is bettre holde thy tonge stille than for to speke" (VII 1218–19). A paraphrastic addition by Renaud to the Latin text, this interpretive comment in *Melibee* follows the French version closely, while also making itself accessible in the tale as English proverbial speech.[26] The proverbial here doubles as expository paraphrase (and like instances discussed earlier is synonymous with material recorded in Whiting's catalogue).[27] *Melibee* absorbs this ambient and dispersed Middle English proverbial lexicon into its prose, where it functions as an intervening layer of vernacular meaning, both supplementing the translation of source

---

[25] J.D. Burnley, "Curial Prose in England," *Speculum* 61 (1986), 593–614 (at 610).

[26] For comparison, see *Liber consolationis et consilii*, ed. Sundby, 60, ll. 6–10. The French text here reads: "C'est a dire, il te vault mielx taire que parler. Par plus fort raison, doncques, se tu as povoir de faire chose dont il te couvienge repentir, il te vault mieux souffrir que commencier." *Sources and Analogues*, ed. Correale, 363. For the relationship of this and surrounding lines to the *Liber consolationis*, see the editor's notes regarding l. 27.12 on the same page.

[27] Whiting, *Proverbs, Sentences, and Proverbial Phrases*, 600 (T366), according to the *Riverside Chaucer* notes. The patterns explored in these examples go beyond self-conscious verbal styling on Chaucer's part; evocative of similar moments in *Boece*, semantic and even syntactic convergence with a source language produces a distinctive text, paradoxically conferring formal specificity on a "close translation." Such traditional formulae for describing medieval translation practices arguably overdetermine our conceptions of literary form, especially when "close translation" is taken to mean the programmatic exclusion of lexical alternatives.

materials, and taking on its own instructive ethical value within the *catena* of linked "resons" comprising Prudence's intricate moral argumentation.

The term "resons," often occurring in the plural, figures prominently in *Melibee* and relates specifically to the question of its form. The section concerning how he should assess the merits of his counsellors' advice concludes with the quote from Alphonsus above, and the hope that he will "understonde by strenger resons" – that is, the various teachings Prudence has just quoted in this dense passage, stretching approximately twenty-two sentences (lines 1200–22) – whether he can put his power to justifiable ends (VII 1220). Earlier, when another of Melibee's venerable old counsellors had stressed the need for "greet conseil and greet deliberacion" in matters of war, emphasizing its unpredictable outcomes and its many deprivations (he invokes the deeply unsettling image of starving pregnant women), he did so, we are told, in an effort to "enforcen his tale by resons," at which point he is interrupted by Melibee's more belligerent advisors (VII 1041–3). Here the *Liber consolationis* cites the first half of Ecclesiasticus 22.6 ("Musica in luctu importuna narratio") but the tale then goes on to elaborate the proper interpretation of the quote, using the expository phrasing of a glossed text: "this is to seyn: as muche availleth to speken bifore folk to which his speche anoyeth as it is to synge biforn hym that wepeth" (VII 1045).[28] Finally, in frustration, the speaker here ruefully notes the truth of the "commune proverbe" that "good conseil wanteth when it is mooste nede" (VII 1048).[29] The *Liber consolationis* quotes this passage as it appears in Albertanus's source, the *sententiae* of Publilius Syrus, the *auctor* perhaps most frequently cited in this section of the story. Chaucer's version builds on the same reference while following the French in labelling Publilius's words as proverbial ("Je voy bien maintenant que le proverbe commun est vray: Lors faut le bon conseil quant le grant besoing est"), and in giving this utterance the status of "commune" speech.[30] An entire sequence of complex moral reasoning culminates in a self-consciously proverbial rendering of an authoritative Latin *sentence*. What might seem like just another proverb in a tale already stuffed full of them instead works against fragmentation and referential selectivity by enacting a shift towards reading on a larger interpretive scale.

---

[28] See, however, Grace, who argues that the authority of such glossatorial stylings is qualified when "contained within speeches of characters": Grace, "Telling Differences," 376.

[29] The repeated use of the phrase "commune proverbe," with discussion of this example, is explored in Betty Bowden, "Ubiquitous Format? What Ubiquitous Format? Chaucer's *Tale of Melibee* as a Proverb Collection," *Oral Tradition* 17.2 (2002), 169–207 (at 191).

[30] *Sources and Analogues*, ed. Correale, 337.

On one level, inscribed textual form matters less for the referentiality of encyclopedic literary-historical works than a cited authority's sentential application as theme or example. Yet to "enforcen" one's tale with "resons" is to impose structure on compilation for the sake of interpretive praxis, in the sense that proverbs accord with Prudence's larger "wille" and "entencioun," inducing Melibee's eventual assent, a moment marked off by her own remarkably effusive foregrounding of their perlocutionary value: "And whan dame Prudence hadde herd the assent of hir lord Melibee … she was wonderly glad in hire herte and seyde: / 'Ther is an old proverbe,' quod she, 'seith that "the goodnesse that thou mayst do this day, do it"'" (VII 1792–4). A French loan term referring to the intellective faculty, Middle English "resoun" denotes the influence of Chaucer's immediate source in Renaud.[31] Nevertheless, the definition more sensitive to plural usage and the explicit notion of "resons" as instances of proverbial wisdom appears under sense 9a in the *Middle English Dictionary*: "A written sentence or verse; a motto, esp. one *engraved, embroidered, or inscribed upon something*; a proverb, saying; a text."[32] Not just external moral concepts, *proverbia* are things inscribed in the textual space of the tale itself, elements of structure and substance. This point is reinforced by a possible architectural metaphor grounded in the paronomastic equivocation between "resons" and "rasens," or timberwork, a Middle English term (and a variant spelling for "resons") with a long if somewhat obscure history in London English.[33] Like beams holding up a building, "resons" supply the connected timberwork bearing the structural weight of the story as a prose treatise. As with all such wordplay (an intrinsic feature of proverbial language) this instance hinges on the linguistic self-consciousness of *Melibee*'s audience, who must not only think through the tale's "resons" in the vernacular, but also imagine the English text as materially necessary for this very purpose. If this pattern refuses to cede semantic authority to the tale's *originalia*, it also envisions the relationship between source and translation as one of self-conscious textual practice.

In addition to *proverbia*, the different terms used by Latin authors from the late twelfth century onwards to characterize the fragmentary traces of classical learning gathered into *florilegia* and other such compilations included *dicta*, *sententiae, abbreviationes, praecepta*, and of course *exempla*, broadly defined. Recast in the tale as "resons," such material takes as its distinctive modality the structure of vernacular logic and argumentation supplied in the form of the English prose treatise. Characters in *Melibee* draw explicit attention to

---

[31] Angelika Lutz, "Norse Loans in Middle English and their Influence on Late Medieval London English," *Anglia* 135.2 (2017), 317–57 (relevant comments at 331).

[32] *MED*, "resoun," n. (2), 9a, italics added.

[33] *MED*, "rasen," n., 1a–b. On paronomasia in proverbial language, see Jakobson, *Language in Literature*, 257.

this discursive process in references to the "resons" by which they seek to bolster their ethical reasoning and attune audiences to the moral complexities of Melibee's dilemma. At the same time, the probative function of "resons" can be distinguished from that traditionally assigned to the proverbial in medieval vernacular ethical discourse. If proverbs exemplify what Anne Middleton has described as the "common voice" of Ricardian poetry – a public and communal poetic cadence addressing itself to the social ideals of Langland and Gower – they also signal the basis on which *Melibee*, as a "moral" treatise, intervenes in fragment VII, where the ethics of poetic form are in question across an unusually wide variety of textual examples (VII 940).[34] As interpellative precepts, proverbs in this sense accord with how scholars have understood their ethical valence in Ricardian moral and theological vernaculars. But the proverbial also asks readers "to accept common forms of speech even where these seem to usurp the poet's peculiar privileges in metaphor, simile and other tropes."[35] Questions framed by the proliferation of common-stock material connect *Melibee* to the *House of Fame*, with its interest in the nature of "tydynges." "Loo, how shulde I now telle al thys?" asks the speaker in that poem as he ruminates on multiplicity and repetition (III.1341). Standing before the labyrinth and the whirling house of rumor, where he has been brought in the course of his dream vision, the speaker anxiously catalogues the disparate fragments of unattributed thought and speech from which he hopes to assemble an authoritative courtly poetic.[36] Adapting Albertanus for his prose treatise places Chaucer in roughly the same relationship to topical compendia and densely proverbial compilations as his poetic persona in the *House of Fame* is to tidings, and calls upon similar organizing strategies. For instance, the anaphoric patterning of lists and catalogues (e.g., III.1961–76) shares syntactical and lexical features sometimes associated with curial prose in the period.[37]

---

[34] Anne Middleton, "The Idea of Public Poetry in the Reign of Richard II," *Speculum* 53.1 (1978), 94–114. For Middleton, this public poetic voice "is neither courtly, nor spiritual, nor popular. It is pious, but its central pieties are worldly felicity and peaceful, harmonious communal existence" (95). On *Melibee*'s proverbs, Jill Mann likewise points to "the communal experience they embody": Chaucer, *The Canterbury Tales*, ed. Jill Mann (London: Penguin, 2005), 1001.

[35] J.A. Burrow, *Ricardian Poetry: Chaucer, Gower, Langland and the 'Gawain' Poet* (New York and London: Penguin, 1992), 140.

[36] "Defined in the *House of Fame* as 'novelries' (*HF*, II.686), tidings are for Chaucer the very figure of replication; distorted in the process of transmission, they are the wayward stuff from which literary tradition is made": Karla Taylor, "Chaucer's Volumes: Toward a New Model of Literary History in the *Canterbury Tales*," *Studies in the Age of Chaucer* 29 (2007), 43–85 (at 58).

[37] Burnley, "Curial Prose." On lists and catalogues in the *House of Fame*, see Wolfram R. Keller, "Performing Generic Exhaustion: Implosive Households in Gavin

For both the *House of Fame* and *Melibee*, form is a question about the aesthetics of multiplicity and surplus meaning, and the process by which textual structures are generated from much smaller units of language and sense. In *Melibee*, the additive logic of prose also serves specific ends, enabling an extended translational mode in which Latin maxims and other such *sententiae* are recast as elements of common parlance, and absorbed into the tale as embodied, ethically situated speech.[38] To some extent, of course, proverbs always operate this way, their relevance being situational, or a function of use and application. Yet they are also claimed – or perhaps reclaimed – by the outsize material presence of *Melibee* as text and translation. Albertanus's use of Aesop as *auctor* is relevant in this respect. It occurs in chapter twenty of the *Liber consolationis*, in a section urging Melibee to reject the counsel of old enemies ("Ne confidatis secreta nec hijs detegatis, cum quibus egistis pugnae discrimina tristis").[39] Here *Melibee* once again mirrors the French text, but Albertanus's reference to a body of writing putatively Aesopian in origin implicates Chaucer's own complex literary positioning as translator and compiler. His reliance on tidings and *proverbia* whose origins are for the most part impossible to trace is a literary-historical problem heightened by the use of *florilegia*, where quotations "float freely about, entirely detached from their matrix";[40] "Aesop" evokes the fragmentary and partial late medieval reception of earlier authors, especially classical ones. Reception in this case, however, produces a citation that materially individuates "Aesop," transferring *auctoritas* from the realm of disembodied tidings to the realm of inscription. And so although Chaucer may indeed have worked exclusively with the French text, one can appreciate the extent to which Albertanus's florilegial citational practices matter to *Melibee*, and how the encyclopedic recontextualization of

---

Douglas's *Palice of Honour*," in *Enlistment: Lists in Medieval and Early Modern Literature*, ed. Eva von Contzen and James Simpson (Columbus, OH: Ohio State University Press, 2022), 135–53, esp. 141–5.

[38] This point is corollary to Burnley's conclusion that in *Melibee* Chaucer reconstitutes the elements of curial style "which his French source had taken the opportunity to create from the general hints in the Latin": Burnley, "Curial Prose," 609. As Jeremy Catto notes, "Chaucer could have adapted the more solemn curial prose of his French source for the Tale of Melibee, the Livre de Melibee et de Prudence, but he preferred to stamp a plainer if still melodious style on English prose narrative": Catto, "Written English: The Making of the Language, 1370–1400," *Past & Present* 179 (2003), 24–59 (at 45).

[39] *Liber consolationis et consilii*, ed. Sundby, 49, ll. 6–7. Translated in the French as "Ne vous fiez point en ceulz a cui vous aurez eu guerre et ennemitié anciennement, et ne leur revellez point voz secrez" (*Sources and Analogues*, ed. Correale, 358), and in *Melibee* as "Ne trust nat to hem to whiche thou hast had som tyme werre or enemytee, ne telle hem nat thy conseil" (VII 1184).

[40] Rouse and Rouse, *Authentic Witnesses*, 124.

108 DAVID LAVINSKY

proverbial material retrieved from the *Liber consolationis* might suggest its place alongside other historical and aesthetic valuations of form in fragment VII of the *Canterbury Tales*.[41]

Textual (in)visibility and the English prose treatise

Proverbial sayings presumably inspired by classical authors such as Ovid or Aesop also appear as interpolations in *Melibee*.[42] Though few in number, these added lines are not found in the tale's Latin or French versions, thereby explicitly demarcating the inclusion of precepts and other moralistic sayings as an aspect of vernacular literary form. But even where the proverbial is implicit, *Melibee* takes measures, as a vernacular text, to prioritize English lexical forms in ways we might not expect given the tale's generally close adherence to its French source materials. Examining the causes for the tale's opening assault, Prudence propounds the "doctrine of Tullius" at some length, drawing on *De Officiis* (VII 1355).[43] The key passages in the *Liber consolationis* derive from *De Officiis* II.18:

> Etenim virtus omnis tribus in rebus fere vertitur, quarum una est in perspiciendo, quid in quaque re verum sincerumque sit, quid consentaneum cuique, quid consequens, ex quo quaeque gignantur, quae cuiusque rei causa sit, alterum cohibere motus animi turbatos, quos Graeci *pathe* nominant, appetitionesque, quas illi *hormas*, oboedientes efficere rationi, tertium iis, quibuscum congregemur, uti moderate et scienter, quorum studiis ea, quae natura desiderat, expleta cumulataque habeamus, per eosdemque, si quid importetur nobis incommodi, propulsemus ulciscamurque eos, qui nocere nobis conati sint, tantaque poena afficiamus, quantam aequitas humanitasque patitur.[44]

---

[41] For brief enumeration of the various compilatory texts used by Albertanus in producing the *Liber consolationis*, see Powell, *Albertanus of Brescia*, 14, n. 31.

[42] See, for instance, *Riverside Chaucer* notes for ll. 1325–6.

[43] See, as well, her earlier reference to the doctrine of Tullius (VII 1201–10).

[44] "And, indeed, virtue in general may be said to consist almost wholly in three properties: the first is [Wisdom,] the ability to perceive what in any given instance is true and real, what its relations are, its consequences, and its causes; the second is [Temperance,] the ability to restrain the passions (which the Greeks call πάθη) and make the impulses (ὁρμαί) obedient to reason; and the third is [Justice,] the skill to treat with consideration and wisdom those with whom we are associated, in order that we may through their co-operation have our natural wants supplied in full and overflowing measure, that we may ward off any impending trouble, avenge ourselves upon those who have attempted to injure us, and visit them with such retribution as justice and humanity will permit": M. Tullius Cicero, *De Officiis*, trans. Walter Miller (Cambridge, MA: Harvard University Press, 1913), 185–7. Passage selectively quoted in *Liber consolationis et consilii*, ed. Sundby, 55, ll. 10–15 and following.

SUPPLEMENTARITY AND ADVISORY ETHICS IN THE TALE OF *MELIBEE* 109

Working her way through these remarks, Prudence concedes that she cannot render a judgement as to the most important questions of causation, including what Chaucer refers to as the "*Causa longinqua*" – idiosyncratically given in the tale as the "fer cause," or "far cause," meaning everything brought about by God – except "by conjectynge and by supposynge" (VII 1395, 1402).[45] "For," Prudence continues, "we shul suppose that they [the assailants] shul come to a wikked ende, / by cause that the Book of Decrees seith, 'Seelden, or with greet peyne, been causes ybroght to good ende whanne they been baddely bigonne'" (VII 1403–4). Here conjecture and supposition are not empty forms of speculation but instead presuppose a heightened attunement to causation – that is, to the causes for assault in the first place, but also to how vengeance itself functions in causal relation to known and unknown future effects: citing what "Tullius clepeth 'consequent,'" Prudence explains to Melibee that "the vengeance that thou purposest for to take is the consequent; / and therof folweth another vengeaunce, peril, and werre, and othere damages withoute nombre, of whiche we be nat war, as at this tyme" (VII 1387–9).

While this somewhat convoluted section does not correspond exactly either to the Latin or the French texts, it roughly follows the main emphases of Albertanus, culminating in a quotation from the Decretals: "quia, ut supra dixi, 'vix bono peraguntur exitu, quae malo sunt inchoata principio.'"[46] A canon law reference revoiced as proverbial speech stands out in a vernacular text based on the work of a thirteenth-century jurist for whom the analysis of cases proceeded according to specific legal and rhetorical paradigms. In *Melibee*, the quote from Gratian serves a more discursive function, both in its sentential content and how it epitomizes the various lessons stemming from the preceding commentary on *De Officiis*. Lexically specific proverbial English is used here to elucidate moral and philosophical concepts from Latin sources. And though not traced as such in the Riverside notes, the line itself is quoted in Whiting, where it appears as "Causes badly begun are seldom brought to good end."[47]

---

[45] Helen Cooper notes that the terms for causality at l. 1395 are Chaucer's addition: Cooper, *Oxford Guides to Chaucer: The Canterbury Tales*, 2nd ed. (Oxford: Oxford University Press, 1996), 314.

[46] *Liber consolationis et consilii*, ed. Sundby, 83, ll. 1–3, though as this phrasing implies, this is the second time this saying has occurred in the text (see 54, l. 21). The French translation is as follows: "Car nous devons presumer qu'il en vendront a male fin, par raison du *Decret* qui dit: A grant pene sont menees a bonne fin les choses qui sont mal commencees": *Sources and Analogues*, ed. Correale, 376. For Chaucer's rendering, see VII 1403–4, discussed above.

[47] Whiting, *Proverbs, Sentences, and Proverbial Phrases*, 75 (C119), citing this instance from *Melibee*, and see 34 (B199) for a related instance. Evidence compiled by Whiting suggests that from about 1300 onwards (with the earliest instances occurring

The didactic appropriation of *proverbia* in *Melibee* stretches all the way back, then, to the moral and philosophical source material that had motivated Latin writing like Albertanus. Indeed, *De Officiis* emerges as a key text throughout this section, in which Prudence holds up Melibee's "wise conseillours" as models of Ciceronian probity and moral rigor (VII 1331). We have already seen how the tale invokes these same counsellors in warning against "hastifnesse," or in acting "hastily or attemprely" in seeking vengeance, and here Prudence's elaboration of what she twice calls "the doctrine of Tullius" is part of the same argument (VII 1380, 1201/1355). Ciceronian ethical terms and categories enter into and shape the deliberative process Prudence describes as propaedeutic to any just assertion of power. For instance, what Cicero refers to in *De Officiis* as "consentynge" (*quid consentaneum cuique rei sit*) – or "accord and consistency" according to the *MED*, citing this singular instance of sense 1b – is an important aspect of this analysis, or whether "thy myght and thy power," as she puts it, "may consenten and suffise to thy wilfulnesse and to thy conseillours" (VII 1382).[48] Already a suggestive idea, "consentynge" is made even more semantically complex through its collocation here with the verb "suffisen," or "to be adequate for a purpose," a frequently repeated term in *Melibee*, in keeping with its analysis of means, causes, effects – that is, the full range of differentiated ethical ideas and actions extending from what Prudence refers to as "wilfulnesse" (VII 1386).[49]

This dense middle section of the tale amounts to a rather extensive vernacular compendium of Ciceronian ethical terms, concepts, and categories, all compiled in view of equipping Melibee to proceed with sufficient deliberation "in this caas" (VII 1342). It is through the deliberative application of such knowledge that Melibee will adequately "purveyen and apparaillen" himself with wise counsel (VII 1342). "For Tullius seith," according to Prudence, "that 'longe apparaillyng biforn the bataille maketh short victorie'" (VII 1347). The term "apparaillen," or "to prepare or equip oneself," is noteworthy for how it insists as an idea on one's immersion in the vernacular semantics by which Prudence seeks to instruct her audience in "the doctrine of Tullius" (VII 1355); this is equally an immersion in vernacular form, since "apparaillen" carries the secondary sense of material adornment, evoking the productive ethical supplementary of *Melibee*'s translated maxims. Having here essentially adorned his source text with a French verb (*appareiller*) whose sense was still new in English, Chaucer ensures the visibility of his own work as

---

in the *South English Legendary*) proverbial English expressions for causal claims occur with surprising frequency. See, e.g., 34–5 (B199–209).

[48] The Latin phrase here comes from *De Officiis*, II.18, cited in *Liber consolationis et consilii*, ed. Sundby, 55, l. 13. *MED*, "consentinge," ger., 1b.

[49] *MED*, "suffisen," v., 1a.

translator.[50] Such usages therefore seem deliberate, a function not only of his close engagement with Renaud, but also of Melibee's own highly specific textuality, and the particular ways in which form attunes one to the ethical meaning of Latin *sententiae* drawn from an authoritative source.[51]

To summarize, then, *Melibee* stages the reception of proverbial wisdom as a prolonged ethical event. The fragmentary and singular *foci* that compilatory works like the *Liber consolationis et consilii* had preserved in decontextualized form – and which might be seen to invite discontinuous, highly selective appropriation, inducing the "hastifnesse" in moral reasoning and decision making so concerning to Prudence – are embedded in an encyclopedic textual space where their relevance for linguistically self-conscious English audiences can be more fully elucidated.[52] Interposed layers of sentential meaning in *Melibee* make this ethical work possible; the result is a translation which at the same time stakes its own claim to formal specificity within the diverse textual field of fragment VII. Perhaps there is also a sense here in which the prose treatise functions as textual correlate to Chaucer's insistence that the storytelling competition make space for "*al* my tale" (VII 966, italics added).[53] The crucial moment for illustrating what this imposition of form and context means in practice is when *Melibee* all but engulfs the reader in a Ciceronian moral lexicon derived from Albertanus's distillation of *De Officiis*. It is here, from VII 1393 onwards, that the focus returns to the tale's opening violence and the audience is compelled to reflect on the relationship between that allegorical episode and the end of the tale, where Melibee finally eschews vengeance, having been persuaded by Prudence to seek reconciliation with his adversaries instead.

Ultimately, no explanation is given for the assault on Prudence and her daughter; it remains unexplained except as an act of God's will (the Ciceronian "fer cause"), with the "cause accidental" described simply as "hate" (VII 1398). Such vagaries give precedence to "the allegorical form of the fiction" in the

---

[50] *MED*, "ap(p)areil(l)en," v., 3a: "to provide (sb., oneself) with clothing, to dress or dress up (in some manner)," with usages becoming far more frequent in the fifteenth century. On "appareillen," see Christopher Cannon, *The Making of Chaucer's English: A Study of Words* (Cambridge: Cambridge University Press, 1998), 241.

[51] Or what Albertanus believed were passages from *De Officiis*.

[52] This is also why it seems unnecessary to focus on equivocations or supposed contradictions in Prudence's teaching, as some critics have, or to invoke consistency as a criterion for evaluating the tale's aesthetics. See, for instance, Daniel Kempton, "Chaucer's *Tale of Melibee*: 'A Litel Thyng in Prose,'" *Genre* 21 (1988), 263–78.

[53] Wallace also draws attention to this line, and to the word "al," though to argue instead that it warns the audience against interrupting Prudence "in her work of managing and dissipating Melibee's rage": Wallace, *Chaucerian Polity*, 228. My point here, in any case, is that *Melibee* does not allow us to transcend textual form and rest complacently on some notion of *sentence*.

tale's closing sequence.[54] Melibee, Prudence stresses, "hast been punysshed in the manere that thow hast ytresspassed," the five wounds corresponding to the corruption of his soul by way of the "fyve wittes" or senses (VII 1419, 1424–5). Critics have often felt it necessary to explain how this moralizing exposition relates to the story itself, especially given the absence of first-order narrative details, such as a concrete motive for the assault.[55] Moreover, it fails to persuade; Melibee remains committed to revenge, promising instead to cast his lot with the goddess Fortune. "I bithenke me now and take heede how Fortune hath norissed me fro my childhede and hath holpen me to passe many a stroong paas," he says, confident that she will now "helpe me my shame for to venge" (VII 1445–6). But if recourse to an allegorical register seems forced or out of place in certain respects, it also follows from the prologue, where pilgrim Chaucer preempts questions about the formal specificity of his own tale: it has many more proverbs than previous versions, he explains, but in essence remains the same text, and shares the same moral. Here, in the same way, allegorical reasoning places the reader at a significant remove from the written word, and is thus presented as a highly extrapolative procedure.

To the extent that allegory is in question, it centers attention once again on the relationship between *Melibee* and its manuscript sources, and the ways in which the tale puts florilegial form to new ethical uses. Often characterized as "an informal collection of Latin maxims," the *Liber consolationis* in fact reflects how twelfth-century authors and compilers had begun to conceive of *ordinatio* as a crucial element in preserving and recalling fragments of antique learning.[56] The topical organization of manuscript compilations gave

---

[54] Taylor, "Social Aesthetics," 316.

[55] Paul Strohm maps out the allegorical "plot" here: "The reader of this passage learns that he has been reading a drama of the psyche; that Melibee's house is his body, that its windows are the five senses which have succumbed to external temptations, that his daughter (named 'Sophie' by Chaucer) is his soul, that Prudence is his own best judgment": Strohm, "The Allegory of the 'Tale of Melibee,'" *Chaucer Review* 2.1 (1967), 32–42 (at 34). Askins, citing Hoffman's article, suggests that Renaud "conflated the five senses and the five wounds of Christ when he described the wounded daughter," and that Chaucer's version follows the French in this respect: *Sources and Analogues*, ed. Correale, 327; citing R. Hoffman, "Chaucer's 'Melibee' and Tales of Sondry Folk,'" *Classica et Mediaevalia* 30 (1969), 552–77. According to Lee Patterson, however, "the apparent discordance between the literal story, in which Melibee's daughter is attacked by three neighbors with whom Melibee eventually becomes reconciled, and the allegorical subtext that identifies these three as the world, the flesh, and the devil is shown to be a discordance only when the Tale is subjected to an overly scrupulous and inflexible exegesis": Patterson, "'What Man Artow?'" 136.

[56] Paul Strohm, *Social Chaucer* (Cambridge, MA: Harvard University Press, 1994), 163.

instructive shape to widely different material while also defining the potential moral application of *proverbia*, sometimes in highly prescriptive ways. Manuscript copies of the *Liber consolationis* reflect these new priorities. In Cambridge, Corpus Christi College MS 306, a London Dominican collection of Albertanus's works dating to the first quarter of the fourteenth century, the text is arranged into numbered chapters, each of which is then given a closely defined topical or thematic focus, made explicit in rubricated chapter headings followed by decorated and enlarged initial capitals indicating the starting point in a sequence of discrete passages.[57] This manuscript also features an opening list of rubrics covering the first three books of the volume's contents (fols. iiir–ivv). Other Albertanus manuscripts employ the same strategies for organizing proverbial and epigrammatic material.[58] The opening table in London, British Library, MS Arundel 248, for instance, delineates individual chapters using two systems, assigning each a number in the left margin, and then also including brief titles or topical headings in the body of the table itself (fols. 1r–3r). Elsewhere in this manuscript, proverbial sayings are catalogued alphabetically (fol. 53r), and epigrams are tabulated using paraphs to distinguish each individual entry in a list (fols. 67v–69v). And in several Albertanus manuscripts, *capitula* tables immediately precede the *Liber consolationis* itself, as in Bodley MS Additional C. 12 (fols. 43v–44r) and Lambeth Palace Library MS 384 (fols. 13r–13v). Users of these manuscripts could navigate their contents as one might a *florilegium* or topical compendium, locating individual chapters with the help of finding aids like tables and rubric lists, and extracting units of sentential reasoning and quotation for a variety of purposes, not all necessarily related to the comprehension of the story as a whole.

No such arrangement is present in Chaucer's most important French manuscript source, and *Canterbury Tales* copies of *Melibee* only sporadically reproduce paratextual elements like descriptive chapter headings or marginal notations.[59] Yet some fifteenth-century vernacular readers and copyists seem to have shared the view that *Melibee*'s archival and encyclopedic scope invited

---

[57] The text is at fols. 7r–28r. Available online: https://parker.stanford.edu/parker/catalog/ts762cz0303.

[58] Durham University Library MS Cosin V.iii.22 and Cambridge Sidney Sussex College MS 48 also both feature lists of rubrics, with minor variations in numbering between them. Information about the former derived from https://reed.dur.ac.uk/xtf/view?docId=ark/32150_slq237hs05z.xml.

[59] On Paris, BN MS fr. 578, see Mario Roques, "Traductions Françaises des Traités Moraux d'Albertano de Brescia," *Histoire Littéraire de la France*, vol. 37 (Paris, 1938), 408–506 (cited in *Sources and Analogues*, ed. Correale, 323). See also Curt Bühler, "The Morgan manuscript (M 39) of *Le livre de Melibee et de Prudence*," in *Studies in Language and Literature in Honor of Margaret Schlauch*, ed. M. Brahmer et al. (New York: Russell & Russell, 1971), 49–54.

highly selective appropriations of its contents. In Huntington Library MS HM 144, for instance, *Melibee* is placed alongside the Monk's tale, and linked to it allegorically, through a moralizing gloss stressing fortune's centrality: "They that this present & forseyde tale haue or shal Reede Remembyr the noble prouerbis that rebukyth Couetise and Vengeaunse takyng in truste of Fortune whiche hathe causyd many a noble Prince to falle as we may rede of them here folluyng" (fol. 99r).[60] This copy also employs the term "Prouerbis" as a running head throughout the tale, elevating sentential content over its narrative structure as treatise or dialogue.[61] As was the case in Cambridge, Corpus Christi College MS 306 and the other manuscripts discussed above, such an arrangement invites selectivity and interpretive discretion by individual users of the book.

This is exactly the discursive problem at stake in the imagined reception circumstances of Chaucer's tale. Wishing that his overbearing wife could learn something from the sagacious example of Prudence, Harry Bailey's "robustly literal" reaction contravenes the interpretive expectations announced in the prologue, when Chaucer pleads with his audience to hear his tale in its entirety ("lat me tellen *al* my tale, I preye") (VII 966, italics added).[62] Presumably, what "al" means here includes some concept of the tale's *sentence* or *moralite*, not just its verbal surface as narrative. At the same time, to treat Prudence's arguments for the triumph of peace over discord as strictly allegorical in nature seems no more warranted.[63] Though the conclusion Harry draws from her instruction is a literal one, he travesties her message through a kind of allegorical logic, by extrapolating a lesson that divests violence and revenge – a crucial emphasis for Albertanus, who, according to Powell, wrote the *Liber consolationis* to address the problem of the vendetta in thirteenth-century

---

[60] Available online: https://hdl.huntington.org/digital/collection/p15150coll7/id/2359. On Huntington Library MS HM 144, see Ralph Hanna, *London Literature, 1300–1380* (Cambridge: Cambridge University Press, 2005), 9, *passim*, as well as Seth Lerer, "'Now holde youre mouth': The Romance of Orality in the *Thopas-Melibee* Section of the *Canterbury Tales*," in *Oral Poetics in Middle English Poetry*, ed. Mark C. Amodio (New York: Routledge, 1994), 181–205, esp. 195.

[61] The same priorities inform the layout of Cambridge, Magdalene College, MS Pepys 2006, a mid to late fifteenth-century manuscript which anthologizes *Melibee* (225–75; the manuscript is paginated) alongside the *Distichs* of Cato (211–24). The text of *Melibee* also uses a different and more pronounced, larger script for the names of the *auctores* cited by Prudence. Consulted in facsimile form, *Manuscript Pepys 2006: A Facsimile*, intro. A.S.G. Edwards, The Facsimile Series of the Works of Geoffrey Chaucer 6 (Norman, OK: Pilgrim Books, 1985).

[62] Burrow, *Ricardian Poetry*, 88.

[63] The attack on Melibee's household, Burrow adds, "is represented as a real event which, by a kind of poetic justice, follows the (metaphoric) pattern of Melibee's sin": Burrow, *Ricardian Poetry*, 80.

SUPPLEMENTARITY AND ADVISORY ETHICS IN THE TALE OF *MELIBEE* 115

Brescia and other northern city-states – of their complex social meanings.[64] In these ways, Harry's reaction both decontextualizes the story he has just heard and subtly attributes his sensibilities as a reader to particular textual circumstances.

As a discursive formation, allegory does not represent the antithesis or subversion of literal reading so much as it does a certain kind of interpretive privilege, one closely associated with topical compendia and encyclopedic textual forms. Margaret Connolly has shown how organizing a manuscript to enable the "selective consumption" of its contents was an authorial signature of compilers in this period.[65] Harry's highly selective reframing of *Melibee* suggests that he considers the tale a kind of compilation. Indeed, his response bears an uncomfortable resemblance in this respect to the way Jankyn discontinuously seizes on brief quotes and sayings from *his* compilation, "Valerie and Theophraste," or *The Book of Wicked Wyves*; both men arbitrarily transfer textual meaning to an external moral and political register they alone define, or attempt to define. Although Alison voices disdain for the antifeminist themes of his citations, in her eyes Jankyn's efforts to establish his authority as a reader are also linked to a specific kind of textual arrangement. She quite specifically characterizes the "volume" of "Valerie and Theophraste," disfigured and cast into the fire moments later, in terms of its proverbial contents, defiantly remarking that "I sette noght an hawe / Of his proverbes n'of his olde sawe" (III 659–60, 681; see, too, 773).[66] By contrast, Melibee's readerly resistance is eventually "overcome," and the connection between advisory ethics and textual form decisively restored (VII 1427). Chaucer's tale thereby challenges

---

[64] On its Brescian setting, see Powell, *Albertanus of Brescia*, 74–86, and 118, describing Prudence's message as "peaceful means over violence." Drawing on Roques's work, Powell points out that Renaud was no less alert to the social topicality his translation may have acquired within Burgundian contexts (124). Marion Turner extends the social meanings of the tale to gender and masculine violence, as does Wallace, who also argues that "one of the most striking aspects of Albertano's *Liber consolationis*" is its "emphasis upon the embodied character of language, and the importance of real (rather than allegorical) bodies." See Turner, *Chaucer: A European Life* (Princeton: Princeton University Press, 2019), 465, and Wallace, *Chaucerian Polity*, 221. See also Carolyn Collette, "Heeding the Counsel of Prudence: A Context for the *Melibee*," *Chaucer Review* 29.4 (1995), 416–33.

[65] Margaret Connolly, "Compiling the Book," in *The Production of Books in England, 1350–1500*, ed. Alexandra Gillespie and Daniel Wakelin (Cambridge: Cambridge University Press, 2011), 129–49 (at 134). Though Connolly's argument here concerns the use of extracts in religious and devotional works, her points might be extended to compilations more generally.

[66] On the fraught poetics of this encounter and its meanings for Chaucer's appropriation of the classical tradition, see Taylor, "Chaucer's Volumes," 75–83.

assumptions of textual transparency and the extrapolative procedures that would render *Melibee* formally invisible.

The patterns tracked in this paper all demarcate the prose treatise as an emergent site of constitutive power in the *Canterbury Tales*, and in Middle English contexts more broadly. But if such a project is premised on the reader's recognition of the tale as didactic allegory, the inclination to focus solely on what Prudence, in her discussion of Cicero, calls the "fer [far] cause" of things – to transfer meaning away from form and language itself – is difficult to sustain (VII 1395); indeed, allegorical signification is the only kind of supplementarity that seems provisional in the story, both because it leaves Melibee unconvinced, as we have seen, and because it eclipses social and communal questions at stake in Melibee's eventual reconciliation with his enemies. Nor is Prudence's didacticism in this sense merely a set *topos* of the tale's family resemblance to the European mirror for princes tradition. Though Melibee "must learn to modify his impulses by attention to good counsel," proper lordship hinges on something more fundamental than moral reform of the kind suggested by the tale's allegorical premise.[67] The means by which Prudence carries out her advisory role instead treat the ethical subject as one altogether enmeshed in semantics. Melibee's restoration depends on his continuous transiting through language in the form of "skiles," "resouns," "wise informaciouns," "techynges," and "conseil" (VII 1870–2). The ethical potential Prudence devises for these terms is inseparable from the work they do within the layered textual space of the tale itself. Chaucer's own word for describing the accumulated effect of Prudence's instruction on her husband is "overcome": "I se wel," he begins to realize, "that ye enforce yow muchel by wordes to overcome me in swich manere that I shal nat venge me of myne enemys" (VII 1427).[68] Tellingly, "overcome" in this sentence figures something rather different from transcendence, allegorical or otherwise. It turns our gaze back towards the plane of inscription, to the "goodliche wordes of dame Prudence," and the embodied textuality Melibee comes to represent (VII 1733). Chaucer's work configures itself accordingly, redistributing its interpretive surplus to sentence-level reasoning and argumentation, and in doing so reimagining the English prose treatise as an immersive ethical form in its own right.

---

[67] Strohm, *Social Chaucer*, 162. Melibee must learn not only to heed good counsel, but how to "examyne youre conseil" by assessing the motives and purposes of various advisors, even friendly ones (VII 1200). Marion Turner notes "the atmosphere of suspicion that pervades the tale": Turner, *Chaucerian Conflict: Languages of Antagonism in Late Fourteenth-Century London* (Oxford: Oxford University Press, 2007), 179.

[68] As Patterson notes, in the French text "Melibée is not 'overcome' but 'enclinée'": Patterson, "'What Man Artow?'" 155, n. 121.

6

Buddha and the Grail: Speaking of the Unstable World in *Barlam and Iosaphat* and Malory's *Le Morte Darthur*

KENNETH HODGES

Two ancient traditions about how to respond to the suffering of the world unexpectedly intersect in fifteenth-century England. The life of Buddha is the ultimate source of *Barlam and Iosaphat*, a popular saint's life, which in the late fifteenth century was translated into Middle English, somewhere around London or the southern Midlands.[1] It resembles the ascetic Christianity displayed in Sir Thomas Malory's version of the Grail quest, translated nearby at about the same time. Both texts emphasize the sorrows that spring from the unstableness of the world and humans' wavering will. In particular, Malory suggests Launcelot's adultery is a symptom of the more fundamental problem of his unstableness. When explaining why Launcelot will not achieve the Grail, the hermit Nacien says:

> For I dare sey, as synfull as ever Sir Launcelot hath byn, sith that he wente into the queste of the Sankgreal he slew never man nother nought shall, tylle that he com to Camelot agayne; for he hath takyn uppon hym to forsake synne. And ne were that he ys nat stable, but by hys thoughte he ys lyckly to turne agayne, he sholde be nexte to encheve hit sauff Sir Galahad, hys sonne; but God knowith hys thought and hys unstablenesse. (729.29–35)[2]

---

[1] *Barlam and Iosaphat: A Middle English Life of Buddha Edited from MS Peterhouse 257*, ed. John C. Hirsh (Oxford: Oxford University Press, 1986), xiii. All references to *Barlam and Iosaphat* are to this edition unless otherwise noted.

[2] All references are to Sir Thomas Malory, *Le Morte Darthur*, ed. P.J.C. Field, 2 vols (Cambridge: D.S. Brewer, 2013).

That Nacien does not mention adultery at all is surprising. The concrete sin he focuses on is not the physical joys of adultery but the physical violence of man-slaying, but seemingly more fundamental than either is the concern with his interior instability. This makes Launcelot's failure not the consequence of a sin unique to him as the queen's lover but of a common flaw shared by many. Launcelot appears to have learned this lesson. When he returns to Guenevere after the Grail Quest, he tells her, "if that I had nat had my prevy thoughtis to returne to youre love agayne as I do, I had sene as grete mysteryes as ever saw my sonne Sir Galahad, other Percivale, other Sir Bors" (791.10–13). He emphasizes not the physical act of adultery but his "prevy thoughtis," suggesting that unstableness of will is the fundamental issue, especially since he says his thoughts "returne," echoing Nacien's claim that Launcelot "by his thoughte" would "turne agayne." Instability is therefore a crucial term for reading the Grail quest, and parallels with *Barlam and Iosaphat* suggest the response is more complex than a simple binary between celestial and terrestrial chivalry. Ascetic renunciation of the world is preferred to and in some ways easier than pursuing salvation while loving an unstable world that tends toward loss and sorrow, but the appropriate responses for individual characters do vary by circumstance.

Language matters: "unstablenesse" is not simply a euphemism for adultery, but a description both of a changing world and of human psychology. It provides the synchronic link between two texts translated in the midst of the turmoil of the Wars of the Roses. It also provides a diachronic explanation for how a life of Buddha could be translated into a Christian saint's life, since the human experience of the unstable world is more general than the religiously specific categories of sin. *Barlam and Iosaphat* fundamentally concerns itself with the griefs and uncertainties of the world, as they drive both Iosaphat's search for Christian stability and his father's misguided efforts to protect his son and to secure his uncertain legacy. The Grail quest, too, responds to the disruptions and instabilities that have been building through the earlier Trystram section. Galahad (an illegitimate child raised apart from his parents), Perceval (a foolish and unpromising younger son), Launcelot (caught in an unstable triangle between his lover and his king), and Bors (overshadowed by his more famous kinsman) find in the Grail quest a promise of more than the upheavals of the secular world. Thus, while Malory criticism has tended to treat the drive for ascetic purity in the Grail quest as the primary narrative impulse and Launcelot's instability as an obstacle to it, in *Barlam and Iosaphat* the recognition of the world's instability and the grief it causes drives the narrative, and ascetic purity is a response, an attempt that is simultaneously a spiritual calling and an earthly solution to some of the earthly griefs instability causes. Applying this to *Le Morte Darthur* suggests the desire to escape the sorrows and dangers of the unstable world might be the root from which the

Grail quest springs; Launcelot's brave devotion to earthly objects inevitably leads to grief but may not inevitably lead away from God.

While there is no evidence that proves one text directly borrowed from the other, the intertextual resonances do tell us how fifteenth-century readers might have responded. Karla Taylor emphasizes that language "offers us a window into the experience of the people who spoke, wrote, heard, and read the texts in which we find it" and celebrates the tools that allow us to look at language not just as the creation of a few master poets, but as an evolving resource shared by communities and shaped by verbal histories.[3] In earlier work, she examines how even conventional language is unstable: "The stability proverbial language promises is doubly deceptive, because the same words can mean various things in various contexts, and because the relationship to reality they propose is not direct, but mediated by desire."[4] In this way, my method here differs from the focus on intertextual allusion practiced by Taylor, and by Andreea Boboc and Elizabeth Allen in this volume; instead, like Colette Moore but in a literary critical vein, I am interested in the place of a loaded word in a late medieval literary system. The parables and symbols of the Grail quest and *Barlam and Iosaphat* are not proverbs, but the sense that familiar moral truths are altered and shaped by their context and history and the desires of their readers and translators still applies. It is appropriate to read the Grail quest remembering that the religious exposition is placed in the mouths of characters and can therefore be analyzed in terms of desires and communities. Careful attention to how each text invokes the unstable pays off, not just in appreciating how each text transforms its sources (whether a non-Christian life of Buddha or a secular tradition glorifying Launcelot's worldly nobility) but also how the texts relate to each other as their translators worked in the unstable end of the fifteenth century.

Assumptions about how a community of readers would respond to these texts, which truths they would accept as stable and religiously absolute and which they would recognize as potentially contestable, underlie our readings of these works. How Christian a text Sir Thomas Malory's *Le Morte Darthur* is (which depends upon the more specific question of how his "Sankgreall" fits with the larger work) has been a topic of sustained debate.[5] If the "Sankgreall"

---

[3]   Karla Taylor, "Language in Use," in *Chaucer: Contemporary Approaches*, ed. Susanna Fein and David Raybin (University Park: Pennsylvania State University Press, 2010), 99.

[4]   Karla Taylor, "Proverbs and the Authentication of Convention in *Troilus and Criseyde*," in *Chaucer's 'Troilus': Essays in Criticism*, ed. Stephen A. Barney (Hamden: Archon Books, 1980), 286.

[5]   An overview of the critics emphasizing the secular is given by Lisa Robeson, "Secular Malory," in *A New Companion to Malory*, ed. Megan G. Leitch and Cory James Rushton (Cambridge: D.S. Brewer, 2019), 191–210; in the same volume, Raluca

is a definitive statement of Christianity, then the return to the concerns of secular knighthood after the Grail quest represent a major failure and perhaps an indictment of chivalry as an institution. If, as I argue, the "Sankgreall" offers one path of several, then it may be possible for characters to have meaningful Christian careers within the roles of conventional earthly chivalry. While the hermits teaching ascetic Christianity during the Grail quest must be taken seriously, they are fallible: one who advises Bors proves to be a demon (742.10–11), and one who counsels Launcelot seems to be well-meaning but is proven wrong (714.11–716.24). This teaches readers to consider the hermits' teachings rather than blindly accept them. Launcelot's final redemption in particular suggests that the Grail hermits do not have the final word on salvation and do not teach the only Christian path.

This invitation to think critically about what is being taught in the Grail quest, coupled with the slipperiness of the word "unstable," opens up interpretive possibilities. The *Middle English Dictionary* suggests that when "unstable" is applied to individuals, it often suggests sinfulness: "Vacillating, irresolute, easily swayed; inconstant, fickle; also, unsteadfast in virtue, susceptible to sin, morally weak."[6] When applied to the world, however, "unstable" has more of a sense of transitoriness and fragility: "(a) Changing, variable, mutable; also, liable to change, volatile ... (b) easily moved, light; not fixed in position, moving; (c) not lasting, impermanent; transitory, fleeting."[7] Thus, when Nacien then asserts that Launcelot, despite honest efforts to forsake sin, will fail because he "ys nat stable" (729.33), his instability tends toward the sinful; however, at the end of the quest, when Galahad's last message to Launcelot bids him to "remembir of this worlde unstable" (787.34–5), the effect is not to emphasize Launcelot's sinfulness but to warn him that the joys of the world are fleeting. This second meaning is closer to the repeated usage in *Barlam and Iosaphat*, where the unstableness of the world is repeatedly invoked as motivation for choosing an ascetic lifestyle and seeking a more

---

L. Radulescu takes a more religious approach in "Spiritual Malory," 211–26. The range of critical opinion is clear in *Malory and Christianity: Essays on Sir Thomas Malory's Le Morte Darthur*, ed. D. Thomas Hanks, Jr. and Janet Jesmok (Kalamazoo: Medieval Institute Publications, 2013). Even approaches that look at the manuscript instead of thematic concerns reach opposite conclusions: K.S. Whetter looks at rubrication and marginalia in the Grail quest to conclude the scribal presentation encourages secular readings in *The Manuscript and Meaning of Malory's* Morte Darthur: *Rubrication, Commemoration, Memorialization* (Cambridge: D.S. Brewer, 2017), 105–58; Radulescu looks at the "Tale of Balin" to draw the opposite conclusion, that Balin was set up to foreshadow the Grail quest and provide a consistent attention to spiritual concerns arising from suffering in *Romance and its Contexts in Fifteenth-Century England: Politics, Piety and Penance* (Cambridge: D.S. Brewer, 2013), 149–97.

6   *MED*, "unstable," 1a.
7   *MED*, "unstable," 1b.

lasting happiness. In light of *Barlam and Iosaphat*, Launcelot's instability, rather than simply a failure to achieve the purity demanded of Grail knights, might be better understood as part of the fundamental human condition of suffering that the Grail is supposed to heal, and it provides more evidence that, despite the rhetoric of some of the Grail hermits, earthly and heavenly chivalry are not opposites but part of a continuum in which imperfect humans struggle with an unstable world. *Barlam and Iosaphat* models an interplay between ascetic, contemplative withdrawal and worldly engagement more complex than is generally recognized in the Grail quest, with holy characters moving back and forth between worldly and spiritual roles instead of simply moving from the earthly to the religious and thence to salvation or a fall back to the world. This provides a framework for interpreting what it means for Bors and Launcelot to re-enter secular life after the Grail quest. While renunciation of the world to focus on spiritual contemplation is recognized in both texts as the superior form of Christianity, both recognize that perversely this can make holiness itself a temptation leading to over-ambitious attempts to claim the spiritual role that end up being more dangerous than accepting the lesser virtues of lay Christianity.

Barlam and Iosaphat centers on the conflict between a holy son and a vicious father, a contrast stronger than between Galahad and Launcelot. The Indian king Avennere, who is persecuting the Christians in his realm, longs for a son, but when Iosaphat is born, it is prophesied that he will turn Christian. Horrified, Avennere confines him so that he will experience only the pleasures of life, but when Iosaphat catches glimpses of the sick, the poor, and the aged approaching death, he questions his tutors about how to understand this suffering. Iosaphat is soon converted by the ascetic Barlam. After long sermons, Iosaphat is tested by a series of temptations, gains and resigns a throne, and dies a hermit. *Barlam and Iosaphat* started as an Indian life of Buddha, circulated in central Asia, and was Christianized in Georgia with the Buddha figure becoming Saint Iosaphat.[8] From Georgian it passed into Greek as *Barlaam and Iosaph*, falsely ascribed to John of Damascus. Then it was translated into Latin. The Latin version circulated widely in Europe, was

---

[8]   For the complicated textual history, see Constanza Cordoni, *Barlaam und Josaphat in der europäischen Literatur des Mittelalters: Darstellung der Stofftraditionen – Bibilographie – Studien* (Berlin: De Gruyter, 2014); Keiko Ikegami, *Barlaam and Josaphat: A Transcription of MS Egerton 876 with Notes, Glossary, and Comparative Study of the Middle English and Japanese Versions* (New York: AMS Press, 1999), 13–65; Donald S. Lopez, Jr., "Introduction," in Gui de Cambrai, *Barlaam and Josaphat: A Christian Tale of the Buddha*, trans. Peggy McCracken (New York: Penguin, 2014); John Hirsh, "Introduction," in *Barlam and Iosaphat: A Middle English Life of Buddha Edited from MS Peterhouse 257*, ed. by John C. Hirsh (Oxford: Oxford University Press, 1986), xiii–xx.

translated into a number of vernaculars, and spread with missionaries back east as far as Japan. In England there are short versions in the *Legenda Aurea*, the *South English Legendary*, and the *Northern Homily Cycle*; Caxton's *Golden Legende*, printed in 1483, two years before he printed *Le Morte Darthur*, includes a short account. It was widely popular: Gower drew on it,[9] it may have influenced the play *Everyman*,[10] and it is the indirect source for the casket scene in William Shakespeare's *Merchant of Venice*.[11] While there are not sufficient grounds to claim *Barlaam and Josaphat* as a source for Malory, it is reasonable to consider it as part of the late medieval horizon of expectations against which early readers would have seen Malory's work. Of particular importance to Malory studies is Cambridge MS Peterhouse 257, much longer than other Middle English versions (because it is based on the longer Latin version and not the shorter version in the *Legenda Aurea*). It was translated into Middle English at about the same time Malory was finishing his work: Caxton's colophon reports Malory finished *Le Morte Darthur* in 1469–70, and Caxton printed it in 1485; on the basis of certain formatting elements derived from print (signatures and catchwords), John C. Hirsh places MS Peterhouse 257 within a few years of 1480.[12] It has the most verbal and thematic parallels with Malory, so it will be the basis for comparison.

Karen Cherewatuk makes the case that fifteenth-century romances should be read in the context of hagiographic texts.[13] More recently, Raluca Radulescu emphasizes penitential hagiographic romances, arguing that the deposition of Richard II and later Henry VI resulted in a literary trend that emphasized misfortune (Job became popular), suffering lords, and concerns with genealogy as a response to political instability.[14] However, exactly how such contexts guide our reading of *Le Morte Darthur* has been controversial. A sizable number of critics have held that *Le Morte Darthur* is fundamentally a secular text, and that Malory included the Grail primarily as a signifier of earthly

---

[9] George L. Hamilton, "Studies in the Sources of Gower," *Journal of English and Germanic Philology* 26.4 (1927), 491–520; Ito Masayoshi, "Gower's Use of *Vita Barlaam et Josaphat* in *Confessio Amantis*," *Eibungaku Kenkyu* (1979), 3–18.

[10] Helen Adolf, "From *Everyman* to *Elckerlijc* to Hofmannsthal and Kafka," *Comparative Literature* 9.3 (1957), 207.

[11] *Barlaam and Josaphat: English Lives of Buddha*, ed. and intro. Joseph Jacobs (London: David Nutt, 1816), lxii; Constanza Cordoni, *Barlaam und Josaphat in der europäischen Literatur des Mittelalters*, 238.

[12] Hirsh, "Introduction," in *Barlam and Iosaphat*, xii–xiii.

[13] Karen Cherewatuk, "The Saint's Life of Sir Launcelot: Hagiography and the Conclusion of Malory's *Morte Darthur*," *Arthuriana* 5.1 (1995), 63–6. She later modifies some of her conclusions about Launcelot but not the argument that hagiography is an important context for *Le Morte Darthur* in "Malory's Lancelot: Not 'Either/Or' but 'Both/And,'" *Arthuriana* 29.1 (2019), 24–33.

[14] Radulescu, *Romance and its Contexts*, esp. 1–39.

honor, either deliberately resisting or blunderingly misunderstanding his source; others have insisted that the Christian commitments of *Le Morte Darthur*, including the decision to include the most religious of the versions of the Grail quest available to Malory, must be taken seriously.[15] Among the latter there is a further split. A few see the religious element as compelling enough to expose the Arthurian court as a tragedy or as a negative exemplum of chivalry.[16] Others do not go that far, suggesting instead that knights must look for ultimate religious salvation not in the practice of chivalry but in the eventual renunciation of the secular world, but that does not condemn the pursuit of chivalry in youth.[17] Still others argue, in the words of Dhira Mahoney, that in fifteenth-century England "Secular and spiritual pursuits could be considered complementary rather than competitive elements of knightly life."[18] Or, instead of merely complementary, they could be fused to provide what Fiona Tolhurst calls "secularized salvation."[19] Underscoring these complications is the problem that the Grail's version of Christianity is not the

[15] Eugène Vinaver's influential commentary boosted secular readings of Malory and verged on suggesting that Malory was a relatively ignorant translator who almost accidentally wrote a work that has lasted over five hundred years, and Larry Benson further argued that *Le Morte Darthur* celebrated secular chivalry in *Malory's* Morte Darthur (Cambridge, MA: Harvard University Press, 1976). On the other side, Charles Moorman took the Grail as a serious critique of Arthurian chivalry in *The Book of Kyng Arthur: The Unity of Malory's* Morte Darthur (Lexington: University of Kentucky Press, 1965), and Sandra Ness Ihle argued that Malory engaged the theology seriously in *Malory's Grail Quest: Invention and Adaptation in Medieval Prose Romance* (Madison: University of Wisconsin Press, 1983). For more recent discussion, see Robeson, "Secular Malory"; Radulescu, "Spiritual Malory"; Hanks and Jesmok, eds., *Malory and Christianity*.

[16] Moorman cites the failure of religion as one of the three major flaws that doom Arthur's reign (*The Book of Kyng Arthur*). Elizabeth Pochoda, *Arthurian Propaganda: Le Morte d'Arthur as an Historical Ideal of Life* (Chapel Hill: University of North Carolina Press, 1971), and Ruth Lexton, *Contested Language In Malory's* Morte Darthur (New York: Palgrave, 2014), also argue that the presentation of Arthur's reign is essentially negative.

[17] See for instance Cherewatuk, "The Saint's Life of Sir Lancelot," or Edward Donald Kennedy, who despite acknowledging how it is Launcelot's love for Guenevere that brings him to salvation, nonetheless sees the triumphant moment of that salvation when he "forsakes the world," in "Malory's Guenevere: 'A Woman Who Had Grown a Soul,'" *Arthuriana* 9.2 (1999), 43.

[18] Dhira Mahoney, "The Truest and Holiest Tale: Malory's Transformation of *La Queste del Saint Graal*," in *Studies in Malory*, ed. James W. Spisak (Kalamazoo: Medieval Institute Publications, 1985), 110; reprinted in *The Grail: A Casebook*, ed. Dhira Mahoney (New York: Garland, 2000), 380.

[19] Fiona Tolhurst, "Slouching towards Bethlehem: Secularized Salvation in *Le Morte Darthur*," in *Malory and Christianity: Essays on Sir Thomas Malory's* Morte

only, or even the standard, version of Christianity. In the Roman church, the eucharistic cup was reserved for priests; the Grail quest's fantasy of knights aspiring to the cup of Christ without being ordained verges on the heterodox: Richard Kaeuper identifies the various iterations of the Grail legend as part of an aggressive knightly lay Christianity that blurred or ignored inconvenient precepts.[20] This suggests it might be critically naïve to take the Grail quest as the final word on Christianity, especially as episodes after the Grail quest (such as the poisoned apple) are intertextually linked to other Christian texts not perfectly compatible with the morals of the Grail hermits.[21] The dubious orthodoxy of the Grail quest leaves open the possibility of more conventional Christian readings in which knights can lead secular Christian lives without seeking to usurp the roles of the clergy.[22] Juxtaposing *Barlam and Josaphat* with the Grail quest offers insight into this vexed relation between ascetic saintliness and secular life.

Unstable Individuals in an Unstable World

The idea of instability, both of a world that is subject to fortune and of individuals who do not and perhaps cannot single-mindedly pursue God, is critical to *Barlam and Iosaphat* and *Le Morte Darthur*.[23] It seems obvious that it is Launcelot's adultery that keeps him from achieving the Grail, but the text gestures to something else as well: his unstableness. Nacien the hermit explains to Gawain that Launcelot will fail because he "ys nat stable, but by his thoughte he ys lyckly to turne agayne ... but God knowith hys thought and his unstablenesse" (729.33–5). By contrast, a hermit found in Bors "so mervales a lyffe and so stable" (732.1–2) that his holiness is clear, just as Iosaphat's teacher Barlam is "a stable man, wyse and redy" (20). Stability

---

Darthur, ed. D. Thomas Hanks, Jr. and Janet Jesmok (Kalamazoo: Medieval Institute Publications, 2013), 127–56.

[20] Richard Kaeuper, *Chivalry and Violence in Medieval Europe* (Oxford: Oxford University Press, 1999), 47 and following.

[21] Kenneth Hodges, "Haunting Pieties: Malory's Use of Chivalric Christian Exempla After the Grail," *Arthuriana* 17.2 (2007), 28–48.

[22] C.S. Lewis, "The English Prose *Morte*," in *Essays on Malory*, ed. J.A.W. Bennett (Oxford: Clarendon Press, 1963), 16–17.

[23] To instability of character and of the world Dorsey Armstrong adds a "social" instability in conceptions of knighthood, suggesting that Palomides and Galahad destabilize the presentation of glorious Christian knighthood, Palomides by testing how Christian or not a knight needs to be, Galahad by testing whether a good Christian can in fact pursue violent secular knighthood: see Armstrong, "Christianity and Social Instability: Malory's Galahad, Palomides, and Lancelot," in *Malory and Christianity: Essays on Sir Thomas Malory's* Morte Darthur, ed. D. Thomas Hanks, Jr. and Janet Jesmok (Kalamazoo: Medieval Institute Publications, 2013), 107–26.

of religious purpose was recognized as necessary for spiritual growth.[24] One sermon cycle puts stableness before even pity and love:

> Thre þingis in specyall be nedefull to every man and woman þat purposithe to preve and to incree in vertu and grace of good lyvyng. The first is *tenor fraternitatis*, the secunde is *humor pietatis*, and the therde is *calor caritatis*. These iij ben nedefull fo every man and woman to plante in þer sowlys and he or sche wyll incree in good lyvyng: stabylnes, moystnes and hete.

> First I sey is stabylnes. For lyke as ȝe see with ȝowre bodily yeen, a plant þat is every day remevyd frome place to place may never preve. The same wyse spiritually: a man or woman may never growe to heuenwarde but if he or sche haue within them the vertu of stabylnes.[25]

Unstableness is linked to sin. Beverly Kennedy points to Walter Hilton and Richard Rolle, who identifies unstableness of thought as a sin of the heart;[26] one can also recall Geoffrey Chaucer's Prioress, invoking "we synful folk unstable."[27] In particular, Nacien's analysis of Launcelot could be an assertion that a temporary desire for holiness is not enough, given that he will return to Guenevere.

But his return to his love represents its own kind of stability. Malory drives home the point in his famous passage comparing true love to May with his own botanical metaphor, when he says:

> For, lyke as wynter rasure dothe allway arace and deface grene summer, so faryth hit by unstable love in man and woman, for in many persons there ys no stabylité. For we may se all day, for a lytyll blaste of wyntres rasure, anone we shall deface and lay aparte trew love for lytyll or nowght, that coste muche thynge. Thys ys no wysedome nother no stabylyté. (841.14–19)

---

[24] Mahoney, "The Truest and Holiest Tale," 121–2; for further discussion, see Janet Jesmok, "Rhetoric, Ritual, and Religious Impulse in Malory's Book 8," in *Malory and Christianity: Essays on Sir Thomas Malory's* Morte Darthur (Kalamazoo: Medieval Institute Publications, 2013), 93–5.

[25] *A Late Fifteenth-Century Dominical Sermon Cycle Edited From Bodleian Library MS E Musaeo 180 and Other Manuscripts*, ed. Stephen Morrison, 2 vols (Oxford: Oxford University Press, 2012), vol. 1, 58–9.

[26] Beverly Kennedy, *Knighthood in the* Morte Darthur, 2nd ed. (Cambridge: D.S. Brewer, 1992), 265–6; Richard Rolle, "Form of Living," in *English Writings of Richard Role, Hermit of Hampole*, ed. Hope Emily Allen (Oxford: Clarendon Press, 1963), 97. Available online: https://archive.org/details/englishwritingso0000roll/page/96/mode/2up (accessed 10 July 2022).

[27] Text from *The Riverside Chaucer*, ed. Larry D. Benson, 3rd ed. (Boston: Houghton Mifflin, 1987), l. 685.

He adds that Guenevere "was a trew lover, and *therefor* she had a good ende" (842.11, my emphasis). And, after the break with Arthur, Launcelot looks back on his career in terms of stability: "Howbehit I wote well that in me was nat all the stabilité of thys realme, but in that I might I ded my dever" (904.21–2). This language suggests there may be forms of stability unacknowledged by the hermits of the Grail quest. It could be argued that Launcelot's effort to fight for political stability shows a fundamental mistake in thinking in earthly rather than spiritual terms. However, as Donald Kennedy has noted, Launcelot finally achieves salvation not by renouncing Guenevere but by staying true to her and following her into religious life.[28] This suggests that Launcelot's struggles for earthly stability, while ultimately doomed to fail, nonetheless prove spiritually valuable.

While Nacien's assessment that Launcelot is unstable encourages us to consider Launcelot's personal spiritual state, Galahad's final words about the world unstable have a different import. The world's instability demands individuals find ways of living in uncertain conditions. *Le Morte Darthur* and *Barlam and Iosaphat* agree the world is essentially unstable. Over and over again, *Barlam and Iosaphat* emphasizes this, and the Christian asceticism that Barlaam preaches is a response to deal with the illness, suffering, and death that Iosaphat sees. For instance, Barlam says:

> [God commanded me to show you the right way] to delyuere þe fro þe erroure of þis world, whych Y loued wel some tyme, and had grete delite þerin, tyl Y considerid in my soule þe vnsikernes of þis lyf here, and how many men han pershyd þerin, some encresynge in þe world, and some discresynge, þat non abode in stedfast state, noþer ryche men in here riches, ne myȝty men in here strengthe, ne ioly men in here lust and lykynge, and þei þat wende to haue lyued stabylly in here vanyte sone fellen and were caste adoun. Al þis was but a while abydynge, but sone passed awey. Al þis Y vnderstode wel, and þat al þe ioye of þe world is but vanyte, and no profyte is þerin. (60–1)

Barlam rejects the world not because it is fundamentally sinful (although it does entice people to sin) but because it is vain and unprofitable. The difference is subtle but significant: if the world is fundamentally sinful, then it must be rejected, and Barlam's and Galahad's ascetic path is the one way to holiness. If, however, the motive in renouncing the world is not to avoid sin but to avoid temptation and sorrow as transitory things pass away, then there is a wider range of ways of negotiating humans' relations to the world, and those who are willing to endure the world's sorrows perhaps can live religious lives within the world. When Galahad entrusts Bors with a last message to

---

[28] Kennedy, "Malory's Guenevere," 41–2.

his father, he says, "salew me unto my lorde Sir Launcelot, my fadir, and as sone as ye se hym bydde hym remembir of this worlde unstable" (787.33–5), his exhortation is a reminder that earthly joys do not last. Bors dutifully does pass on Galahad's message, telling Launcelot to "remember of thys unsyker worlde" (789.5–6). But the effect of the message is altered by the messenger: Galahad is preparing to leave the world unstable in search of heavenly joy; but Bors himself is making the transition back from the religious isolation of the Grail quest to the worldly community of Arthur's court. Whether Launcelot is to follow his son's lead in renouncing the world or his cousin's in engaging the world while remembering not to depend upon its pleasures is unclear.

A tempting reading is that people who embrace the unstable world make themselves unstable, and those who renounce the world in favor of the stable and eternal become stable themselves. Terrestrial chivalry is unstable; celestial, stable. Thus Donald Kennedy writes, "What is at issue … is Lancelot's insta-bility, his inability to renounce the unstable world he must abandon if he is to be saved."[29] However, the relation between unstable individuals and the unstable world is not as straightforward as it appears. In Barlam's analysis, it is fear that causes the instability of the world to result in unstable lives:

> Se now how mankende is vexid and turbelid by þe wykkyd enmye, þe world, and neuer may abide in one state, but is now here, now þere, now in one degree and now in anoþer, as a dowve þat fleeth fro þe egyl or an hawke. Now she is in o place, and now in anoþer, now amonge trees, now amonge busshys, now amonge stonys, now amonge þornys, for to hyde hereself, and neuer may fynde syker reste, but euer mevyth aboute in grete drede an trybulacion. So it fareth by hem þat dreden to leese þe welfare and þe prosperyte of þis world. (61)

At first glance, Barlam's image of a frightened dove seems far removed from Malory's intrepid Launcelot. Yet Malory does repeatedly speak of Launcelot's fears: his pious "drede of God" (206.13; VI.10), but he also "drad sore" Melleaguance's treason against Guinevere (847.26; XIX.4), and of course fear of shame, both present and future. When Arthur banishes him, he laments:

> [H]it grevyth me sore, for I shall departe with no worship; for a flemyd man departith never oute of a realme with no worship. And that ys to me grete hevynes, for ever I feare aftir my days that men shall cronycle uppon me that I was fleamed oute of thus londe. And ellis, my fayre lordis, be ye sure, and I had nat drad shame, my lady Quene Gewnyvere and I shulde never have departed. (903.22–9; XX.17)

---

[29] Kennedy, "Malory's Guenevere," 41.

These fears move Launcelot: although he may move nobly in quest and battle, like the dove he is regularly in motion until the revelation of his sin and the loss of Guinevere and Arthur cause him to abide in his hermitage. His repentance brings not just holiness but also stillness.

But what if it is possible to engage with the world without fearing and fleeing loss? Bors seems to model a stoic acceptance of whatever comes. When Mordred and Aggravayne catch Launcelot in Guenevere's chambers, Bors counsels him, "all ys wellcom that God sendyth us, and as we have takyn much weale with you and much worship, we woll take the woo with you and we have takyn the weale" (878.6–9). Their allies agree: "lat us take the wo and the joy togydir" (878.14–15). Bors then repeats his advice: "be myne advice, ye shall take the woo wyth the weall" (879.29–30). Bors is teaching what it means to engage with the world while avoiding the fearful unstable flight from sorrow, and that is to accept sorrow and pain as the price for living in the world. Arthur seems more disturbed. When he has his frightening vision of the instability of the world in his dream of the wheel of Fortune (920.15–25; XXI.3), it is after his disappointments have provoked him into a killing rage against Guenevere and Launcelot and led him to break the fellowship of the Round Table he had founded. When Arthur departs for Avalon and Bedivere laments, Arthur answers "In me ys no truste for to truste in" (927.5; XXI.5). Surely part of the enigmatic meaning since he has lost faith in the worldly projects he had set his hand to, that leaves the knights who follow him with nothing in which to set their trust. Launcelot, unlike Arthur, does maintain his love for Arthur and for Guenevere (his magnanimity perhaps aided by being more sinning than sinned against). Perhaps, like Bors, he has found a way to engage with the secular world at the price of accepting its sorrows.

If the world need not be absolutely rejected, then the dichotomy between celestial and terrestrial chivalry becomes blurred.[30] *Barlam and Iosaphat* uses language similar to the Grail quest's distinction between celestial and terrestrial chivalry: early in the text, a retired knight turned holy says "we vsed þe knyȝthode of þis world" (7) before converting to spiritual things. But in *Barlam and Iosaphat*, the terrestrial and the celestial are not simple opposites. It is knowledge of this world that leads Iosaphat to holiness. Iosaphat begins removed from the world, in a palace his father King Avenerre has designed to show his son only the pleasures of the world, but this isolation from the world is meant to encourage his sin. Going out into the world and seeing suffering is a necessary step that causes Iosaphat to seek religious answers about how to deal with the instability of the world. His time in the world leads to his final withdrawing from the world, based not on pleasure and ignorance but on faith and wisdom. It is thus not surprising that, although Barlam briefly tells

---

[30] Tolhurst, "Slouching towards Bethlehem," 131.

Iosaphat the story of Eden, the dangers of the knowledge of good and evil are not greatly emphasized (25–6). More forceful is the parable of the unicorn, in which a man is pursued by a fierce unicorn and falls into a pit with a dragon at the bottom. He catches himself halfway down on a little green tuft, but two mice, one black and one white, are gnawing it. However, a bush above drips honey in his mouth, and it is so sweet he is happily distracted until the mice gnaw the bush away and he falls into the dragon's mouth. The explanation is that the unicorn is death, which always pursues humans; the pit is the world, the green tuft fragile worldly prosperity, the two mice gnawing it away are night and day (representing time), the dragon is hell, and the honey is worldly joy (55–6). Here the threat seems willful ignorance rather than forbidden knowledge. Worldly joy may not be sinful but it is distracting, and the wise use their perception of the instability of the world to motivate their holiness.

This might suggest a form of religion in which life is lived in phases, living in the world initially and then withdrawing from it as years and wisdom accumulate. The middle stage of experiencing the world's sorrow might be said to correspond to Malory's questing knights, exposing themselves to injury to build their worthiness. Dhira Mahoney suggests that for Malory celestial chivalry might usually be most appropriate in the final stages of a knight's life, after a more worldly career while younger.[31] This may fit Launcelot's conversion at the end of his life, and it can be adjusted to fit Galahad, who, although only fifteen years old at the start of the Grail quest (656.31), dies after seeing the mysteries of the Grail. However, a number of characters return to the world after religious experiences, including Bors and Launcelot, suggesting that transformative religious events need neither be reserved for the end of life nor result in an absolute withdrawal from the world.

Certainly, in *Barlam and Iosaphat*, spiritual development is not a matter of simple linear movement from the secular world to spiritual withdrawal. Characters move back and forth from seclusion to worldly engagement, their roles marked by changes of clothing. Barlam, knowing of Iosaphat's spiritual distress, changes clothes and leaves the desert to go back to the secular world (19). Just before Iosaphat asks to be baptized, there is a long discussion of Barlam's clothes (77–9), and immediately after baptism, Iosaphat is rebuked for offering Barlam and his spiritual fellows a worldly gift of good clothes (80–1). (In addition to the discussion of worldliness, this exchange is also part of *Barlam and Iosaphat*'s concern with wealth and poverty, an issue absent in the Grail quest.) The issue comes up again when Barlam departs: Iosaphat takes Barlam's hair shirt to wear under his courtly clothes and gives Barlam a new hair shirt in return (94). Iosaphat buries his father not in royal clothes but in a penitent's garb (163). When he is done mourning his father,

---

[31] Mahoney, "The Truest and Holiest Tale," 122–3.

Iosaphat joins Barlam in the desert, casting off his fine clothes and wearing a hair shirt (167). In a final proof of holiness, when King Barachia opens up the grave, "he sawe þe bodies of Barlam and Iosaphat in a feyre and clere coloure with here clothis hole and sounde" (178). In both texts, even though clothing seems to signify religious purity or worldly vanity, the changeability of the garments trouble the binary between terrestrial and celestial modes of living. At the boundary between public vision and private feeling, able to be exposed or hidden, allowing access to public spaces or encouraging private religious thought, clothes allow characters to pass back and forth between religious and secular realms, putting on roles as needed.

Even Iosaphat, sheltered and eager to renounce the world, must engage the world on multiple occasions. When Barlam departs after baptizing Iosaphat, he does not allow Iosaphat to accompany him, but insists he stays longer in the courtly world. King Avennere's final strategy to seduce Iosaphat away from Christianity is to make him king of half of Avennere's land, in hopes that "þe grete besynes þat he shal haue aboute his temporal gooddys shal make hym to turne" (154). Iosaphat shows his worthiness not by refusing to go into the world but by living in the world as a good Christian king, converting his people, including ultimately his father. (Galahad, of course, is briefly made king of Sarras (786.32–3) but the episode has less narrative significance.)

A strange and underanalyzed adventure in the Grail quest similarly suggests there is a path to holiness that does involve temporarily leaving a life of religious withdrawal to return to the world to protect other worldly people, and, as in *Barlam and Iosaphat*, clothes play a role in the interpretation. Launcelot finds a dead old man wearing a fine shirt. A hermit interprets this to mean that he was damned for returning to secular life, thus breaking his vow to be a holy man. So far, it seems a perfect warning to Launcelot about the perils of instability and returning to a worldly life after turning to religion. However, the hermit then (with no narrative comment!) summons a demon, which contradicts the hermit, saying the dead man is saved, explaining that he had returned to secular life to protect his nephew and been murdered for it, but his clothes were given miraculous power to testify to his holiness. Launcelot takes the dead man's hair shirt to wear (716.16–19), which Launcelot continues to wear under his courtly finery for his return to Arthur's court after his closest approach to the Grail (776.1–4). Thus what appears to start as an exemplum to warn Launcelot against returning to the world ends up affirming the virtue in returning to secular matters to protect those left behind. Launcelot's confused counselor discovers the simplistic insistence on renouncing the world and never returning to it does not fit with the complex bonds of human life. Other hermits acknowledge Launcelot's worldly responsibilities. One instructs him "ye shall no more com in that quenys felyship as much as ye may forbere" (696.27–8), the qualifier acknowledging the political realities that the best knight in the queen's affinity must have political contact with her. Launcelot's response is a commitment to the path of knighthood: "From hensforewarde I caste me, by the grace of God, never to be so wicked as I have bene, but as to sew knyghthode and to do fetys of armys" (697.35–698.2). The answer is apparently acceptable, because the hermit assigns "suche penaunce as he might do and to sew knyghthode" (698.3–4). Launcelot's continued pursuit of knighthood appears to be endorsed by hermits and adventures in the Grail quest. Instead of the simple binary of celestial versus terrestrial, Launcelot's failings lie in the details of how he returns to the world.

The Perfect as the Enemy of the Good

Launcelot's worldly engagements may be a licit form of Christianity, but, as he is constantly reminded, it is less prestigious than Galahad's disengaged purity. The glory of ascetic renunciation tempts ambitious knights such as Launcelot and Gawain, but aiming that high brings with it the danger of falling short, especially since such a commitment makes previously acceptable behaviors sinful. Both texts suggest that the desire to pursue divine mysteries is actually dangerous to sinners. When Barlam comes to see Iosaphat, he pretends that the intangible knowledge of Christianity he brings is a precious jewel, but when a skeptical guardian asks to see it, he warns that sin can lead to blindness and that what is holy can hurt those unprepared for it:

> [I]t wyl be sey of no man clerly, but of hym þat is chaste in body, and in no manere synne defouled. And if eny man loke þeron and be nat chaste in body, but be defouled in synne, he shal in þe siȝt þerof be blynde and gon out of his mende. (20)

This language is reminiscent of a hermit's warning to Launcelot:

> And for youre presumpcion to take uppon you in deadly synne for to be in Hys presence, where Hys fleyssh and Hys blood was, that caused you ye might nat se hyt with youre worldely yen, for He woll nat appere where such synners bene but if hit be unto theire grete hurte other unto theire shame. (695.35–696.5)

The association with blindness that Barlam warns of is echoed in the failure of Launcelot to see and confirmed later when he is told "ye shall have no power to se hit, no more than a blynde man that sholde se a bright swerde" (716.6–7), and ultimately when he is struck down in Corbenic he loses the power of his hearing and sight (774.20–1). More generally, the Grail quest is repeatedly marked as hazardous. The Siege Perilous destroys anyone unworthy who sits in it (80.29–31). Balin's sword, which comes floating down the river at the start of the Grail quest, will wound anyone who attempts to draw it and fails (668.21–3). Bagdemagus is likewise hurt for daring to bear the shield that is

132 KENNETH HODGES

meant for Galahad (678.14–679.25). The Ship of Faith to which Percivale's sister leads Percivale, Bors, and Galahad warns those of insufficient belief (752.12–28). The sword of the strange girdles that Galahad receives has a similar threat (753.22–5, 756.14–17). In *Barlam and Iosaphat*, the warning of danger might be literally understood, since King Avenerre is enthusiastically martyring all the Christians he can catch, but in Malory the question of why pursuing Christian truths should be so dangerous is less easily dismissed. If the Grail quest is meant to be the standard of Christianity for all believers, these repeated dangers seem strangely distant from the easy yoke Jesus promised. It makes better sense if the texts are distinguishing between the heroic rigors of ascetic saintliness and the softer, safer Christianity open to the masses. The Grail's covered appearance at Arthur's feast of Pentecost to the whole court represents the grace available to all Christians; Gawain's rash vow to see it uncovered is the result of a hubristic discontent with the rewards of common Christians and aspiring to a higher degree of Christian perfection than he has earned.

The distinction in modes of Christianity is part of Barlam's early teaching. When Iosaphat asks nervously whether, if he sins after baptism, he will lose all grace and be damned, Barlam reassures him that the remedy for instability is penance:

> For Almy3ty God, þat became man for saluacion of mankende, / knewe well þe infirmyte of man, and his vnstabylnes. And because þat he wolde nat þat we pershyd after oure bapteem, as a wyse leche he ordeyned for us a remedie to reforme us to grace a3en. And þat is penaunce. (47)

This is presumably the standard lay life, and Barlam elaborates on the theme of penance for several pages. When Iosaphat expresses dissatisfaction with the pains of penance and desires to live more perfectly, then Barlam teaches him about the martyrs and desert fathers who chose a difficult but more perfect path:

> [Iosaphat said] "How shoulde Y do for to keep meself clene from synne after my bapteme? For if a man falle into synne a3en he muste þerfor do penaunce, and lyue in grete laboure and sorowe, wepynge and waylynge for his synne. And þat is ri3t harde and hevy for a man to do. Therefore Y wolde fynde a syker wey, þat Y my3t parfytly keep þe comaundmentys of God and neuer to falle into synne after it is for3eue me."

> Barlam answerid a3en and seide: "Treuly, Syr, þou seist wonder wel. It is gretely desired, but it is ful laberous, and / inpossible it is to ley a stykke on þe fyre and brenne nat. So it is ful harde to a man þat leuyth in seculere lyf, in grete besynes, in sturbel, in delite, in iolite, in riches, to keep parfytly þe comaundementis of God, and neuer to trespas in hem, and to keep hym clene fro synne." (50)

Like Iosaphat, Launcelot desires to forsake the world in pursuit of perfect holiness, and his failure is perhaps more grievous because he made the attempt rather than being content to accept the life of sin and penitence that living in the secular world entails. This forces him into the other form of Christianity Barlam speaks of, labor and sorrow, weeping and wailing for sin.

The dangers of aspiring above one's degree of holiness are taught through similar episodes of seduction that involve the temptation of sinning to save someone else. King Avenerre to ensnare Iosaphat puts beautiful women as his servants and instructs them to seduce him (136–45). The most beautiful, the daughter of the king of Syria, taken as a slave and given to King Avennere, nearly succeeds. Iosaphat is stirred by what he chooses to believe is pity for her plight and decides to convert her. She offers to convert if he will marry her. When he exclaims that "þouȝ Y desire gretly þy saluacion, it were hevy and greuous to me to defoule my body with eny fleshly weddynge" (140), she gives a spirited defense of marriage as suitable for Christian life, citing multiple bible verses. He concedes marriage is lawful to most, but not to those sworn to virginity, "Treuly Womman, al þis is sothe þat þou hast seide. It is leefful to haue a wyf, to hem þat wyll haue one, but nat to hem þat haue made a vowe and a behest to keep here maydenhode clene unto Cryste" (140–1). She proposes that if he will sleep with her once, she will convert, and they can both repent and live ascetically ever after. (One is reminded that Bors had one sexual encounter in which he engendered Elyne le Blank but repented and became a Grail knight.) Iosaphat is sorely tempted, but desperate prayer and a miraculous vision save him. Although the primary concerns are the ways in which religious young men can rationalize lust as pity and the morality of sinning to achieve someone else's salvation, it is worth pausing on the question of why the one-night stand is more tempting than the offer of marriage, when marriage is lawful for Christians and fornication is not. Iosaphat is spiritually ambitious, and marrying would drop him down into a less exalted form of Christianity. Sleeping with the princess once, however, and repenting afterward would preserve mostly intact his ambitions for spiritual grandeur. Barlam's teaching that unstableness is intrinsic to the human condition, not something that can be avoided by force of will, and that the path of salvation is one of penance instead of perfect purity, can easily be twisted into license for indulgence. Iosaphat's desire to achieve the spiritual heights thus has made a range of otherwise acceptable behavior like marriage sinful, increasing the chances that he will fall, and it has perversely made the short-term sin more attractive than the long-term public acknowledgment of a lesser form of Christian life. The desire for spiritual perfection has become the enemy of an acceptable good.

Malory includes an episode similar to Iosaphat's temptation, but his version leaves the middle option of marriage out, and it makes the episode a stark warning of what it means to value souls instead of lives. During the Grail quest, a devil in the form of a priest tells Sir Bors that he will meet a woman who loves him, and that if he denies her desires, she and (for unexplained reasons) Sir Launcelot will die; the seeming priest says Bors should sleep with her, and to refuse her to keep his chastity would in fact be vainglory. Bors does meet the woman and he does refuse her. She threatens that she and twelve of her gentlewomen will commit suicide. He refuses; they jump; he crosses himself, and they are revealed to be devils (Malory 738.28–740.35). In Malory the test is black and white: the temptress is a demon, not a woman; there is no mention of possible marriage; and the threatened suicide makes it clear lives as well as souls are at stake. The moral explanation for Bors's choice to defy the seeming priest is brief: "Than had he of hem grete pité; natforthan he was nat uncounceyled in hymselff that levir he had they all had loste their soules than he hys soule" (740.25–7), with the tortured grammar and the multiplication of negatives reflecting the emotional difficulty of the choice. In *Barlam and Iosaphat*, there is more nuance, and, although devils urge on both Barlam and his would-be seductress, the major players are human.[32] Bors's adventure teaches the ruthless lesson that the proper concern of Christianity is souls, not lives; Iosaphat's infatuation teaches more about human emotion and what forms of life might be permissible.

Barlam and Iosaphat's open acknowledgment that ascetic virginity is not the only acceptable form of Christianity is instructive for Malory scholars in evaluating the Grail quest's role in *Le Morte Darthur*. The quest teaches a powerful form of Christianity, and those who undertake the quest and slide away from it may well be sinful; but this binary excludes a middle form of Christianity. The people who do not participate in the Grail quest, whether married characters (including Gareth and Arthur himself) and unmarried characters not dedicated to celibacy (Palomides), may point to forms of lay Christianity not explored in the Grail quest. Malory seems fond of Pelleas and Nyneve, several times inserting mentions of their happy, enduring marriage (a marriage he invented), and early in the text lists Pelleas as one of the knights achieving the Grail (143.23–4), suggesting at one point he considered a less ascetic quest in which a married knight might succeed. Since the Grail quest teaches an elite Christianity, Launcelot's struggles to reconcile the various secular and religious elements of his life after the Grail quest perhaps should

---

[32] *Barlam and Iosaphat*'s nuance compared to Bors's more straightforward temptation allowed for a range of translators' responses: Constanza Cordoni documents a variety of reactions to the princess in European versions of *Barlaam and Josaphat*, ranging from a misogynist assumption that women are frequently allied with devils to Rudolf von Ems's vigorous defense of women and fleshly love; the variety of interpretation revealing the provocative openness of the story: Cordoni, *Barlaam and Josaphat in der europäischen Literatur des Mittelalters* (Berlin: De Gruyter, 2014), 293–5.

Arthur, Guenevere, and the World

When Bors and Iosaphat face their choices about whether to sin to save women's lives or souls, the women serve primarily as temptresses. Guenevere is a more complicated case. Edward Donald Kennedy understands the Grail quest to demand that Launcelot "renounce the world and Guenevere,"[33] but she is not a symbol of the world. Guenevere not only saves her own soul, but she inspires Launcelot to save his. In some ways it is Arthur more than Guenevere that represents the unstable world. Arthur's link to mutability is suggested by his dream of Fortune's wheel (920.15–24). Malory's uncertainty about his death, the possibilities that he might return, end up with his famous circumlocution about Arthur's death that uses the key words "world" and "change" as subtle reminders of the instability of the world: "here in thys worlde he changed hys lyff" (928.26). His death, releasing knights from loyalty to a worldly king, prompts a wave of people to renounce the world. Before Launcelot and Guenevere is Bedivere. The sole male, non-magical witness to Arthur's departure, he in his grief joins a hermit (formerly the Archbishop of Canterbury) in "prayers and fastynges and grete abstynaunce" (928.31–2). When Launcelot, freshly departed from Guenevere at the nunnery in Amesbury, encounters Bedivere and the former archbishop, Bedivere's news of Arthur provokes Launcelot to exclaim against the world and immediately precedes his religious commitment:

> But whan Syr Bedwere had tolde his tale al hole, Syr Launcelottes hert almost braste for sorowe, and Sir Launcelot threwe hys armes abrode, and sayd, "Alas! Who may truste thys world?"
>
> And than he knelyd doun on his knee and prayed the bysshop to shryve hym and assoyle hym; and than he besought the bysshop that he might be his brother. Then the bysshop sayd, "I wyll gladly," and there he put an habyte upon Syr Launcelot. And there he servyd God day and nyght with prayers and fastynges. (934.17–25)

Launcelot's ties to this unstable world include Arthur and his court, not just his adulterous love for Guenevere, and his grief at worldly losses aids his repentance.

---

[33] Kennedy, "Malory's Guenevere," 41.

136 KENNETH HODGES

When Guenevere and Launcelot part, they negotiate his relation to the world and his changed circumstances. She bids him marry: "Sir Launcelot, go thou to thy realme, and there take the a wyff, and lyff with hir wyth joy and blys. And I pray the hartely to pray for me to the Everlasytnge Lorde that I may amende my mysselyvyng" (933.10–13). This suggestion of marriage, like the Syrian princess's proposal to Iosaphat, is acceptably Christian – Guenevere asks for Launcelot's prayers – but it is a step down from Launcelot's ambitions for perfection, both as a lover and as an ascetic Grail seeker. Launcelot rejects the idea that he would "turne agayne unto my contrey and there to wedde a lady" (933.14–15). His language echoes Nacien's condemnation that "he ys nat stable, but ... he ys lyckly to turne agayne" (729.33). His refusal to turn again to his own lands thus is an assertion of his own stability. Guenevere, at once elated and doubtful at his commitment to follow her into religious life, repeats the language of turning: "A, Sir Launcelot, if thou wylt do so and holde thy promise! But I may never believe the ... but that thou wylt turne to the worlde agayne" (933.20–2). Guenevere here decidedly does not position herself or their love as part of the unstable world Launcelot is to renounce. Rather, her fear that Launcelot will turn to the world is a fear that he will turn away from her. Malory's narrative remarks in the earlier 'love and summer' passage, in which he denounces those who turn away from love as unstable and claims Guenevere had a good end because she was a good lover, here prove true. Guenevere and Launcelot are able to use their love to move away from the world – but not each other – and earn their penitent salvation.

However, Launcelot and Guenevere's love is not the only form of earthly love acknowledged by the texts. Raluca Radulescu explores Launcelot's duties to his familial and spiritual lineages (forward and back) in the Grail quest.[34] Bors's love for his enraged and betrayed kinsman Lionel is heart-breaking; and while Bors made the right choice to rescue a virgin rather than Lionel, the text in no way suggests his love for his kin is inappropriate for a Grail knight. Likewise, *Barlam and Iosaphat* celebrates family. In her discussion of the importance of family, Constanza Cordoni suggests that King Avennere functions as a prodigal father, occasioning Iosaphat's joy upon his conversion.[35] The funerals at the end affirm that Iosaphat and Launcelot can acknowledge earthly bonds with repentant sinners without sacrificing their commitment to

---

[34] Radulescu, *Romance and its Contexts*, 149–97; Karen Cherewatuk also explores the relations between fathers and sons in *Marriage, Adultery and Inheritance in Malory's* Morte Darthur (Cambridge: D.S. Brewer, 2006), 90–9.

[35] Constanza Cordoni, "Es geschieht in den besten Familien: *Barlaam and Josaphat* und das Problem der Familie," in *D'orient en occident: les recueils de fables enchâssées avant les Mille et une nuits de Galland (Barlaam et Josaphat, Disciplina Clericalis, Roman des sept sages)*, ed. Yasmina Foehr-Janssens and Marion Uhlig (Turnhout: Brepols, 2014), 185–6.

heavenly concerns. The deaths of holy figures such as Barlam, Iosaphat, and Launcelot, followed by evidence of their ascension, is a familiar trope; having these religious figures mourn at funerals is less standard. When Iosaphat buries Avennere, the text shows not just philosophical resignation to death but great grief. He inters his father with "grete wepynge," and for seven days he "neuer arose from his grave, and neuer he þouȝt on mete, ne drynke, ne slepe, but euer he was in prayer" (163). There is a momentary hint of bitterness when in a dream he sees a spirit bringing crowns both for him and for his father, and he wonders if it is fair for his father to have just as much reward as his son (no one ever said familial love is perfect), but he quickly acknowledges that grace is infinite (176–7). When Barlam dies, Iosaphat also registers great grief with strong weeping (173, 175). There is no suggestion that his faith is less because he grieves the early deaths of mortal men. Launcelot's grief for Arthur and Guenevere has been treated more suspiciously. Within the text, a hermit claims he displeases God for mourning for Guenevere and Arthur so greatly, but Launcelot strongly defends himself, and the text seems to validate his view (936.26–937.5). Critics, too, have wondered at his grief, which seems to mix penitential awareness of sin with a continuing earthly love.[36] Barlam's mourning suggests that Malory is not alone in allowing earthly love to express itself in earthly grief, even in high religious context. Malory's earlier dictum "firste reserve the honoure to God, and secundely thy quarel muste com of thy lady" (841.28–9) does not require renunciation of the love of earthly objects, just its subordination. That Launcelot turns away from the world while maintaining his bonds to both Arthur and Guenevere is in keeping with what *Barlam and Iosaphat* teaches.

---

[36] For recent contributions, see Cherewatuk, "Malory's Lancelot: Not 'Either/Or but 'Both/And,'" who finds the closing richly ambiguous, with evidence of sincere repentance mingled with evidence Launcelot is still setting too high a priority on Guenevere; Corey Olsen sees the doubling but reads Launcelot's grief at the funeral as evidence of sincere and discerning penitence in "Adulterated Love: The Tragedy of Malory's Lancelot and Guinevere," in *Malory and Christianity: Essays on Sir Thomas Malory's* Morte Darthur, ed. D. Thomas Hanks, Jr. and Janet Jesmok (Kalamazoo: Medieval Institute Publications, 2013), 29–55. In the same volume, Janet Jesmok disagrees, arguing that Launcelot remains trapped by the physical, stable only in the practice of earthly chivalry: see Jesmok, "Rhetoric, Ritual, and Religious Impulse in Malory's Book 8," 92–106. K.S. Whetter argues that the text, and the manuscript presentation of the text, show a secular and not a religious focus in *The Manuscript and Meaning of Malory's* Morte Darthur, 190–1.

Conclusion

As Malory critics increasingly recognize that religious texts, especially saints' lives with touches of romance, are an important part of the horizon of expectations for Malory and his readers, *Barlam and Iosaphat* as translated in MS Peterhouse 257 offers a particularly fertile field for comparison. The texts share a deep concern with the unstable world, with how to balance worldly and heavenly concerns, similarities expressed in language, in imagery (such as the shifts in clothing when passing from the secular to the religious world or temporarily returning) and trials, such as the temptation of saving a woman's life or soul by sinning. *Barlam and Iosaphat* is in some ways more tolerant than Malory's Grail quest, showing sympathy with deeply flawed characters such as Ʒardan, the servant with conflicted loyalties who warns King Avennere of Iosaphat's conversion (91–3), or the captive Syrian princess who attempts to seduce Iosaphat, or even King Avennere himself, whose desire for a son and a stable succession, and his desire for what he perceives to be his son's happiness, go so horribly wrong. *Barlam and Iosaphat* is also more concerned with worldly wealth and less with worldly prowess than Malory (even if Gui de Cambrai's early thirteenth-century French translation invents a war between Iosaphat and his father for a demonstration of crusading valor). Nevertheless, it offers an instructive example of the mixing of aristocratic and ascetic ideals. It suggests that Launcelot's return to the world after the Grail quest is more defensible than some critics have allowed. Launcelot's adultery is sinful, both in its fleshly lust and in the lovers' disordered spiritual priorities, but the remedy need not be the complete renunciation of each other and of the world. Galahad sets a model for responding to the unstable world by abandoning it; so, too, does Iosaphat, although his great weeping at the deaths of his father Avennere and his mentor Barlam show his remaining worldly attachments to those he loves. Bors sets a model for accepting the price of grief for worldly bonds, whether it is suffering Lionel's rage or counselling Launcelot to accept whatever God sends when his adultery is discovered and the realm descends into civil war. The late conversion of King Avennere provides a model of how even great sinners can find grace. Launcelot and Guenevere end up somewhere in between; penitents like Avennere, but together finding a measure of spiritual wisdom and holy desire that seems more than merely penitential.

Barlaam and Iosaphat started as a life of Buddha, and by the time it was translated into the late Middle English of MS Peterhouse 257, it had crossed over several religions, numerous cultures and languages, and many centuries. It is a reminder of the web of connections that cross the boundaries of period, nation, language, and religion that we use to define our disciplines. Yet if the radical translations testify to the instability even of religious texts, there is a stability in the concerns about how to respond to the sorrows and uncertainties of the world. The "Sankgreall" too, though to a lesser extent, had crossed over generic, cultural, and linguistic lines. The dramatic diachronic fluctuations of meaning in these texts may attract the most attention, but the synchronic interplay is also illuminating. Malory and the unknown translator of *Barlam and Iosaphat* produced works that are in intertextual conversation with each other and more generally with late fifteenth-century English concerns with instability and penitence. Although from very different literary traditions, these works are connected through the language they use, and that language matters.

PART IV

THE AESTHETICS OF LANGUAGE IN MIDDLE ENGLISH LITERATURE

7

Facing the Reeve: Reason, Resonance, and the Tragedy of the Local in the *Canterbury Tales*

STEPHANIE L. BATKIE

> "*The face, what a horror.*"[1]
> – Deleuze and Guattari, *A Thousand Plateaus*

Nobody much likes the Reeve, it seems. And with good reason.[2] From the first, he is singled out from the pilgrim group not because of boisterous (but apparently affable) revelry like the Miller, or divine justice made manifest by providential election like the Knight, but because of his querulous, personal complaints. In our first real encounter with him, the Reeve objects to the Miller's declaration that he will tell a disordered tale, both because of his station (and condition) among the pilgrims and his choice of content. "Lat be thy lewed dronken harlotrye," he cries out, before the Miller has said much at all (I.3145). The Reeve's protest might be premature, but his assumptions about the Miller's story are not exactly inaccurate. After all, the narrator also breaks in several lines later with his well-known (if possibly feigned) reluctance to

---

[1] Gilles Deleuze and Felix Guattari, *A Thousand Plateaus: Capitalism and Schizophrenia*, trans. Brian Massumi (Minneapolis: University of Minnesota Press, 1987), 190.

[2] The critical consensus on this is nearly universal. Approaches to the Reeve range from uneasiness to fury, and recent investigations into sexual violence in the tale comprise some of the most important and revelatory readings of the text we have. See, most notably, Carissa Harris, *Obscene Pedagogies: Transgressive Talk and Sexual Education in Late Medieval Britain* (Ithaca: Cornell University Press, 2018), 26–66. The exception to this within the scholarly conversation might be the interest in the Reeve as a dialect-speaker – although even his northern provenance is sometimes read as being associated with a "devilish character," as in Deborah S. Ellis, "Chaucer's Devilish Reeve," *Chaucer Review* 27.2 (1992), 153.

repeat the "cherles tale" (I.3169).[3] Nevertheless, the Reeve's initial exchange with the Miller is so emphatic that his objection colors how the pilgrims (or at least the Host) see him from that point on: he is a sermonizer for the narrator (I.3899) and an improper and unwelcome preacher for the Host (I.3903). First impressions matter, and the Reeve is now solidly defined by his contest with his churlish counterpart.

Acts of definition like this surround the Reeve and make him one of the most delineated and localizable figures of the pilgrim group. He is famously identified by his dialect as a northerner, and his portrait, prologue, and tale are all place-bound.[4] He is geographically situated by the language he speaks, the setting of his tale, and by the comfortable "wonyng" he gains the use of (I.606–8). Even his complaints about his aging body pin him down. This localized identity manifests and maintains the durable structures of power the Reeve exists within, and as a member of an interstitial estate, the Reeve is caught between the spheres he occupies. Not quite a franklin and more than a common laborer (despite his training as a carpenter), Oswald is plotted out by intersecting social and economic structures. "The Reeve embodies the inertia of those who maintain strong social networks, untouched by the dynamic mobility of those with weaker ties to several networks," as Karla Taylor writes, and in this she gives us an angle on the character that demonstrates the pleasures and perils of inhabiting structures of power.[5] In the

---

[3] The narrator and the Reeve are aligned in their appraisal of the Miller, to the point that the two share strategies of warding off (on the part of the narrator) or scolding (on the part of the Reeve). The famous advice the narrator offers in light of the Miller's subject matter, that readers might "Turne over the leaf" (I.3177), echoes with the Reeve's own admonition to the Miller himself that "Thou mayst ynogh of othere thynges seyn" (I.3149).

[4] This is a quality of the tale that has been noted from Tolkien onward. See J.R.R. Tolkien, "Chaucer as Philologist: The Reeve's Tale," *Transactions of the Philological Society* 33.1 (1934), 1–70; W.W. Allman, "Sociolinguistics, Literature, and the Reeve's Tale," *English Studies* 85.5 (2004), 385–404; Phillip Knox, "The 'Dialect' of Chaucer's Reeve," *Chaucer Review* 49.1 (2014), 102–24; Joseph Taylor, "Chaucer's Uncanny Regionalism: Rereading the North in the Reeve's Tale," *JEGP: Journal of English and Germanic Philology* 109 (2010), 468–89. The same is true of the clerks in the tale. See Andy King, "'Fer in the North; I Kan Nat Tell Where': Dialect, Regionalism, and Philologism in Chaucer's Reeve's Tale," *Nottingham Mediaeval Studies* 57 (2013), 89–110. For a contrasting view on the Reeve's northernism, see S.C.P. Horobin, "J.R.R. Tolkien as a Philologist: A Reconsideration of the Northernisms in Chaucer's Reeve's Tale," *English Studies: A Journal of English Language and Literature* 82.2 (2001), 97–105.

[5] Karla Taylor, "Language in Use," in *Chaucer: Contemporary Approaches*, ed. Susanna Fein and David Rabin (University Park: Penn State University Press, 2010), 110.

Reeve, *status* become stasis, and he embodies the position of a rigid and circumscribed subject inasmuch as he strives to be effective, measurable, and secure in his position.

My contention is that the Reeve poses a particular problem in the *Canterbury Tales*, and I would like to propose that he also offers an unexpected solution. He is someone we are asked to take at face-value – including in his capacity for violence and deceit. The suspicion and fear he engenders in those around him is hard-earned and proper, and while I do not think this is an unfair response to the character, I do think it is one Chaucer works hard to make sure we come to easily. Without denying the unpleasantness and the dislike Chaucer cultivates around him, I suggest that Oswald is also one of the most *tragic* of the pilgrims setting out from the Tabard. The Reeve embodies the ramifications of a figure inhabiting a *status* that makes plain the gap between what a person is capable of and what he desires. Chaucer gifts Oswald with a skill in language that is truly extraordinary; throughout his prologue and tale, the Reeve exhibits a mastery over how his language sounds that opens his speech up to possibility and potential.[6] This sounded space is de-localized and untraceable – and it is one that the Reeve himself would certainly not recognize or desire, despite his potential involvement with it. In fact, Chaucer shows us how, even as the poetics of his speech map out new (if unexplored) geographies of meaning, Oswald turns away from the abeyant sense-structures embodied in his language at almost every turn. As we shall see, wherever the Reeve's language begins to open up into multiplicity and polyvalence, he chooses legible and reactionary structures; when soundplay starts to offer a supple sense of meaning and identification, he turns back towards rigid and striated forms of capture; at the moments where escape from the conjuncture of place and meaning begins to glimmer, Oswald clings to a *status* that locally defines him.[7]

---

[6] While I am arguing here for seeing the Reeve's language as skillful, I am not prepared to read into it, as Derek Pearsall does, "an impression of pure joyous energy." Skill does not necessarily imply something we should delight in, and I find the Reeve presenting a chilling tension between these two poles, as well as the clear limits of (textual) "pleasure." See Derek Pearsall, "Towards a Poetics of Chaucerian Narrative," in *Drama, Narrative, and Poetry in the Canterbury Tales*, ed. Wendy Harding (Toulouse: Presses Universitaires du Mirail, 2003), 107.

[7] My formulation of these binaries comes from Deleuze and Guattari's notions of faciality, strata, and regimes of signs. In addition, Fred Moten's discussions of the ensemblic and his investigation into place and meaning (place/meant and displacement) in Amiri Baraka's work feature largely in my thinking. See Deleuze and Guattari, *A Thousand Plateaus*; Fred Moten, *Black and Blur* (Durham: Duke University Press, 2017); Fred Moten and Nehal El-Hadi, "Ensemble: An Interview with Dr. Fred Moten," *M.I.C.E.* 4 (2017), https://micemagazine.ca/issue-four/ensemble-interview-dr-fred-moten.

Famously impotent in the flesh, the Reeve is also impotent in his failure to see the potential for escape offered to him by the same tools he uses to fix himself in place. His localization (as an off-putting character, as marked by geographical ties, and as determined by his economic position) is accomplished through his ability to use reason, argument, and cleverness to produce reward. Rational, reasonable speech paves the path to profit – even if that speech might harm others in the process. If the Reeve can make language do what he requires, he is right to do so according to the structures he exists within. Moreover, the mode of capture we see in the Reeve comes through this commitment to the rational, "reasonable" language of commerce and exchange, language that for all its claims to truth and equity is nevertheless so often deployed for deceit and exploitation of others. The Reeve has learned well the art of mercantile speech that presents economic predation as defensible and just, but I would like to propose that Chaucer uses this not just as censure but as a tragic loss of what language might otherwise offer. In this article I will argue that, in forcing us to face the tragedy of the Reeve, Chaucer conceives in him an impotence that signifies beyond the physical, and that he uses him to chart out the limits of language's ability to escape the emergent social regimes the Reeve and all the pilgrims circulate within. In this effort, as we shall see, the Reeve is not just miserable; he is sacrificed.[8]

Resonance Machines and Sounding out the Supple

"Becoming-other is the madness of the imagination."[9]

The sound of Oswald's language is perhaps the most imaginative and unexpected thing about him. While we are not provided with a description of what his physical voice sounds like, throughout his prologue and tale we can hear how his language exercises sound in a variety of careful ways.

---

[8]   In my thinking of the Reeve as scapegoat or sacrifice, I am indebted to my notes from one of Karla's graduate seminars, carefully preserved in the margin of a fraying *Riverside Chaucer*. In addition to these, I also am grateful for Alcuin Blamires's argument about the Reeve as a social and economic scapegoat who is fixed as a point of surveillance on behalf of aristocratic authority, and for Anne McTaggart's argument, *pace* René Girard, tracking the consolidation of power as the Reeve attempts to access despotic authority. See Alcuin Blamires, "Chaucer the Reactionary: Ideology and the General Prologue to the Canterbury Tales," *Review of English Studies* 51.204 (2000), 523–39; Anne McTaggart, "What Women Want?: Mimesis and Gender in Chaucer's Wife of Bath's Prologue and Tale," *Contagion: Journal of Violence, Mimesis, and Culture* 19.1 (2012), 41–67.

[9]   Brian Massumi, *A User's Guide to Capitalism and Schrizophrenia* (Cambridge: The Massachusetts Institute of Technology Press, 1992), 108.

Equally weaponized and opportunistic, the Reeve's sonorous poetics are unquestionably masterful in their construction. But the sound of his words should also be heard within what sound can do more broadly. In this tale, sound *resonates*. For Middle English, the idea of resonance is expressed in the verb *resounen*, a word Chaucer uses elsewhere to describe the way Palamon's "youlyng and clamour" ring off the walls of his prison: the great tower "resouneth" with his woe (I.1275–8). For as long as the cries last, they define the prison-space, filling and even creating it.[10] But *resounen* as a word echoes with another, a term deeply important to (if never directly used by) the Reeve: *resoun*. To be reasonable, to exercise rational judgment, and to have reason is, for the Reeve, directly connected to a sense of order and what is proper (or available) to a given time and place. This, in large part, is where we can locate the "clerkly" quality that defines him as strongly as do his geographic origins.[11] His dedication to what is *resonable* is no doubt what prompts his initial ire over the Miller's interruption, and it animates his response. Oswald answers the Miller's unreasonable attack, and he does so in a way that reasonably returns slight for slight and blow for blow. This effect, of course, is the famous interest in quiting we associate with the Reeve, but I would like to consider his desire for vengeance as one that includes both sides of the *resounen/resoun* pun: his response must be equitable in that it is justified in its aims, and it also must occupy the space created by the Miller's terms. Oswald must re-sound the Miller's language back to him in order to counter the effects he objects to.

Considering the slippery conjunction of reason and resonance in the Reeve allows us to see how his language unexpectedly opens up transversal geographies that slip free of his enunciated desire for rational response. That is, attending to sounded language can show us not only what the Reeve reasonably wants, but what his resonant language is capable of.[12] Both reason and resonance happen in the space "in between." Directed, rational sound moves

---

[10] "Sound is a vibration that travels through the air to implant itself in flesh. But its force ripples far beyond merely human environs. Sound saturates, renders air thick with narrative": Jeffrey Jerome Cohen, "Heavy Atmosphere," in *Contemporary Chaucer across the Centuries*, ed. Helen M. Hickey, Anne McKendry, and Melissa Raine (Manchester: Manchester University Press, 2018), 92.

[11] For the implications of Oswald's clerkliness, see Edward Vasta, "How Chaucer's Reeve Succeeds," *Criticism* 25.1 (1983), 1–12.

[12] My interest in these two terms follows that of Veit Erlmann, who uses them to establish the Cartesian subject, and the deconstructionist perspective of Derrida and Jean-Luc Nancy. See Veit Erlmann, *Reason and Resonance: A History of Modern Aurality* (New York: Zone Books, 2014); Jacques Derrida, *Margins of Philosophy*, trans. Alan Bass (Chicago: University of Chicago Press, 1982), ix–xxix; Jean-Luc Nancy, *Listening*, trans. Charlotte Mandell (New York: Fordham University Press, 2007).

from speaker to listener to penetrate the ear and orient the figure in space; it arranges speaker and auditor in their relation to one another, plotting them out in a legible field. But resonance, I argue, works differently. Resonance lingers, overlays, echoes, and reverberates. It resists establishing a point of origin, and it ripples outward in all directions. In this way, and importantly for understanding the sound of the Reeve, the space created by the resonant machine is anything but punctual or local; it is not a mappable territory in which we can locate the speaking or listening subject with certainty, and its "betweenness" is not one that stretches between identifiable points.[13]

While resonance brings the interstitial space into being, giving it longitude and latitude, it does so in a way that resists the ability of that space to be plotted – or to emplot. Deleuze and Guattari project that art might generate a form of transversal movement that resists the localizing power of the point or the axis:

> Opposed to the punctual system are linear, or rather multilinear, systems. Free the line, free the diagonal: every musician or painter has this intention. One elaborates a punctual system or a didactic representation, but with the aim of making it snap, of sending a tremor through it.[14]

In a complementary way, Fred Moten proposes we imagine "a geography of displacement. A geography that's not predicated on the fiction of a fixed point. You could even call it, not necessarily a relational geography, but a relativistic geography."[15] Here, longitude and latitude do not offer the punctual system of Mercator, but rather the affective field of Spinoza; they map extension

---

[13] I am indebted to Adin Lears's work on echo and resistance as a model for how "the felt qualities of sound would eventually contribute to its associations with a knowledge more immediate and visceral than the supposedly more detached and rational understanding offered by vision." See Adin E. Lears, *World of Echo: Noise and Knowing in Late Medieval England* (Ithaca: Cornell University Press, 2020), 22. For more on literary uses of medieval sound, see Andrew Albin, "The 'Prioress's Tale,' Sonorous and Silent," *Chaucer Review* 48.1 (2013), 91–112; John M. Ganim, "Chaucer and the Noise of the People," *Exemplaria* 2.1 (1990), 71–88; Adin E. Lears, "Noise, Soundplay, and Langland's Poetics of Lolling in the Time of Wyclif," *Studies in the Age of Chaucer* 38 (2016), 165–200.

[14] Deleuze and Guattari, *A Thousand Plateaus*, 295. Here I am using "longitude" and "latitude" in their terms: "On the plane of consistency, *a body is defined only by a longitude and a latitude*: in other words the sum total of the material elements belonging to it under given relations of movement and rest, speed and slowness (longitude); the sum total of the intensive affects it is capable of at a given power or degree of potential (latitude). Nothing but affects and local movements, differential speeds" (260).

[15] Moten and El-Hadi, "Ensemble: An Interview with Dr. Fred Moten."

and flow, moving outward and beyond. As Moira Gatens explains, "[t]he two axes – longitude and latitude – together provide an immanent appraisal of any given body *rather than a taxonomic reading*. That is to say, this cartography maps any given thing in terms of the internal composition of its parts and its powers for affecting and being affected."[16]

For a space to map *without localizing* – this is what the resonance machine offers. Rather than fixing a subject within a legible and traceable system of coordinates, it responds through a sense of relative movement and speed rather than absolute location.[17] The milieu that emerges (and the affective power it contains) works on others through social rather than Cartesian cartography and moves through the shifting ethologies of extensive parts and capacities. In short, the resonance machine opens a path to *haecceity*, to a position that is unfixed and without edges.[18]

And curiously enough, there is a strong element of this in the way the Reeve's language works. Resonance is there from the beginning. Consider one of the densest sonic passages in the *Reeve's Prologue*, and certainly one of the most evocative. In the oft-discussed image of the empty wine cask as an analogy for old age, reverberations come thick and fast:[19]

> … As many a yeer as it is passed henne
> Syn that my tappe of lif bigan to renne.

[16] Moira Gatens, "Feminism as 'Password': Re-Thinking the 'Possible' with Spinoza and Deleuze," *Hypatia* 15.2 (2000), 64, emphasis mine.

[17] "Moving along this transversal line, which is really a line of territorialization, there is a *sound block* that no longer has a point of origin, since it is always and already in the middle of the line; and no longer has horizontal and vertical coordinates, since it creates its own coordinates; and no longer forms a localizable connection from one point to another, since it is in 'nonpulsed time': a deterritorialized rhythmic block that has abandoned points, coordinates, and measure …": Deleuze and Guattari, *A Thousand Plateaus*, 296, emphasis in the original.

[18] "There is a mode of individuation very different from that of a person, subject, thing, or substance … [it consists] entirely of relations of movement and rest between molecules or particles, capacities to affect and be affected": Deleuze and Guattari, *A Thousand Plateaus*, 261.

[19] Susanna Greer Fein's masterful reading of the sounds of the wine-cask passage is the best example, as found in "'Lat the Children Pleye': The Game Betwixt the Ages in the Reeve's Tale," in *Rebels and Rivals: The Contestive Spirit in the Canterbury Tales*, ed. Susanna Greer Fein, David Raybin, and P.C. Braeger (Kalamazoo: Medieval Institute Publications, 1991), 73–104. Additional and detailed readings of the sonic-image of the wine-cask can be found in Carol Falvo Heffernan, "A Reconsideration of the Cask Figure in the Reeve's Prologue," *Chaucer Review* 15.1 (1980), 37–43; A.H. Maclaine, "Chaucer's Wine-Cask Image: Word Play in the Reeve's Prologue," *Medium Aevum* 31 (1962), 129–31.

150 STEPHANIE L. BATKIE

> For sikerly, whan I was bore, anon
> Deeth drough the tappe of lyf and leet it gon,
> And ever sithe hath so the tappe yronne
> Til that almoost al empty is the tonne.
> The streem of lyf now droppeth on the chymbe.
> The sely tonge may wel rynge and chymbe
> Of wrecchednesse that passed is ful yoore;
> With olde folk, save dotage, is namoore! (I.3889–98)

The echoes between the "tonne" (I.3894) of the cask and the tongue which speaks of it, the sound of dripping liquid falling on the rim, the reverberating space of the empty chamber, and the actual repetition of words themselves all serve to drive home the way in which the Reeve is attentive to the way sound becomes sense. The reverberation between "chymbe" (n. the cask-rim) and "chymbe" (v. to chime) in the final lines stands out as a particular poetic flourish, as do the extra rhythmic (and rhyming) beats between "is ful yoore" and "is namoore." The surplus of sound-painting in the passage both draws the lines together even as it also opens up echoing spaces between them. Like the hollow body of the cask, the sound of the lines unfolds in the space required to produce resonance; the resonance in turn makes us aware of the space it exists within. But the multiplication of the echoes makes this a zone, a milieu, that is manifested without punctual orientation – it expands and contracts, shifts and reverberates, even as it describes the Reeve as an embodied subject. The space of his flesh drifts into resonant, echoey indeterminacy the more we listen to its figurative and figuring sound.

As tongues and tonnes converge, the Reeve's repetitions create new spaces, spaces in which resonance penetrates to the semantic as well as the sonorous register. His language here does more than ring out a bit of *rime riche*, as impressive as that effect might be. Rather, multiplicities of meaning continue to displace the punctual and open diagonal or transversal lines that resist strict emplotment. The effect of this is to augment what might otherwise be familiar tropes of polyvalence or ambiguity by sounding them within the resonant sphere. To return to the passage above, in the description of the cask/ body, the Reeve complains "Of wrecchednesse that passed is ful yore," in which "wrecchednesse" is a term that contains both the sense of "misery" and "wickedness" – two characteristics that will carry two very different meanings as part of the analogy. In the first, Oswald is complaining about the general wretchedness of life; in the second, he laments the wicked antics of his past that he can no longer fully participate in. The same is true for "dotage" in the next line, which can refer to "senility" or "decay," but also "folly" or "foolish love." In his age, Oswald can be left with any of these – but also with all. He is not singular or even located with a singular aging body; he is multiple and multiplied by the resonances through which his language moves. Thus, the Reeve's polyvalence crosses the registers of sound as well as sense, generating a field of potential for his body and for his *status* that gathers its meaning by resisting the local and the definitive.[20]

In this way, the sound of the Reeve's language allows him an enormous amount of flexibility in terms of what he asks his speech to do, and it demonstrates what this resonance is capable of. We don't see the Reeve coming more into focus through these resonant poetics; we see him rather diffuse into a range of possibilities, none of which are absolute, singular, or localized. The same is true when we move from the *Prologue* to the narrative agenda of the *Tale*. For all that the story is narrativized, it retains the lyric resonance of Oswald's non-narrative, embodied self-figuration from the wine cask.[21] For example, when it comes to a moment in the tale that seems to present a minor narrative detail, that of the plans Malyne's family has for her marriage prospects, lyric resonance intrudes upon what amounts to a plotting-out of her imagined future and her grandfather's figured past:

> His purpos was for to bistowe hire hye
> Into som worthy blood of auncestry,
> For hooly chirches good moot been despended
> On hooly chirches blood, that is descended.
> Therefore he wold his hooly blood honoure,
> Though that he hooly chirche sholde devoure. (I.3981–6)

On the one hand, the passage locates and localizes Malyne within the poles of masculine desires, past and present. It fixes her in place, tracing out the

---

[20] This resistance offered by the resonance machine is where we might locate both the literary and the revolutionary. What it does not do is make things clear – quite the opposite. For Glissant, "The literary text plays the contradictory role of a producer of opacity." And for Moten, "Opacity implies a sort of blurring or obscuring, a complication, but it also still implies the capacity to see through it, to see through that complication, and to see through it even if that seeing through produces something others might want to think of as a kind of distortion or a lack of clarity." It is in this opacity and resistance to the legible that we begin to hear what is possible in the Reeve's language. See Édouard Glissant, *Poetics of Relation*, trans. Betsy Wing (Ann Arbor: The University of Michigan Press, 1997), 115; Moten and El-Hadi, "Ensemble: An Interview with Dr. Fred Moten."

[21] Moten argues that lyric form interrupts the "convergence of literary meaning and bourgeois production that comes into its own with that reification of the sentence that animates and is animated by the rise of novelistic techniques of narration. Such disruption is noisy; and such unruly and ongoing reemergence of sound in literature is crucial because the lyrical interruption of narrative marks a different mode, within the same mode, of literary production ... this mode is shaped by resistances": Fred Moten, "Not in Between: Lyric Painting, Visual History, and the Postcolonial Future," *The Drama Review* 47.1 (2003), 128–9.

lines of her life on the existing map of filiation, expectation, and *status*. On the other hand, the kinship between this moment and the echoing "chymbe/chymbe-ing" of the empty wine cask is strong, with a pulsing sense of repetition used for deliberate effect. The Reeve effectively leaves Malyne behind, expectations and all, to focus on ecclesiastical critique. The semantic overlay conjured up by repetition of "hooly" creates a field of interpretation in which the aspect of Holy Church (and the body of Christ, not that of a young girl) is doubled, refracted, and degraded through the Parson's various earthly attentions. The succession of "hoolys" act as a sardonic mimic to the devotional meter of prayer, wherein the Reeve opts not to solidify through repetition but to fragment through resonance. Indeed, the lines have an almost Gowerian quality inasmuch as the Reeve (or Chaucer) lodges his critique of the Parson's unholy attachment to earthly and monetary lineages within the disintegration of ecclesiastical sense and meaning within his own text.[22] Rather than using repetition to encode and strengthen the Church's presence in the poem, the Reeve (and Chaucer) asks us to watch it evaporate with each new iteration.

In a similar, but even more immediate act of resistance, when we come to the climax of the fabliau Oswald tells, we find an unexpected loss of localization within resonant and repetitive structures. In this case, within pronouns. After the bed-trick with the Miller's wife is revealed, Aleyn and Symkyn's struggle in the darkened bedchamber is so chaotic that the two characters begin to lose their bodily distinction:

> And by the throte-bolle he caughte Alayn,
> And he hente hym dispitiously agayn,
> And on the nose he smoot hym with his fest.
> Doun ran the blody streem upon his brest;
> And in the floor, with nose and mouth tobroke,
> They walwe as doon two pigges in a poke;
> And up they goon, and doun agayn anon,
> Til that the millere sporned at a stoon ... (I.4273–80)

---

[22] This is a technique Gower uses to great effect, although more in his Latin than in his English verse. Indeed, it is tempting to see more broadly in the Reeve as well a shadow of Chaucer's "moral Gower." For Gower's Latin wordplay, see Stephanie L. Batkie, "The Sound of My Voice: Aurality and Credibility in Gower's *Vox Clamantis*," in *John Gower: Others and the Self*, ed. Russell A. Peck and R.F. Yeager (Cambridge: D.S. Brewer, 2017), 32–49; Matthew W. Irvin, "Genius and Sensual Reading in the *Vox Clamantis*," in *John Gower, Trilingual Poet: Language, Translation, and Tradition*, ed. Elisabeth Dutton, with John Hines, and R.F. Yeager (Cambridge: D.S. Brewer, 2010), 196–205.

Just who is doing what to whom here? The language is masterful in its ability to render the confusion of the melee as extending to the de-individuation of the combatants. The pronouns are singular, but they are not attached to a discernable individual, and as fists cross from one body to smash into another, the flow of violence renders the two men as a conjoined entity within the field of the fight. The singular becomes plural, escaping grammatical number, and the two dissolve, indistinct, into the field of their private combat. They are no longer punctual, but multiple.

Moreover, the Reeve structures the entire fabliau to lead us to this precise moment, in which two bodies physically and poetically collapse into one another – and in many ways, this is exactly what the Reeve gains through his larger choice of form, intentionally or no. For all their delight in transgressing boundaries, fabliaux exist within an unstratified regime of signification; in Deleuze and Guattari's terms, they are segmented but not stratified, meaning that the multiplicities they contain are supple rather than rigid, overlapping and smooth rather than hierarchical and organized. Their pleasures lie in the successive combinations of spheres of influence, overlaying and crossing one another without necessarily becoming organized and hierarchized. (At least, not until the end – a feature we shall return to below.) Within the tale the Reeve tells, we encounter intersecting elements of clerical identity (and anticlerical sentiment), economic spheres of influence (marked by the presence of absence or university oversight), professional identities and the ambitions that come with them, the micro-politics of the village of Trumpington, the conflict between age and youth, geographic and geological identities in the cultivation of the natural world, sexual desire and exploitation coming into contact with economic desire and exploitation – and on and on. Fabliaux work through the teller's ability to construct and deploy these overlapping spheres, managing them in such a way that characters and circumstances allow them to emerge and to affect. Who is Alisoun without John? Who is John without Nicolas? Likewise, who is Symkyn without Malyne? Or without the two clerks? Who are the clerks without their horse? The singular and differentiated flow into elastic identities that are difficult to disentangle. As such, the fabliaux function around (at least initially) the sense of multiplicity and "a relatively supple line of interlaced codes and territorialities …"[23]

Within the moment of the fight, I would argue that Chaucer allows Symkyn and Aleyn to become part of Deleuze and Guattari's supple line, even if only momentarily – violence draws them together, and it will eventually separate them as well. A quick crack across the Miller's skull neatly returns them to their divided and divisive bodies once more, but reading their momentary conjunction as potential rather than critique (or humor) is instructive. The

---

[23] Deleuze and Guattari, *A Thousand Plateaus*, 223.

violence of the fight is not a problem in that it removes the ability of each character to function as rational, distinct human subjects. What the fight shows us is the potential in what Brian Massumi has called "the connective freedom of fractality."[24] In becoming indiscernable from one another, in becoming multiple, the brawlers fulfill the fullest line of the fabliau-form in that they embody the overlapping, disorienting spheres through which fabliau operate. The pronoun confusion in the passage demonstrates how the echo, the reverberation, the resonance of the fight transcends rigid structures and is held and suspended in the moment before the blow to Symkyn's head brings it all crashing back into alignment – the alignment that becomes so satisfying for the Reeve.[25]

The effect of all three of these passages (the empty cask, the outline of Malyne's marriage prospects, and the fistfight) is to shift the relationship between speech and the sense of the stable, interior subject. Neither the Reeve, nor the Church, nor the characters in the tale emerge as plotted, localized figures in these moments – they resist the subject-position we might otherwise expect from a tale-teller so concerned with authoritative and institutional states. As much as the Reeve seems to be creating a universalizing exemplum in the *Prologue* or a familiar and legible critique in the *Tale*, his language creates meaning by actively resisting set coordinates in which to locate *status* within the formal or stylistic mode. Resonance and echo create a poetics that works against locating the subject within the bounds of individuating language, flowing instead between moments of repetition in de-localizing, rhythmic refrain.

[24] Massumi, *A User's Guide to Capitalism and Schrizophrenia*, 107.

[25] This is true outside the tale as well. After all, it is not just in the indistinct pronouns of the brawl in which characters blend together. In the *Reeve's Tale*, we have an aging and (seemingly) sexually-challenged miller who monopolizes the economic conditions of his area up against the cleverness and quiting-desires of two lewed-minded clerks. The Reeve, as an aging, sexually-challenged economic authority who attempts to use clerkly language to quite his foe maps onto both categories. Likewise, Robyn is a lusty and vigorous miller who levels a (narrative) attack against an aging and foolish carpenter by telling a tale about the ends of clerical trickery. He also embodies multiple perspectives in the *Reeve's Tale*. We might similarly find echoing, resonant spaces for Absolon, Nicholas, and John to assert their own connections with the Reeve's characters and narrative positions.

Tragic Rigidity at the Threshold of the Local

"Morality (molarity) is the delirium of Reason."[26]

All this is, to say the least, unexpected to get from the Reeve, and it is an effect that works directly counter to his desires. Whenever he can, the Reeve will return again and again to *status*, to the signifying power of the static systems he cannot bring himself to leave because more than anything else, the Reeve needs to *win*. And he needs to win along lines that are impossible to separate from the confining systems of value and desire within which he circulates. He does not desire escape; he desires *position*, and this he effectively accomplishes. As we know, he is grounded in his geographic origins, both linguistically and economically; he is located in and by the comfortable property he enjoys (I.606–8). He is singled out as "devilish" in his preaching by the Host (I.3903), and is clerkly in his appearance (I.588–90). He is enclosed in his aging body,[27] and his rural, post-1381 context colors the way he understands and participates in affective social structures.[28] A series of lines converges on the definitive point through which we locate and comprehend him. It is quite true that the Reeve opens up questions for readers (and pilgrims) about his lack of social legibility: he embodies in his economic and social dealings the secrecy, hiddenness, and craftiness that is also attached to him in *The General Prologue* (I.609).[29] Unlike some of his fellows, however, the Reeve's ability to access the possibilities of language is read as solely negative. We do not even need to go as far as Symkyn's teasing of the young clerks about their education in logical argument, an "art" that nevertheless cannot "make a place / A myle brood of twenty foot of space" (I.4123–4). The Reeve's articulation of resonant meaning is captured always by his desire for profit and power, both economic as well as social. And rather than the questions we get about language-use from someone like The Wife of Bath, Oswald is cast as an *exemplum* of what we must be on guard against. This places him in a position defined by a tension between his position, which is fixed by inertia and *status*, and how much mobility and potential his language is capable of.

---

[26] Massumi, *A User's Guide to Capitalism and Schrizophrenia*, 108.

[27] A. Everest Carol, "Sex and Old Age in Chaucer's Reeve's Prologue," *Chaucer Review* 31 (1996), 99–114; Heffernan, "A Reconsideration of the Cask Figure in the Reeve's Prologue"; Maclaine, "Chaucer's Wine-Cask."

[28] See Brantley L. Bryant, "Accounting for Affect in the 'Reeve's Tale,'" in *Medieval Affect, Feeling, and Emotion*, ed. Glenn Burger and Holly A. Crocker (Cambridge: Cambridge University Press, 2019), 130–50; Holly A. Crocker, "Affective Politics in Chaucer's Reeve's Tale: 'Cherl' Masculinity after 1381," *Studies in the Age of Chaucer* 29 (2007), 225–58.

[29] For more on secrets and "pryvetee" in the Reeve (and in Fragment 1 more generally), see Vasta, "How Chaucer's Reeve Succeeds," 3–4.

What is noteworthy (and tragic, I would argue) is how he inhabits that tension. We might find that, in Oswald, Chaucer opens the multiplicity of the echo up into a quantum field rather than a fixed point, demonstrating what Deleuze and Guattari suggest when they write, "A punctual system is most interesting when there is a musician, painter, writer, philosopher to oppose it, *who even fabricates it in order to oppose it, like a springboard to jump from.*"[30] We might follow the Reeve as Chaucer's creation of a supple character who slips free of the grip of the economic and social patterns surrounding him. But this is clearly not what happens. Rather than work as an exemplar of escape, the Reeve compulsively cedes the resistance-potential of his language to the very systems of desire and power that define and confine him, and the resonance Chaucer provides him is recoded by something quite different. It is recoded by reason.

Resoun for the Reeve, not *resounen*, is critical to the language he uses within his professional capacity. He is neither a braggart nor a bully who overtakes by oppositional force. Instead, he constructs systems of signification that allow him to manage meaning in a way that plays by the rules even if it changes the stakes of the game. He tricks and deceives, but does not do so in a way that opens him to charges of illegality or outright fraud:

> Ther koude no man brynge hym in arrerage.
> Ther nas baillif, ne hierde, nor oother hyne,
> That he ne knew his sleighte and his covyne;
> They were adrad of hym as of the deeth. (I.602–5)

In this, Oswald's facility with language is one of the most important pieces in his arsenal, used to deceive, exploit, and profit. His language has power because he uses it to redraw the lines of the map for his own ends. Deborah S. Ellis notes that this ability gives the Reeve, in large part, his devilish quality: "Much of the Reeve's devilishness is expressed through the paradox of reality becoming merely verbal," and that "Language is the vehicle for damnation."[31] Susanna Fein sees the threat of force issued by the Reeve as tied to both his linguistic cunning and the work he does, noting the Reeve/*reve* pun that inflects "his professional name, his practices, and the tenor of his tale ..."[32] And of course, Chaucer himself makes plain the connection between the language the Reeve is able to marshal and the treachery that marks his office. These "slightes" are very real, and they pose a distinct and dreadful threat to those around him. As Alcuin Blamires writes, the Reeve is the pilgrim "who comes closest to making people squeal," and much of his professional and social

[30] Deleuze and Guattari, *A Thousand Plateaus*, 295, emphasis mine.
[31] Ellis, "Chaucer's Devilish Reeve," 150, 55.
[32] Fein, "Lat the Children Pleye," 77.

REASON, RESONANCE, AND THE TRAGEDY OF THE LOCAL 157

power comes through his ability to make language (his and that of others) do what he wants.[33] The Reeve uses words as weapons, and for them to be effective they need to be appropriate; they need to respond in kind to achieve the position of justified, reasonably-owed profit the Reeve desires.[34]

We see this pattern emerge most clearly (and most miserably) through the Reeve's dedication to the quiting-structure initiated by the Miller and the Host in his prologue and his tale. The adversarial nature of the Reeve's language requires opposition, and moreover requires opposition the Reeve can capture and recast for his own purposes. As we have seen, Oswald's speech relies on the kind of clerical wit Harry Bailey finds so irksome to establish himself amongst the company (I.3899–905). But this wit requires instigation to work – it requires the Miller. In his presentation of himself and of his tale, the Reeve cleverly recasts the terms and structures the Miller uses in order to seize their signifying potential for himself. As he does elsewhere in his life, he will take the structures surrounding him and rework them to establish a base for his own power.[35]

Such is, in a broad sense, how the Reeve functions: he works through "esement." As a term, "esement" has two important valences for the Reeve. First, it might be taken simply as "compensation" or "redress" – the definition the *Middle English Dictionary* cites when it comes to its use in the *Reeve's Tale* proper.[36] When the extent of Symkyn's treachery comes out, Aleyn argues that,

> Som esement has lawe yshapen us,
> For, John, ther is a lawe that saw thus:

[33] Blamires, "Chaucer the Reactionary: Ideology and the General Prologue to the Canterbury Tales," 525.

[34] This is, I think, the quality that separates the Reeve from someone like the Pardoner. The Pardoner acknowledges and even celebrates his deceit, offering only the thinnest of justifications for it. The Reeve, on the other hand, wants to believe he is in the right because his language-use opens a path for him to read himself as virtuous. In this way, he ties his economic success to his moral success in a way that might be familiar to modern readers from similar moves in modern economic and religious discourses.

[35] This pattern is one that Deleuze and Guattari also are interested in, and it will provide the basis for their arguments about the relationship between the subject of enunciation (the subject that seeks to articulate himself) and the subject of statement (the subject that exists within established regimes of significance and signification). In their reading, the two subjects are irrevocably linked, as the regime that provides the ability to articulate anything, including oneself, is also the mechanism that defines and subjectifies it. In the same way, the Reeve is bound by the terms of the Miller as the material with which he tries to assert his own mastery. See Deleuze and Guattari, *A Thousand Plateaus*, 133.

[36] See *MED*, "esement," def. 3.

> That gif a man in a point be agreved,
> That in another he sal be releved.
> ... And syn I sal have neen amendement
> Agayn my los, I wil have esement. (I.4179–86)

The tit-for-tat logic here echoes the larger interest the Reeve himself has in accounts and reckoning – activities at which he obviously excels. Payment is due and must be paid, one way or another. But the passage also invokes another use of "esement" as a legal category – the "lawe" Aleyn refers to: "The right or privilege of using something not one's own, such as a pasture, a forest, a waterway, a well, domestic facilities, etc."[37] The Latin use of the term (*aisiamentum*) is used throughout medieval legal charters and rolls in this way, alongside the more general sense of "profit" or "advantage," to indicates *usufruct* rather than *dominium*.[38] To access something through the legal category of "esement" is to have the right to make use of it without controlling or otherwise exerting dominion over it; it allows for a figure to profit without ownership. This is in keeping with how the Reeve functions in his professional dealings, and it is likely the way he holds rights over the land on which he lives. It is also how his language works. When the Reeve attempts to quite the Miller, he begins by making use of the terms through which the Miller enters the conversation; he profits from the discourse initiated and dispensed by his adversary. We can see the Reeve's ambitions surface in how he recasts resonant potential to fit his own petty (but reasonable) ends, yoking any winning he might muster to this ability to legitimately capture the sounds of others.[39]

This is where the Reeve's talents really shine. For example, at the very end of the Reeve's prologue speech, in which he announces his intention to outdo the Miller's perceived criticism, he shows us just what he can do:

---

[37] See *MED*, "esement," def. 2.

[38] *Dictionary of Medieval Latin from British Sources*, ed. R.E. Latham and D.R. Howlett (London: Oxford University Press for The British Academy, 1975), "aisiamentum." See, for example, its use in the *Liber custumarum* regarding a dispute over access to the Thames: *Munimenta Gildhallæ Londoniensis: Liber Albus, Liber Custumarum, Et Liber Horn*, ed. H.T. Riley, 3 vols (London: Longman, Brown, Green, Longmans, and Roberts, 1860), vol. 2, part 2, F.242.b, 444.

[39] And this is the epitome of how the Reeve embodies what Carissa Harris calls "felawe masculinity," in which "obscene sexual storytelling is an integral part of rape culture: it fosters masculine community and functions as a means for asserting one's gendered identity within the group ... it serves as a social weapon to settle conflicts and establish hierarchies among men": Harris, *Obscene Pedagogies*, 46. The Reeve's language is bound to this "fellowship" and he has no interest in language that does anything but exemplify its parameters in order to outdo others within those same parameters.

REASON, RESONANCE, AND THE TRAGEDY OF THE LOCAL   159

> ... Right in his cherles termes wol I speke.
> I pray to God his nekke mote to-breke;
> He kan wel in myn eye seen a stalke,
> But in his owene he kan nat seen a balke. (I.3917–20)

The terms of his speech are laid out clearly: he will take up the forms of the Miller's language and volley them back in a way that vindicates Oswald's own position and causes the most possible social and personal harm. The final lines, most tellingly, provide a succinct example of this by turning to a rather ironic reference to Matthew 7:3 (*Quid autem vides festucam in oculo fratris tui et trabam in oculo tuo non vides?*). This is all well and good. But the "balke" that closes out the final couplet is also akin to those which proved intrinsic to John's humiliation and the fabliau-justice at the end of the *Miller's Tale*: the family climbs "Into the tubbes hangynge in the balkes" (I.3626). The "beam" in question is both the scriptural impediment to clear judgment and that which John foolishly suspends himself from so that Nicholas and Alisoun might have their fun. As the final word before the tale begins, it is neatly chosen.[40]

We find a similar attention to careful but opportunistic language threading throughout Oswald's closing appeal to the company as well, in which he invites his listeners to admire his cleverness. In response to the Host's urging that he, in effect, "get on with it" rather than nattering on about his bodily condition, the Reeve unfurls exactly the kind of subtle jab we saw above:

> "Now, sires," quod this Osewold the Reve,
> "I pray yow alle that ye nat yow greve,
> Thogh I answere, and somdeel sette his howve;
> For leveful is with force force of-showve." (I.3909–12)

As another justification for his quiting-attempt, the claim that he will "hoodwink" the Miller is cast here in terms of recognized, outward deception – similar to the "sette hir aller cappe" that concludes the Man of Law's portrait in the *General Prologue* (I.586), as editors often note. But the metrics of the last line of the quotation actually sound out the argument the Reeve would like to put forward: that his ability to exert the force he has at his disposal not only answers the Miller, but exceeds him. The line itself is beautifully balanced, with the repetition of "force" perched on either side of the caesura,

---

[40] In a similar gesture, we might think as well of the analogy the Reeve makes between his declining age and the "open-ers" of the medler-fruit (I.3870–1) in light of the ribald play of the openness of various asses in the Miller's tale. The "wehee" of the clerks' lost horse (I.4066) also brings to mind that "coltes tooth" that gives Oswald such trouble (I.3888) but also Alison's famous "'Tehee!' quod she" (I.3740).

effectively formalizing the claim the Reeve is aiming for. He will match strength with strength, and he will do so using the same terms to offer an equal fight. Or – nearly equal. The metrics of the line requires that a reader sound the final -e on the first "force" (but not the second) to maintain the rhythm of the passage, while the syntax aligns the first "force" with that of the Reeve's response and the second with the instigating "blow" from the Miller. The effect is both sly and precise – a succinct portrait in miniature of the language the Reeve uses here and deploys, presumably, as part of his office as well.[41] In order for his language to appear to himself and others as justified, the Reeve must follow claims to "appropriate" parity, just as he does in his economic dealings. He offers a price for goods, and that price needs to seem (at least broadly) reasonable. But it also must provide him a profit, that little bit extra. It is in this ability to balance these two poles of parity and surplus that the Reeve finds his power. Contrary to the layered echo and overlap of resonance, reason for the Reeve is strictly controlled and any excess is compressed into carefully deployed production. Thus, in the contest with the Miller above, we have a distinction with a difference as Oswald answers Robyn's "force" in terms that are clearly set down to emphasize their compatibility in a kind of sonic and poetic stasis, but he uses them in such a way that nevertheless allows him to showcase his careful skill and to broadcast that he will emerge the better, more potent speaker.

But success is not without cost. What is given up is the potential resonance Chaucer winks at elsewhere in the Reeve's speech, potential that is aggressively stifled by Oswald's insistence on following the call and response form to which he so fervently commits. Even the neat axiomatic of satisfaction he expresses by the end of his tale ("A gylour shal hymself bigyled be" (I.4321)) feels stale by the time we get to it, and as listeners we are clearly aware that the disagreeable Cook seems to be the only one who appreciates Oswald's "jape of malice" (I.4338).[42] The sound of the *Reeve's Tale* becomes increasingly bound to his localizing, quiting impulses, and a flattening or muting effect takes precedence in order to fit Oswald's petty, narrative ends.

This is particularly evident when it comes to the physical space containing the climactic action of his tale, which takes place in an environment that is almost non-sensible: Symkyn's small bedchamber follows no sonic logic

---

[41] For a longer analysis of the way in which the Reeve's language signifies the kind of deception upon which he must depend as part of his office, see Ellis, "Chaucer's Devilish Reeve."

[42] This is perhaps to be expected. Joseph Taylor has found in the Cook something of a kindred sonic spirit to the Reeve inasmuch as the Cook's tale also maintains a careful control over its soundscape as a site of political and social affect – a "biopolitical milieu": Taylor, "Quiet Riot," 182, *passim*.

whatsoever. When the family retires around midnight after indulging in good, strong ale, things get loud:

> This millere hath so wisely bibbed ale
> That as an hors he fnorteth in his sleep,
> Ne of his tayl bihynde he took no keep.
> His wyf bar hym a burdon, a ful strong;
> Men myghte hir rowtyng heere two furlong;
> The wenche rowteth eek, *par compaignye*. (I.4162–7)

The noise in the bedchamber is so great that Aleyn and John are kept awake, thereby providing ample opportunity for the ensuing bed-swapping and sexual assaults:

> Aleyn the clerk, that herde this melodye,
> He poked John, and seyde, "Slepestow?
> Herdestow evere slyke a sang er now?
> Lo, swilk a complyn is ymel hem alle;
> A wilde fyr upon their bodyes falle!
> Wha herkned evere slyke a ferly thyng?" (I.4168–773)

The bedchamber becomes a site wherein sound reverberates to the extent that it creates narrative progress.[43] In this case, the night-sounds of Symkyn and his family are described with exasperated sarcasm by Aleyn. The effect of these sounds, beyond being a moment of realistic detail, is that the students are kept awake and irritated enough to take action against the Miller for his earlier slights against them. Yet curiously, at the end of the tale the same space that projected sound at the beginning of the night so effectively now exhibits a peculiar silencing effect. When Aleyn mistakenly finds himself in bed with the Miller, the brawl that ensues is both violent and bloody; what it is not, however, is *loud*. Somehow, Symkyn and Aleyn end up battered and rolling on the floor, like "two pigges in a poke" (I.4278) until the Miller stumbles on a stone and falls on top of his wife – whereupon she is rudely awakened, and takes matters quite literally into her own hands. Prior to this bodily contact both she and John remain asleep, blissfully unaware of their surroundings despite what must certainly be an audible commotion taking place inches away from their bed.

As a counterpoint to the collapsing pronouns of the fistfight we saw earlier, the strange silence of the bedchamber transforms what we might see as a reasonable expectation of resonance (how noises would logically echo in the

---

[43] For the echo-chamber of the bedroom, see Michael W. Twomey and Scott D. Stull, "Architectural Satire in the Tales of the Miller and Reeve," *Chaucer Review* 51.3 (2016), 331.

room) for a different kind of reason: that required by the quiting-agenda of the Reeve's fabliau-milieu. As discussed above, fabliaux embrace supple identities that overlap, merge, and bifurcate in an endless circulation of subjects. That is, until their conclusion. More than other examples of Chaucerian fabliaux, I would argue that the Reeve's adoption of the form, while an obvious attempt to answer the *Miller's Tale* in kind ("with force force of-showve"), betrays how deeply his desires determine the tenor of the story. He needs this tale to end reasonably, properly, with everyone receiving their due (I.4313–17). As Brantley Bryant has observed, "The *Reeve's Tale* shows the interpersonal and affective consequences" of the kind of narratives the Reeve would be familiar with constructing as part of his professional life – the accounts and ledgers that transpose evolving relationships and values into tidy columns of figures.[44] "Manorial accounting relentlessly includes and flattens," and we know that the Reeve is an expert in managing his books.[45] The reckoning the Reeve is after constructs Symkyn's house as muffled, as deadened, as a space where sound and resonance cannot circulate. Pronouns might momentarily slip free, but bodies never do. They are returned to their appropriate places in the end, and the Reeve revels in the commensurate flattening out of the multiplicity of the fabliau-form into his own conception of stratified, rigid, and reason-able justice.

Which brings us, once more, to Malyne. As stifling as the sound of the Miller's house is in the Reeve's hands, Oswald's muffling technique is used most viciously against this young girl, whose silencing lands dully within the space of the bedchamber and provides the most insidious of all the examples of the loss or limits of the resonance machine in the Reeve's portrait, prologue, or tale. She, like everything else in this story, is instrumentalized in service of narrative "satisfaction," and this is especially true when it comes to what happens to her body.[46] Her muted cries at the moment of her sexual assault are unheard and un-hearable, and it is the narrative's convenient silences that makes what happens to her, for the Reeve, an act of swiving rather than

[44] Bryant, "Accounting for Affect," 131.

[45] Bryant, "Accounting for Affect," 119–23. For more on the Reeve's capabilities as a bookkeeper, see R.H. Parker, "Accounting in Chaucer's Canterbury Tales," *Accounting, Auditing & Accountability Journal* 12.1 (1999).

[46] As Holly Crocker argues, this is part of a larger pattern of churlish masculinity: "By governing women, who are explicitly identified with affect in this tale, men distinguish themselves from one another. Just like anything else, women become weapons in a competitive universe where a class of men, elsewhere called 'cherls,' vie for dominance over one another": Crocker, "Affective Politics in Chaucer's Reeve's Tale," 228.

rape.[47] That renders her, in his ears, a wench rather than a daughter.[48] Using the terms of rape-narratives for the pleasure and acknowledgement of his fellows, the Reeve doubly mutes Malyne: first, in the moment Aleyn overrides her ability to consent or "crie" (I.4196), and again on the morning after, when she bids her "deere lemman" (I.4240) farewell.[49] This leave-taking has been much discussed because of the interpretative problems it poses to readers:

> "Now, deere lemman," quod she, "go, far weel!
> But er thow go, o thyng I wol thee telle:
> Whan that thou wendest homward by the melle,
> Right at the entree of the dore bihynde
> Thou shalt a cake of half a busshel fynde
> That was ymaked of thyn owene mele,
> Which that I heelp my sire for to stele.
> And, goode lemman, God thee save and kepe!"
> And with that word almoost she gan to wepe. (I.4239–48)

For some, this becomes a heartbreaking instance in which we see a young girl, in the aftermath of rape, turning to the familiar amorous discourse of love and leave-taking as a trauma response to make the world livable after her assault.[50] She makes the deliberate choice, in other words, to turn Aleyn into a lover rather than a rapist to save herself. For others, a turn to philologic concerns open up more positive avenues of interpretation that make Malyne's consent after the fact something she offers in the hope of a future relationship with the

---

[47] Helen Barr makes clear the violent and vivid register "swiving" should indicate for Chaucer: the closest translation into modern idiom shouldn't be "laid with" or "made love to" as some editors would have it, but "fucked." Throughout her analysis of the *Canterbury Tales*, she finds that "A clear pattern ... emerges about the particular kind of sexual activity that 'swyve' represents: it is crude, transgressive, masculinist, forceful, and competitively vengeful. And it is also part of a literary game": Barr, "Swiven," in *A New Companion to Critical Thinking on Chaucer*, ed. Stephanie L. Batkie, Matthew W. Irvin, and Lynn Shutters (Leeds: Arc Humanities Press, 2021).

[48] See the excellent historical and literary analysis in Carissa Harris, "Chaucer's Wenches," *Studies in the Age of Chaucer* 45 (2023), 35–72.

[49] For the difficult valences of *lemman* in light of medieval consent-discourse, see Susan Signe Morrison, "Consent and Lemman in Geoffrey Chaucer's the Reeve's Tale," *Notes and Queries* 68.1 (2021), 45–9. For a deeper reading of this moment within "Chaucer's important critique of obscene comic discourse" and a suggestion of how the Reeve might be seen as resisting the fabliau model, see Nicole Nolan Sidhu, "'To Late for to Crie': Female Desire, Fabliau Politics, and Classical Legend in Chaucer's Reeve's Tale," *Exemplaria* 21.1 (2009), 3–23.

[50] Leah Schwebel, "Chaucer and the Fantasy of Retroactive Consent," *Studies in the Age of Chaucer* 44 (2022), 345.

student who forced his way into her bed.[51] Personally, I would like to see her "deere lemman" as furious, vengeful sarcasm, in which she mockingly uses the language of romance in an attempt to wound her attacker as best she can. I want her tears to be angry and accusing, and her mocking inclusion of the "oh, and one more thing –" of the stolen loaf to be a final twist of the knife. I want her to bitterly reveal how stupidly Aleyn has been tricked and (more importantly) with her help. God help him, indeed – he might have "swived" her, but she fucked him over first. But even before this resonant reading begins to surface, the Reeve just as cruelly closes it down. This passage is presaged by Aleyn's own naming of Malyne as his "sweete wight" and his declaration that he will be "thyn awen clerk, swa have I seel!" (I.4235–9). The sex apparently went on "al the longe nyght" (I.4235), with the young man working hard at his task, and the dawn is forcing him to reluctantly leave her, with no sense of shame or responsibility. Within these contexts, Malyne's voice might sound one way in my head, but in the tale it does what the Reeve needs it to do. Narrative force here is too strong, and the Reeve uses it to override Malyne's potential meanings in a bitter echo of Aleyn's "labors" throughout the night.

Thus, as much as I would like it to be otherwise, I do not think that we can see in Maylene's inability to "crie" (I.4196) or in Aleyn's departure an opening for ambiguous polyvalence; she is not given the chance to become resonant in the way the Reeve's lyrical self-description from the wine cask opens up to a field of multiplicities. Her silencing is instead a narrative tactic aimed at the vengeful emplotment the Reeve is attempting to accomplish with his tale. She is positioned, physically and narratively, in such a way as to close out the mechanism of the story; she becomes part of the "esement" for the clerks and the quiting of the Miller by being placed in a recognizable and measurable *status*. This denial of potential resonance (or resistance) in and for her character subsequently collapses the overlapping spheres of the narrative space into ordered and stratified patterns that mark the Reeve's understanding of the fabliau form, those "proper" patterns meeting the larger ends he finds both reasonable and satisfying – and expects us to as well.

Propriety is what is owed at the end of the day, after all, and the clerks gallop off with their various prizes, leaving the Miller and his family in their dust. To accomplish this, however, the narrative climax of the tale requires the erasure of resonance from the fabliau-space it operates within. We are left, then, not with the multiplicity and suppleness of the resonance machine, but instead with a figure and tale marked by stratification and rigidity. Oswald's need for equity thus runs in line with his turn to the rational, to the reasonable,

---

[51] Thomas J. Farrell, "Scribes, Critics, and Malyne's Tears," *Chaucer Review* 59.1 (2024), 56.

and even to the juridical as a source of his authority.[52] As such, we might well accord with the charges laid at his door regarding his "clerkliness" in that his language allows him to win out in a dialectical field, which in turn binds the success he has to his ability to overturn and overcode the discourse used first against him. Any mastery he achieves is that of adaptation and appropriation, and for all that his aims here are to end the conflict by emerging as the better, more justified party, the party by whom "esement" is rightfully (and decisively) managed, his winning creates a true – but dead – end. His conclusion will never liberate him as a masterful subject, but rather more firmly encodes him as subjected, willingly operating within signifying structures set out before him. Quiting thus becomes another mode of capture, bolstered by its claims to legal and moral authority. Moreover, it is undergirded by the Reeve's own desires, sexual and social, to be a man of means and ends. His bodily impotence is ironically mirrored here in his inability to locate a mode of speaking that gives him true autonomic agency; he can only manage to respond, never to initiate. As he famously observes, "For whan we may nat doon, than wol we speke" (I.3881). The way he understands satisfaction and *status* will permit him no other path.

Facing the Reeve

This leaves us in an unpleasant place, there is no doubt. It is not surprising that most critics find little pleasure in the *Reeve's Tale*, despite its impressive language, and neither the Reeve nor his offering come across as delivering *solas* to anyone – apart from Oswald. (And perhaps the equally unloved Cook.) But I would argue that the Reeve presents us with something more than a nasty character who tells a nasty tale; he presents tragedy. Not intentionally, of course, but unmistakably. This is not a sense of tragedy that induces pity or fellow-feeling, but rather one that distances, that deadens, and that chills. He contains a tragedy that he himself cannot or will not see, and it is this particular form of impotence that gives the tale, I would argue, its heft and that makes it singularly transfixing among the rest in the collection: Chaucer sacrifices Oswald's potential on the altar of Oswald's *status*-bound desire. Oswald, as the narrativized version of his estate, wants to be a man of ends. In his professional life, he derives great pleasure (and profit) from winning out over his adversaries, who appear to include almost everyone he comes into contact with. And as a pilgrim and member of the Canterbury company, much the same is true. The goal in both spheres is

---

[52] For the intricate way the Reeve relies on legal notions of justice and complaint, see the exceptionally thorough analysis in Arvind Thomas, "Fighting Force with Force: How the Reeve Makes His Day; or, Chaucer Stands His Ground among Jurists Past and Present," *Studies in the Age of Chaucer* 42 (2020), 27–72.

to win, and winning means bringing things to a conclusion and controlling the parameters of any exchange to his own benefit. The Reeve wants to end the Miller's interruption of the orderly progression from Knight to Monk in the tale-telling game; he wants to end (before it begins) the bawdy tale he correctly anticipates; he wants to end the sense of being made a public fool of in the eyes of his fellow travelers, and he wants to end the feeling of an unanswered slight that impugns his sexual dignity and social position. In each part of his life he desires closure – he desires *satisfaction*. The fact that this sense of satisfaction has disappeared from his sexual life is surely not immaterial to his insistence upon finding it elsewhere.

Clad as he is in a body that no longer offers him the sexual satisfaction of his youth, the Reeve searches for the same form of pleasure and completion by other means – in this case, in economic achievement and in the micropolitics of Harry Bailey's tale-telling game. His desires are entirely focused on the rewards that come from his commitment to the quiting-structure and from his need to reclaim his position in a masterful and rational manner. In so doing, Oswald assumes an identity-structure located within the signifying structures surrounding it, favoring familiar networks of antagonism, profit, and masculinity over the multiplicity and resonance otherwise suggested within his own language. If we are to truly face the Reeve, this is where it must happen. For Deleuze and Guattari, the Face, or faciality, is generated by the tension between social structures of significance and the articulation of the individual subject from within those same structures; the one provides a communal system of signification through which legibility is possible, and the other attempts to resist by creating individual signification grounded in the singular subject.[53] Moreover, the Face always emerges as a politics that expands to encompass everything around it: "The machine is called the faciality machine because it is the social production of face, because it performs the facialization of the entire body and all its surroundings and objects, and the landscapificaton of all worlds and milieus."[54] The face and the conditions of its emergence are

---

[53] To use Deleuze and Guattari's terms more overtly, the structures of significance that form the linguistic stratum become the white screen upon which the subject is projected; in this way, the screen becomes the structure by which legibility of a subject is possible. In turn, the subject responds by creating a series of black holes within or throughout the screen in which they attempt to locate their individual semiotic resonance. The combination of the two forms the face, with its smooth cheeks and the holes of the eyes, ears, nose, and mouth. For the presence of faciality in medieval texts, and in Chaucer in particular, see Jamie K. Taylor, "Toward Premodern Globalism: Oceanic Exemplarity in Chaucer's Man of Law's Tale," *PMLA* 135.2 (2020), 261–4.

[54] Deleuze and Guattari, *A Thousand Plateaus*, 181.

always intertwined and local in that the one becomes a product of the other.[55] Thus, the connections between the Reeve's successful business dealings and a silenced bedchamber are real and pervasive. The Reeve's desire for despotic mastery, his desire for the *status* of the Jurist-Priest, expands to suffuse all aspects of his speech and any story he might tell.[56] Everything returns to the center point of his desire, and nothing escapes him.

The trouble is, the Reeve desires the Face. Like all faces, it is horrifying, but what I would like to offer here is that it is his need for it that is tragic. The Reeve's social and economic positions place him in an interstitial role in which he becomes the fulcrum between aristocratic signification and the products of physical labor. On the one hand, he draws his ability to navigate the duties and advantages of his post because of his access to the signifying systems of aristocratic identity. Not noble himself, he nevertheless makes use of how value and meaning are structured by those he "serves." On the other, he maintains an individual subjectivity through his willingness and ability to manipulate these structures to his own ends, and to do so with deliberation and intent. Rather than subservience to aristocratic figures, the Reeve embodies productive resistance to the structures associated with them. This resistance is personal and profitable, as we know, and it offers the Reeve a sense of individuality that distinguishes him from his peasant peers and from the land-owning nobility.[57] The problem is that the Reeve seeks not resistance but stability. To be landed, to be grounded. Ethan Knapp has argued that Chaucer's characterizations render individual details of a portrait as significant: the gait of a horse, the shape of a haircut, the color of a stocking. He finds that these elements "... work in a constellation of pseudoheraldic emblems (clothing, faces, emblematic mottos)," indicating their use as part of heuristic structures of recognition that merge the individual with the tropological.[58] Knapp's connection to the heraldic, a system of signification associated with aristocratic status and identity, is important for understanding the problem

---

[55] "It is not the individuality of the face that counts but the efficacy of the ciphering it makes possible, and in what cases it makes it possible. This is an affair not of ideology but of economy and the organization of power (*pouvoir*). We are certainly not saying that the face, the power of the face (*la puissance du visage*), engenders and explains social power (*pouvoir*). *Certain assemblages of power (pouvoir) require the production of a face*, others do not": Deleuze and Guattari, *A Thousand Plateaus*, 175, emphasis in the original.

[56] Deleuze and Guattari, *A Thousand Plateaus*, 351–2.

[57] Taylor, "Language in Use," 109.

[58] Ethan Knapp, "Faces in the Crowd: Faciality and Ekphrasis in Late Medieval England," in *The Art of Vision: Ekphrasis in Medieval Literature and Culture*, ed. Andrew James Johnston, Ethan Knapp, and Margitta Rouse (Columbus: Ohio State University Press, 2015), 213.

of the Reeve's desire. He can never achieve the kind of easy certainty he imagines comes from aristocratic security – but he wants to. He wants to be seen as embodying fruitful, satisfying power that shapes the world, body and soul, and this too tracks Knapp's arguments about identity. In reading the figure of Constance in the *Man of Law's Tale*, Knapp focuses on the moment in which her visage appears amidst her accusers in the trial scene (II.645–58). The paleness of her appearance engenders pity as readers take in her plight, and this response is partly what marks her as an affective center to the tale. Her face defines her as a moment of lyric emotion within the shifting crowd: "… one might say that to have a face is to have a stance, that where the crowd is in continual movement, the face is fixed in space and in meaning."[59] Constance is clearly not in control of her surroundings, but she certainly embodies constancy and her participation in tropological meaning is satisfying to a reader like the Reeve. "[We] can see this face plucked out of the crowd because it has now simultaneously become an individual and a type," as Knapp writes, and it is in this balance between extended, structuring meaning and subjective focalization that we can locate Oswald's desire for *status* and singularity.[60]

Chaucer uses the tension between the liberating and resistance forms of the Reeve's speech and the static immobility of *status* – what Knapp calls "a tragic finitude"[61] and Karla Taylor terms "inertia."[62] The Reeve desires heraldic signification in the visual field, and he seeks out the kinds of capture he imagines in aristocratic significance. However, to achieve this, he must also embrace the more shifting and nomadic qualities of his own language. As nasty, brutish, and (increasingly) short as the Reeve's life is, Chaucer uses him to experiment with the pull between language and desire and to test out how difficult it is for one to escape the other. We see a similar tension between desire and social constraint in the portrayal of Criseyde as willful subject and as object of exchange, as Elizabeth Allen argues in this volume. The Reeve puts language in Oswald's mouth that runs counter to and exposes the limits of his desires, and the resonant potential of his language is sacrificed so the estates satire can proceed and, perhaps, be challenged in less challenging ways.

---

[59] Knapp, "Faces in the Crowd," 216. It is important to note here that Knapp's interest in the face derives more from Benjamin than from Deleuze and Guattari, and as a result his argument considers the way in which faces emerge and interact with the crowd through the image of the *flâneur* rather than the white wall/black hole system. This allows him to think through Chaucer's negotiation of the lyric and narrative modes in a way that would also be fascinating for the Reeve, but these are beyond the scope of this article.

[60] Knapp, "Faces in the Crowd."

[61] Knapp, "Faces in the Crowd," 217.

[62] Taylor, "Language in Use," 110.

The Reeve will thus be sacrificed at the edge of an undiscovered country he cannot see or hear, despite tracing its outlines.[63]

Forfeiting one unpleasant character to discover these limits feels like a worthwhile choice on some level, but it is an effect that reinforces all the other ways in which the Reeve becomes a scapegoat among the pilgrim company. And it is easy, I think, to accept all of this and abandon the Reeve, a sacrifice of one unhappy character to establish the productive lines of narrative and satire that will carry us forward into the rest of the collection. We watch the pilgrims unite against him, and a more consolidated sense of what productive discourses are available emerge in the wake of his departure from the narrative field. But I would also argue this only works if we recognize the danger the Reeve poses (and the tragedy he embodies). If we fall into the pattern of his desire, a pattern that can never be fulfilled and will end benefiting only the regimes of signification he cannot escape, we are lost. And these desires are extremely durable, fixed in place by the emerging social structures that solidify the more we engage with them. If we look the other direction, however, other fields of possibility emerge in which individuation, esement, and the Reeve's particular version of mastery are not the end; more productive desires begin to emerge in the spaces between. If there is something that might revive the Reeve for us (if not for him), I think it must be this. In dissolution lies potential and possibility, and clean lines and edges are not the only end; even the aging body might be escape rather than closure. "Til we be roten" after all, "kan we nat be rype" (I.3875).

[63] We return here to the potential offered by Moten's "geography of displacement." This is a landscape the Reeve will not or cannot recognize. See Moten and El-Hadi, "Ensemble: An Interview with Dr. Fred Moten."

8

"Borne to Blisse": Souls in Flight and (In)Authentic Vision in Chaucer's *Canterbury Tales*

ASHBY KINCH

Astute readers of Karla Taylor's *Chaucer Reads 'The Divine Comedy'* will recognize in my title a reference to a key concept in her elucidation of Chaucer's reading of Dante's *Commedia*: authentication, and its spectral double, the inauthentic. Authentication in her work refers to the literary devices a poet deploys to establish the credibility of both the narrator (primary) and the world he has constructed (secondary).[1] That's no mean feat in Dante's *Commedia*, whose credibility is staked to its comprehensive synthesis of Christian theology. Since, as Taylor puts it, "death marks a radical break with the past," Dante co-opts this stance of conversion as a mark of radical rupture, tied to the linguistic performance of the "eternal present" of the literary text, effectively inventing a formal system that insulates his text from the ravages of the world.[2] The eternal present with which Dante's poem conspicuously ends is contrasted with the narrator's return – "gia volgeva il mi disio e 'l velle" ("my desire and will had already rotated/revolved") – by Dante's use of a verb in imperfect tense (*volgeva*) against the present tense of that famous last line: "l'amor che move il sole e l'altre stelle" ("the Love that moves the sun and other stars," *Par.* XXXIII, 143–5). Language matters deeply to Dante's authentication of the reader's experience of the *Commedia*, because it aligns a theological vision with a core premise of the work: that the "converted" narrator, now "dead" to his previous self, can view not just his own life, but the lives of others, in the clear light of transcendent vision, authenticated by the beauty of poetry.

---

[1] Karla Taylor, *Chaucer Reads 'the Divine Comedy'* (Palo Alto: Stanford University Press, 1989), 18 ff., on "primary" and "secondary" authentication.
[2] Taylor, *Chaucer Reads*, 92–6.

But the kind of transcendent vision in which Dante traffics triggered Chaucer's skepticism on both literary and ethical grounds. In Taylor's reading of *Troilus and Criseyde*, Chaucer acknowledges his conceptual limits that "render the objective report of Troilus' end inauthentic," and thus exposes Dante's transcendent ideal as "attainable only inauthentically – that is, as a figment of reified desire."[3] That contrast between authenticity and inauthenticity highlights the high stakes of a literary text that claims to speak of the world beyond human experience, as set against the way Chaucer places limits on poetry, which "makes him turn back to the world, to see how he, his characters, and his audience may struggle toward knowledge and moral vision with the strictures of experience *unfolding in time before death*" (my italics).[4] Within the narrative community of *Troilus and Criseyde*, this question of the limits of "conversion" is explicitly foregrounded in Criseyde's response to Antigone's Song in Book II, to which her company listens in rapt delight. In this moment of interpretive exchange between characters in their social field, Chaucer highlights the gap between "objective history" and "subjective experience," in Taylor's terms,[5] through Criseyde's befuddled response to the song's intense expression of love, the beauty of the song enhancing her sense of wonder. Criseyde's leading query – "Lord, is ther swych blisse among / Thise loveres, as they konne faire endite?" (II. 885–6) – is answered by a layered, qualified response that moves through the conventional (of course, love is blissful!), to the restrictive qualification (not every lover experiences "the parfit blisse of love," II. 891), before ending with Antigone's final recourse to a telling comparison: "Men moste axe at seyntes if it is / Aught fair in hevene. (Why? For they kan telle) / And axen fendes is it foul in helle" (II. 894–6). That conjunction of the discourses of love and post-mortem experience perfectly analogizes Criseyde's skepticism as a form of readerly resistance that is overcome, in the end, by art. If the exchange makes her "somwhat able to converte" (II. 901–3), Antigone's song has given powerful expression to the possibility of a transformative experience, not some "objective report" from the post-mortem sphere: saints and fiends are inaccessible, but art is in our immediate plane of experience.

Here and throughout Chaucer's corpus, we are implicated in the text as readers whose interpretive choices are foregrounded: we are most likely to be seduced by the inauthentic visions of others to the extent that we forget that fact. This emphasis on reading is another salient through-line in Taylor's work, which argues for Chaucer's awareness of the need to build new interpretive and ethical capacities in the readers of vernacular fiction. This problem is dramatized in the *Canterbury Tales* project by readers who

---

[3]   See Taylor, *Chaucer Reads*, 202, 194.
[4]   Taylor, *Chaucer Reads*, 202.
[5]   Taylor, *Chaucer Reads*, 197.

172   ASHBY KINCH

are "disgruntled, skeptical, disorderly, and above all deaf."[6] Chaucer's sense
of the need to invent a new audience raised the stakes for his examination
of reading practices, which he embedded in the *Canterbury Tales* as one of
its constituent features: we read both with and against the narrators and their
characters, making constant judgments about what we can and cannot trust
in their discourses, attuned to the reality of our shared powers of deception,
including self-deception.

Bringing these two strands of Taylor's work together (a critique of authentication strategies and an emphasis on reading practices), I offer in tribute a
critical analysis of three verbo-visual images (or image texts)[7] of the soul in
flight in the *Canterbury Tales*: in the *Summoner's Tale*, the *Merchant's Tale*,
and the *Second Nun's Tale*. In each case, Chaucer's deployment of the image
highlights the ethical stakes of storytelling, and hence reading: the speakers use
these images to authenticate their claims to an insight about the post-mortem
world, but the contexts force the reader to reflect on the dangers of an uncritical
acceptance. An iconographic figure like this strives to generate an unmediated
experience through recourse to the "absent-presence" of an image driven by
powerful intuitions and desires (for hope, for release, for persistence, for
transcendence). Chaucer was writing during a period in which image practices
of all kinds were proliferating in a wide range of media: illustrated books;
wall paintings in both sacred and secular spaces; stained glass throughout the
remodeled churches of the late fourteenth century; wood sculptures of saints;
and decorative objects of all sorts, from ivory sculptures to meta-images like

---

6   Karla Taylor, "Chaucer's Volumes: Toward a New Model of Literary History
in the Canterbury Tales," *Studies in the Age of Chaucer* 29 (2007), 43–85 (at 46).

7   I cite here the well-known coinage by W.J.T. Mitchell, *Picture Theory: Essays
on Verbal and Visual Representation* (Chicago: University of Chicago Press), 94–107.
Medieval scholars have been exploring this conceptual terrain to account for the mobile
way that a Latin term like *imago* squints at both verbal and visual formulations. See
V.A. Kolve, *Chaucer and the Imagery of Narrative: The First Five Canterbury Tales*
(Stanford: Stanford University Press, 1984), especially the introduction, where he
stresses the way medieval faculty psychology blurs the boundary between word and
image. See also Olivier Boulnois, *Au-delà de l'image: Une archeologie du visuel
au Moyen Âge v–xvi siècle* (Paris: Des Travaux/Seuil, 2008), who uses the term
"image-object" to stress the physical material of made objects over their mental or
psychological content, the former distinguished by Aquinas as *ars*, the latter as *scientia*,
348–9. See also Jessica Brantley's excellent study, *Reading in the Wilderness: Private
Devotion and Public Performance in Late Medieval England* (Chicago: University
of Chicago Press, 2007), on the text-image interfaces in a Carthusian miscellany,
which works with Mitchell's core concept to generate a rich interpretive context for
devotional reading.

Absolon's shoes "With Poules wyndow corven" (I. 3318).[8] In the essay that follows, however, I hold the rich visual tradition of the soul in flight at the margin of discussion and focus on mediating structures of language that draw attention to the medium of language into which the device is inextricably woven.[9] The image of the soul in flight functions as a recursive device that moves the reader back and forth across the larger text, functioning like the astrological exordium in the *Man of Law's Prologue*, which looks back to the *General Prologue* and anticipates the *Parson's Prologue*.[10] This cross-textual reading practice functions like other conceptual tensions that have attracted critical attention – "game" and "earnest," for example – to develop a set of questions about the implications of the narrative strategies each speaker employs to authenticate their claims to a vision of the spiritual world.

Even though it appears last in the *Canterbury Tales*, Maximus's vision from the *Second Nun's Tale* comes first in the essay that follows, and I return to it in the end, as a means of demonstrating that even the most straightforward convention is subject to poetic mediation. Indeed, analysis of these images highlights what Taylor refers to as Chaucer's investment in the "problem of communicating unshared experience."[11] The conventionality of the iconography of the soul in flight suggests the consummate shared cultural experience: wall paintings, devotional books, and narrative images of a soul released from the body of a dying person are so ubiquitous that they might seem beyond the powers of critique. But reading these rhetorical instances across the *Canterbury Tales* reveals Chaucer's investigation of the gaps in our experience, the blindspots – literal and figurative – that open up when we examine the motives of this image as a device for authenticating vision. They provide

---

[8] Ashby Kinch, *Imago Mortis: Mediating Images of Death in Late Medieval Culture* (Leiden: Brill, 2013).

[9] Though I do not fully explore Chaucer's visual sources here, I have done so elsewhere in a collection with a range of exciting new studies on Chaucer's engagement with visual culture: see Susanna Fein and David Raybin, eds., *Chaucer: Visual Approaches* (University Park: Pennsylvania State University Press, 2016). V.A. Kolve's groundbreaking work, *Chaucer and the Imagery*, and the collection of his individual studies, *Telling Images: Chaucer and the Imagery of Narrative II* (Palo Alto: Stanford University Press, 2009), are essential, as is H.A. Kelly's skeptical take on Chaucer's interest in visual arts, "Chaucer's Arts and Our Arts," in *New Perspectives in Chaucer Criticism*, ed. Donald M. Rose (Norman: Pilgrim Books, 1981), 107–20.

[10] Taylor, "Chaucer's Volumes," 49, 55, on the exordium and the Man of Law's practice of citation as a grounded in his reading style. Chaucerians so effortlessly read "across" the *Canterbury Tales* project, we can forget how sophisticated a readership this kind of reading implies, a problem that Taylor explores fully in this essay, and which Chaucerians in every generation carry out as a practice, even when they do not fully theorize it.

[11] Taylor, *Chaucer Reads*, 188.

opportunities for us to reflect on what we see in words, what we do not see, and what we can (and cannot) think about those acts of seeing and not seeing. Reading them closely, we become more finely attuned to the ethical dangers that come from being too easily seduced by the images of others, especially as they take the shape of language in a context of manipulation, deceit, and desire, the overlapping contexts that define the *Canterbury Tales* project.

The imagery of post-mortem ascent is ubiquitous in medieval culture, which vested its hope for redemption in a figurative paradigm of escape from the trappings of the world.[12] This feature of mainstream religious culture is hardly unique: many cultures across the world have evolved figures of a soul ascending, often in the form of birds, to a paradisal space.[13] In medieval post-mortem iconography, the soul in flight belongs to a strand of images that strive to affirm the glorious possibility of spiritual re-birth, which in turn drives Christian redemptive poetics. But souls in flight pose a bit of an embarrassment to a visual artist, who is stuck with the problem of "depiction": how do these souls move? What do they look like? Late medieval culture evolved a specific version of this visual image in response to this problem: a naked homunculus ascending from a dying person, whose final breath is presumed to push forth this spirit.[14] This soul is often figured with specific childlike characteristics, an evocation of neoteny that picks up a key strand in Christian discourse on becoming like a child before God.[15] In Books of Hours, especially those illustrating the Office of the Dead, the naked soul in flight, hovering without wings, becomes a standard visual cipher of the soul escaping the body, or

[12] For an excellent summary of the evolution of the "voyage of the soul," see Claude Carozzi, *Le Voyage De L'Âme Dans L'Au-Delà D'Après La Littérature Latine (Ve–XIIIe Siècle)* (Rome: École Française de Rome, 1994).

[13] For a broader discussion of the motif in relationship to cultural beliefs about birds, see Christopher M. Moreman, "On the Relationship between Birds and Spirits of the Dead," *Society & Animals* 22.5 (2014), 1–22.

[14] Moshe Barasch, "The Departing Soul: the Long Life of a Medieval Creation," *Artibus et historiae* 26.52 (2005), 13–28, focuses on the "pneumatic" feature of this motif, with the spirit's association with breath framing the way artists represent the moment of death. For detail on this motif with respect to the Dormition of the Virgin, see also Jean-Claude Schmitt, "L'Exception Corporelle: À Propos De L'Assomption De Marie," in *The Mind's Eye: Art and Theological Argument in the Middle Ages* (Princeton: Princeton University Press, 2006), 151–85.

[15] Stephen J. Gould is most well-known for advancing this concept, which describes animals who retain traits of a prior developmental stage even as they age. It is interesting that two medieval scholars, L.O.A. Fradenburg, *Staying Alive: A Survival Manual for the Liberal Arts* (Santa Barbara: Punctum Books, 2013), 242, and Susan Crane, *Animal Encounters: Contacts and Concepts in Medieval Britain* (Philadelphia: University of Pennsylvania Press, 2012), 21–2, have used the concept to discuss intersubjectivity in human relationships with animals.

attempting to escape: in one sub-type, common in the depiction of the Dives and Lazarus myth, a devil appears to snatch the soul emerging from the mouth at the moment of death, with no opportunity for an angel to intervene, because Dives has not repented. Though many late medieval images depict a "battle for the soul" around the deathbed, they usually resolve in favor of the souls as the angels intervene.[16] In English Books of Hours in the late medieval period, the *commendatio animae* is most often depicted with naked souls swaddled in cloth held by an angel who flies them to heaven.[17] The visual invention of the cloth resolves the otherwise ambiguous question of how these souls levitate without wings: they are simply *carried* by angels with wings.

Late medieval culture was, of course, saturated with images – Camille famously referred to the "explosion" of images in the fourteenth century – but a persistent strand of theological distrust of images framed them as mere vehicles for transmission of ideas for the illiterate (*libri laiocrum*); or, worse, as misleading, and thus dangerous, stimuli to affective response.[18] The soul in flight is an obvious instance of precisely the kind of image that might draw the ire of rationalist theologians. Happily, we have direct evidence of one such voice from the medieval period: a thirteenth-century English Franciscan, Thomas Docking, who registered his dissatisfaction with the falsity of the image of the soul departing a body. The soul does not share any bodily features

[16] Philippe Ariès, *The Hour of Our Death* (New York: Oxford University Press, 1981), 108, notes that the "battle for the soul" reflects a shift in attention to the high spiritual stakes in the deathbed scene, a new spiritual drama in the late medieval period. There are other iconographically significant instances of the Devil successfully snatching a soul from the mouth of the dying: e.g., Judas Iscariot, whose suicide from despair signaled his damnation. I thank the anonymous reviewer for the suggestion to include this "paired" instance.

[17] See Roger S. Wieck, *Painted Prayers: The Book of Hours in Medieval and Renaissance Art* (New York: George Braziller, 1997), 117–32, and "The Death Desired: Books of Hours and the Medieval Funeral," *Death and Dying in the Middle Ages*, ed. Edelgard E. DuBruck and Barbara I. Gusick (New York: Peter Lang, 1999), 431–505, for an excellent overview of the images of the Office of the Dead and the prevalence of the *commendatio animae* in English Books of Hours. One clever artist in the Sherbrooke Missal connects this soul-as-child motif to the impact of communion on our spiritual destiny by depicting a man kneeling at an altar and lifting a naked soul in cloth up to God as his offering. See William Marx, "Iconography and Meaning in the Sherbrooke Missal," *English Manuscript Studies 1100–1700*, ed. A.S.G. Edwards (London: British Library Publishing, 2002), 154–76, 103–5.

[18] See Michael Camille, *The Gothic Idol: Ideology and Image-Making in Medieval Art* (Cambridge: Cambridge University Press, 1989), 160, 215–19. This debate about images played out over centuries – arguably, we are still having it – and I am simplifying a complicated discussion to narrow to this singular image, and to pivot away from the visual sources, which are beyond the scope of this paper.

and is not visible to us (*quia aut omnio nullum corpus secum gerunt aut nullum corpus nobis visible*), Docking notes.[19] He implicitly rebukes those who claim that spiritual vision allows us to see invisible things (who knows what a soul looks like in this world open only to spiritual vision?). Docking, a neo-Aristotelian rationalist, sees this little naked soul propagated throughout his culture, and it irks him that people would consume it irrationally.

But despite their dubious accuracy from a rational perspective, these kinds of images serve a powerful function in Christian discourse, including hagiography and monastic discourse. They crystallize a moment of release, which is a key element in the drama of Christian thought. This function is exemplified in Chaucer's use of the image at the midpoint of the *Second Nun's Tale*. Cecile's ministry has led to the conversion of her husband, Tiburce, and his brother, Valerian, into *miles Dei* who are willing to defy the command of the prefect, Almachius, that all citizens worship the image of Jupiter. After performing "manye wondres" (VII. 358), they are arrested, but manage to convert their "tormentours," as well as the Prefect's assistant, Maximus, who spirits them away to his house. They continue to preach there up to the point that they are brought to the temple where they "losten both hir hevedes" (VIII. 398). At this juncture, the narrative takes a focalizing turn, and suddenly we see the execution through the eyes of Maximus himself, whose conversion in faith enables his vision of an unseen world: "he hir soules saugh to hevene glyde / With aungels, ful of cleernesse and of light" (VIII. 403). That verb "glyde" echoes the convention of a smooth ascent of a saved soul, used in religious writing but also used to describe the movement of light and stars in

---

[19] Thomas Docking, *Commentary in Deuteronomy*, is cited in Michael Camille, "The Illustrations in Harley MS 3487 and the Perception of Aristotle's *Libri naturales* in Thirteenth-Century England," in *England in the Thirteenth Century: Proceedings of the 1984 Harlaxton Symposium*, ed. W.M. Ormrod (Woodbridge: Boydell Press, 1986), 31–44 (at 39). There, the discussion focuses on the influence of neo-Aristotelian commentaries on natural philosophy. See A.G. Little, "The Franciscan School at Oxford in the Thirteenth Century," *Archivum Franciscanum historicum* 19 (1926), 803–74 (at 846–50), for Docking's career, and this comment on images of the soul, 848. See Cecilia Panti, "The Theological Use of Science at the Oxford Franciscan School: Thomas Docking, Roger Bacon, and Robert Grosseteste's Works," in *The Franciscan Order in the Medieval English Province and Beyond*, ed. Michael Robson and Patrick Zutshi (Amsterdam: Amsterdam University Press, 2019), 181–210, who explores the "theological use" of scientific examples in Docking's *Deuteronomy*. Docking sits in a line of English neo-Aristotelian Franciscans who were crucial to the normalizing of scientific concepts in their theological commentaries, in a lineage that goes back to Robert Grosseteste and Adam Marsh, Docking's teacher, and forward to Thomas Bradwardine, famously cited by Chaucer in the *Nun's Priest's Tale* (VII. 3242).

SOULS IN FLIGHT AND (IN)AUTHENTIC VISION IN CHAUCER 177

the sky.[20] Maximus's experience, as told through the elevated discourse of hagiography, exemplifies the special powers of vision accorded to people of faith, a theme that runs through Chaucer's Cecilia legend and unifies its idea of an elevated sensorium available to the elect of the faith.[21] The passage appears straightforwardly to conform to the conventional iconography: even the addition to his source of the line "ful of cleernesse and of light" appears to nod to contemporary iconography of the Office of the Dead, especially the *commendatio animae* discussed above.

The passage also draws upon the deep conceptual roots of post-mortem vision as an answer to the skeptical query of rationalists, the driving concept of Book IV of Gregory the Great's *Dialogues*. Not coincidentally, Book IV's "miracles" directly address the post-mortem state of souls, which was highly influential in the evolution of practices and beliefs about the reciprocal relationship of the living and the dead. Gregory is answering in this *Dialogue* the question put to him by his interlocutor, Peter, who says: "I once witnessed the sudden death of a monk. At one moment he was speaking to me and the next moment I saw him dead. But I did not see whether or not his soul departed. And I find it difficult to accept on faith what I cannot see."[22] He expects to see the soul, and fails to, which Gregory attributes to a misplaced attention: "It was a mistake on your part even to try to see an invisible being with your bodily eyes. For it was with spiritual vision, purified by acts of faith and abundant prayers, that many of our people were able repeatedly to observe souls leaving the body." Gregory then recounts specific instances of spiritual insight into the Afterlife, including the passage that leads to the famous Trentals (discussed below), beginning with specific, named instances of monks with access to the unseen spiritual world at the moment of death: Germanus "being carried up to heaven in a ball of fire" and an assembled community seeing the soul of Abbot Spes "escape from his body in the form of a dove."[23] Witnessing these moments – and passing them forward as stories

---

[20] *MED*, "gliden," sense 1a: (a) To pass through the air, sky, etc.; glide smoothly and uninterruptedly; of light: to come, shine.

[21] Spiritual vision and the interplay of images has long been a focal point of criticism of this tale, on which see Carolyn Collette, "A Closer Look at Seinte Cecile's Special Vision," *Chaucer Review* 10.4 (1976), 337–49; and Katherine Little, "Images, Texts, and Exegetics in Chaucer's Second Nun's Tale," *Journal of Medieval and Early Modern Studies* 36.1 (2006), 103–34. Kolve's predictably brilliant reading of the "Iconography of St. Cecilia," in *Telling Images*, 199–222, is grounded in a claim that the tale is "the most absolute of the Canterbury narratives – uncompromised by irony, unmediated by larger context, and uncolored by the idiosyncrasies of a personal narrative voice" (221).

[22] Gregory the Great, *Dialogues*, trans. Odo John Zimmerman, in *The Fathers of the Church: A New Translation. Vol. 5* (New York: Fathers of the Church, 1959), 196.

[23] Gregory the Great, *Dialogues*, 200–3.

within the community – authenticates the work of the monastic community in steering the living toward beneficent deaths, and then communicating that vision to others in a kind of self-confirming circularity of authentication. In Chaucer's hagiography of Cecilia, Maximus becomes a figure for this clerical privilege of witness of the unseen spiritual world.

While Chaucer presents Maximus's vision as "authentic," the clerical figure at the heart of the *Summoner's Tale* – a corrupt Friar seeking a deathbed gift from a family in grief – lays claim to a similar post-mortem "vision." This authentication gesture fails, and thus undermines the very clerical privilege he espouses. The tale begins with a scene in which our fraudulent Friar visits a village church where he urges the "folk in chirche" (III. 1735) to purchase "Trentals," the cycle of thirty prayers for the souls of the deceased that are modeled on a key episode at the end of Book IV of Gregory the Great's *Dialogues*.[24] As with post-mortem "vision," Gregory's claim to the efficacy of the trental is grounded in the spiritual labor of the community, but its origin is Gregory's "strong compassion" for a fellow monk, Justus, whose corpse has been cast into a manure pile in punishment for violating the rules of communal life.[25] It is a story not only of redemption, but also of compassion. Their thirty days of prayer liberate him from his perilous state, and impart a key lesson of compassion, core to Christian ethics, for even those who have wronged you. In contrast, Chaucer focuses our attention on the sociology of the Trental at the outset of the *Summoner's Tale* by listing the payments the friar solicits: a "kechyl" (mass-cake), a bit of cheese, a bushel of wheat, malt or rye, brawn (a piece of undyed cloth) (III. 1746–53). Chaucer's diction of the common market evokes the homely gifts from people without any ready cash, sharpening the contrast with the Friar's contemptible lack of compassion for the poor.[26] In exchange for their largesse, his companion writes their names in a wax tablet, and he erases them later. The theory behind the efficacy of

[24] See Richard Pfaff, "The English Devotion of St. Gregory's Trental," *Speculum* 49.1 (1974), 75–90, on the evolution of the Trental in the Sarum rite, a distinctively English form that spreads the thirty prayers over the course of a year through ten feast days at each of which three prayers are said. A verse tale called "The Pope trental," or "The guldene trental" circulated in fourteenth-century England, and two versions are recorded in the famous Vernon MS (Bodl. Eng. Poet. A.1). The Vernon MS names the specific feast days, so there is no doubt that it was established liturgical practice in Chaucer's day, which appears to be the precise target of the Summoner's biting satire. By the fifteenth century, the number of manuscripts attesting to the story has exploded, and it is regularly called "Trentalle Sanctri Gregorii." See *Trantalle Sancti Gregorii*, ed. Albert Kaufmann (Amsterdam: Rodopi, 1890).

[25] Gregory the Great, *Dialogues*, 268–9.

[26] Takami Matsuda, "Death, Prudence, and Chaucer's 'Pardoner's Tale,'" *Journal of English and Germanic Philology* 91.3 (1992), 313–24, also stresses this aspect of the Friar's over-selling of the Trental (at 318). And of course this scene is key to

SOULS IN FLIGHT AND (IN)AUTHENTIC VISION IN CHAUCER 179

the Trental is that the spiritual purity of the person praying determines the effectiveness of the prayer, details that the Friar lays out later in his exchange with Thomas's wife, using the language of vision to mystify clerical insight into "secree thynges":

> Oure orisouns been moore effectueel,
> And moore *we seen* of Cristes secree thynges,
> Than burel folk …
> And therefore *may ye se* that our preyeres –
> I speke of us, we mendynantz, we freres –
> Been to the hye God moore acceptable
> Than youres, with youre feestes at the table (III. 1870–2, 1913–14)

Of course, that is precisely what the story's protagonist, Thomas, objects to: he claims to "have spent upon diverse manere freres / Ful many a pound; yet fare I never the bet" (III. 1950–1). He's sick, presumably on his deathbed, and he has yet to see a return on his investment.

This gap in the Friar's credibility sets the context for the pathos-laden moment in which Thomas's unnamed wife mentions her recently dead child to the Friar. What the woman wants when she addresses the Friar is not totally clear; she merely says, "My child is deed withinne this wykes two, / Soone after that ye wente out of this toune" (III. 1852–3). But as with the village folk at church, the Friar plays on this woman's grief by quickly interrupting her with an image that exploits her deepest hope by laying false claim to Gregory the Great's visionary tradition: "His deeth saugh I by revelacioun" (III. 1854), he says, using a loaded word that suggests a mystical access to a world beyond our mundane physical experience. "I dar wel seyn that, er that half an hour / After his deeth, I saugh hym born to blisse / In myn avision, so God me wisse" (III. 1856–8). The repetition of two different terms for the same vision (revelacioun/avision) undermines rather than re-enforces its veracity. The image is clearly meant to stir the woman's affect. But the Friar converts the simple lie – vague in its details, but affirming her hope for her child's salvation – into a much more elaborate scene that involves his entire convent, re-socializing this image into an instrument to vaunt fraternal piety, which perversely aligns perfectly with Gregory the Great's authentication of group vision. While it might be excused in short form as a harmless bit of sympathetic rhetoric, as he expands the "revelacioun" we see yet again his institutional machinations, as his ultimate goal is to press for a deathbed donation for the chapter of his convent. He claims that two other people, the *fermerer* and the *sexteyn*, both

---

establishing the Friar's class aspirations over and against his duty, a tension that culminates in his full exposure in the bravura fart-explication scene in the tale's conclusion.

friars of over fifty years, also had the vision, and that latter figure is key: the sexton's job is to care for the liturgical vestments and vessels. The friar thus conjures for this grieving mother an image of the whole institutional infrastructure of a fraternal convent praying on behalf of her child, turning the wheels of eschatology with their simple, poignant improvised ritual: "*Te Deum* was oure song, and nothyng ells" (III. 1866). Among the scenes of horrific fraudulence in the *Canterbury Tales*, this cynical exploitation of the emotions of a grieving mother might well be the worst, and certainly worse ethically than the transactional fraudulence with which the story begins. In the opening section of the tale, the Summoner summarizes the defrauding of the citizens with the phrase: "He served hem with nyfles and with fables" (III. 1758–60). "Nyfles" repays scrutiny, especially in a story that focuses ironic attention on comestibles,[27] including the villagers who buy Trentals with food, and the Friar's own indulgence in food. "Nyfle" is an Anglo-Norman word for a wafer cake, a pleasing but nutrition-less confectionary dessert.[28] As a zeugma, the phrase here links together a physical object with a keyword in the lexicon of invention; a "fable" suggests both a falsehood and a thing that must be interpreted. The verb "served" complements the confection, but ill-fits the second component: one does not "serve" fables. Resolving this zeugma into "silly stories" (as the Riverside does) dissolves the metaphorical component, which artfully highlights the alimentary thread of the whole story: we take in our food, and it all heads out the same direction eventually, but we are perverse if we make our mouths the exit orifice.

Among those "nyfles" is, of course, the image of the child's soul in flight with which the Friar seduces Thomas's wife. Having played this role of giving a human face to the psychological abuse of the Friar, she gives way to her husband, who, having witnessed this scene at his sickbed, has retribution on his mind. The tale culminates, famously, in a reverse seduction: at the deathbed to solicit a gift, the Friar finds himself uncomfortably in bed with Thomas, rooting around in his underwear. The incident at the bed powerfully reverses the mechanism of self-deceiving credulity that the Friar cynically exploits in the wife's desire to believe: this Friar believes so deeply in his own preaching prowess that he thinks, contrary to all indications, that he has convinced

---

[27] See Susan Crane's excellent discussion of the animal subtext of food in "Cat, Capon, and Pig in the Summoner's Tale," *Studies in the Age of Chaucer* 34.1 (2012), 319–24.

[28] See *Anglo-Norman Dictionary*: https://anglo-norman.net/entry/niule. "Nyfles" is probably miscategorized in the *MED*, which places it under the sense of a "trick or a jest." But both examples under "jest" involve food, which is the primary etymology, and connects the Anglo-Norman usage with the Middle English. Later attestations with the clear sense of a "styled kerchief" would be secondary metaphorical derivations connected to the word's sense of a food with no nutritional value.

Thomas to give a big donation. This thoroughgoing self-deception leads him to stick his hand under the bedcovers to receive the gift that Thomas has, as he puts it, "held in pryvitee" (III. 2143), and then grope around under his "towel" (III. 2148) to seek it out. While funny, the *Summoner's Tale* derives its anti-fraternal satire from a nervously pointed critique of what was, for late medieval religion, a high-stakes affair: death (the child), and the cure of souls in preparation for death (Thomas).[29] Wisdom famously exhorts the Dying Man in Suso's *Horologium Sapientiae*, an influential *ars moriendi* text, to open the "eye of his mind" (oculum mentis); Thomas on his death-bed opens his nether eye, hardly a sign of his privileged access to an unseen spiritual world. The "exchange" that Thomas suggests in his fart is a re-adjustment of the market expectations of the very idea of intercessory prayer. When faith in that system is ruptured, the whole system dissipates, like the gift-fart, which lives its most powerful life in secondary, symbolic discursive exchange. But that fart is in some ways a misdirection away from the core spiritual depravity that has been called to the surface: the willful manipulation of the spiritual hopes of a family who has lost a child, whose father is sick and in peril of death.

An old man's lack of spiritual preparation for his own death provides a crucial sub-text for the *Merchant's Tale*, as well. Indeed, the image of the soul in flight, deployed by Justinus at a key moment when he hopes to convince January to think on death rather than marriage, perfectly ironizes Gregory the Great's dictum in his *miracula* that "we arrive at a true understanding through images."[30] The relationship between images and desire is foregrounded in this tale in the key passage between the two counsel scenes when January, having decided to marry, ruminates on various women of the town in a kind of masturbatory reverie beginning "heigh fantasye and curious bisynesse" (IV. 1577), and ending "this was his fantasye" (IV. 1610). In medieval faculty psychology, "fantasye" carried the freighted sense of images in the mind untethered by rational control; "curious" could signify restlessness and potentially moral danger.[31] The language of this passage thus emphasizes January's disordered

---

[29] There is of course a massive amount of criticism on the fart, and its explication, too numerous to cite, but here I want to draw attention to critics who have focused on the deathbed context: Patrick Gallagher, "The 'Summoner's Tale' and Medieval Attitudes Towards Sickness," *Chaucer Review* 21.2 (1986), 200–12; and Carl Phelpstead, "'Th'Ende is Every Tales Strengthe': Contextualizing Chaucerian Perspectives on Death and Judgement," in *Chaucer and Religion*, ed. Helen Phillips (Cambridge: D.S. Brewer, 2010), 97–110, esp. 98–105, as he is one of the few critics to discuss the experience of child mortality, and connects this with the risk of an unrepentant death that hovers over the scene.

[30] Gregory the Great, *Dialogues*, 242.

[31] See *MED*, "curious," especially the way meanings associated with exploring the occult or the inner recesses shade into moral danger. Chaucer likely would have

mind, his lack of control of the images that run through it. This characterization of his cognition thus frames our attention to the second counsel scene, in which January cautions Placebo and Justinus that he wants assent rather critique (IV. 1619–20), a kind of Trumpian parody of real debate. Justinus, on the contrary, wants January to approach his decision to marry in the more serious light of the expected penitential disposition of an older man, who should be turning his thoughts to death and his soul's condition in the Afterlife, not marriage. And, in a very strange way, January *is* worried about the Afterlife, but in a manner that demonstrates the limits of his cognitive ability. He opens his presentation of his final qualms with "o thyng priketh in my conscience" (IV. 1635). Chaucer's readers would have heard in that phrase allusion to the tradition of vernacular moral instruction initiated by the thirteenth-century French text *Somme le Roi* by Friar Laurent, which was translated in one tradition as *The Book of Vices and Virtues*, in another as "Handlyng Synne," and in yet another as "Ayenbit of Inwit," or "pricke of conscience." All of them are grounded in the fundamental medieval penitential admonition: look to your final end. But we know all too well that it is not just his conscience that is pricked. The fabliau segment of the story, including two awful sex scenes, is replete with uncomfortable detail about the various drinks and foods January consumes – a kind of dietary Viagra – to give greater vitality to his prick, rather than prick to his conscience.

When January turns to his counsellors to relieve his conscience in light of an unexpurgated sexual desire that drives his choice, Chaucer expertly provides us with a portrait of January's mental disorder, using language that mixes registers indiscriminately to come to a strange conclusion. January gives a little speech in which he recalls that "no man han parfite blisses two – / This is to seye, in erthe and eek in hevene" (IV. 1639–40). So far so good: he seems to have internalized a key medieval preaching theme that "hevene is boght so deere / With tribulacioun and greet penaunce" (IV. 1648–9). But the problem is that his understanding of "parfit blisse" and "hevene" includes some scrambling of the metaphorical and the literal, such that the "parfit felicitee" he hopes to have in his upcoming marriage – and again, it is a decidedly sexual "felicitee" that he is thinking of – will give him "myn heven in erthe heere" (IV. 1647). Chaucer plucks this piece of language from the more carnal side of the lyric tradition of *fin' amor*, where a lover's body (or love itself, or sexual consummation) is described as a paradise.[32] The way this language

---

known of Augustine's well-known critique of *curiositas*, connected with the "restless mind" in Joseph Torchia's study, *Restless Mind: Curiositas and the Scope of Inquiry in St. Augustine's Psychology* (Milwaukee: Marquette University Press, 2013).

[32] See, for example, the line from *Mosti riden by Rybbesdale* in the Harley Lyrics: "hyre tyttes aren anunder bis / as apples tuo of parays. / Ouself ye mowen seo" (58–60), in Susanna Fein, with David Raybin, and Jan Ziolkowski, eds., *The Complete Harley*

of heavenly sensuality sticks in January's head right next to this other, more serious thought of moral discernment reminds us that Chaucer is remarkably acute in staging the manifold ways in which bad reading manifests itself as bad thinking, and vice versa. January knows that he needs to be thinking about death, but at the same time he knows that he cannot stop thinking about sex; his weak intellectual toolkit will not allow him to disentangle the two threads. He needs help resolving his cognitive dissonance from his "bretheren tweye," whom he beseeches: "Assoileth me this question, I preye" (IV. 1653–4).

What follows is a staggering moment of *ressentiment*, as Justinus recognizes his brother's self-deceiving stupidity and cannot imagine a way of disentangling it: he simply gives up on trying to straighten him out. Like many cynical intellectuals in the face of a recalcitrant man of power and wealth, he resorts to mockery: "Justinus, which that hated his folye, / Answerede anon right in his japerye" (IV. 1655–6). His "japerye" places the reader in the position of seeing past January, laughing at him, and thus giving up completely on counsel. This reaction inside the text justifies the reader's own jaded *jouissance* in the raveling out of the plot to its ironic end. This passage signals to the reader that he is a worthy of derision because he is beyond help, whether of his friends, or of any authorities Justinus might cite to make his case: "And for he wolde his longe tale abregge, / He wolde noon auctoritee allegge" (IV. 1657–8). What's the point in citing authorities for an audience that fails to understand them? Authentication strategies are lost on those who cannot parse simple distinctions. This cognitive deficit destabilizes civic discourse, a problem Chaucer explores through what Taylor terms a "social aesthetics," forms that emerge with the new behavior and ideology of figures like the Merchant, our narrator.[33]

Justinus thus directly warns January that his married life may not produce as much bliss as he anticipates, by suggesting that only a "high myracle" could achieve it. In the course of this mockery, Justinus recycles key terms from the culture of the deathbed that suggest his real purpose is to continue to "prick" the kind of ethical self-awareness that comes from facing one's mortality. He frames God's moment of "mercy" within the context of the

---

2253 Manuscript, vol. 2 (Kalamazoo: Medieval Institute Publications/TEAMS, 2014), 146.

[33] See Karla Taylor, "Social Aesthetics and the Emergence of Civic Discourse from the *Shipman's Tale* to *Melibee*," *Chaucer Review* 39.3 (2005), 298–322; and Karla Taylor, "Chaucer's Reticent Merchant," in *The Idea of Medieval Literature: New Essays on Chaucer and Medieval Culture in Honor of Donald R. Howard*, ed. James M. Dean and Christian Zacher (Newark: University of Delaware Press, 1992), 189–205.

administration of last rights: "er ye have youre right of hooly chirche,"[34] before which he may well have a chance to "repente of wedded mannes lyf" (IV. 1662–3). The opportunity – the necessity, of course – to confess before receiving Final Communion and Last Rites was a cultural arena with great weight and significance in the late medieval period, but particularly vexed in the late fourteenth century when the decreasing number of available clergy led to an increase in attention to the importance of lay preparation for the moment of death. A moral layman would be prepared to "assoil" himself; a rich man like January should be able to employ a chantry priest and a confessor.[35]

In twisting the knife further, Justinus uses the major term of warning – "Dispeire yow noght" (1669) – that signals in the *Ars moriendi* tradition the most dangerous state in which to die. He then immediately echoes a cherished convention of the deathbed scene in the late medieval period, namely, that the more you suffered in life, and particularly in your dying, the faster your movement through Purgatory would be: "Peraunter she may be youre purgatorie! / She may be Goddes meene and Goddes whippe" (IV. 1670–1).[36] Indeed, the exasperation to which January's monologue drives Justinus signals for readers Chaucer's serious concern, escalating throughout the tale, for the consequences of January's neglect of his own mortality. As an old man who

---

[34] The word "rite" here clearly squints at both marriage and last rites, but the point I am making is that Justinus makes one more (vain) attempt to direct January toward mortality over marriage.

[35] Especially pertinent is Vincent Gillespie's point in "Vernacular Books of Religion," in *Book Production and Publishing in Britain 1375–1475*, ed. Jeremy Griffiths and Derek Pearsall (Cambridge: Cambridge University Press, 1989), 325, that the late medieval lay appropriation of penitential texts as spurs to *contemptus mundi* and "encouragement to self-knowledge and self-assessment." See also Amy Appleford, *Learning to Die in London, 1380–1540* (Philadelphia: University of Pennsylvania Press, 2014), an excellent granular account of the deep penetration of death preparation texts into lay civic self-understanding. Nicholas Watson, "Chaucer's Public Christianity," *Religion & literature* 37.2 (2005), 99–114, develops the broader problem of whether a person's ignorance was a barrier to their salvation. See James R. Goldstein, "Future Perfect: The Augustinian Theology of Perfection and the Canterbury Tales," *Studies in the Age of Chaucer* 29.1 (2007), 87–140, for a response.

[36] This line is, of course, the exact line the Wife of Bath herself uses in the passage in which she, in a moment either of passing guilt or glib irony, describes herself as a "purgatorie" to her fourth, deceased husband (III. 496–500), part of the "phantom debate" that Tison Pugh identifies in "Gender, Vulgarity, and the Phantom Debates of Chaucer's *Merchant's Tale*," *Studies in Philology* 114.3 (2017), 473–96, and a topic that has vexed critics since Walter Skeat. For my part, the whiff of death discourse that hovers over this intertextual exchange sharpens up the stakes of January's caustic remark, by highlighting how both characters (Wife, January) fundamentally misconceive the work of death.

married a young woman to engender an heir, he has already violated a crucial principle of penitential discourse, which is to turn away from one's investment in continuity. The echoes of the discourse of death preparation here remind the reader of a deeper moral failing: that January's misunderstanding of the rhetoric of marriage as a heaven is sign of his dangerous lack of attention to "final things." Chaucer's language evokes this subtle interweaving of two strands of rhetoric that deepen the tale's larger consideration of sexual desire, blindness (literal and figurative), and deceit (including self-deceit).

Justinus cinches his point with our third image of the soul in flight, the wording of which suggests how a smart man might signal his subtle distaste for these false images of transcendence: "Thanne shal youre soule up to hevene *skippe* / Swifter than dooth an arwe out of a bowe" (IV. 1673). The soul "skipping" to heaven is meant, sarcastically, to undermine the childish view of the iconography that sees the soul moving to heaven too easily, without the labor and struggle that had come to define post-mortem iconography. This kind of reductive quip is a "nyfle" one tells a child or an ignorant peasant, not a full-grown adult entering his life's last stage. The second part of the image, marking time with the swift flight of an arrow from a bow, is likely borrowed from Dante, figuring an instantaneous arrival that suggests simultaneously the menacing subtext of death's arrow or spear. Dante uses the arrow image to describe Phlegyas and Geryon in the *Inferno*, and in both cases the emphasis is speed.[37] In this context, that would be a further ironic re-writing of January's cognitive state: he seeks an instantaneous gratification, which the bow image superficially affirms, even as it re-directs the reader's attention to the ironic inversion of his goal (he will suffer for whatever worldly pleasure he vainly pursues). In addition to this possible allusion to Dante, the image occurs in the context of two references to the Wife of Bath: one a citation

---

[37] See Dante, *Inf.* VIII, 13–16 (1970), describing the movement of the boat of Phlegyas: "Corda non pinse mai da sé saetta / che sì corresse via per l'aere snella, / com' io vidi una nave piccioletta / venir per l'acqua verso noi in quella" ("A bowstring never sent an arrow flying / Through the air as swiftly as the little boat I saw / come across the water at us in an instant"). But see also *Inf.* XVII, 136, where Geryon, in the circle of Fraud is (multiply) described, sitting on a boundary, then flying, before leaving suddenly: "si dileguò come da corda cocca" ("he vanished like an arrow from a bow"). Ronald Martinez, in Dante Alighieri, *Inferno* (Oxford: Oxford University Press, 1996), 273, notes that this image is used frequently in thirteenth-century writing on physics, and cites Aquinas, *Summa theol.* 1a, q. 1, a.2: "Thus an arrow directs itself to its determined end because it is set in motion by the bowman, who directs his action to an end." If this sub-text is in Chaucer's mind, it is ironized due to January's disorganized mind. See also Dante, *Par.* XVII (1970), where Dante seeks Beatrice's counsel on his future misfortune, hoping that deeper understanding will slow down sudden arrival: "ché saetta previsa vien più lenta" ("the arrow one sees ahead of time arrives more slowly"; *Par.* XVII, 27).

of the Wife's line about subjecting her fourth husband to a "purgatorie" (III. 489), and the other Justinus's inexplicable reference to the Wife of Bath as an authority on marriage (IV. 1685–7). This dense network of intra- and inter-textual allusions, two of which use the language of Purgatory,[38] teach the reader to think "across" the *Canterbury Tales* project about the moral and ethical stakes of our images of death, dying, and the Afterlife. This rhetorical image of a soul flying at great speed to Heaven looks back to the Friar's and forward to Maximus's vision as an agent of conversion. Justinus's image thus poses the obverse problem of the Friar's: its explicit artificiality as image is the construct of a rhetorician deceiving his audience, but also evidence that an audience who is ineducable will never be able to discern the difference between rhetoric and reality. Literary reading and civic life depend on parsing this distinction.

When we return to Maximus's vision in the *Second Nun's Tale*, conditioned by re-reading these prior images, we see how much language matters, especially in a poem where language is shaped into the forms of polished poetic style. Chaucer alters his sources here in subtle ways to craft lines that reflect the deep interpenetration of word and image, as he exploits the full resources of his poetry to maximize the cognitive impact of the image. Chaucer's account of Cecilia is largely a "faithful" translation of a Franciscan abridgement of a very old Latin hagiographical text, and close study has shown he probably had access to two separate abridgements, and connected them himself.[39] In this image, however, he makes a telling translation decision that focalizes our attention on Maximus's mediating role, and complicates any direct narrative of his vision. The passage clarifies that the "conversion" he produces comes from a two-stage process of *seeing* and then *reporting*:

> This Maximus, that *saugh* this thyng bityde,
> With pitous teeris *tolde* it anonright,
> That he hir soules *saugh* to heven glyde
> With aungels ful of cleernesse and of light,
> And *with this word converted* many a wighte (VIII. 400–4;
> my italics)

---

[38] See Matsuda, "Death, Prudence," 319.

[39] See Sherry Reames, "The Second Nun's Prologue and Tale," in *Sources and Analogues of the Canterbury Tales*, ed. Robert M. Correale with Mary Hamel (Cambridge: D.S. Brewer, 2002), 491–527 (at 494–6). Lynn Staley, "Postures of Sanctity," in *The Powers of the Holy: Religion, Politics, and Gender in Late Medieval English Culture*, ed. David Aers and Lynn Staley (University Park: Pennsylvania State University Press, 1996), 179–260, makes the case that Chaucer's version edits the text to focus on the contrast between the early church and Chaucer's present, and to emphasize the "emptiness of imperial systems that locate value in power" (at 207).

The key phrase "with this word" is not in his source, but it is crucial:[40] words are the Chaucerian medium, and they are the matter of the storytelling that allows Maximus to convey to his listeners whatever subjective experience he has had. "With this word" provides narrative agency, and marks the culmination of a movement from vision to narration to conversion. He uses repetition of the word "saugh" both to link, and differentiate, two acts of vision that otherwise might escape observation: Maximus sees the execution (an event in the visible world), and starts to tell the story, which then requires him to narrate seeing the souls (an event visible only to him). Further, Chaucer arranges the object (hir soules) of the verb "saughe" to create a metrical effect that is re-enforced by word painting in the line. "Saugh" comes at the center of the line in this arrangement, marking its caesura and ensuring a consistent iambic line (That hé hir soúles *saúgh* to heven glyde; my italics). The consonantal elision of "soules saugh" has the effect of merging his sight with the souls at the phonic level, poetically suggesting the rapturous effect of this spiritual vision. In interlocking phrases that balance seeing and telling, Chaucer pivots back and forth from vision to narration to model the process of "conversion" with verbs in the third stress position (saugh, tolde, saugh, converted): the only way Maximus can share his subjective experience of a new spiritual reality is to tell the story, which returns to a visual image told in words.[41] Though these poetic master-stokes do not (necessarily) sow doubt as to the content of the experience, Chaucer's version stresses that the power of conversion is the power of image transmission: "aungels ful of cleernesse and of light" do not convert "many wight"; *Maximus* does so as a verbal mediator of the visionary image. As instrument of conversion, the "word" does not reproduce inner experience, but produces social exchange and discourse, including the ability to read fully – to read closely – its poetic performance. Chaucer's per-form-ance in this five-line sequence masterfully highlights the concepts of the passage in a mimesis that also underscores the poet as a mediator:

[40] The *Legenda* text insists on the truth-value of his claim through his assev-eration in an oath (Latin: *cum iuramento asseruit*; Reames, "The Second Nun's," 513), while the Franciscan abridgment of the story (*In festo Sancte Ceilie virginis et martyris*) reports it in primary narration with a focus on his emotional state, as would befit the "liturgical" use of this text, which quotes a person recounting a first-person vision: "Then with tears Maximus said [*cum lacrimis narrante Maximo*], '*I saw* shining [*fulgentes*] angels of God carry their souls to heaven,' and many believed [*crediderunt*]," in Reames, "The Second Nun's," 523.

[41] Little, "Images, Texts," 120, makes a similar observation about the shared "inter-pretive function" of revelation in this moment. The sense of agency in the tale, and the sensory and cognitive abilities that flow from it, is powerfully elucidated by Elizabeth Robertson, "Apprehending the Divine and Choosing to Believe: Voluntarist Free Will in Chaucer's *Second Nun's Tale*," *Chaucer Review* 46.1–2 (2011), 111–30, in the context of voluntarist free will as a necessary adjunct to the conversion.

Chaucer's conspicuous artistry draws attention to poetic craft, the mediating structure of significance produced through the matter – sound, especially – of language. The vision is only as compelling, only as authentic, as the form in which it is conveyed. Maximus's vision is authenticated, but we have no better way of corroborating his vision than we do Friar John's: they are both mediated, after all, by human language, and only a secondary value judgment can determine their ethical import.

Chaucer worried, habitually, about the misuse of emotional images, and the culture of death of his period threw up a great variety of them, stimulating people to intense and dangerous feelings (of fear, of hatred of the body). This chastened penitential fear in death discourse can be channeled into irrational forms in any cultural moment, with disastrous consequences. Throughout his corpus and across his career, Chaucer appears skeptical of this cultural change, though perhaps partly because of a suspicion – not exactly monastic at its root – that the content of the images themselves played a highly prejudicial role in cultivating an unmanageable anxiety. To the extent that clerical institutions affirmatively mediate the needs of communities they serve – and here Maximus is a more positive clerical stand-in set against the Summoner's Friar – these images are fictions that, like literature, can foster growth. To the extent, however, that they are *mere* rhetoric, tools of deception of others or of the self, they are corrupt or salvific on a scale determined by an ethical analysis of the speaker, not the image itself. These images also provide an expanded gloss on a key moment, much commented upon by critics, where the soul in flight is *missing*: the death of Arcite in the Knight's tale. Presented with the opportunity to authenticate his narrative through a visionary moment, available in his source,[42] the Knight disclaims knowledge of where Arcite's soul went when "his spirit chaunged house" (I. 2809). In doing so, Chaucer marks a boundary, both spiritual ("I nam no divinistre," I. 2811) and textual ("Of soules fynde I nat in this registre," I. 2812), which suggests a profound discomfort with describing this post-mortem space.[43] The rhyme here, with its clash of concepts, does powerful work in refusing either to textualize the sacred or sacralize the textual. Both moves would be inauthentic.

Chaucer makes us wary of visions that rely on narrative authentication strategies that threaten to falsify, or simply to overwhelm, our emotional

---

[42] The moment is an exemplary instance of Chaucer's creative, and aggressive response to his sources: two different Boccaccio texts are violated in the course of this "translation": both *Il Teseida*, in which Arcite's "end" is edited out, and *Il Filostrato*, where Troilus's "end" is re-directed by including the soul in flight motif.

[43] I wholeheartedly endorse D. Vance Smith's recent claim, in *Arts of Dying: Literature and Finitude in Medieval England* (Chicago: Chicago University Press, 2020), that "this moment, in fact, signals the poem's general discomfort with talking about the state of death" (107).

experience, as well as to mislead us in ways that make us more susceptible to the visions, or depredations, of others. Chaucer focuses attention in these images of the soul in flight on the danger of those who repress that knowledge – like January – or who abuse the grief of others by re-directing it to an inauthentic vision of bliss motivated by greed – like Friar John. And through that reflection, Chaucer reminds us that skeptical reading makes us vigilant, less inclined to yield to the visions of heavenly bliss sold by the merchants of death, when our experiences of grief, of life in this mortal coil, are real enough. Language matters, and so does reading: the how and why of it, its strange circuitry and recursion, as well as its capacity to befuddle and liberate, illuminate and confuse. If the core of Chaucer's poetic vision is a meditation on, in Taylor's phrase, the "strictures of experience unfolding in time before death,"[44] and I think it is, then we are ethically responsible for the stories we tell one another about that time. Whether our souls glide or skip to heaven, are born to bliss, or whether they exist at all, we are responsible for the stories that testify to our shared mortality, our impending deaths, and our authentic hopes and fears about the deaths of those whom we love.

[44] Taylor, *Chaucer Reads*, 203.

PART V

LANGUAGE BETWEEN TEXTS: INTERTEXTUALITY ON THE LEVEL OF LANGUAGE

9

Treason and the Royal Person: Chaucer to John Lane

ANDREEA BOBOC

Treason seems a strange offering for a mentor's *Festschrift*. Allowances might be made, however, when the focus is on John Lane, a poet who, more than two hundred years after the completion of the *Canterbury Tales*, breathes life into a tale Chaucer left unfinished, a tale in which a royal heroine counters treason with prudence. Given Karla Taylor's own attention to "Prudence's hard-fought battle to deter Melibee from revenge on his enemies, by propounding a new vocabulary of public life,"[1] and our stimulating conversations about law and literature, this essay hopes to qualify as a loyal tribute.

John Lane completed his continuation of Chaucer's *Squire's Tale* c. 1615 and revised it in 1630. Its two versions exist in the Bodleian Library in Douce MS 170 and Ashmole MS 53, respectively, and have been collated and edited by Frederick Furnivall.[2] Lane continues Chaucer's tale by drawing on medieval discourses of prudence as put forth by the *Tale of Melibee*. Prudence informs the feminine governance embodied by Canace, John Lane's heroine, who reassembles a royal personhood fractured by treason and war. Through her unfailing love and prudence, Canace turns treason into an opportunity for the enthroned king to practice wise governance and consolidate his royal person.

Precious little has been written about John Lane, but he seems to have been invested in female leadership.[3] His poem, "An Elegie vpon the Death of the

---

[1] Karla Taylor, "Social Aesthetics and the Emergence of Civic Discourse from the *Shipman's Tale* to *Melibee*," *Chaucer Review* 39.3 (2005), 298–322 (at 311).

[2] *John Lane's Continuation of Chaucer's Squire's Tale*, ed. Frederick. J. Furnivall, with notes by W.A. Clouston (London: Kegan Paul, Trench, Trübner and Co. Ltd, 1888–90).

[3] Sidney Lee informs us that Lane "lived on terms of intimacy with Milton's father," and that he was "personally known to Milton's nephew, Edward Phillips, who

high and renowned Princesse our late Soueraigne Elizabeth," written in 1603, conveys his admiration for Elizabeth I. Lane's continuation of the *Squire's Tale* is a nostalgic revisiting of that glorious period of female leadership, whereby the most prudent and pacifist character is the king's daughter, Canace, a Stuart development of Lady Prudence, who in the *Tale of Melibee* brokered peace between her husband and his treasonous enemies. This essay investigates how the legal personhood of the queen-to-be, Canace, is informed by prudence and love in dealing with traitorous relatives. To this end, I am drawing on the formal changes in the law of treason (statutory and judicial, medieval to early modern) and on the trial transcripts of Guy Fawkes and his co-conspirators after their failed Gunpowder Plot (1605).

The plot of Lane's tale is rather convoluted. Cambuscan, the king, promises the hand of his daughter, Canace, and kingdom to a knight able to vanquish everyone else in a joust. Apart from Canace, Cambuscan has two sons – his first-born, Algarsif, is rapidly acquiring a bad reputation, so much so that Cambuscan considers disinheriting him; by contrast, his second son, Camballo, is careful and wise. The king is seeking to marry off his children all at once, but Algarsif is revolted that Canace will get the lands to which he feels entitled according to the law of primogeniture.

Under the nefarious influence of the witch Vidrea, Algarsif takes revenge against the king by drumming up an army and taking the city Fregilia from which he intends to defeat the royal troops. Only Canace is aware that her brother Algarsif operates under Vidrea's black magic – her father and especially her mother, Queen Ethelta, are incensed with Algarsif and vow that all traitors will be punished. Ethelta even demands his death. A civil war ensues, in which Cambuscan, Camballo, and the loyalist troops fight against Algarsif, his rebel troops, and Vidrea's dark magic.

After several battles and numerous turns of fortune, the royalists win, and the traitors are defeated. Under Canace's guidance, Alfgarsif repents and is ultimately pardoned by his parents. To prove his good intentions, Algarsif defeats the giant Horbello to save the realm. The remaining traitors are either punished or commit suicide out of guilt.

This essay is divided into three sections: a contextual assessment of how semantic changes in the law of treason from medieval to Stuart times might have informed Lane's creation; a psychological portrait of the Stuart traitor as a seduced young man by the example of the rebellious but repentant Algarsif; and a discussion of Canace, the heroine of the poem, as an *exemplum* of a Stuart Lady Prudence with roots in the Chaucerian tradition. I conclude with some thoughts on what Lane's poem offers to the semantics of early modern treason.

---

was born in 1630." See *Dictionary of National Biography*: https://en.wikisource.org/wiki/Dictionary_of_National_Biography,_1885-1900/Lane,_John_(fl.1620) (accessed 9 July 2022).

Treason and the Stuart Royal Person

About the aesthetic merits of Lane's continuation little complimentary has been said. To be sure, Lane found a staunch defender in Edward Phillips, who describes him as:

> ... a fine old Queen Elizabeth gentleman ... whose several poems, had they not had the ill fate to remain unpublisht, – when much better meriting than many that are in print, – might possibly have gain'd him a name not much inferiour, if not equal, to *Drayton*, and others of the next rank to *Spencer*.[4]

Yet Furnivall calls Lane's continuation "miserable," with "frightful word-coinages" that necessitate a glossary,[5] while Sidney Lee deplores Lane's "attempts [at] an archaic style and ... many pseudo-archaisms."[6] This perspective brightens, however, when we shift our interpretive focus from the aesthetic to the legal because Lane's continuation provides fascinating insight into how royal personhood, initially ruptured by discourses of treason and absolutism, is then repaired by Chaucerian discourses of prudence.

In *The History of English Law*, Pollock and Maitland observe that "treason is a crime which has a vague circumference, and more than one centre."[7] From medieval to Stuart England there are significant shifts in the law of treason as its circumference expands and its number of centers increase. These shifts correspond to discursive changes as more expressions of treason are criminalized during the early modern age.

Initially, medieval treason – whether petty or high – was a violation of trust between two people. During the reign of Edward I, armed group resistance to the king began to count as treason, rather than mere personal resistance.[8] Later, petty treason, perpetrated by a wife against her husband, a clergyman against his prelate, or a servant against his lord, was differentiated sharply from high treason perpetrated against the king. From 1351, the circumference of treason (and correspondingly, of treason's semantic field) increases to include the death of the queen and the crown prince and the killing of the king's chancellor, treasurer, or judges in the execution of their duty.[9] Congruently,

---

[4] *John Lane's Continuation of Chaucer's Squire's Tale*, x.

[5] *John Lane's Continuation of Chaucer's Squire's Tale*, xii and xv.

[6] Lee, in *Dictionary of National Biography*.

[7] Frederick Pollock and Frederic W. Maitland, *The History of English Law before the time of Edward I*, 2nd ed., vol. 1 (Cambridge: Cambridge University Press, 1968), 503.

[8] Arnold Blumberg, "Drawn and Quartered: The Law of Treason in Medieval England," *Medieval Warfare* 5.2 (2015), 49–52 (at 49).

[9] Treason Act 1351 c. 2 (Regnal. 25_Edw_3_Stat_5): https://www.legislation.gov.uk/aep/Edw3Stat5/25/2/section/II (accessed 26 July 2022).

the legal personhood of the sovereign expands to include these persons in addition to the person of the king. Finally, there is a further expansion in the circumference of the semantic field of treason: as we move into early modern and Stuart England, treason shifts from a crime against the monarch to a crime against the state.[10] Once treason becomes an affair of state, the monarch and the people of the realm become bound together in a corporate *persona ficta*, a new legal understanding of royal personhood. "Treason" thus comes to gather both personal (betrayal) and political (sedition) terms in ways that increasingly conflate individual desire and corporate harm. As we shall see later, magic and witchcraft also become part of the semantic field of treason.

In his continuation to the *Squire's Tale*, John Lane grapples with the consequences of these semantic shifts in the law of treason when he makes the traitorous crown prince Algarsif break asunder the legal person of the sovereign and Canace, the king's daughter and deputy, put it back together. To repair the legal person, Lane draws on medieval discourses of love and prudence in ways that directly challenge early modern discourses of treason. When she saves her kingdom by healing the wounds caused by treason and by forgiving those lead astray by witchcraft, Canace provides a Stuart exemplar of a feminine royal person defined by clemency and prudence with roots in the Chaucerian tradition. Once Algarsif is forgiven, he earns back his place into the royal personhood by defeating a giant and protecting the realm.

Just as treason has more than one center, so too has royal personhood in John Lane's continuation of Chaucer's *Squire's Tale*. Treason in John Lane's continuation starts out as personal betrayal when the crown prince, Algarsif, opposes the king, but soon expands into a crime against the realm when Algarsif causes sedition and infighting, pitting brother against brother and father against son. In so doing, Lane reminds his audience of James I's acrimonious conflicts with his subjects, particularly with the House of Commons.[11]

Some of James's subjects would have experienced these conflicts as a personal betrayal. James's authoritarian views of kingship, expounded in his 1598 work, *The True Law of Free Monarchies*, and his 1599 *Basilikon Doron*, were at odds with the English tradition of mixed government, according to

---

[10] D. Alan Orr, *Treason and the State: Law, Politics and Ideology in the English Civil War* (Cambridge: Cambridge University Press, 2007). I am arguing here for an expansion of treason, rather than a transition from a personal crime against the monarch to an impersonal crime against the state – Orr's argument – because the 1351 statute of treason was never repealed, though it has been changed to reflect present times. For instance, as the law of primogeniture has been updated to include women, the Treason Act 1351 has too been updated to protect the monarch's eldest child rather than the monarch's eldest son (under the Succession to the Crown Act 2013): https://www.legislation.gov.uk/ukpga/2013/20/schedule/enacted (accessed 27 July 2022).

[11] Thomas Cogswell, *James I: The Phoenix King* (New York: Penguin, 2017).

which power was shared among the monarch, the House of Lords, and the House of Commons. As Elizabeth Allen reminds us, "the feudal bond at the heart of English kingship entails a reciprocalist legal idea of treason as a personal betrayal across hierarchy: either the lord or the subject can betray the feudal bond."[12] Consequently, some of James's subjects must have loathed being reminded that:

> ... the kings were the authors and the makers of the laws, and not the laws of the kings ... To dispute what God may do is blasphemy ... so it is sedition [treason] in subjects to dispute what a king may do. ... The king is above the law, as both author and giver of the strength thereto, yet a good king will not only delight to rule his subjects by the law, but even conform his own actions thereunto. ... Yet he is not bound thereto but of his good will, and for good example giving to his subjects.[13]

By placing his self-interest above the interests of his subjects, James creates disharmony within the realm and disrupts his corporate royal personhood, which includes the state and implicitly his subjects, in the name of whom the early modern state is formed. In contrast, Lane's fictional king, Cambuscan, is deeply invested in a royal personhood that encompasses a peaceful realm: he is "sorrowfull for Fregiley, his [seditious] towne" (Pt. III, l. 397), and pities both the state of his daughter (who is duly distressed at her brother's treason) and the state of the realm torn asunder by civil war: "hee, pittienge her state and the common state" (Pt. III, l. 399).

Like Elizabeth before him, James summoned his Parliament to deal with specific business and then dismissed it, occasionally dissolving it (in 1614 and 1621), when "he felt it was encroaching on his royal prerogative."[14] But while Elizabeth couched her disagreements in the language of love by presenting herself first as a bride and then as a mother to the nation, "James's fondness for lecturing his subjects at length in rambling speeches on constitutional theory was not something they shared and it often provoked them to deliver indignant replies."[15] Thomas Howard, the 1st Earl of Suffolk, wrote in 1611 that Elizabeth "talk[ed] of her subjects' love and good affection," while James

---

[12] Elizabeth Allen, *Uncertain Refuge: Sanctuary in the Literature of Medieval England* (Philadelphia: University of Pennsylvania Press, 2021), 121.

[13] James VI, *The True Law of Free Monarchies* (1598), cited in Angus Stroud, *Stuart England* (London and New York: Routledge, 1999), 27.

[14] Stroud, *Stuart England*, 29.

[15] Stroud, *Stuart England*, 29. Some indignant replies are listed on 28. For Elizabeth I's language of love as a language of politics see, for instance, her "Golden Speech": https://www.nationalarchives.gov.uk/education/resources/elizabeth-monarchy/the-golden-speech/https://www.nationalarchives.gov.uk/education/resources/elizabeth-monarchy/the-golden-speech/.

"talketh of his subjects' fear and subjection."[16] Perhaps one of these indignant subjects was Lane himself because, as we shall see below, his Canace deploys a political language of prudence and love in a nostalgic adaptation of Chaucer.

The idea of mutual affection between a king and his subjects, in which the king's clemency and the subjects' obedience must needs reside, did not originate with Elizabeth I; it was an Edwardian idea (1 Edward VI c. 12).[17] Edward VI was at pains to repeal the many definitions of treason of the "verie streighte, extreme, and terrible" King Henry VIII,[18] under whose rule high treason found its greatest circumference, and formulate penalties for treason in more moderate terms. Though Edward's Treason Act from 1457 was replaced by Mary I's in 1553, its core component, the 1351 Statute of Treason, has never been repealed and so its formulation about "compass[ing] or imagin[ing] the death" of the sovereign lives on. It is precisely this formulation that focuses our attention on the next center within the semantic field of treason in James I's reign and Lane's creation: witchcraft.

James I's concerns about witchcraft grew after the 1590 plots to kill him through magical means (the so-called North Berwick affair). P.G. Maxwell-Stuart describes the situation as follows:

> … there came to light four separate plots to injure or kill the king by magic. One was to raise a storm while he was at sea on his way to Denmark; a second involved a magical consecration of a picture of the King; a third centered on a wax image of James, consecrated after a similar fashion; and the fourth involved expressing venom from a toad, mixing it with other noxious substances, and placing it over or under a doorway through which the King was sure to pass quite frequently.[19]

That James took seriously the power of magic to harm him and his bride, Anne of Denmark, is evidenced by his reaction to the verdict reached by an assize in the trial of Barbara Napier, who was accused of attempting to sink the royal ships.[20] Napier was the only principal in the Berwick trial who escaped burning, and perhaps punishment altogether, since there is no record of her

---

[16] *The Norton Anthology of English Literature*, ed. Stephen Greenblatt, Katharine Eisaman Maus, and George Logan, 10th ed., vol. 2 (New York and London: Norton & Company, 2018), 892.

[17] See https://archive.org/details/statutesatlarge00raitgoog/page/490/mode/2up (accessed 27 July 2022).

[18] John Bellamy, *The Tudor Law of Treason* (London: Routledge and Kegan Paul, 2013 [1979]), 48.

[19] P.G. Maxwell-Stuart, "King James's Experience of Witches and the 1604 English Witchcraft Act," in *Witchcraft and the Act of 1604*, ed. John Newton and Jo Bath (Leiden: Brill, 2008), 29–46 (at 34).

[20] See *The Survey of Scottish Witchcraft Database*: http://witches.shca.ed.ac.

execution. Her political connections helped her to get convicted of the lesser charge of consulting with witches, but not of treason, a capital crime.[21] The king was so infuriated by the verdict that he put the original jury on trial on the charge of acquitting a witch.[22]

Barbara Napier's case is compelling because she was accused of performing white magic, a respectable variety of medieval sorcery since it involved understanding and taking advantage of natural phenomena. By the middle of the thirteenth century, William of Auvergne had conceptualized natural magic as part of natural science.[23] And Richard Kieckhefer reminds us that "educated clerics thought of magic as a rational activity."[24] One of them, Thomas Aquinas, took this line of thinking a step further by arguing that "if something followed 'right reason' it meant that it was for the common good, and anything for the common good therefore agreed with natural law."[25]

Before the publication of *Malleus Maleficarum* in 1487, medieval clerics might not have even taken black magic (witchcraft) all that seriously. The canon *Episcopi*, first recorded in the tenth century and included in Gratian's *Corpus Iuri Canonici*, a foundational canon law text for the Middle Ages, taught that night-flying and shapeshifting were illusions, mere "phantasmata, that is, images impressed on the mind but without physical reality," and that those who believed in such things were not true believers in Christ.[26]

This is not, however, the view James I takes in his *Demonology*, in which only one kind of magic exists – black – and all sorcery becomes "treason against God."[27] Donald Tyson argues that James's book "arose as a direct visceral reaction to the North Berwick trials and the supposed plots against his life by magic."[28] At the same time, James I might also have viewed witchcraft as an excuse for absolutism, since it allowed him to undercut the affective unity of royal personhood and concentrate it in his own person. When

---

uk/index.cfm?fuseaction=home.caserecord&caseref=C%2FEGD%2F103&search_type=searchaccused&search_string=lastname (accessed 27 July 2022).

[21] Donald Tyson, ed., *The Demonology of King James I* (Woodbury: Llewellyn Publications, 2011), 209.

[22] Tyson, *The Demonology of King James I*, 210.

[23] Guillelmus Alvernus, *De Universo*, i.l.43, in *Opera omnia*, 1 (1674; repr. ed., Frankfurt am Main, 1963), 648 ("in ea parte naturalis scientiae, quae vocatur magica naturalis"). Cited in Richard Kieckhefer, "The Specific Rationality of Medieval Magic," *American Historical Review* 99.3 (1994), 813–36 (at 819).

[24] Kieckhefer, "The Specific Rationality of Medieval Magic," 832.

[25] Diana Wood, *Medieval Economic Thought* (Cambridge: Cambridge University Press), 22.

[26] Robert Bartlett, *The Natural and the Supernatural in the Middle Ages* (Cambridge: Cambridge University Press, 2008), 80–1.

[27] Tyson, *The Demonology of King James I*, 180.

[28] Tyson, *The Demonology of King James I*, 6.

he ascended the English throne, he had escaped several treasonous attempts on his life perpetrated with the aid of black magic. It was in James's interest to present himself as a Christian knight wreaking vengeance upon the devil, who, according to one of the Berwick witches, regarded James as "the greatest enemy he hath in the world."[29]

The passing of the Witchcraft Act in 1604, shortly after James ascended the throne, made it a felony punishable with death to practice "witchcrafte, inchantment, charme, or sorcerie"; such felons could not apply for sanctuary or benefit of the clergy.[30] There is, however, little evidence that the Act prompted James to increase the persecution of witches: "Indeed, we can actually see the King leaning towards the opinion that several cases brought into court were impostures rather than genuine instances of witchcraft."[31] Perhaps James hoped that his uncompromising anti-magic stance would be shrewd politics and divert attention from his homosexuality, favoritism – he was in the habit of promoting young men for "no other reason ... but handsomeness" – and profligacy, which would plunge England deeper into debt.[32]

True to its early modern context, dark magic in John Lane's continuation of the *Squire's Tale* belongs to the semantic field of treason and imperils royal personhood. Only by casting back to the Middle Ages is Lane able to deploy a more nuanced understanding of magic, whereby intention is what sets good (white) magic apart from bad (dark). In his continuation, Lane is careful to differentiate between the two kinds of magic: while Algarsif, under the destructive spells of the wicked witch, Vidrea, starts a self-serving war, commits treason, and dismantles the royal personhood, his sister Canace deploys several white magic accoutrements (a mirror, a ring, a brass horse) to restore peace to the realm and repair the royal person.

Algarsif: A Portrait of the Traitor as a Seduced Young Man

It is essential to contextualize Lane's plot by relating it to two discursive traditions: moral and psychological discourses that carry forward from Chaucer through Elizabeth I and legal discourses from the documentary context of treason laws and James I's own writings on dark magic.

By reading Lane's continuation of Chaucer's *Squire's Tale* against *The Trials of Guy Fawkes* and his co-conspirators, one gains an appreciation for the psychology of the young traitor, Algarsif, as a victim of Vidrea's seduction – the political act of leading someone astray to such a degree that they commit

---

[29] Tyson, *The Demonology of King James I*, 4.

[30] See https://encyclopediavirginia.org/entries/an-acte-against-conjuration-witch-crafte-and-dealing-with-evill-and-wicked-spirits-1604/ (accessed 27 July 2022).

[31] Maxwell-Stuart, "King James's Experience of Witches," 45.

[32] Francis Osborne, *Traditional Memoirs*, quoted in Stroud, *Stuart England*, 34–5.

treason. Seduction acts as a mitigating circumstance by turning Algarsif into an auxiliary to the crime of treason, not a principal. To be sure, the law did not recognize accessories to treason: "Those who participated actively in a traitorous plot were principals."[33] This is, in effect, Queen Ethelta's reaction when Canace argues Algarsif was seduced and therefore deserves forgiveness: by his exercise of reason, Algarsif knew he involved himself in betraying his parents and his country; therefore, there can be no reconciliation with him (Pt. IV, ll. 204–10).

This absolutist view of the traitor as fully culpable is challenged by the trials of Guy Fawkes and his co-conspirators and Lane's continuation of Chaucer's *Squire's Tale*. While we have no evidence that Lane drew on these trial transcripts when he composed his poem, the "Powder Treason" and subsequent trials were shocking enough to the English imaginary that they would likely have been dissected for many years afterwards by the intellectual elite of the day to which Lane belonged given his close association with Milton's family. Indeed, so scandalous was the Gunpowder Plot that it received its own calendar date, 5 November, commemorated as deliverance from treason by an act of Parliament in 1606 (today's "Bonfire Night" or "Guy Fawkes's Day").[34]

Both Lane's poem and contemporaneous trial transcripts seek to offer seduction as a motivation for treason perpetrated by the seduced (and implicitly, less culpable) traitor. This reasoning introduces a separation of principal offenders (the seducers) from auxiliaries (the seduced) in a manner foreign to the contemporary law of treason. I shall discuss below Canace's defense of her brother Algarsif on the basis of the temptations of magic. But turning first to the trial transcripts, one finds that seduction figures prominently among the conspirators' motives for treason. In the findings of the prosecutors, the principal offenders are separated from the auxiliaries:

> For the Persons offending, or by whom, they are of two sorts; either of the Clergy, or Laity: and for each of them there is a several Objection made. Touching those of the Laity, it is by some given out, that they are such Men, as admit just Exception, either desperate in Estate, or base, or not settled in their Wits; such as are *Sine Religione, Sine Sede, Sine Fide, Sine Re, & Sine Spe*; without Religion, without Habitation, without Credit, without Means, without Hope. But (that no Man, tho' never so wicked, may be wronged) true it is, **they were Gentlemen of good Houses, of excellent Parts, howsoever most perniciously seduced, abused, corrupted, and jesuited, of very competent Fortunes and States**. ... For I never yet

---

[33] J.H. Baker, *An Introduction to English Legal History*, 4th ed. (London: Butterworths, 2002), 528.

[34] Philip Williamson and Natalie Mears, "James I and Gunpowder Treason Day," *The Historical Journal* 64.2 (2021), 185–210.

knew a Treason without a Romish Priest; but in this there are very many Jesuits, who are known to have dealt and passed thro' the whole Action ... **So that the principal Offenders are the seducing Jesuits; Men that use the Reverence of Religion, yea, even the most sacred and blessed Name of Jesus, as a Mantle to cover their Impiety, Blasphemy, Treason and Rebellion, and all manner of Wickedness;** (emphasis mine)[35]

Moreover, when some of the co-conspirators defend their motives and ask for mercy, they also talk in their mitigation pleas about their love and friendship towards someone who had embroiled them in the treasonous plot. Ambrose Rookwood, for instance, would have never committed treason were it not for his love of his friend, Mr. Catesby:

But *Ambrose Rookwood* first excused his denial of the Indictment, for that he had rather lose his Life than give it. Then did he acknowledge his Offence to be so heinous, that he justly deserved the Indignation of the King, and of the Lords, and the Hatred of the whole Commonwealth; yet could he not despair of Mercy at the Hands of a Prince, so abounding in Grace and Mercy: **And the rather, because his Offence, tho' it were incapable of any Excuse, yet not altogether incapable of some Extenuation, in that he had been neither Author nor Actor, but only persuaded and drawn in by** *Catesby*, **whom he loved above any worldly Man: And that he had concealed it not for any Malice to the Person of the King, or to the State, or for any ambitious Respect of his own, but only drawn with the tender Respect, and the faithful and dear Affection he bare to Mr.** *Catesby* **his Friend, whom he esteem'd dearer than any thing else in the World.** (emphasis mine)

Similarly, Sir Everard Digby found himself drawn into the plot because of the friendship he bore Mr. Catesby:

The first Motive which drew him into this Action, was not Ambition or Discontentment of his Estate, neither Malice to any in Parliament, but the Friendship and Love he bare to *Catesby*, **which prevailed so much, and was so powerful with him, as that for his sake he was ever contented and ready to hazard himself and his Estate.** (emphasis mine)[36]

---

[35] "XIX. *The Trials of* Robert Winter, Thomas Winter, Guy Fawkes, John Grant, Ambrose Rookwood, Robert Keyes, Thomas Bates, *and Sir* Everard Digby, *at* Westminster *for* High-Treason, *being Conspirators in the* Gunpowder-Plot. 27 Jan. 1605. 3 Jac. l.": http://www.armitstead.com/gunpowder/gunpowder_trial.html.

[36] "XIX. *The Trials of* Robert Winter, Thomas Winter, Guy Fawkes, John Grant, Ambrose Rookwood, Robert Keyes, Thomas Bates, *and Sir* Everard Digby, *at* Westminster *for* High-Treason, *being Conspirators in the* Gunpowder-Plot. 27 Jan. 1605. 3 Jac. l.": http://www.armitstead.com/gunpowder/gunpowder_trial.html.

While the trial transcripts seem designed to mitigate the traitors' guilt by showcasing their vulnerability to personal seduction (love of friends), Lane's poem shows how political seduction operates in a young, impressionable man like Algarsif.

Algarsif is a disenchanted young prince who does not have any true friends, and therefore, no strong defense;[37] he is vulnerable to flattery;[38] and he nurses against his father a grudge, which renders him an easy prey for Vidrea (Pt. III, ll. 193–232). His associates are self-interested plotters, forgers, and parasites. The most dangerous of these "fleshe-flies" (Pt. III, l. 243) are the flatterers, who compare him favorably with his father, though, as Lane tells his audience, Algarsif is like his father in shape only; his character is untrue (Pt. III, l. 202).

Surprisingly, his parents are not thinking of bypassing Algarsif in favor of Camballo, his temperate, self-controlled, and witty younger brother. Instead, they plan to pass on the corporate nature of royal personhood (which includes the realm) to Canace and a knight worthy enough to win her in battle, thereby ensuring that the sovereign body and corporate polity are safeguarded both by Canace's wisdom and her future husband's exceptional martial prowess. With this solution in mind, why not sacrifice Algarsif, whose sole contribution to the polity is civil war and the attempted destruction of the royal person?

Eliminating Algarsif would have fissured royal personhood in ways detrimental to its affective and corporate nature, a form of regicide that might have proved unpalatable to Lane's audience. Treason, instead, allowed Lane to imagine a king (Cambuscan) for whom treason was an opportunity to practice wise governance and consolidate his royal person with the help of his prudent and loving daughter, Canace.

Unlike Cambuscan, James I ruthlessly deployed his deliverance from the Gunpowder Treason in the same way he did his escape from the magic of the North Berwick witches: as a sign of divine favor that confirmed his "chosen" status. He "claimed that the Gunpowder Plot's failure should be seen as a God's act of pardoning both him and the entire state of England; this pardon meant that James could subsequently embody the ideal theological-political ruler – and thus the only one truly free of divine intervention – initiating God's apocalyptic reign on earth."[39] Indeed, a mini apocalypse followed. The interrogation and judgment of the traitors was a task James I reserved for his attorney general, the illustrious Edward Coke, who was assisted by the Privy Council. Steve Sheppard notes that "although he [Coke] develops clear

---

[37] Compare *Tale of Melibee*, l. 1161: "a true friend is a strong defense."

[38] Compare *Tale of Melibee*, l. 1175: "you shall also avoid the advice of all flatterers."

[39] Bernadette Meyler, *Theaters of Pardoning* (Ithaca: Cornell University Press, 2019), 84.

evidence of their guilt, he also is, again, unusually cruel."[40] The trial resulted in the hanging, drawing, and quartering of the perpetrators, with the additional spectacle of castrating and disemboweling a fully conscious Everard Digby. By showing no mercy toward the perpetrators, James I aimed to discourage any future treason and legitimize his absolutist ambitions.

Tucked in James I's library, there was, however, another argument for how the royal person might deal with traitors: mercy. The French jurist Jean Bodin (1530–59) made room for mercy when he outlined his theory of sovereignty, on which James I drew when he developed his own theory of the divine rights of kings. The treason against James I had proved a victimless crime; the plot was discovered before anybody was injured physically. There remained, of course, the injury to the royal person. But even in this case, Bodin argues, mercy is the best response of a sovereign: "Of all the graces and pardons that a prince can giue, there is none more commendable, than when he pardoneth the injuries done against his owne person."[41] Mercy is the path taken by Duke Vincentio in Shakespeare's *Measure for Measure*, first performed in 1604 with James I in audience, a play which Bernadette Meyler analyzes as "a dramatic exception."[42]

Similarly, Lane's continuation of the *Squire's Tale* is a poetic exception since mercy is also the path taken by King Cambuscan after the intercession of his daughter, Canace. Showing mercy to traitors becomes an unanticipated way for Cambuscan to strengthen his royal personhood. This exception to strict justice, however, is contingent on providing insight into the psychology of the early modern traitor. Alfgarsif is presented not only as one led astray (seduced) but also as conflicted and honorable, a person who in the end rejoins the right path and the fight for the common good. Although the Gunpower trial transcripts imagine a path to mitigation, they cannot go so far to imagine rehabilitation, in part because of James's brutal response. But rehabilitation is the province of Lane's poem. Cambuscan's pardoning of Algarsif echoes Melibee's reconciliation with his foes, who are ultimately forgiven because of Prudence's intercession.

The audience becomes privy to Algarsif's crisis of conscience when he takes responsibility for his bad decisions and owns his dishonorable behavior. Informed that Cambuscan has come to wreak vengeance on his conspiracy, Algarsif re-becomes his father's son, from being merely the pawn of the witch Vidrea: "For nature, natural, wrought in his blood, / of kindlie kind, to thincke what hee hathe donn / without forgettinge hee's his fathers sonn" (Pt. VII, ll. 32–4).

---

[40] *The Selected Writings of Sir Edward Coke*, ed. Steve Sheppard, vol. 1 (Indianapolis: Liberty Fund, 2003), xliv.

[41] Jean Bodin, *Six Bookes*, 175, cited in Meyler, *Theaters of Pardoning*, 83.

[42] Meyler, *Theaters of Pardoning*, 84 ff.

TREASON AND THE ROYAL PERSON: CHAUCER TO JOHN LANE   205

His examination of conscience takes place when he retires to a secret grove, where he blushes at his own sins (Pt. VII, l. 47); a soliloquy frames his words as sincere remorse:

> "I my owne selfe have my owne selve vndon.
> I have provokd my ffather and my mother;
> I have brought down againste mee my stowt brother;
> and, for my pleasures, vauned my swoord gainste them,
> to th' slaunder of all sonns, and shame of men" (Pt. VII, ll. 48–52)

Distraught, Algarsif weeps and calls on Nature to annihilate him. His shame and distress prove not only his potential for redemption but also Canace's good instincts as a judge of his character: he is merely weak, not bad. He resolves to repent, stop the war, and throw himself on the mercy of his father:

> "I will repent this villanye,
> sithe to repent dothe dissaffect so farr,
> as cause to no cause nature dothe abhorr.
> sighinge, I will submitt mee to my ffather,
> and throwe my iuste death at his foote for favor;
> then, if hee kill mee for m'vntruithes mistake
> perhaps hee'l save his sonn for's ffathers sake
> so stirr no further wars, ne colles promove
> then that his mercie have for subiect loue" (Pt. VII, ll. 70–8)

Algarsif's weakness is again on display when the royalists attack and he vacillates in his resolve. He feels responsible for starting a war and then abandoning his men mid-fight. He realizes that, if he were to give in, he would have to accept either death or exile. (At the end of the poem he is exiled, but not as a traitor; rather, he is married off to a foreign princess whom he follows abroad.) Moreover, Vidrea advises Algarsif to continue the war, reminding him of his father's intention to deny him his land right according to the law of primogeniture. She teaches Algarsif how to falsify the words of his father and persuade his men that they are fighting not for his inheritance but for their freedom from the alleged tyranny of the enthroned king.

Algarsif has a second moment of contrition and shame (he blushes again) when, from the rebel city, Fregiley, he sees his father reconnoitering in preparation for battle:

> Now, when Algarsife his owne ffather sawe,
> some nature strooke his hart throughe with some awe,
> and shame (which in the best blood blussheth ever)
> diverts his eies, and hunge adowne his feather
> caractringe this confession on his will [i.e. stamping it on his
>   will so as to show it]
> "Lo, I, which have requitted good with ill" (Pt. VII, ll. 337–42)

Though he will again vacillate from shame to *falsarie* (Pt. VII, l. 615) and *villanye*, there is another glimpse of his virtue when his generals justify the killing of a captive and Algarsif reprimands them (Pt. VIII, ll. 406–14). Afraid she might lose him as her pawn, Vidrea uses Algarsif's virtue against him by seeding unrest among his generals and leading them to believe that they lost the war because of his treason. When Algarsif is charged with treason by his generals and imprisoned, his soldiers demand his release, proving their love and loyalty to him. Just before his treacherous generals are ready to hand him over to Camballo, his brother, Algarsif repents again and rues his errors of judgment which had led to his father's death in battle (Pt. X, ll. 152–92). Miraculously revived by King Thotobun's white magic, which also produced Canace's magic objects and the Horse of Brass, King Cambuscan sets Algarsif free, though he initially refuses to forgive him.

Nevertheless, by the exercise of prudence, love wins out and mercy conquers all – "Justice turnes lover; Mercie all subdeweth" (Pt. X, l. 575). The rebel city, Fregiley, becomes Canacamor and is gifted to Canace as dowry on her marriage to Akafir. Algarsif repents further (Pt. XI, ll. 67–108), and because of Canace's unwavering intercession, he is forgiven by his parents and married off to Theodora, the daughter of King Bunthoto of India, but not before he earns everyone's respect by vanquishing the Giant Horbello. On this occasion, Cambuscan finally entrusts his first-born son with the Horse of Brass and shows him how to steer it, so that he wins the battle against Horbello. For his bravery and return to honor, Algarsif gets Theodora's dowry, which consists of India, Judea, Palestine, and some Arab countries, and is gifted the Horse of Brass. The treacherous masterminds are sentenced, but not to death: Vidrea is imprisoned, the generals are branded, and Quidavis, a Judas figure who betrayed Cambuscan for a fee, hangs himself.

In the character of Algarsif, Lane dissects the psychology of the royal traitor, his motives, and his ensuing pangs of conscience. Rather than evil, the traitor appears as an honorable but weak and conflicted young man, easily seduced, and easily manipulated. By giving Algarsif a conscience in turmoil, Lane makes the psychology of the royal traitor available to the semantic field of early modern treason and prepares his literary redemption, which is engineered by his prudent and loving sister, Canace.

Canace: A Stuart Lady Prudence

In early modern times, prudence had become less idealistic and more practical, namely "the virtue of making moral choices and acting on them," whereby an individual was allowed *in extremis* to abandon the loftiest moral route and embark on what was morally feasible in a given situation.[43] The danger here, as Edward Vallance points out, "was that rationalizations of this kind could easily shade into the 'false prudence' of mere cunning, the self-interested preference for survival above necessary sacrifice."[44] This is not the road taken by Lane's Canace, who would have profited greatly from her brother's betrayal and subsequent elimination. Why does Lane construct Canace as an *exemplum* of medieval prudence rather than of its early modern counterpart? As I will demonstrate below, her wisdom feeds largely on medieval discourses of prudence as a feminine aristocratic virtue (including the Chaucerian Prudence in the *Tale of Melibee*).

The medieval semantic field of prudence includes not only the usual suspects – intelligence, discretion, foresight, shrewdness, and knowledge – but also "the wisdom to see what is virtuous."[45] Carolyn P. Collette reminds us that "*Prudence* had historically been associated with men and with rulers rather than with female deportment"; by the later Middle Ages, however, "*Prudence* developed a gendered form: it became a female science of actions within human relations, particularly marriage, in order to obtain desired goals, a science of patience and indirection, of self-effacement and strict control of emotion."[46]

Canace's prudence is effectively medieval. She deploys tears frequently. Her weeping, as she urges those around her to virtuous action, is however self-effacing; it underscores her femininity and youth, and protects her wisdom from the egos of those around her, who are older, more established, or male; it also improves the effectiveness of her counsel by rendering her arcane knowledge less intimidating. Lane makes his Canace weep publicly, thus bringing into the political sphere the domestic, garden-enclosed weeping from the *Squire's Tale*.

Weeping charges prudence with legal and political implications: while Chaucer's Canacee wept for a betrayed falcon, Lane's Canace weeps for her traitorous brother, whom she aims to recuperate into the royal personhood. For a good part of the poem, Canace laments the impeding war and her brother's betrayal, as she unsuccessfully intercedes with her parents on his behalf. Unlike Prudence, who relies on reason and authorities to assuage Melibee's anger and desire for revenge, Canace relies on arcane information obtained through white magic. Because she never takes the lead in political affairs,

---

[43] Edward Vallance, "The dangers of prudence: *salus populi suprema lex*, Robert Sanderson, and the 'Case of the Liturgy,'" *Renaissance Studies* 23.4 (2009), 534–55 (at 534).

[44] Vallance, "The dangers of prudence," 534.

[45] *MED*, "prudence," 2 (a).

[46] Carolyn P. Collette, "Heeding the Counsel of Prudence: A Context for the 'Melibee,'" *Chaucer Review* 29.4 (1995), 416–33 (at 420–1).

and because her weeping renders her innocuously feminine, she benefits from her father's guidance and learns magical military secrets that would have been the prerogative of a male heir (for instance, how to steer the brass horse by turning a pin in its ear). In this way, she remains available at the center of power, best positioned to make her next move. Remarkably, when King Cambuscan departs for war, he deputizes her, not the queen, to lead the country in his absence.

Lane's continuation of the *Squire's Tale* is not, however, an argument for feminine prudence as a better alternative to male statesmanship. Lane makes it clear that Cambuscan is a "good kinge" (Pt. IV, l. 51), and a "prudent kinge" (Pt. VII, l. 209) torn between his duty as a father and as a king. Neither are women uniformly good leaders. Queen Ethelta, Canace's mother, relies on personal, destructive emotions to inform her value judgments in a political situation. She is "so transported into ire" (Pt. IV, l. 5) by Algarsif's betrayal that she cannot sleep at night; she denounces her son in public, advocating death for his treason, a logical crowning of his previous inequities:

> false caitiff, traitor! thy stolne liberties
> thy pleasures vnrestraind, thy surquedries
> thy gracinge publicke ill, good in private
> thy surphetes, luxuries, plottinges in state
> weare presages enuff, what thow wooldst bee (Pt. IV, ll. 41–5)

Unlike Canace, who focuses her efforts on keeping the corporate royal personhood intact, Queen Ethelta is bent on excising Algarsif from the collective royal personhood. Speaking to the army leaving for war, she elevates her personal grievance against her son[47] to the rank of state politics when she demands that the king's army not take him prisoner: "but hee is false and so of right ought die" (Pt. V, l. 511). In so doing, she imprudently invites treason to wreak havoc from within the royal person, in which the royal family and the realm are bound together as a corporate *persona ficta*.

Ethelta's wrathful washing of dirty linens in public indicates a lack of self-governance and endangers royal personhood, which for centuries had prudently veiled itself in an aura of mystery (*corantos* – court reports disguised as personal letters – the ur-newspapers – do not start to circulate until the 1620s).[48] By contrast, Lady Prudence merely pretends to become angry for the profit of her husband and, ultimately, of the community: "I make no semblant of wratthe ne anger, but for youre grete profit" (l. 1706). Similarly, when Canace expresses emotion, she does so to influence others to better

---

[47] Algarsif is described as "a most wicked boy" who has forsaken his natural duty to filial gratitude (Pt. V, l. 483).

[48] *OED*, "coranto," n. 2.

TREASON AND THE ROYAL PERSON: CHAUCER TO JOHN LANE   209

ends – for instance she faints to prevent her mother from taking vengeance on her brother and later cries to engineer their reconciliation (Pt. X, ll. 227–46).

Unlike her mother, Canace seeks to understand her people's motivations to serve them well. Like her father, who tries to find "how to fitt love, and iustice remedie" (l. 258) by retiring in private to ponder the queen's desire for revenge, the mercy suit of his daughter, and the falsehood of his son, Canace thoughtfully takes her time to arrive at a decision.[49] Through her magical devices, she learns that her brother has been ensnared by the "divelishe witche" (Pt. IV, l. 69), who has stung Algarsif "snake-wise" (l. 195), leaving no doubt about the enemy the royal person faces and must defeat: not simply Vidrea but the devil himself, cause of mankind's fall.

Lane is careful to differentiate between white (preserving) magic – a tool of the royal person – and black (destructive) magic – a tool of the devil and his subservient witch. This opposition casts the royal person as a defender of the faith and vanquisher of dark forces, just as James I presented himself publicly. Canace, however, is antithetical to James because she weaponizes omniscient white magic that is medieval in its scope and beneficial in its consequences.[50] While James I figures black magic as a pretext for reducing the corporate royal personhood to a binary (king versus traitorous subjects), Lane counters James I's absolutist discourse with an affective and prudential language. This language of rehabilitation has its roots in Chaucer, and Canace deploys it with white magic to reintegrate her traitorous brother into the royal person.

As Canace seeks to understand her brother's reasons for sedition, she uncovers the motivations of his seducer. Vidrea is narcissistic (she "fell to self likinge" – Pt. IV, l. 115), who strives for prominence through promiscuity and rabblerousing. She has been squarely rejected by her own family. Her father, Lord Homnibone, is a respectable magician who, recognizing she is beyond help, banishes her, and makes sure she no longer gains access to state secrets:

> and raught the sorceresse fast by the throte
> without regarding ought the strumpetes note,
> in whome was left no matter to amendment
> after all favors reft weare for avengement.
> "Counterfeate" (quoth hee), "packe thee, with thy
> crewe!"
> so her and hers quite out of dores hee threwe,
> and locked the gates with suche a secret seale,
> as near [i.e. never] more state newes shoold to her reveale.
>   (Pt. IV, ll. 141–8)

---

[49] Compare *Tale of Melibee*, l. 1163: "in olde men is the sapience, and in longe tyme the prudence."

[50] Here, too, she is similar to her father, Cambuscan, who uses white magic tactically in battle (Pt. VII).

While Homnibone's action might seem advisable for how rulers should deal with traitors jeopardizing the royal person, Canace recognizes that Algarsif's behavior is amendable. He is young and impressionable and has fallen victim to dark forces. Moreover, his rebellion feeds on a sense of injustice because his parents, worried about the company he keeps and his prospects, have circumvented the law of primogeniture and promised the kingdom to Canace and her future husband.

For all these reasons, Canace argues that their parents should forgive him and reincorporate him into the royal person. Where the queen sees mere treason and ingratitude, Canace sees the vulnerability and naïveté of her brother, who, like many other young men, has fallen victim to the "... falshode (which this witch termes veritie)! / ... tonge-plages (cowardlie scurrilitie)!" (Pt. IV, ll. 158–9). Canace is keenly aware of the sins of the tongue (tonge-plages) and the damage they can inflict on the royal person. The Tudor tongue had always been suspected as a locus of treason. Under Henry VIII, judges had inferred through "broad construction" of the 1351 statute that "even the mere expression of opinion could in some cases constitute high treason."[51] By the second half of the sixteenth century Henry's statutes of treason had been repealed and, although people were still arrested under James I for offensive speech against the king, they no longer lost their lives for uttering mere words.[52]

Canace's prudence is reflected in her speech, in which truth and sweetness can coexist; she is described as a "trewe-sweete oratresse" (Pt. IV, l. 149). Enticing speech is an aristocratic virtue of the highest importance for a ruler – in Chaucer, Prudence reminds Melibee of Salomon's wisdom: "swete words multiplien and encreescen freendes and maken shrewes to be debonaire and meeke" (l. 1738). In contrast, Algarsif is a "peltinge [i.e. paltry] orator" (Pt. V, p. 55), who promises bribes to all who side with him against the king. Since glibness is treacherously connoted as being a characteristic of Vidrea (Pt. IV, l. 169), Algarsif's deficient rhetoric paints him as a victim rather than as a perpetrator, bolstering Canace's plea he should be forgiven. Like Melibee, he is young and needs direction, and is no match for the "hegge" (hag) (Pt. IV, l. 154) who has torn him away from the corporate royal person and deployed him as a vehicle of treason.

Both Canace and Prudence are "covered" by male authorities, but while Prudence holds the *maistrie* over Melibee in Chaucer's tale, in Lane's poem, Canace's agency is always relegated to second place, after the agency of her father.[53] If Cassiodorus, Cato, Solomon, and God are some of Prudence's

---

[51] Baker, *An Introduction*, 528.

[52] David Cressy, *Dangerous Talk: Scandalous, Seditious, and Treasonable Speech in Pre-Modern England* (Oxford: Oxford University Press, 2010).

[53] Covered as in *femes covert*: Prudence as a wife by her husband, Canace as a daughter by her father.

TREASON AND THE ROYAL PERSON: CHAUCER TO JOHN LANE   211

authorities, Canace's prudence is mirrored by that of her father's, who is constrained, however, by justice, that is, by the obligation to give each of his subjects their due. The queen echoes the justice argument when she rejects Canace's plea for the life of her brother lest she seems partial, and therefore, unjust:

> I love my sonn while hee dothe vs partake;
> but hee is gonn. Now love I iustice better;
> my iustice shall my love paye, trew loves debter,
> my iustice is my selfe, and I am it,
> which iustice cann no partial love admitt. (Pt. IV, ll. 224–8)

It is this pursuit of justice and impartiality that compels King Cambuscan to start a war he wholeheartedly detests. He recognizes the need to eliminate treason but realizes that, in so doing, he would also destroy his city Fregiley where the seditious have taken cover, and therefore, a piece of his realm and royal personhood.

Canace is predictably against the war; her prudence opposes the advice of the many who welcome it. Here, too, Lane draws heavily on Chaucer: The "vulgar['s]" desire for war in Part V of Lane's continuation echoes "Werre! Werre!" (l. 1036) – the rallying cry of the young, imprudent folk in the *Tale of Melibee*. Unable to stop the war, Canace begs her parents to allow her to address the army. Her speech comes right after the queen's, who had just ordered the army to eliminate her treasonous first-born; Ethelta's rigidity recalls Prudence's warning against the hardness of one's heart, which leads to arrogance and evil: "he that thrugh the hardynesse of his herte and thrugh the hardynesse of hymself hath to greet presumpcioun, hym shal yvel bityde" (l. 1317).

Compared with her mother, who "did abound in all masculine honor" (Pt. V, l. 96), Canace embodies self-effacing love: "All this while, meeke Canac stood backe behind, / vnmentioned, vunthought on, as out of kind, / was hid in teeres, lost, or gonn out of sight; / for love is gonn, wheare rigor gettethe might" (Pt. V, ll. 515–18). Lest some might mistake her tears for weakness, Lane immediately compares her humble demeanor with the sun's shade that, by its contrast, increases the sheen of the sun's rays: "yet, as the sonn, mantled in watrie clowd, / keepes home his glories (to none elles alowd) / till, breakinge throughe, the more his bewties seeme, / as advmbration, it presentes more sheene" (Pt. V, ll. 519–22). And indeed, Canace's effect on the troops, who had just acclaimed the queen's revenge speech with cries of "Amen, amen!" (Pt. V, l. 512), is transformational: the soldiers experience a change of heart and agree to take Algarsif prisoner and, rather than kill him, hand him over to his father for correction.

To make the royal person whole again, Canace deploys the language of love as language of politics. When she urges the army to spare her brother's life, she reminds soldiers not only of their duty to the royal person – "remember that by dutie natural, / yee owe obedient Love to th' blood roial" (Pt. V, ll. 565–6) – but also of their duty to themselves, as Christian knights, to exercise mercy: "thincke on his faultes with love, let pittie move / elles hee's no martial man that hath no love. / ô, then brave martial men, Ne lett bee sedd, / pittie, for lacke of love, in yee is dead!" (Pt. V, ll. 567–70).

Canace's appeal for mercy runs counter to the queen's demand for just deserts, but the king is secretly pleased with his daughter, mercy being a paramount aristocratic and Christian virtue: "Cambuscan likd all well his daughter did / Yet weetelie [i.e. shrewdly] in his countenance it hid" (Pt. V, ll. 589–90). This is precisely why he deputizes her, and not his imprudent queen, to rule the realm in his absence.

Canace's love preserves the royal person through the exercise of mercy. An exemplary queen-in-training, Canace urges the martial men: "but let love pittie keepe this glorie still; / more honorable 'tis to save then kill" (Pt. V, ll. 573–4). The substitution of conflict with love, peace, and forgiveness is of course true to the advice of Chaucer's Prudence. Yet far more than a Christian virtue, a ruler's ability to inspire love is also about strategy and self-preservation. Prudence reminds Melibee that an aristocrat's best defense is being loved by one's subjects and neighbors: "the gretteste and strongeste garnysoun that a riche man may have, as wel to kepen his persone as hi goodes, is / that he be biloved with hys subgetz and with his neighebores" (ll. 1356–7).

Interestingly, the medieval connection between prudence, vulnerability, and power finds an echo in Elizabeth I. Canace's definition of the martial man as a loving man (compare above: "elles hee's no martial man that hath no loves") and her deployment of feminine vulnerability as an asset echo Elizabeth I's *Speech to the Troops at Tilbury* (1588). Elizabeth addresses the troops as "my loving people" and makes her safety contingent on their loyal hearts: "I have placed my chiefest strength and safeguard in the loyal hearts and goodwill of my subjects."[54] Her physical vulnerability – "I know I have the body but of a weak and feeble woman" – binds the men of arms closer to her physical person because she stirs in them the obligation to protect, a chivalric virtue. However, just as Lane's fictional Canace, Elizabeth I reminds the troops of their obligation to her royal person: "but I have the heart and stomach of a king, and of a king of England too."[55] Elizabeth's vulnerability becomes an asset when, though a woman, she declares herself ready to risk

---

[54] *The Norton Anthology of English Literature*, vol. 2, 235. This is not the only example – Elizabeth's "Golden Speech" skillfully employs the language of love to justify taxation.

[55] *The Norton Anthology of English Literature*, vol. 2, 235.

her life, providing an example for the martial men to follow suit: "rather than any dishonor shall grow by me, I myself will venter [i.e. risk] my royal blood."[56] Canace also deploys femininity to her advantage but with a different goal: to persuade the troops to show mercy to her brother, and thereby, limit the damage to the royal person.

Like Elizabeth I, Canace succeeds because she can access proprietary knowledge. But while Elizabeth obtains information from a network of spies organized by Walsingham, for Canace there is always white magic involved.[57] Because Canace's priority is her people, she deploys magic to unite the belligerent parties behind the common goal of achieving peace in the realm. Love and magic work in tandem to heal the ruptures caused by treason; even the king, who had been presumed dead in battle, returns to life and rule.

But the imaginative resources of Lane's poem remain most prominently with Chaucer. Throughout the poem Canace maintains a bird's-eye view of worldly affairs, a view she acquires when she is on the flying brass horse. This scene foreshadows his later entrusting her with the reins of the kingdom. A good ruler, the poem suggests, is always well-informed and privy to all kinds of covert undertakings. Like her counterpart in Chaucer's *Squire's Tale*, Canace exercises powers not limited to human affairs. She understands the language of birds, whose betrayals mirror those of humans, and succeeds in steering them as well towards a loving, peaceful relationship.

What seems a mere instance of Lane's early modern humor is actually a medieval "use of birds for marking human status," which Susan Crane has analyzed in the *Squire's Tale*, noting that Canacee and the female falcon are linked through "an analogous superiority and a metonymy of hearts."[58] Lane continues the episode of Chaucer's tale dealing with avian betrayal according to a medieval paradigm, whereby "the superior merit of female falcons, … who are larger and bolder than the male tercels, is appropriate for an adventure illustrating female excellence."[59]

After reconciling the people of her realm, Canace strives to reunite the birds: she reconnects a traitorous tercel to his beloved, but only after she has prudently made sure that the tercel, who has betrayed his falcon, will amend his philandering ways. With disputes among her human and feathered subjects resolved, Canace's own legal person is no longer for the birds. She has come into her own as a prudent settler of disputes, transcending her *feme covert* status as a daughter and future wife. Canace's peace-making abilities among

[56] *The Norton Anthology of English Literature*, vol. 2, 235.

[57] Stephen Budiansky, *Her Majesty's Spymaster: Elizabeth I, Sir Francis Walsingham, and the Birth of Modern Espionage* (New York: Penguin Books, 2006).

[58] Susan Crane, "For the Birds: The Biannual Chaucer Lecture," *Studies in the Age of Chaucer* 29 (2007), 21–42 (at 28–9).

[59] Crane, "For the Birds," 28.

her avian subjects also enrich the collective royal person with judicial skills that transcend the realm of human affairs.

Given the poem's focus on the excellence of a young queen-in-training, it is no wonder that the royalist Lane dedicated the 1630 (revised) version of his poem to Charles I's teenage wife, Henrietta Maria. From 1528, the royalists came to associate Henrietta Maria with the language of love. Charles I suddenly turned into a besotted husband, after his favorite, George Villiers, the 1st Duke of Buckingham, was assassinated.[60] Recent research on Henrietta has placed her at the center of Carolinian artistic activity. Karen Britland has shown how the king and queen were fond of communicating through theater plays, which they gifted to each other as birthday presents.[61] The queen's patronage would have been very desirable for a poet like Lane.[62]

Conclusion

Ultimately, John Lane delivers a pacifist ending in the tradition of the *Tale of Melibee*: Algarsif is recuperated as an honorable son (and future ruler) and Canace's insight into her brother's true character – informed by her prudence and sisterly love – is verified. By providing us with a window into the thought processes of the prudent sovereign and the recovering traitor, John Lane's poem offers a psychological dimension to the cultural life of treason in the seventeenth century. Prudence and love emerge as the most significant attributes and the ultimate safeguards of the corporate royal person. A prudent king knows that ruling solely by force (without love and mercy) does not win his subjects' hearts and might encourage them to treason. In the words of King Cambuscan:

> What conquest is (quod hee) to vanquishe foes,
> if I, by killing them, theire hartes doe lose?
> but everie mastrie makes not victorie,
> vnlesse the hart be vanquishd willinglie;
> nor force alone cann stowtest hartes subdewe
> but stowborne hartes may yeeld to meeke virtue.
> Ile try th'conclusion, wheather force or love
> have greater force sterne soldiers hartes to move. (Pt. VIII, ll. 333–40)

---

[60] Barry Coward and Peter Gaunt, *The Stuart Age: England 1603–1714*, 5th ed. (London: Routledge, 2018), 187.

[61] Karen Britland, "Queen Henrietta-Maria's Theatrical Patronage," in *Henrietta Maria: Piety, Politics and Patronage* (London: Routledge, 2016), 57–72 (at 60 ff.).

[62] Sophie Tomlinson, *Women on Stage in Stuart Drama* (Cambridge: Cambridge University Press, 2005), and Karen Britland, *Drama at the Courts of Queen Henrietta Maria* (Cambridge: Cambridge University Press, 2006).

Cambuscan's words echo Edward VI's statute of treason, whereby subjects readily obey out of love a sovereign who rules with clemency and indulgence:

> Nothing being more godly, more sure, more to be wished and desired betwixt a Prince, the Supream Head and Ruler, and the Subjects, whose Governor and Head he is, than on the Prince's Part great Clemency and Indulgency, and rather too much Forgiveness and Remission of His Royal Power and just Punishment, than exact Severity and Justice to be Shewed; and on the Subjects behalf, that they should obey rather for Love, and for the necessity and love of a King or Prince, than for fear of his strait and severe Laws (1 Edward VI c. 12)

It is hard not to view Lane's poem as a criticism of the absolutist streak of James I, or perhaps of his son, Charles I, who managed to quarrel with Parliament (hostile to his spending and his protégé Buckingham) and dissolve it at its very first session in 1625.[63] The poem's sensitive subject matter coupled with Lane's desire to win the patronage of Queen Henrietta might well have been among the reasons why the poem went unpublished until 1888 (though it most likely circulated among Lane's literary friends). A devotee of Lady Prudence and Elizabeth I, Lane rewrites the Stuarts' relentless conflicts with their subjects. Poetry offers a refuge and a language to express a different view of sovereignty. For Lane, language matters because he counters a seventeenth-century legal vocabulary of absolutism, witchcraft, and treason with moral and psychological discourses of prudence, mercy, and love derived from an earlier historical moment and imaginative context. His most important offering to the early modern semantics of treason (and the history of early modern ideas), however, remains the psychology of the seduced but repentant (and therefore redeemable) royal traitor.

[63] Stroud, *Stuart England*, 49.

10

Tears Of Survival: Myrrha And Criseyde

ELIZABETH ALLEN

Virgil associates Troy with loss, exile, and mourning: with Aeneas's loss of his wife Creusa and his father Anchises, and with the communal *lacrimae rerum*. Yet Troy survives collapse in numerous ways. Its survivors go into exile and form new communities, like Deiphobus's civic simulacrum at Buthrotum. The tears of things also power Aeneas's honorable *peitas*, driving his war against Turnus and marriage to Lavinia, fulfilling the civic obligation to rebuild and found an empire. Depictions of Troy survive both textually and culturally, from the painted temple at Carthage (as depicted in the *Aeneid*) to the New Troys of London and other western cities . Exile in these instances becomes foundational.

Criseyde's exile from Troy, by contrast, is associated with irremediable wrongdoing and betrayal. She can neither return nor lay a foundation for some new Troy. Chaucer's *Troilus and Criseyde* is not interested in Troy's potential for renewal but in her peculiarly intimate and feminine actions: her gradual loss of faith and abandonment of Troilus, and of Trojan community, in their darkest hour. Her "sliding" heart is evidence of a failure to fulfill her promise to Troilus and her broader obligation to Trojan community, so that she is inevitably marginal to any coherent narrative of Troy's triumphant rebirth. Indeed, her abandonment of Troilus has often been taken quasi-allegorically as the beginning of the end for the city itself.[1]

Yet the poem's local language – syntax, metaphor, allusion, stanza structure, pacing – often resists such large-scale judgments. One allusion in Book IV disrupts with particular force the relation between Criseyde's intimate and communal obligations, and the corresponding sympathy of the poem's

---

[1] In "Antiquity and Beyond: The Death of Troilus," in *The European Tragedy of Troilus*, ed. Piero Boitani (Oxford: Clarendon Press, 1989), 1–20, Piero Boitani writes that Troilus's name "contains both the beginning and the end of Troy" (5).

TEARS OF SURVIVAL: MYRRHA AND CRISEYDE

audience. After reporting the parliament's decision to trade Criseyde to the Greeks, Chaucer depicts a scene of the lovers' meeting in which he compares their tears to those of the incestuous Myrrha:

> The woful <u>teeris</u> that they leten falle
> As bittre weren, out of <u>teris</u> kynde,
> For peyne, as is ligne aloes or galle –
> So bittre <u>teeris</u> weep nought, as I fynde,
> The woful Mirra thorugh the bark and rynde –
> That in this world ther nys so hard an herte
> That nolde han rewed on hire peynes smerte. (IV. 1135–41)[2]

The stanza's formal and syntactical complexity enhance the already strong tendency for rhyme royal stanzas to slow narrative propulsion and encourage "critical engagement with the narrative."[3] The allusion to incest is couched among a series of disruptive linguistic effects (periphrasis, syntax inversion, negation) and formal effects (enjambment, listed metaphors) that shape the depiction of the lovers' sorrow into something at once grand and awkward: a set of small-scale resistances to the larger-scale plot, the emerging gendered constraints upon Criseyde, and the terms of her communal obligations.

The story is told by Orpheus in Ovid's *Metamorphoses*, Book X. When Myrrha falls in love with her father, Cinyras, she tries to hang herself. Her nurse finds the noose, makes her confess, and brokers disguised nightly visits with her father, who, when he discovers her identity, tries to kill her. The now pregnant Myrrha flees from Cypress to what is now Yemen. There she becomes the myrrh tree, which splits to give birth to Adonis. The tree's resinous sap leaks through the bark and hardens to create the medicinal myrrh.

Troilus and Criseyde alludes frequently to Ovid, most often in the interchanges between Troilus and Pandarus in the role of poet and teacher of love.[4] Sometimes, Criseyde's Ovidian references fantasize a pastoral past in order

---

[2] All quotations from *Troilus and Criseyde* are from *The Riverside Chaucer* (Boston: Houghton Mifflin, 1987).

[3] For an account of rhyme royal's tendency to disrupt narrative flow and encourage self-consciousness about narrative temporality, see Elizabeth Robertson, "Rhyme Royal and Romance," in *The Transmission of Medieval Romance: Metres, Manuscripts, and Early Prints*, ed. Ad Putter and Judith A. Jefferson (Cambridge: D.S. Brewer, 2018), 50–68 (at 52). For an account of rhyme royal as emphasizing "middles" rather than ends, see Claire M. Waters, "*Makyng* and Middles In Chaucer's Poetry," in *Readings in Medieval Textuality: Essays in Honour of A.C. Spearing*, ed. Cristina Maria Cervone and D. Vance Smith (Cambridge: D.S. Brewer, 2016), 31–44.

[4] John Fyler, *Chaucer and Ovid* (New Haven: Yale University Press, 1979).

to resist the tragic future.[5] Frequently, however, the poem channels Ovidian irony and political alienation: Jeremy Dimmick remarks that Ovid models "an *auctor* perpetually falling foul of authority."[6] Jamie Fumo takes this further to show how Chaucer's provocative misquotation encourages readers to use Ovid as "funnels of signification" not stable loci of meaning.[7] Karla Taylor finds that Ovid provides Chaucer a locus for examining "his own literary making" in the *Canterbury Tales*.[8] With respect to *Troilus and Criseyde*, Andrew Galloway remarks that the "politically and emotionally oppressive world of Troy is dotted with allusions to Ovid, featuring his most unsettling images and narratives."[9] The reference to Myrrha, like others to Philomela, Oenone, and Medea, is just such an unsettling narrative. Why would Chaucer cite a tale of incest at a moment of mutual sorrow between lovers? How does Myrrha's sorrow reflect upon the sorrow of the lovers? A story so laden with taboo seems oddly suited to the scene of exogamous courtly love on the brink of loss. Yet, as I shall argue, incest also marks a tension between difference and likeness that simultaneously isolates the lovers and disrupts their intimacy, entangling this moment of shared grief with questions of community.

Community might be thought of as grounded in what is "common," that is, shared or similar among members: sympathy, loyalty, shared customs. From the poem's opening, Criseyde has been set apart within her community. Her father is a traitor, so that she is accepted on sufferance. Her precarious social place points to the hierarchical – rather than lateral – ordering of civic life, both its intimate judgments of her based on her family, and its structures of differential power based on her sex, marital status, and kinship. If community demands resemblance, then, its operations continue through complex mutual relations based on various social roles; if members of the community mirror one another affectively and socially, through sympathy and conformity to custom, they also differ structurally from one another, for example across gender and rank. Community, that is, entails reciprocal obligations that are

---

5   Elizabeth Allen, "Flowing Backward to the Source: Criseyde's Promises and the Ethics of Allusion," *Speculum* 88.3 (2013), 681–720.

6   Jeremy Dimmick, "Ovid in the Middle Ages: Authority and Poetry," in *The Cambridge Companion to Ovid*, ed. Philip Hardie (Cambridge: Cambridge University Press, 2006), 264–87 (at 264).

7   Jamie C. Fumo, "'Little Troilus': *Heroides* 5 and its Ovidian Contexts in Chaucer's *Troilus and Criseyde*," *Studies in Philology* 100.3 (2003), 278–314 (at 282).

8   Karla Taylor, "The Motives of Reeds: The Wife of Bath's Midas and Literary Tradition," in *Later Middle English Literature, Materiality, and Culture: Essays in Honor of James M. Dean*, ed. Brian Gastle and Erick Kelemen (Newark: University of Delaware Press, 2018), 25–41 (at 26).

9   Andrew Galloway, "Ovid in Chaucer and Gower," in *A Handbook to the Reception of Ovid*, ed. John F. Miller and Carole E. Newlands (Hoboken: John Wiley & Sons, 2014), 188–201 (at 192).

not symmetrical: what an individual member owes depends on their role and responsibility, their status within the group, their family and good name.[10] What does Criseyde owe her community, in the context of her widowhood, her family, and her sex? Arguably, she owes it her survival in two senses: she owes her survival to Hector's gracious protection and the royal family's support; and, in turn, her existence on sufferance entails an obligation to stay alive, in order to carry out the exchange between Troy and the Greek camp that brings back Antenor. Her survival in the latter sense is obligatory, yet possible only by betraying the very city to which she owes it.

As Karla Taylor and others have taught a generation of readers, Chaucer's language does not allow us to rest easy casting Criseyde as betrayer, and detailed observation of that language depicts conflicting features of Criseyde's character and social world that resist the inevitability of bad faith. She is at the mercy of circumstances within which she also exerts some choice; she appears variously as mourning woman, object of exchange, victim of circumstance, and agent of decision. Her "choice" to leave Troy and Troilus (rather than, as he suggests, eloping with him) highlights the asymmetry of the obligations that create her membership in the community in the first place, based as they are on hierarchies of status and sex. If her survival appears as a social and communal act, the nature of the community itself comes into question, its customary sympathy and the workings of pity in general revealed as effects of social hierarchy. At the same time, both Criseyde and those around her remain affectively linked through a shared sorrow whose depth and scale cannot simply be dismissed as tainted by hierarchy. Her tragedy differs from Stephanie Batkie's account of the Reeve's tragedy in this volume, but the two characters both confront the painful gap between will and social constraint. As we will see, the Myrrha stanza shows Criseyde – and her audience – balancing painfully on the fulcrum between sympathy (linked to desire) and social obligation.

[10] I draw on ideas of community as articulated by Robert Esposito, *Communitas: The Origin and Destiny of Community*, trans. Timothy Campbell (Palo Alto: Stanford University Press, 2010). Esposito usefully insists that community is not "an aseptic enclosure within which [members] can establish transparent communication or even a content to be communicated" (7). Instead, "The subjects of community are united by an 'obligation,' in the sense that we say 'I owe *you* something,' but not 'you owe *me* something' ... The common is not characterized by what is proper but what is improper, or even more drastically, by the other" (6–7). This sense of community as a fundamental alienation from the self emerges, I argue, more strongly with respect to Criseyde because her obligations differ from those of Troilus.

Bitter Tears

The Myrrha reference comes when the lovers first meet after the parliament has decided to trade Criseyde; they are too sad to speak and can only collapse into one another's arms. Their sorrow is mutual, so alike in intensity as to be indistinguishable: "The lasse woful of hem bothe nyste / Wher that he was" (IV. 1132–3). The lovers weep together mutely, and their tears are even bitterer than Myrrha's: "So bittre teeris weep nought, as I fynde, / The woful Mirra thorugh the bark and rynde" (IV. 1138–9). Yet the scene boomerangs away from the disruptive comparison. There is a Pyramis-and-Thisbe-like drama as Criseyde faints for sorrow, and Troilus, thinking her dead, resolves to kill himself; awakening and horrified to learn his plan, she shifts from grief to a far more pragmatic and voluble discourse about the ways in which she might imagine her return. The work of the scene displaces initial sorrow: as Criseyde comforts Troilus, she imagines her survival and submission to her fate.

Still, the Myrrha stanza pulls us to linger on the depth and bitterness of the lovers' grief. Elsewhere in *Troilus*, bitterness in love conventionally turns into sweetness and enhances its pleasure – especially for Troilus. In one of Pandarus's many proverbs, bitterness normalizes Troilus's suffering in love: "For how myghte evere swetnesse han ben knowe / To him that nevere tasted bitternesse?" (I. 638–9). As bitterness has from the beginning of the poem been associated with the conventional, paradoxical pain of being in love (e.g., I. 384–5), such pain has been assuaged when it leads the lovers to find sweet company (III. 1212–22).[11] In Book IV, however, the repetition of bitterness instead makes us aware of both lovers' mutual and unalleviated suffering. Their sorrow is conveyed in formal repetitions that cycle through the stanza – "woful teeris … / bittre … teris / peyne … / bittre teeris … / woful … / peynes smerte" – expressing their resistance to impending separation. Conventional phrases – bitter as gall, bitter tears, bitter as myrrh, hard hearts – contribute to the sense that their grief is widely shared and even communally agreed upon, and the stanza's final lines involve the narrator and audience in their shared grief. The allusion to Myrrha is couched in language that almost quells the transgressive story of incest and metamorphosis. In these ways, the stanza's energies are dedicated to a vocabulary of emotional likeness – repetition,

---

[11] The bitterness/sweetness dichotomy is most often attributed to Troilus. Jennifer Garrison, "Chaucer's *Troilus and Criseyde* and the Dangers of Masculine Interiority," *Chaucer Review* 49.3 (2015), 320–43, finds in Troilus's courtly suffering a form of masculine abjection that consolidates power by denying its connection to the social world, so that Troilus's obsession with his own inner state constitutes a privileged denial of masculine violence. I argue that courtly suffering also generates a fantasy of community, based in shared suffering, with complex consequences for both Troilus and Criseyde.

TEARS OF SURVIVAL: MYRRHA AND CRISEYDE

shared affect, communal agreement – that wards off the social differentiation that will mark the "chaungyng of Criseyde."

At the same time, the stanza also immediately complicates the lovers' pain. Its single sentence stacks three comparative constructions. Comparison, of course, begins with a claim of similarity, but it also introduces difference. Conventional figures of speech like "bitter as gall" also emphasize similarity, inasmuch as they rely on audience agreement: their conventionality assumes communally shared understanding. Meanwhile, however, the stanza's comparisons are phrased through negation: the lovers' tears, *unlike* normal tears, are metaphorically bitter as aloe or gall; even Myrrha does *not* weep such bitter tears; there is *no* heart so hard that it would *not* pity the lovers. The negations suggest emphasis, but they also create a series of distinctions – among tears' degrees of bitterness, between the lovers' tears and those of Myrrha, and between those with hard hearts and those who pity them. The syntax, too, introduces difference. The first comparison, through the use of modifying phrases, introduces a series of syntactical distances and disruptions: "The woful <u>teeris</u> that they leten falle / As bittre weren, out of <u>teris</u> kynde, / For peyne, as is ligne aloes or galle." Their tears are syntactically separated from "bittre" and again from "peyne." These tears, which the passive lovers "leten falle," take on a quasi-agential status as the subject of the stanza's single sentence. They are strange tears, "out of teris kynde," which the Riverside glosses as "unlike the nature of tears": the lovers' tears are unnaturally bitter, beyond the norms and conventions of sorrow.[12] Formally, the enjambed "For peyne" suggests another likeness-with-difference, as the outward expression of sorrow – tears – is caused by, but distinguished from, the emotional state that produces them – pain.

Thus, by the time we get to the vehicles of the first metaphor, "ligne aloe or gall," the clause has been disrupted several times: linguistically, through negatives and modifiers, and formally, through enjambment. The effect is enhanced by the third line's awkward rhythm, with its early heavy caesura after "peyne." To be sure, the comparison conveys a proverbial similarity between tears and aloe and gall.[13] Yet there are differences between the two vehicles of the metaphor, aloe and gall, that echo the differences between feeling and expression already implicit in the clause. The sap of aloe leaves (or *lignum*, "wood") is a topical painkiller and anti-inflammatory as well as a laxative, with eastern and southern provenance, where it grows in dry climates – such

---

[12] *Riverside Chaucer*, n. 1136.

[13] Gall is proverbially bitter: Whiting cites "The dove has no gall" (D364); the contrast between honey and gall (H433, 438); and the contrast between sugar and gall (S871). See Bartlett Jere Whiting with Helen Wescott Whiting, *Proverbs, Sentences, and Proverbial Phrases From English Writings Mainly Before 1500* (Cambridge, MA: The Belknap Press of Harvard University Press, 1968), "gall."

as that of Troy, perhaps.[14] Extracts from the much more common and, for England, local oak galls were used to control diarrhea. Unlike sap, plant galls do not originate within the plant, but form on the outside.[15] The comparison thus juxtaposes exotic and local (eastern and western) plants, whose medicines derive from within and from outside the plant body. Are the lovers' tears entirely integral, or are they separable from their inner state?[16]

The stanza's multiplication of vehicles (aloe, gall, later myrrh) calls attention to choices one might make in writing such comparisons. Oak galls, in fact, were also used in making ink, marking the juncture between bitterness and its expression in language. The hint that writing about pain is itself painful crosscuts referentiality with enactment, metaphor with metonymy, invoking a topos from texts like Ovid's *Heroides*, whose wronged women associate suffering and death with writing.[17] Dido, for example, associates writing, sword, tears, and blood in her compressed farewell: "I write, and the Trojan's blade is ready in my lap. Over my cheeks the tears roll, and fall upon the drawn steel – which soon shall be stained with blood instead of tears."[18] Suicidal response to love will come to the fore later, but here, the *Troilus* stanza's weeping lines point away from a single, inevitable doom and toward a sense

---

[14] *De proprietatibus rerum* locates it in India and Persia: Bartholomeus Anglicus, *De proprietatibus rerum*, trans. John Trevisa, ed. Stephen Batman (Ann Arbor: Text Creation Partnership, 2011 [1582]), XVII, cap. 6. Available online: http://name.umdl. umich.edu/A05237.0001.001 (accessed 30 August 2022). See also *MED*, "lignum aloes," which locates the plant in the middle east or India; and *OED*, "lign-aloes," which locates it in Mexico.

[15] *OED*, "gall," n. 3, notes that galls are formed by insects and used for ink and dyes; they are formed by a tug-of-war between bacterial, fungal, or other attackers and plant antibodies. Because they are an immunological response of the plant, they contain chemicals that can be therapeutic for humans. Seema Patel, Abdur Rauf, and Haroon Khan, "The relevance of folkloric usage of plant galls as medicines: Finding the scientific rationale," *Biomedicine & Pharmacotherapy* 97 (2018), 240–7.

[16] The etymologically distinct humoral term "gall" refers to bile and the bile-producing organs in the body. See Batman, ed., *De proprietatibus rerum*, V, cap. 40. Both uses of "gall" are associated with humoral bitterness; and both plant galls and animal bladders (galls) were used medically.

[17] Chaucer's narrator often adopts this Heroidean image, as in the poem's opening invocation to the fury: "Thesiphone, thou help me for t'endite / Thise woful vers, that wepen as I write!" (I. 6–7). Boethius, too, evokes tearful composition. Perhaps the closest image to Myrrha's weeping is Dante, *Inf.* XIII, where the suicides weep through their injured branches.

[18] "scribimus, et gremio Troicus ensis adest, / perque genas lacrimae strictum labuntur in ensem, / qui iam pro lacrimis sanguine tinctus erit": Ovid, *Heroides. Amores*, trans. Grant Showerman, rev. G.P. Goold (Cambridge, MA: Harvard University Press, 1914), VII, 184–6.

of multiplicity. Alongside the Riverside's gloss, we might also understand tears "out of kynde" as indicating the variety of possible types of tears: "out of all the possible natures tears might have." The implied conventional comparison "bitter as gall" is syntactically interrupted and doubled with aloe, suggesting different kinds of bitterness. Gall's connection to ink suggests, further, an artificial or constructed grief, calling attention to the narrator's choice in selecting his comparisons.[19] The impression is that the narrator casts about for medicinal remedies even as he describes a sorrow that tilts toward self-destruction. The stanza's first simile, then, undercuts the unmediated mutuality of the lovers' sorrow by pointing to the multiplicity of its expression and to the narrator's presence, and his choice of words, in writing – and himself seeking remedy for – their sorrow.

Nonetheless, at the same time, the vocabulary of likeness comes to the fore in the stanza's middle line, insisting on the unified or shared sorrow of the lovers. Across the first three lines (IV. 1135–8), the words "tears" and "bitter" have been separated ("The woful teeris ... bittre were ... out of teris kynde"). Now in the stanza's pivotal line (IV. 1139) they are brought together ("So *bittre teeris* weep nought, as I fynde"), as if these particular lovers were the occasion for the narrator to gather, or even derive, the cliché "bitter tears."[20] The central fourth line, formally surrounded by the rest of the stanza, encloses these lovers' suffering, almost as though their singular woe could take them out of the society that infringes on their love. It would seem that here, the narrator's description has created a tableau of the lovers' conventional, recognizable, singular, and wholly mutual sorrow: an enclosed image of likeness. Moreover, here the tears are like another medicine, myrrh: "– So bittre teeris weep nought, as I fynde, / The woful Mirra thorugh the bark and rynde –" (IV. 1139–40). The properties of myrrh – the tree's hardened sap – include, besides its bitterness and hardness, its use as an analgesic and an expectorant, as an ingredient in perfume, and as an embalming substance.[21] Aloe, gall, and myrrh share an impulse toward healing (even preserving) love. Spiritually, myrrh is

---

[19]   Jamie Fumo points out the relational and performative character of tears in the poem, arguing for their empowerment of Criseyde as emotional agent who can resist convention: Fumo, "Criseida Lacrymosa? Rereading the Weeping Criseyde," *Chaucer Review* 54.1 (2019), 35–66.

[20]   For evidence that "bitter tears" is a cliché even in Middle English, see *MED*, "bitter," 2 (c).

[21]   "*Mirrum* is an oyntment made of Mirra, and of other spicery. By vertue thereof sinewes and other members of feeling be comforted, and humours in the ioynts and toes be wasted. By the good smell thereof spirits of feeling be restored & comforted, & slaieth with bitternesse lice and wormes, & letteth breeding thereof, & abateth stinking sweats, & keepeth & saueth bodyes whole and sounde, that they rot not": Batman, ed., *De proprietatibus rerum*, XVII, 102–3.

not infrequently associated with contrition, as in the *Book to a Mother*: "Murre, þat kepiþ bodies fro rotinge, bitokeneþ bitter penaunce and sorwe þat schal saue þi soule fro rotinge in sinne."[22] Mary Carruthers links Troilus's tears throughout the poem to monastic ideals about contemplative reading, which benefits from the reader's readiness to weep: she describes a mode of reading that softens the heart and allows physiological restoration.[23] The stanza calls up the idea that "bitter teres" could offer consolation.

Yet the language here resists remedy. Syntactically, the second comparison has disrupted the first, as the Riverside's editorial em-dashes indicate.[24] The whole comparison is negatively phrased. The periphrasis – the reference to myrrh indirectly through Ovidian allusion to its source – calls attention to a difference between painful tenor (lovers' sorrow) and restorative vehicle (myrrh). The lovers' tears may be metaphorically *like* bitter medicine, but they fall short of real cure.

Furthermore, the cliché of bitter tears elides a question of perception: at the literal level, who is perceiving the bitterness here and finding remedy? Is the lovers' suffering turned into tears that they can taste, ingest, and find healing? It is worth noting that in the parallel scene in Boccaccio's *Il Filostrato*, the lovers drink each others' tears despite their bitterness, whereas in Chaucer the experience of bitterness is far less grounded in sensory experience.[25] Does the sensing of bitterness also, or instead, belong to the sympathetic onlookers? Does bitterness, expressed, itself produce the restoration, the tears of Myrrha producing myrrh? Who is that restoration for? The stanza labors to overcome questions of perceptual difference and insist on shared feeling; to create likeness between sorrow and its expression; and, in turn, to link lovers and witnesses. But its formal disruptions undercut its depiction of shared feeling and the healing power of mutual sorrow.

---

[22] *MED*, 1 (b).

[23] Mary Carruthers, "On Affliction and Reading, Weeping and Argument," *Representations* 93.1 (2006), 1–21 (at 7).

[24] Stephen A. Barney in the Norton Critical Edition of Chaucer's *Troilus and Criseyde* (New York: W. W. Norton & Company, 2006), follows the Riverside, as does Barry Windeatt in his edition of *Troilus and Criseyde* (London: Penguin, 2003). James M. Dean and Harriet Spiegel (Peterborough: Broadview, 2016) start a new sentence with the Myrrha lines: "So bitter teeris weep nought, as I fynde, / The woful Mirra thorugh the bark and rynde, / That in this world ther nys so harde an herte / That nolde han rewed on hire peynes smerte." This punctuation strengthens the causal chain between Myrrha and the hard hearts: the lovers tears are "so bitter … that in this world ther mys so harde an hearte."

[25] "They kissed each other sometimes and drank the falling tears without care that they were bitter beyond their nature": Barney, *Troilus, Il Filostrato* IV, st. 115, 280–1.

Bark and Rind

Myrrha appears as part of a network of proverbial language about trees that occurs throughout the poem. As Karla Taylor brilliantly traces it in *Chaucer Reads 'The Divine Comedy'*, such tree proverbs begin with the narrator's assertion in Book I: "The yerde is bet that bowen wole and wynde / Than that that brest" (I. 257–8).[26] Proverbs, writes Taylor, appear linguistically and referentially stable – they are traditional language that is portable across situations and through time. This proverb establishes an apparently consistent distinction between a stick (or reed, sapling, etc.) that bends and a tree that breaks and falls. It is generally "better" to be flexible like the reed: the narrator here hopes the previously callow Troilus will bend to the power of love. The proverb sets up a language pattern that relies on generalization to indicate an apparently stable truth about the benefit to Troilus of being the "yard that bends."

But as Taylor shows, proverbs do not actually refer to the same truths consistently. In line with Troilus's association with the bending reed, Pandarus echoes a Virgilian simile to liken Criseyde to a stable oak:

> So reulith hire hir hertes gost withinne,
> That though she bende, yet she stant on roote;
> What in effect is this unto my boote?
> Thenk here-ayeins: whan that the stordy ook,
> On which men hakketh ofte, for the nones,
> Receyved hath the happy fallyng strook,
> The greete sweigh doth it come al at ones. (II. 1377–83)

In the *Aeneid*, Troy's fall is represented in the famous epic simile of an ancient ash tree struck by blows until its crashing fall (II. 626–31).[27] Pandarus imagines Criseyde standing rooted and apparently pitiless, but actually all the more rigidly vulnerable to the ax of love and its "happy fallyng strook." Then, later, a new take on the proverb (this time echoing Dante) indicates the way in which Troilus's love makes *him* the rigid oak, encasing him in sorrow, as if bound within the bark of a tree:

> And as in wynter leves ben biraft,
> Ech after other, til the tree be bare,

---

[26] Taylor, *Chaucer Reads*, 132–74.

[27] Chaucer here capitalizes on the mutability of the image that is already evident in the *Aeneid*, where sturdy trees do not necessarily succumb: Aeneas unmoving and pitiless in the face of Dido's pleas is compared to an oak that stays standing (*Aeneid*, IV. 438–49). Lindsay Ann Reid, "Virgilian and Ovidian Tree Similes in *Troilus and Criseyde* 2.1373–84," *The Explicator* 72.2 (2014), 158–62.

> So that ther nys but bark and braunche ilaft,
> Lith Troilus, byraft of ech welfare,
> Ibounden in the blake bark of care,
> Disposed wood out of his wit to breyde,
> So sore hym sat the chaungynge of Criseyde. (IV. 225–31)

Here it is Troilus who is rooted; Criseyde is set to become, as Taylor writes, "the bending reed, surviving each storm because of her lack of firmness."[28] The binding of Troilus within the bark of his own sorrow, as the leaves of his love float away, lodges him firmly within the tragic core of the poem. Encased in his immutable love, he has no way to bend or adapt to "the chaungynge of Criseyde" – a punning phrase that refers, first, to the negotiated exchange of Criseyde for Antenor and, second, to the impending change in her affections. If Criseyde is the "yard that bends," then the flexible branch is no longer "better" than the one that breaks. Further, the application of the "yard that bends" proverb has been reversed, from Troilus as reed and Criseyde as tree, to Criseyde as reed and Troilus as tree, frustrating the ostensible consistency of the proverb itself. If proverbs are patterned, repeated, and traditional forms of language – figures of speech whose meaning is consistent across changing situations – Chaucer's tree images instead provide "an example of a failed attempt to secure stability through language."[29] For Taylor, ultimately, this mutability is part of Chaucer's searching analysis of the "gaps and failures" inherent in any use of conventional language.[30] Her insight applies not only to proverbs about "the yerd that bends" but also, as we have seen, to the clichés within the Myrrha stanza – "bitter tears," "bitter as gall" – which seek a vocabulary of likeness, of consistency and conventionality in language that hint at the remediation of sorrow through resistance to change, but that reveal, in the attempt, "gaps and failures" both linguistic and thematic.

Chaucer's reference to Myrrha as tree picks up the proverbial contrast between reed and rooted tree. Myrrha's weeping "thorugh the bark and rynde" specifically cites Ovid's description of Myrrha's metamorphosis, during which, as her body parts become branches, she settles and sinks her face down to meet the tree's bark or carapace ("subsedit mersitque suos in cortice vultus," 498).[31] Myrrha's body solidifies into bark, becoming the body of the tree. Chaucer's image also invokes Ovid's flow of tears: "yet she weeps, and the warm drops spill from her tree trunk" (598; "flet tamen, et tepidae manant

---

[28] Taylor, *Chaucer Reads*, 161.

[29] Taylor, *Chaucer Reads*, 162.

[30] Taylor, *Chaucer Reads*, 173.

[31] Quotations in Latin and translations in English are from Ovid, *Metamorphoses, Volume II: Books 9–15*, trans. Frank Justus Miller, rev. G.P. Goold (Cambridge, MA: Harvard University Press, 1916).

ex arbore guttae," 500).[32] Bound within the tree, Ovid's Myrrha labors and gives birth, weeping; her liquid tears harden even as her child grows up into the beautiful (but doomed) Adonis. Myrrha's tears blur the line between what hardens and what flows, what remains inside the bark and what comes out, even what is dead and what lives on. In Ovid, metamorphosis encapsulates this painful in-between state. In a prayer to the gods to which I will return, Ovid's Myrrha has asked for precisely this punishment, wanting, she says, to join neither the living nor the dead.

If Chaucer's reference to this Ovidian moment returns to the contrast between rigid oak and bending yard, it does not use the contrast to distinguish the lovers from one another; instead, *both* of them resemble Myrrha, in her combination of hard and soft, solid bark and liquid flow. In this sense, the narrator recruits Myrrha as an image of resistance or refusal to choose between life or death, to bend or break, to change, to separate. In this way, the allusion's metaphorical effects support the vocabulary of likeness that has developed through the stanza. There is no bending yard versus falling oak. Even in referring to a metamorphosis, the stanza's use of the tree proverb keeps differentiation at bay, as though the lovers' undifferentiated sorrow might actually ward off change itself. Indeed, as often in Chaucer, the literal bodily transformation of Myrrha is unavailable to Troilus and Criseyde: metamorphosis is not what the stanza depicts. It will not be what the rest of the scene depicts, either, despite the structural allusion to another Ovidan metamorphosis related by Orpheus, "Pyramis and Thisbe," when Troilus imitates the Ovidian lover's misapprehension of his beloved's death and (nearly) kills himself.

Resistance to change belongs to the lovers themselves, of course, but the stanza also assigns it to readers. After comparing the lovers' bitter tears to those of Myrrha, the narrator closes the stanza by interpellating its audience. Here is the whole stanza again:

> The woful teeris that they leten falle
> As bittre weren, out of teris kynde,
> For peyne, as is ligne aloes or galle –
> So bittre teeris weep nought, as I fynde,
> The woful Mirra thorugh the bark and rynde –
> That in this world ther nys so hard an herte
> That nolde han rewed on hire peynes smerte.

---

[32] Even the transformation itself implies a liquidity as Myrrha "mersit" (submerges) her face into the tree. Orpheus's description of her laboring and childbirth further emphasizes the sense of Myrrha's bodily entrapment within a rigid frame, which is wet with falling tears and rent asunder when Adonis is born: "arbor lacrimisque cadentibus umet ... fissa cortice vivum / reddit onus" (Ovid, *Met.* X, 509–13).

The lovers' bitter tears, says the narrator in those emphatic negatives, would inevitably invoke the sympathy of others; he denies anyone would fail to sympathize. The couplet's recourse to the cliché of the hard heart softened renders pity conventional, that is, communally agreed upon.[33] The tears repeated in the stanza's first five lines – and associated with the outward expression of feeling, and with ink and poetry – are absent in the result clause. The narrator instead depicts a community of readers who share the feelings of the characters, as if without mediation or hierarchy: audience, narrator, and lovers are bound by shared sorrow.[34] The meeting of the two grieving lovers expands throughout "this world." The stanza's couplet clinches formal effects – emphatic negatives, looping repetitions, conventional language, expanded scale – that ward off differentiation; the couplet imagines feeling shared by everyone. Any gap opened by Myrrha's morally problematic desire for her father, her discovery and exile, and her painful metamorphosis is elided in a vocabulary of likeness extending straight from sorrowing lovers to even the hardest of hearts.

The tight connection between the lovers and their audience, however, is as subject as the rest of the stanza to the "gaps and failures" embedded in the narrator's language. If the phrase "bittre teeris" unites disparate words into a conventional figure, "ther nys so hard an heart" subtly splits another conventional figure. Like tears, hearts can vary in their kind or degree of hardness. If the negative form of the claim here is designed to be emphatic, "nolde" in an initial stressed position in the final line still suggests some might *not* wish to entertain that pity.

Moreover, at the level of syntax, the final couplet is not a culmination but a digression. Although the whole stanza seems to be a single clause disrupted by the Myrrha allusion, the link among first and third clauses is not as tight as it looks. That is, the couplet's initial "That" looks like an intensifier, as in, "their tears were *so bitter ... That* the hardest heart would pity them." But with "as"

---

[33] Once again, the stanza "takes apart" a conventional figure of speech, hard-heartedness, so as to make us aware of its operations. The word "hard-hearted" is attested from Old English *heordheartness*, in *OED* "hard-hearted" and in *MED* "hard-herted." The specific variants of hard hearts – hearts of stone, iron, and steel – are proverbially paired with the notion of melting or softening with tears, pity, or love. See Whiting, *Proverbs, Sentences, and Proverbial Phrases*, H277: "A heart of stone (iron, steel) would melt."

[34] Compare Ruth Evans's insight about the poem's construction of pity as a form of hospitality: the "ethical injunction to remember 'passed hevynesse' is something close to Jacques Derrida's idea of hospitality as an act that is 'not governed by duty' but which is graciously offered beyond debt and economy'" (130). The poem frequently suggests that pity should transcend social duty in precisely this way. See Evans, "Tie Knots and Slip Knots: Sexual Difference and Memory in Chaucer's *Troilus and Criseyde*," *Medieval English Literature* 1 (2016), 128–43.

instead of "so" in the second line, the complex syntax and hence the causal intensity is not borne out. Thus the pitying hearts are less inevitably bound to the lovers' pain than it may first seem: "They wept tears as bitter as aloe or gall, *so* there is no heart so hard that it would not have pity." Implicitly, the tears are *so* bitter *as* to soften the hard heart, but again, the tears are separated from the resulting pity in such a way as to disrupt causation in portraying the shared feeling to which the stanza overtly lays claim.[35] Empathy appears here as a mediated conclusion rather than a spontaneous response.

The Myrrha stanza devotes much of its syntactical and formal energy to a vocabulary of likeness designed to imagine not only the lovers' mutuality but also a community that mirrors their feeling. The stanza is only one of the narrator's many claims and exhortations to compassionate response. From the poem's opening, he has called upon his audience to recall their own joy and pain in love, which (he imagines) will motivate sympathetic prayers for both the poem's characters and the narrator himself, in his efforts to represent "Swich peyne and wo as Loves folk endure" (I. 34). In writing their woe, he says, he seeks "to have of hem compassioun, / As though I were hire owne brother dere" (I. 50–1). This lateral, brotherly compassion brings narrator, audience, and characters into continual (and sometimes uncomfortably vicarious) identification with one another.[36] It often overrides distinctions in role, status, sex, or individual experience to emphasize instead the ethical power of empathetic response – even, here, in the face of the incest taboo.

Yet throughout the poem, and with particular force in the final two books, the narrator's calls to pity or compassion introduce difference and mutability. In the Myrrha stanza, we have seen the ways in which verbal arrangements put pressure on the vocabulary of likeness: forcing distance between the elements of conventional figures of speech; opening gaps between feeling and expression, and among different forms of expression; multiplying the vehicles of conventional metaphors; attenuating the syntactical connections within and between clauses; and finally, of course, estranging conventional language by citing a highly charged and thematically disturbing Ovidian tale. It is through that allusion that we can start to understand the way in which "the chaungyng of Criseyde" destroys the narrator's fantasy of a community formed through affective identification, and the way in which Criseyde is made the figure for that destruction.

---

[35] On the effects of editorial punctuation here, see n. 22. It is possible to re-punctuate so as to tighten the causal link between Myrrha and the softening heart, but it is not possible to tighten the link between the lovers' tears and the softening hearts.

[36] On Pandarus's vicarious desire and the way it implicates the reader, see Taylor, *Chaucer Reads*, esp. 78–132.

Incest and Community

If what Karla Taylor finds is that Troilus and Criseyde switch places in the course of the poem – she becomes the flexible reed and he, the stable oak – then in Myrrha's tears we have an image of the sheer pain of conjunction, rigid *and* flowing, implying an erotic unity that makes and ekes out bitterness. Entwined and mutely weeping, the lovers perform a kind of futile self-enclosure, an intimacy in the face of fatherly politicking and parliamentary decision-making that seems to cordon them off from history. When the narrator merges audience feeling with that of the lovers, he brings the audience, too, into this pattern of resistance to change.

The allusion to Myrrha participates in that dense mutuality by spinning the stanza back in literary time to a story in which a daughter is enclosed within a recursive desire (incest) and then within a tree. The reference to incest intensifies the lovers' enclosure and the vocabulary of likeness: incest, by definition, resists the differentiation of the daughter from her family through exogamy.[37] Thematically, the taboo and its transgression at the heart of the Myrrha tale still sit awkwardly within the love between Troilus and Criseyde.[38] Even in Ovid, Myrrha's desire for her father actually introduces difference, starting with a crucial deception when she hides her identity from him in order to consummate their union.[39] And later, her father's discovery that his young lover is his daughter introduces another difference, exile, as she flees south from Cyprus across the Arabian Peninsula into Sabaea. The story, as Michael Putnam shows, unfolds as a meditation on exile as its heroine enters a "new world of apartness" that calls up the exile of Aeneas and of Ovid himself.[40] If Chaucer's stanza seems to represent a vortex of mutual sorrow into which the lovers pull every compassionate heart, the Myrrha reference associates such sorrow with epic and tragic exile at various allusive levels, expanding the stakes and the scale of the lovers' grief.

---

[37] John Fyler connects incest to problems of excessive likeness in "Domesticating the Exotic in the *Squire's Tale*," *English Literary History* 55.1 (1988), 1–26. On incest in medieval literature more generally, the classic account is Elizabeth Archibald, *Incest and the Medieval Imagination* (Oxford: Oxford University Press, 2001).

[38] Wetherbee suggests that Pandarus's vicarious intimacy does approach an incestuous intimacy. Carolyn Dinshaw calls his vicarious presence "almost obscene": Dinshaw, *Chaucer's Sexual Poetics* (Madison: University of Wisconsin Press, 1989), 48. But the Myrrha stanza frames the lovers alone far more strongly than it gestures toward Pandarus, detaching her incest from simple association with his vicarious desire.

[39] This deception is what Dante blames her for – he places her with the falsifiers in the eighth circle of Hell (*Inf.* XXX, 34–48).

[40] Michael Putnam, "Ovid, Virgil and Myrrha's Metaphoric Exile," *Vergilius* 47 (2001), 171–93 (at 175).

TEARS OF SURVIVAL: MYRRHA AND CRISEYDE

To observe the full scope of the allusion here is to see afresh the lovers' grief, especially that of Criseyde; and it is to recontextualize Criseyde's eventual turn toward what Winthrop Wetherbee calls "practicality" – her emergence out of the mute and involuted embrace with Troilus, her refusal of suicide, and her acquiescence to the trade. For Wetherbee, Chaucer's Myrrha allusion points to the nurse who saves Myrrha from suicide by arranging her incestuous consummation; the nurse points toward Pandarus's machinations that allow the lovers to come together. It is true that the lovers' meeting in Book IV is suggested by Pandarus to assuage Troilus's grief (IV. 1114–20).[41] Yet while Wetherbee's comparison between the sympathetic responses of two over-active procurers is evocative and attentive to sexual excess, he misses Chaucer's emphasis on the mutuality of the lovers' sorrow, underestimating as a result the sheer devastation wrought by Troy's political plan and reducing the magnitude of Criseyde's grief. As Taylor and others have long seen, Criseyde's concern with survival is part of Chaucer's exploration of the effects of gender and status on the way her love and loss play out within the community.[42] The poem's very first scene depicts Criseyde before parliament, after her father has betrayed the city, pleading for her life: the problem of her place in the community governs the entirety of the plot and every decision she makes.

How, then, does Criseyde, in particular, respond to the mapping of wartime politics onto the love affair? The Myrrha stanza appears at the beginning of the scene in which she will decide how to respond. What conduct is proper to a person whom the community has agreed to trade away? As I argued above, the stanza's vocabulary of likeness forms a bulwark against separation. It also invokes the sympathy of others, conjuring a community based on fellow-feeling. What role does such pity have in the context of the trade? The parliament has acted on a form of community based less on affect than on hierarchy, less on mutual recognition than on exchange. The Myrrha reference, with its see-sawing between likeness and difference, tests out options for responding to a sudden shift – not in civic organization per se, but in Criseyde's range of acceptable actions. The reference experiments with both tragic self-destruction and epic grandeur, unfolding alternatives that the lovers – in particular, Criseyde – will shortly decide to refuse. Inasmuch as these experiments recall the nurse's and Pandarus's sympathy, the effect

---

[41] Winthrop Wetherbee, *Chaucer and the Poets* (Ithaca: Cornell University Press, 1984), 87–110.

[42] Criseyde's concern for her safety throughout the poem is linked, according to Taylor, to Chaucer's argument about the domain of poetry. Through comparison with Dante, Taylor's work on the *Troilus* shows a sustained conceptual disagreement between the two poets about the role of poetry in representing the temporal world (Chaucer) versus leading us toward salvation (Dante).

232   ELIZABETH ALLEN

is less a moral critique of sexual excess than an examination of the structure and function of sympathy itself.

Seen in this way, Chaucer's reference to Ovid's Myrrha elevates the sheer indecision of the moment. Myrrha's metamorphosis in Ovid harks back to an arboreal metaphor from earlier in the tale, when Myrrha suffered suicidal torment. Wholly absorbed by the passion she knows is wrong, Myrrha is about to hang herself:

> [She] is filled now with despair, now with desire to try, feels now shame and now desire, and finds no plan of action; and, just as a great tree, smitten by the axe, when all but the last blow has been struck, wavers which way to fall and threatens every side, so her mind, weakened by many blows, leans unsteadily now this way and now that, and falteringly turns in both directions; and no end nor rest for her passion can she find save death.[43]

These lines, in turn, cite Virgil's comparison of Troy's fall to the felling of an oak – the same image that Pandarus used in Book II to urge Troilus to fell the "sturdy ook" that was Criseyde. In Virgil, the image personifies the besieged city as a soldier about to fall. In Ovid, the image is both feminized and narrower in scope, containing only the isolated Myrrha, soon to be interrupted by her nurse. Myrrha's wavering here like a swaying tree depicts not the inevitable fall, but reed-like indecision, as Myrrha hesitates between suicide and incest. Adducing a pattern of Virgilian allusions in the Myrrha story, Julie Dyson argues that Ovid uses them to diminish his literary "father."[44] Such skepticism about the epic grandeur of Troy's fall pervades the *Metamorphoses* and, as I have written elsewhere, often accompanies Ovidian allusions in *Troilus and Criseyde*.[45] At the same time, the allusion to the fall of Troy in Myrrha's dark narrative elevates her inner torment, the conflict between her resistance and her eventual acquiescence to the desire she knows to be wrong. This suffering is both intimate and social: Myrrha construes the social taboo as a legitimate, yet unwelcome, limit on her desire. Her desire, then, figures a disordered relation to community, and suicide captures her resulting isolation. Myrrha's swaying tree is, in this sense, both an indication of and a foil for community responsibility.

---

[43] "Et modo desperat, modo vult temptare, pudetque / et cupit, et, quid agat, non invenit, utque securi / saucia trabs ingens, ubi plaga novissima restat, / quo cadat, in dubio est omnique a parte timetur, / sic animus vario labefactus vulnere nutat / huc levis atque illuc momentaque sumit utroque, / nec modus aut requies, nisi mors, reperitur amoris" (Ovid, *Met.* X, 371–7).

[44] Julia T. Dyson, "Myrrha's Catabasis," *The Classical Journal* 94.2 (1998–9), 163–7.

[45] Allen, "Flowing Backward," 685. On the anti-epic impulse of the *Metamorphoses*, see Philip Hardie, "Ovid's Theban History: the First 'Anti-Aeneid'?" *Classical Quarterly* 40 (1990), 224–35.

However equivocally and even satirically, Myrrha's tree invokes the epic world in which the grandeur of the tree's crashing to the ground indicates the terrible destruction of an entire heroic culture. In comparing the bitterness of the lovers' tears to myrrh and comparing their grief to incestuous Myrrha's, Chaucer does more than show the mute self-enclosure of their sorrow. He also asserts its locatedness within a web of imagery that connects a woman's intimate, transgressive self-destruction to the fall of the great city. Chaucer's stanza thus contains a reminder of Criseyde's involvement in Troy's inevitable tragic ruin. His allusion insists – against the grain of the stanza's intimacy and stasis – that Troilus and Criseyde are sorrowing within, and because of, a broader political community on a grand scale. The poem remains, like Dyson's Ovid, skeptical about the stature and the ethical values of that political community. But the Trojan world visible through the Myrrhan tree symbolically elevates the lovers' struggle; reminds readers of the wider civic context and the city's martial threat; and, as in Myrrha's desperate recourse to suicide, shows the limits of their power to resist the force of the communal decision.

Criseyde's swoon acknowledges and seeks a way out of the impending political fall. In the stanzas that follow the allusion, the lovers seem momentarily to calm themselves, as their "woful weri goostes tweyne" return to their bodies – only for Criseyde's "woful spirit" to pass out of its proper place as she falls into a swoon. Criseyde's limbs grow cold and her eyes roll back in an imitation of death so convincing that Troilus takes his sword out of its sheath and begins to bid the world goodbye. It is as if the allusion to the tree had allowed Myrrha's intended suicide to "leak" into the poem's action. Indeed, Criseyde's faint also resembles the quasi-death of Myrrha, who begs for metamorphosis as a liminal solution, neither death nor life:

> O gods, if any there be who will listen to my prayer, I do not refuse the dire punishment I have deserved; but lest, surviving, I offend the living, and, dying, I offend the dead, drive me from both realms; change me and refuse me both life and death![46]

Myrrha's language here implies a kind of contagion that often accompanies incest, a sense that her outrage must not be allowed to spread, and that only a liminal existence – a fertile body enclosed in the bark of the tree – can adequately express her suffering while containing it, keeping it from the rest of the world. Criseyde's quasi-death resembles the wretched in-between state of Myrrha in the tree, and the echo of Myrrha's distraught plea enhances Criseyde's similarly suspended state – between union and separation, living and dead. In this context it is no accident that Orpheus is the teller of Ovid's

---

[46] "o siqua patetis / numina confessis, merui nec triste recuso / supplicium, sed ne violem vivosque superstes / mortuaque exstinctos, ambobus pellite regnis / mutataeque mihi vitamque necemque negate!" (Ovid, *Met.* X, 483–7).

tale: the Orpheus who has lost Eurydice and sings in Apollo's grove, suspended between catabasis and eventual dismemberment and death. These Ovidian suspensions mirror the liminal status of Criseyde, while also pointing out a crucial difference: Myrrha can beg for metamorphic change, but Criseyde's "chaungynge" offers no bodily shapeshifting as either containment or release.

The Myrrha stanza, then, lends Criseyde's faint a tragic seriousness, suggesting the liminal and passing character of a catabasis. Her swoon separates her from Troilus and particularizes her suffering, breaking the mutuality of their sorrow and marking the extremity of her specific grief, which has had the stamp of death from when she first learned her fate earlier in Book IV. There, when the Trojan women visited to confirm the rumors of her impending trade, her spirit already left her body (IV. 699) and, in the women's unconsoling company, "she felte almost hire herte dye / For wo and wery of that compaignie" (IV. 706–7). After they departed, she retired to her chamber, rending her face and hair in a classical image of grief; her rhetoric escalated into another kind of catabasis, an imagined death, with her and Troilus reunited in Elysium like Orpheus and Eurydice (IV. 788–91). The scene paints Criseyde as profoundly alienated from the "claustrophobic town of gossip" ostensibly pitying her plight.[47] Similarly, after greeting Troilus, her swoon isolates her: she is cold, speechless and unresponsive, as though already separate from both Troilus and the community that has traded her away.[48] Yet she does not die a heroic, sacrificial death. Thinking her dead, Troilus begins to bid the world farewell in a very different, more communal mode, in language that encompasses the world, the gods, the city "which that I leve in wo" (IV. 1205), and his father and brothers. The difference in their communal language indicates a difference in role and obligation – hers to go into exile, his to belong and to fight. That other exile, Aeneas, also sojourns in the underworld, where he hears the prophecy of empire from his father, Anchises. By contrast, Criseyde's prophetic father is a traitor, not a harbinger of Roman ascendancy. He betrayed the city to which, as a result, she now owes her exile. If Criseyde's swoon has something of the cosmic grandeur of that signal future traveler in the land of the dead, her kinship and her sex inhibit any entitlement to exceptional heroism.

Criseyde embraces her communal obligation, though, as much as it differs from Aeneas's *pietas*. Her Myrrhan sojourn in the quasi-death of the swoon

---

[47] Daniel Davies, "'Wereyed on every side:' Chaucer's *Troilus and Criseyde* and the Logic of Siege Warfare," *New Medieval Literatures* 20 (2020), 74–106 (at 98).

[48] In "Troilus' Swoon," *Chaucer Review* 14.4 (1980), 319–35, Jill Mann notes the way in which the swoon preserves the lovers' mutuality. Chaucer places Troilus's swoon in Book III, whereas in Boccaccio's *Il Filostrato*, Troilus swoons publicly after learning Criseyde will be traded for Antenor – in close proximity to Criseida's swoon.

prompts a transformation: when Troilus kisses her, she comes to and is horrified to see his drawn sword: "Allas, how neigh we weren bothe dede!" (IV. 1232).[49] Although initially this cry frames their recovery as mutual, the sympathy between the lovers has fractured, first because of her swoon, a separate encounter with death, and afterwards because she veers decisively *away* from both mutual sorrow and self-destruction. She chooses instead the opposite response, embracing survival and looking outward toward the larger social system of the war as she seeks to comfort Troilus.

That is, at the point of death, Criseyde becomes newly conscious, like Aeneas emerging from the Sybil's cave, of what she owes to her community. The nature of her debt has to do with precisely that which is transgressed in father-daughter incest: what Gayle Rubin calls "the traffic in women" constituted by exogamy. According to a logic of exchange, the incest taboo prevents the customary transaction between one head of family and another that ties together a (male) community by extending its network of obligation and inheritance.[50] Trading prisoners of war is a structure of exchange: after a Trojan loss, the two sides call a truce in order to exchange prisoners and ransom, "for the surplus yeven sommes grete" (IV. 60). The negotiation of an exchange of prisoners reaches Calchas's ears and prompts his request, which he frames as a transaction: having lost all his goods when he left Troy behind to help the Greeks, he wants to "redeem" his child (IV. 108) as a reward for his prophetic services. To be sure, he also uses emotional terms, regretting having abandoned her – "How myghte I have in that so hard an herte?" (IV. 95) – and begging for succor – "ye lords rewe[th] upon my sorwe" (IV. 98). His remorse for his own hard heart and his need for pity, however, appear in a context of political acquisition, so that his paternal affection seems a thin cover-up for the structure of exchange. This transactional situation assigns a communally agreed upon value: Criseyde is "worth" Antenor plus Thoas (IV. 138). Hector's resistance to the trade on the grounds that she is not a prisoner indicates her exchange value even in denying its legitimacy: "We usen here no wommen for to selle," he insists (IV. 182). The Middle English "sellen" encompasses gift giving and reward as well as exchange, making clear the range of customary terms for such traffic. As scholars have long pointed out,

---

[49] A swoon is "a way of creating a 'fresh start' in the narrative," writes Mann, "Troilus' Swoon," 328. Having suffered a kind of catabasis, Criseyde now begins to counsel survival even at the cost of the mutuality she and Troilus have discovered. Dyani Johns Taff, "Secrecy and Alternate Endings," *Studies in Philology* 116.4 (2019), 617–39, argues that Criseyde's swoon suggests a tragic double suicide but then "truncates" the possibility (at 636).

[50] Gayle Rubin, "The Traffic in Women: Notes on the Political Economy of Sex," in *Feminist Anthropology, a Reader*, ed. Ellen Lewin (Malden: Blackwell Publishing, 2006), 157–210.

Hector's gesture to custom ironically recalls Helen's abduction, crucial sign of a culture in which women *are* in fact given and sold and stolen, fought for and redeemed.[51]

The structure of Criseyde's situation is clear from the opening stanza of Book IV. While Antenor must be freed from prison because he is valuable for his qualities and actions – his boldness and capacity to fight – Criseyde's value does not "belong" to her. As a woman, she does not need to be a prisoner to be traded. Once this transactional structure emerges, its power becomes nearly impossible to resist because anything said in parliament reiterates the woman's absence and reduction to an object; even Hector can only be her "protector," as though he were her lone unhappy escort, confronted by an enemy in the forest of Logres.[52]

Yet, as the comparison to that quintessential romance trope of the traffic in women suggests, women differ from objects of exchange (for example, money) inasmuch as they are human beings with will and desire. According to the custom of Logres, an unaccompanied woman is not available for the taking; that is, there is a basic structural alternative to being trafficked, in the figure of the woman traveling alone, whose will should be respected. When Troilus, in parliament, is silent in response to the proposal that Criseyde be exchanged, he refuses to claim her as object – a resistance to transaction that has, in fact, often defined his conduct toward her.[53] He thinks to himself instead about her reaction if he were to reveal their love and decides not to argue in parliament without her assent (IV. 165). That is, his response assigns value to that which does "belong" to her, her own desire. As conventional to erotic love as Troilus's secrecy may be, its function here is to inhibit his public participation in the traffic of women and to preserve his crucial attention to Criseyde's will.

Troilus's habit of inhibition, in fact, leaves space throughout the poem for Criseyde's idiosyncratic reactions and the suggestion of her independent

---

[51] Dinshaw, *Chaucer's Sexual Poetics*, 28–64, was the first account to apply Gayle Rubin's analysis of the traffic in women to Criseyde.

[52] "In those days the practices and liberties were such that if a knight came upon a girl – be she lady or maid-in-waiting – he would no more treat her with dishonor than cut his own throat should a noble reputation concern him ... But if she was under the escort of one knight, another, anxious to fight for her and successful in winning her in armed combat, might do with her as he pleased without receiving censure or shame": Chrétien de Troyes, *Lancelot; or the Knight of the Cart*, in *The Complete Romances of Chrétien de Troyes*, trans. David Stanes (Bloomington: Indiana University Press, 1990), 186.

[53] Some readers have understood Troilus's silence in more skeptical terms as a self-centered disavowal of authority, for example, Garrison, "Masculine Interiority," 333.

desire. The subtle operations of her consent are the primary topic of Books II and III. In the consummation scene, Troilus so inhibits his own desire that he falls into a swoon of his own, allowing Criseyde to become the desiring subject, touching him, kissing him, and begging him to speak to her. Although the scene is also marked by Pandarus's intrusions – throwing the fainting Troilus into bed, retiring only as far as the fireplace – the narration also leaves space for *both* lovers' desire, as when Troilus speaks to her "as fil to purpos for his herte reste" (III. 1131; "as was appropriate to ease his heart") and she in turn speaks to him "as hire leste" (III. 1132). By withholding the content of their speech here and elsewhere, the narrator points instead to the reciprocal structure of their desire, tenuously separate from Pandarus's machinations. Later, a vocabulary of mutual, specular desire is achieved through the narrator's use of undifferentiated plural pronouns, so that each enjoys the other (e.g., III. 1310–44). Metaphorically, too, the lovers are depicted in terms that emphasize mirroring or resemblance, not differentiation, ringing another change on the image of the flexible versus rigid tree: "And as aboute a tree, with many a twiste, / Bytrent and writhe the swote wodebynde, / Gan eche of hem in armes other wynde" (III. 1230–2). Who winds about whom here? Withheld content, plural pronouns, the vine simile, and many of the other rhetorical effects of the consummation scene are designed to indicate Criseyde's desire and, even more, to use a language of likeness to depict mutuality. In Book III, such language is designed to resist gender hierarchy and suggest an alternative to the traffic of women to which Criseyde knows she is at risk from the poem's start. The narrator's prominence, along with that of Pandarus, continually reminds us that the depiction of this alternative is partial and fabricated, so that the poem suggests, rather than firmly defines, Criseyde's independent will.[54] A structure that privileges her independent desire, that is, exists as a precarious and gestural alternative to the far more practically functional structure of the traffic in women.[55] Later, waking from her swoon, she faces the fact that, by deciding she can be traded, the Trojan

[54] "Chaucer gestures toward a female autonomy not wholly confined by the strictures of romantic love, without, however, actually representing it," writes Karla Taylor, "Inferno 5 and Troilus and Criseyde Revisited," in *Chaucer's Troilus: "Subgit be to alle poesye": Essays in Criticism*, ed. R.A. Shoaf (Binghamton: SUNY Press, 1992), 252.

[55] Criseyde's independent desire or will remains a subject of debate. Another essential account, Elizabeth Robertson, "Public Bodies and Psychic Domains: Rape, Consent, and Female Subjectivity in Geoffrey Chaucer's *Troilus and Criseyde*," in *Representing Rape in Medieval and Early Modern Literature*, ed. Elizabeth Robertson and Christine M. Rose (New York: Palgrave, 2001), 281–310, articulates the complexity of her consent within a context of rape established both by Pandarus's suggestion that Troilus abduct her and by allusions to rape even in the love scenes.

aristocracy have (re)asserted the hierarchical structure of gender and status that the lovers, however temporarily and even accidentally, found ways to resist.

In Book IV, the "chaungyng of Criseyde" imposes the communal pattern that the lovers have tried to evade, and as we have seen, their initial response is to wind all the more tightly about one another, merging and hardening into the Myrrhan tree of solidifying tears. To compare the lovers' mutuality to incest, as we have seen, might seem to mark it as erotically excessive; but actually, the allusion produces a tension between desire and communal obligation, and it is this tension that draws in the sympathetic audience imagined in its final couplet. The couplet merges lovers and readers in a lateral intimacy that implies a community built on mutual sympathy – a community that seems to evade mediation, as the hardest hearts respond directly and inevitably to the lovers' pain. Such an image of compassion resists not only the reality of separation but also the mediatory structure of the traffic in women.

After her swoon, Criseyde does recognize that she has been placed in a position of exchange and agrees to occupy that position, against the grain of her profound sorrow, because it is the condition of her survival, or what Holly Crocker calls her "embodied endurance."[56] Criseyde's decision to acquiesce to the trade – if this can be called a decision – differentiates her from Troilus and, eventually, from her sympathetic audience as well. Her speech to him, arguing that her departure could be temporary, is full of admonitions: "Lo, herte myn, wel woot ye this" (IV. 1254); "Now herkneth this" (IV. 1296); "Have here another wey" (IV. 1366). She appeals to what he sees and knows, what is well understood and believable. In effect, she summons a new vocabulary – an apparently "practical" discourse full of phrases that diminish the magnitude of the lovers' woe, make virtue of necessity (IV. 1586), and put their "disese" and annoyance into a context of a future joyful reunion (IV. 1303 ff.), as though bitter pain in love could still now turn to sweetness. Her arguments move away from Ovidian and Virgilian allusion, disavowing Myrrhan torment, suicide, and the epic downfall of the city as she tries to imagine a concrete future that does not entail downfall at all.

In seeking survival, Criseyde casts about for local and communal mechanisms by which she might return to Troy after the trade. She is "killing death," preventing her own and Troilus's demise, drawing herself and him out of the mute vortex of their shared sorrow. In the process she sidelines the vocabulary of likeness and accepts the logic of sexual difference that makes her exchangeable. Whereas earlier, haunted by death, Criseyde envisioned her existential isolation, now she strongly registers the social presence of both Troilus and the imperatives of the wartime community. Parliament has decided to trade her, which, she says, she cannot resist (IV. 1296–302). Yet her whole

---

[56] Holly Crocker, *The Matter of Virtue: Women's Ethical Action from Chaucer to Shakespeare* (Philadelphia: University of Pennsylvania Press, 2019), 44.

family is in Troy except her father (IV. 1331–3); how can she possibly dwell among the Greeks? (IV. 1362–3); and yet peace may be coming (IV. 1346); if peace comes, she has friends in court to take her part (IV. 1391–3); she can manipulate her father easily to let her go (IV. 1395 ff.). If her imagined return is an impractical fantasy, it is in the service of a political survival in the camp, where she can imagine procuring a safe conduct, or there may even be a truce. Like Dorigen in the Franklin's tale, she is trying to stave off sacrificial self-destruction.

It is worth lingering on the asymmetry that defines her speech here. In turning away from the deathlike involution of the Myrrha stanza, Criseyde chooses to acknowledge her debt to her community; paradoxically, that debt consists in her departure and survival in the enemy camp. To die would be to make herself a sacrifice and transgress the terms of her obligation. To elope with Troilus would be to betray the city. She is in this bind because of her sex, which both makes her blameworthy and limits her power to determine her own fate. If her choice to accede to the trade is not accompanied by the concern for gods and family piety that Troilus summoned on the brink of suicide, that lack shows more about the seriousness with which she approaches death – and the Trojan negotiators' contrasting assertion that her life is owed in trade – than about the "practicality" of Criseyde's survival.

In this context, incest marks the bind: it suggests that Criseyde's departure is prompted not simply by politics but by social taboo. As we have seen, because Myrrha appears in Chaucer's stanza as the already-changed and grieving tree, the stanza does not point directly to a simple correspondence between her desire for her father and the lovers' desire to stay together. Instead, the allusive tree partakes in patterns of tension between stasis and change, likeness and difference; it magnifies the lovers' grief, tilting Criseyde's sorrow in particular toward self-destruction and death. More than this: the allusion points to the conflict between desire and cultural imperative – incest and the rule against it – that governs the lovers' and the narrator's fantasies of likeness or co-feeling in this stanza. Myrrha's suffering presence marks a profound rupture between the lovers' desires and their duties to the community. The asymmetry of their respective social duties differentiate them and isolate Criseyde. More particularly, alluding to incest emphasizes the logic of the taboo: incest avoidance is what enables the traffic in women. To figure the lovers' scene of mutual love in terms that approach incest is to make forceful and fundamental Criseyde's separation. It is to dramatize the immovability of the hierarchy to which she is subject and the foundational character of the cultural imperative according to which, Myrrha-like, she must catapult herself away, detach herself from her beloved, and go into exile. At the same time, the mutual grief expressed through the Myrrha stanza expresses the sheer pain of abiding by cultural obligations, and the way in which such suffering will continue – across Arabia in Myrrha's case, and in Criseyde's, across the border between Troy and the Greek camp. Finally, when Criseyde approaches and crosses that border, she differentiates herself from Troilus in order to undergo the required "chaungyng." She is immediately understood as a woman who can and must be trafficked, who connects the warring sides, who will become, as Diomede immediately calls her, "my lady fre" (V. 144) as he seeks to prove that Greeks are just as true and kind as Trojans (V. 124–6).

In one sense, then, Criseyde's trade reveals how closely the two sides are knit together. As a woman given in marriage mediates the bond between male heads of household, so too Criseyde's exchange enables agreement between the warring sides. It is as though the war were reduceable to two equal forces competing over a prize, with Criseyde's trade symbolically mirroring Helen's abduction; the war essentially consists of a single community in conflict yet bound by the traffic in women. As much as the lovers sought ways of resisting the traffic in women – and as much as their grief itself approaches reciprocity – Criseyde's status as object of exchange is what she "owes" Troy. That status is fully realized during and after the trade, so that the Greek camp becomes the mechanism by which her debt to the wider community is enforced or, as Carolyn Dinshaw puts it, "she in fact acts in the best interests of Troy in the repair of its losses in battle and in the reestablishment of truce or temporary equilibrium of the siege."[57] She joins the Greek community, that is, as an exchanged and therefore exchangeable woman, accompanied, in the terms of the Custom of Logres, and the logic of her acquiescence to Diomede's protection is the logic of her role in such a structure. Diomede's wooing makes apparent that he sees her as an object to be won from the tenuous protection of her father. When he first delivers her to her father's tent, and later, repeatedly, visits her in the tent, he emphasizes the way in which she is under Calchas's jurisdiction, asking her why her father has delayed so long in marrying her (V. 862–3). The temporary character of Calchas's dwelling, and his status as an outsider, render her available, albeit more for "fishing" than for marriage.

In another sense, the trade reveals difference, not only between male and female, but also between the besieged citizens of Troy and the empowered Greek attackers.[58] The trade, then, damages the alternative structures of community based on pity that the poem experiments with or gestures toward. It undercuts the possibility of autonomous feminine desire; hence it disables a crucial aspect of the compassion that the poem has cultivated. The narrator has continually implied that we might not only pity Troilus but also feel with or alongside Criseyde. The poem's opening proem calls upon *all* lovers, even those falsely injured by wicked tongues, "be it he or she" (I. 39): the

---

[57] Dinshaw, *Chaucer's Sexual Poetics*, 57.

[58] Davies, "Logic of Siege Warfare," shows the military differences between attackers and besieged in order to elucidate Criseyde's subjection to the "engin" of both love and war.

implication from the outset is that Criseyde, like all lovers, may be worthy of empathy. The narrator's efforts in Book V show at once how possible and how thwarted is the impulse toward such pity: "But trewely, how longe it was bytwene / That she forsok hym for this Diomede, / Ther is non auctour telleth it, I wene" (V. 1086–8). Ignorance of the facts baffles the narrator and implies blame, even though he struggles to pity her: "I wolde excuse hire yet for routhe" (V. 1099). What frustrates the narrator's will to pity her and renders his efforts a form of condemnation is the fact that not just the timing of her betrayal, but the very suggestion of her independent will has receded before a cultural imperative that renders her mediatory rather than agential. It is because she is trafficked that the narrator cannot find access to her intentions.

The poem has nonetheless been built on a fantasy of resemblance among the feelings of lovers and their witnesses, a shared feeling that continually overcomes socially derived barriers such as Troilus's shame and Criseyde's fear and even Pandarus's clumsiness in love. Pandarus's response to Troilus's love is to promise to share his pain (I. 589); the narrator plans to write the lovers' woe as though he were their brother; he begs for all lovers to pray for both his characters and himself (I. 29–46). The Myrrha stanza rings a variation on this emotional sharing, as we have seen. Myrrha's sorrow invokes pity: Myrrha does not kill herself because, hearing her complain, the nurse is filled with empathy and enables transgression rather than allow the girl's death.[59] The narrator Orpheus, too, especially at the moment of the metamorphosis, renders Myrrha sympathetic, in a "shift in tone from antipathy to sympathy toward his protagonist."[60] In the course of *Troilus and Criseyde*, pity is often suspect, particularly, as Taylor shows, when it aligns with Pandarus's vicarious desire, involving witnesses in others' affairs in ways that risk invasiveness.[61] The social nature of shame and fear are thus never fully offset by Pandarus's or anyone else's pity.

But there is more than vicarious desire at stake in the stanza's conventional claim that even the hardest of hearts would pity the lovers. The stanza, clinched in this way, imagines a world in which the lovers remain equivalent and wound about each other. At the same time, it mystifies the impending force of the traffic in women and the reduction of Criseyde to survival; it evades gender

---

[59] "She took the weeping girl on her aged bosom, and so holding her in her feeble arms she said: 'I know, you are in love! and in this affair I shall be entirely devoted to your service, have no fear; nor shall your father ever know'" (Ovid, *Met.* X, 406–10; "gremio lacrimantem tollit anili / atque ita conplectens infirmis membra lacertis / 'sensimus,' inquit 'amas! et in hoc mea (pone timorem) / sedulitas erit apta tibi, nec sentiet umquam / hoc pater'").

[60] Putnam, "Metamorphic Exile," 171.

[61] Taylor connects Pandarus's vicariousness to readerly complicity in *Chaucer Reads*.

difference. In what follows, Criseyde will become less accessible to pity, not simply because the narrator does not know when or why she betrays Troilus, but because she is subsumed into a communal structure oblivious to her sorrow or ambivalence. The poem's brotherhood of pity pretends that Criseyde's feeling is the same as Troilus's, rather than a gendered set of bonds from which Criseyde has already, in effect, been excluded. In this sense, the lateral pity that readers are assigned throughout the text, as much as it earlier allowed gestures to Criseyde's interiority and the lovers' mutuality, now obscures the hierarchical – and finally unpayable – nature of Criseyde's communal debt.[62]

The conventional formulation that ends the Myrrha stanza returns in Book V, as Criseyde grieves for her losses, remembering what she had desired:

> In al this world ther nys so cruel herte
> That hire hadde herd compleynen in hire sorwe
> That nolde han wepen for hire peynes smerte,
> So tendrely she weep, bothe eve and morwe.
> Hire nedede no teris for to borwe!
> And this was yet the werste of al hire peyne:
> Ther was no wight to whom she dorste hire pleyne. (V. 722–8)

Though we begin with even the hardest heart weeping for her pain, the effect is disrupted by the mention of borrowed tears, as though Criseyde's grief might somehow not "belong" to her. Moreover, despite the conventionality and apparent stability of the "no heart so cruel" figure, its context has shifted: whereas in the Myrrha stanza, the hard heart concluded the stanza, softening in response to the lovers and confirming the brotherhood of pity, here the cruel heart's struggle to sympathize opens the stanza. As the stanza continues there is no one to mirror her sorrow; the specific loss of Troilus blurs into a more sweeping lack of any audience to hear her complaint. The stanza moves away from the vocabulary of likeness, showing how profoundly the lateral bonds of sympathy have been thwarted by the traffic in women. Criseyde does not need to borrow tears, but neither can she share them, and it is this consequence of her communal action that clarifies her exclusion from the brotherhood of pity and consignment to isolation, long before her acquiescence to Diomede.

---

[62] Esposito, *Communitas*, describes the character of *munus* or social debt as unending, "a gift that does not belong to the subject, indeed weakens [*reduce*] the subject and that hollows him out through a never-ending obligation" (17). Community thus brings its members close to death by withdrawing them from their subjectivity, a liminal situation that resonates with Criseyde's situation here (10–11).

KARLA TAYLOR'S PUBLISHED WRITING

"Proverbs and the Authentication of Convention in Troilus and Criseyde," in *Chaucer's 'Troilus': Essays in Criticism*, ed. Stephen A. Barney (Hamden: Archon, 1980), 277–96

"A Text and Its Afterlife: Dante and Chaucer," *Comparative Literature* 35.1 (1983), 1–20

"From *superbo Ilion* to *umile Italia*: The Acrostic of *Paradiso* 19," *Stanford Italian Review* 7.1–2 (1987), 47–66

Chaucer Reads 'The Divine Comedy' (Palo Alto: Stanford University Press, 1989)

"Chaucer's Reticent Merchant," in *The Idea of Medieval Literature: New Essays on Chaucer and Medieval Culture in Honor of Donald R. Howard*, ed. James M. Dean and Christian K. Zacher (Newark: University of Delaware Press, 1992), 189–205

"Inferno 5 and *Troilus and Criseyde* Revisited," in *Chaucer's Troilus: "Subgit be to alle poesye": Essays in Criticism*, ed. R.A. Shoaf (Binghamton: SUNY Press, 1992), 239–56

"Chaucer's Uncommon Voice: Some Contexts for Influence," in *Boccaccio and the "Canterbury Tales": New Essays on an Old Question*, ed. Leonard M. Koff and Brenda Deen Schildgen (Vancouver: Associated University Presses, 2000), 47–82

"Social Aesthetics and the Emergence of Civic Discourse from the *Shipman's Tale* to *Melibee*," *Chaucer Review* 39.3 (2005), 298–322

"Chaucer's Volumes: Toward a New Model of Literary History in the Canterbury Tales," *Studies in the Age of Chaucer* 29 (2007), 43–85

"Chaucer and the French Tradition," in *Approaches to Teaching Troilus and Criseyde and the Minor Poems*, ed. Tison Pugh and Angela Weisl (New York: Modern Language Association, 2007), 33–8

"Writers of the Italian Renaissance," in *Oxford History of Literary Translation in English, Volume 1 (to 1550)*, ed. Roger Ellis (Oxford: Oxford University Press, 2008), 390–406

"Inside Out in Gower's Republic of Letters," in *John Gower, Trilingual Poet: Language, Translation and Tradition*, ed. Elisabeth Dutton, with John Hines, and R.F. Yeager (Cambridge: D.S. Brewer, 2010), 169–81

"Language in Use," in *Chaucer: Contemporary Approaches*, ed. Susanna Fein and David Raybin (University Park: Pennsylvania State University Press, 2010), 99–115

"Reading Faces in Gower and Chaucer," in *John Gower: Others and the Self,* ed. Russell A. Peck and R.F. Yeager (Cambridge: D.S. Brewer, 2017), 73–90

"The Motives of Reeds: The Wife of Bath's Midas and Literary Tradition," in *Later Middle English Literature, Materiality, and Culture: Essays in Honor of James M. Dean*, ed. Brian Gastle and Erick Kelemen (Newark: University of Delaware Press, 2018), 25–41

"What Lies Beneath," in *John Gower in Manuscripts and Early Printed Books,* ed. Martha Driver, Derek Pearsall, and Robert F. Yeager (Cambridge: D.S. Brewer, 2020), 71–88

What We Think of When We Think of the Prioress's Tale, ed. with Susan Nakley, a special issue of the *Chaucer Review* 59.3 (2024)

"Sin," in *The Routledge Companion to Global Chaucer*, ed. Craig E. Bertolet and Susan Nakley (New York and London: Routledge, 2025), 426–36.

INDEX

abbreviationes in florilegia, 105
absolute token frequencies of borrowed suffixes, 51–5
Adonis, 227
adultery in *Le Morte Darthur* (Malory), 117–18, 124, 138
Aeneas, 225 n.27, 230, 234, 235
Aeneid (Virgil), 9, 216, 217, 225
Aesop, 107, 108
aesthetics, social, 183
affect
    and assembly terms, 83–7, 90
    and connotation, 73
    and mattering of language, 19
    and pleasure, 28, 29, 30
    scholarly interest in, 16–19, 28–9
    and surface reading, 4, 28, 29, 30
affective reading, 4, 28, 29, 30
agency, 11, 74, 165, 187, 210–11
aging and *The Reeve's Tale* (Chaucer), 149–51, 155
Aleyn (*The Reeve's Tale*), 152–4, 157–8, 161–4
Algarsif (*The Squire's Tale* [Lane]), 194, 196, 200–1, 203–6, 208–10, 211, 214
allegory
    and borrowed suffixes, 49
    and *The Tale of Melibee*, 36, 96, 98, 111–12, 114–16
Allen, Hope Emily, 30
aloe, 221–2, 223, 229
"An Elegie vpon the Death of the high and renowned Princesse our late Soueraigne Elizabeth" (Lane), 193–4
angels, 175, 176, 186, 187
animals
    birds, 174, 207, 213–14
    and predevelopment stages, 174 n.15
    and soul in flight imagery, 174
Anne of Denmark, 198
Antenor (*Troilus and Criseyde*), 219, 226, 235–6
antonyms and borrowed suffixes, 66
apparaillen term, 110
Arcite (*The Knight's Tale*), 188
arrow imagery, 185
Arthur (*Le Morte Darthur*), instability of, 128, 135
artificial intelligence, 81, 89
assembly and congregation terms
    as assemblages themselves, 89
    in Chaucer, 73–4, 87–90
    and connotation and context, 74–7, 80–9
    overview of, 34–5, 73–4
    qualitative approaches to, 82–90
    quantitative approaches to, 80–2, 89
    semantic field analysis, 78–80
    table of occurrences, 91–2
Auerbach, Erich, 32
Augustine, St, 182 n.31
authentication, 170–2, 173–4, 176–80, 183, 188–9
authority
    in *Canterbury Tales*, 12–13, 186, 210–11
    female, 12–13
    and readers, 13
Avennere (*Barlam and Iosaphat*), 121, 128, 130, 132, 136–7, 138
Ayenbite of Inwit, 50

Baayen, Harald, 51
Bagdemagus (*Le Morte Darthur*), 131–2
Bailey, Harry (*Canterbury Tales*), 114–15, 157

INDEX

Balin's sword, 131
Barlam (*Barlam and Iosaphat*), 121, 126, 127, 128–30, 131, 132, 137
Barlam and Iosaphat
   ascetic *vs.* lay Christianity in, 36, 117–21, 126, 127, 128–35, 138–9
   and instability of world, 36, 117, 120–1, 124, 126, 127, 132, 138
   links with *Le Morte Darthur*, 117, 119, 122, 138–9
   mourning in, 136–7
   overview of, 36, 117–21
   plot, 121
   textual history and dissemination of, 121–2, 138
Barthes, Roland, 75
Basilikon Doron (James I), 196
Bedivere (*Le Morte Darthur*), 135
Benveniste, Émile, 4
Best, Stephen, 20, 28
betrayal in *Troilus and Criseyde* (Chaucer), 16, 216, 219, 241, 242
birds, 174, 207, 213–14
bitterness
   in *Troilus and Criseyde*, 220–5, 226, 227–30
   and writing, 222–3
Black Lives Matter, 90
black magic *see* magic
Blamires, Alcuin, 146 n.8, 156–7
Bloomfield, Leonard, 32–3, 75
Boccaccio, Giovanni, 188 n.42, 224, 234 n.48
Bodin, Jean, 204
Boece (Chaucer), 103 n.27
Bolling, George Melville, 33
Book of Margery Kempe (Allen), 30
Books of Hours, 174–5
Bors (*Le Morte Darthur*)
   and demons, 120
   return to secular world, 121, 126–7, 129, 136, 138
   and sex, 133, 134
   and stability, 118, 128
Bradwardine, Thomas, 176 n.19
breath and soul in flight imagery, 174 n.14
Brembre, Nicholas, 83, 90
Britland, Karen, 214
Buddha, life of *see Barlam and Iosaphat*
Burnley, David, 42, 46–7, 71

Camballo (*The Squire's Tale* [Lane]), 194, 203
Cambuscan (*The Squire's Tale* [Lane])
   as Gengis Khan, 37
   and mercy, 204, 205, 206
   and royal personage, 197, 198, 208
   and treason, 194, 211, 212, 214–15
Canace (*The Squire's Tale* [Lane])
   and magic, 200, 206, 207–8, 209, 213
   and mercy, 204, 205
   and prudence, 193–4, 198, 206–14
   and treason and royal personage, 193, 194, 196, 198, 200, 201, 203, 213
Canterbury Tales (Chaucer) *see under* Chaucer; *specific Tales and characters*
Cassiodorus, 96 n.2
catabasis, 234
catalogues, 106
Catesby, Robert, 202
Caxton, William, 122
Chang, Ku-ming Kevin, 22, 23
Charles I, 214, 215
Chaucer, Geoffrey
   and assembly terms, 73–4, 87–90
   Boece, 103 n.27
   borrowed suffixes, 42, 43, 45–50, 53–68, 70–2
   Canterbury Tales
      and audience, 16–17, 171–2
      borrowed suffixes in, 42, 45–50, 53–68, 70–2
      end rhymes in, 60–3, 65
      Ovid's influence on, 12–13, 108, 218
      quiting, 147, 154 n.25, 157, 159, 160, 162, 164, 166
      and transcendence, 170–1
      and translanguaging, 47–8
      see also *specific Tales and characters*
   Canterbury Tales General Prologue
      and allegory, 112
      and authorial intention, 97, 99
      and compilation, 101 n.19
      and end rhymes, 65
      and Man of Law, 159, 173
      and Parson, 173
      and Reeve, 144, 145, 146–51, 154, 155, 157, 158–9
      and soul in flight, 173
      and *The Tale of Melibee*, 114
      and Wife of Bath, 65, 101 n.19

INDEX

247

The House of Fame, 106–7
in overview, 4, 5–17
rhyme scheme experimentation, 60
and role of poetry, 5–6, 231 n.42
Troilus and Criseyde
allusion in, 6–7
and authentication, 171
and betrayal, 16, 216, 219, 241, 242
bitterness in, 220–5, 226, 227–30
and community obligations, 37,
216–19, 220–1, 229, 230–42
female subjectivity in, 11–12
and incest, 37, 217, 218, 230–40
instability of language in, 7–9
as reaction to Dante, 6–8
tense in, 6–7
and tree proverbs and imagery, 9,
37, 225–9, 232, 237
and weeping, 217, 220–5, 226–30,
242
see also Myrrha allusion in *Troilus
and Criseyde* (Chaucer)
Cherewatuk, Karen, 122
children and soul in flight imagery, 174,
175, 185
Christianity
and assembly terms, 85–7, 89
borrowed suffixes and Christian
discourse, 57, 59–60, 65, 71
critique of Church in *The Reeve's Tale*,
152
Le Morte Darthur as Christian text,
119–20, 123–4
Christianity, ascetic *vs.* lay
in *Barlam and Iosaphat*, 36, 117–21,
126, 127, 128–35, 138–9
and dangers of renunciation, 131–5
in *Le Morte Darthur*, 36, 117–21,
123–4, 126–8, 129, 131–5, 138–9
movement between in *Barlam and
Iosaphat*, 121, 128–30
renunciation as prestigious, 118–21
Cicero, 108–10, 111, 116
class
and *-age* suffix, 59, 60
and the Miller, 143–4
in *The Reeve's Tale*, 10, 36–7, 143–6,
167–8
in *The Summoner's Tale*, 179 n.26
in *The Tale of Melibee*, 14
see also status
The Clerk's Tale (Chaucer), 15

close reading, 27
clothing, 129–30, 138
code-switching
and borrowed suffixes, 34, 42, 43,
47–9, 60, 65, 71–2
vs. translanguaging, 47
cognitive processes discourse and
borrowed suffixes, 59, 60, 71
Coke, Edward, 203–4
collectivity discourse and borrowed
suffixes, 58 *see also* assembly and
congregation terms
collocational analysis, 80–1, 88–9
colonialism and philology, 23, 24
community
obligations in *Troilus and Criseyde*, 37,
216–19, 220–1, 229, 230–42
and pity, 228, 240–1
readers as, 228
as theme in Middle English literature,
37–8
compilation, 101, 102–3, 115
concordances and lexical analysis, 81, 89
Confessio Amantis (Gower), 10, 42, 50,
53–69, 70, 71, 72
congregacioun term, 78, 79, 82, 83, 84,
87–90
congregation terms *see* assembly and
congregation terms
connotation
and assembly terms, 73, 74–7, 80–9
shifts in, 77, 89–90
as term, 73, 75
context
and frequency, 87
local, 87
quantitative approaches to, 80–2, 89
contrition and myrrh, 224
conventicle term, 78, 79, 83–6, 90
Corpus of Middle English Prose and Verse
and assembly terms, 79–80, 84, 91–2
as tool, 13
couplets and borrowed suffixes, 42, 45,
60, 67–9, 70
Criseyde (*Troilus and Criseyde*)
and betrayal, 16, 216, 219, 241, 242
and community obligations, 37, 216–19,
220–1, 229, 230–42
Culler, Jonathan, 27
curious, as term, 181–2
Cursor mundi, 50
custume/volume rhyme, 12

248 INDEX

Dante
  arrow imagery in, 185
  female subjectivity in, 11
  and lexical pairs, 12
  and Myrrha story, 225, 230 n.39
  and role of poetry, 5–6, 231 n.42
  transcendence in, 170–1
  Troilus and Criseyde as reaction to,
    6–9
De Officiis (Cicero), 108–10, 111, 116
death
  in *Canterbury Tales*, 181–6, 188, 189
  Myrrha as neither living nor dead, 227,
    233–4, 241
  quasi-death in *Troilus and Criseyde*,
    233–5
  see also soul in flight
decomposability and borrowed suffixes,
    34, 42, 43, 45–6, 55–7, 70
Decretals, 103, 109
Deleuze, Gilles, 143, 145 n.7, 148–9, 153,
    156–7, 166–7
Demonology (James I), 199
demons in *Le Morte Darthur* (Malory),
    120, 130, 134
denotation, 73, 75
density, lexical, 55–7, 70
derivations
  diversity of types, 42, 43, 56, 69–70
  frequency of, 46, 52–3, 69
  and learning, 52–3
  motivations for, 43–4, 63–7, 70–1
  see also suffixes, borrowing of
Derrida, Jacques, 228 n.34
description and philology, 29, 30
devil
  and James I, 200
  in *Le Morte Darthur*, 134
  Reeve as devilish, 143 n.2, 155, 156
  and soul in flight imagery, 175
  in *The Squire's Tale* (Lane), 209
dialogue
  and *Liber consolationis et consilii*, 96
    n.3
  and *The Tale of Melibee*, 96, 100, 114
  and *Troilus and Criseyde*, 7
Dialogues (Gregory I), 177, 178, 179
dicta in florilegia, 105
Dinshaw, Caroline, 30, 230 n.38, 240
Disciplina Clericalis, 103
discourses and borrowed suffixes, 41,
    43–4, 47, 52, 57–60, 65, 71, 72

distant reading, 13–14, 27, 35
Divine Comedy (Dante), 6–7, 9, 11, 170–1,
    185
Docking, Thomas, 175–6
doublets, 14, 15, 74, 77, 90, 97, 100

economics
  economic power in *The Reeve's Tale*,
    157–8, 160, 166
  and Friar (*The Summoner's Tale*),
    178–80
  and Trentals, 178–9
Edward VI, 198, 215
Elizabeth I, 37, 193–4, 197–8
end rhymes and borrowed suffixes, 34, 41,
    43–4, 45–6, 60–72
enticing speech, 210
enunciation, subject of, 157 n.35
Episcopi, 199
esement term, 157–8, 164, 165, 169
espace term, 100–1
Ethelta (*The Squire's Tale* [Lane]), 194,
    201, 208, 210, 211, 212
ethics
  and economic success, 157 n.34
  and fraud, 177–81
  and hastiness, 100–3
  and integrity, 15
  and proverbs, 108–16
  in *The Reeve's Tale*, 157 n.34
  in *The Summoner's Tale*, 177–81
  in *The Tale of Melibee*, 100–3, 104–6,
    108–16
Everyman, 122
exempla in florilegia, 105
exile
  of Myrrha, 228, 230
  in *The Squire's Tale* (Lane), 205
  in *Troilus and Criseyde*, 216, 217, 234,
    239
  in Virgil, 217

fabliaux, 152–4, 159, 162, 164, 182
face
  and faciality, 145 n.7, 166–8
  of king in Gower, 15
falcons, 207, 213
farts, 180–1
Fawkes, Guy *see* Gunpowder Plot
Fein, Susanna, 156
feminine rhyme, 44
fight in *The Reeve's Tale*, 152–4, 161–2

INDEX

Fisher, John, 50–1
flâneurs, 168 n.59
florilegial form
    and *Liber consolationis et consilii*, 99
    organization and structure, 112–13
    and *The Tale of Melibee*, 36, 97–108,
        112
Foucault, Michel, 75
Fox, Denton, 54
fraud, 177–81
Friar (*The Summoner's Tale*), 177–81, 186,
    188, 189
The Friar's Tale (Chaucer), 45
Furnivall, Frederick, 193, 195

Galahad (*Le Morte Darthur*)
    death of, 129
    and instability, 118, 120, 124 n.23,
        126–7
    as King of Sarras, 130
    renunciation of secular world, 126–7,
        131, 132, 138
gall, 220, 221, 222, 223, 226, 229
gathering terms *see* assembly and
    congregation terms
Gawain (*Le Morte Darthur*), 131, 132
gender
    and community obligations in *Troilus
        and Criseyde*, 217, 218, 219, 231,
        239, 242
    masculinity and obscene storytelling,
        158 n.39
    prudence as feminine aristocratic
        virtue, 207, 208
    as scholarship area, 10–13
    see also masculinity; women
Gengis Khan *see* Cambuskan (*The
    Squire's Tale*)
geography
    of displacement, 148–9, 169 n.63
    and the Reeve, 10, 144, 145, 146, 155
    resonance and space, 147–50
gliding and soul in flight, 176–7
Golden Legende, 122
Golden Speech (Elizabeth I), 197 n.15, 212
    n.54
Gower, John
    and *Barlam and Iosaphat*, 122
    and borrowed suffixes, 42, 43, 50,
        53–69, 70, 71, 72
    influence on *The Clerk's Tale*, 15
    rhyme in, 15, 60–3

and stability, 6
and wordplay, 152
grace, 137
Gregory I, 177, 178, 179, 181
Guattari, Felix, 143, 145 n.7, 148–9, 153,
    156–7, 166–7
Guenevere (*Le Morte Darthur*), 126,
    135–6, 137, 138
Gunpowder Plot, 194, 200–4
Gurd, Sean, 29

hagiography
    and *Le Morte Darthur*, 122–3, 138
    and *The Second Nun's Tale*, 176, 177,
        178, 186
hard-heartedness, 228, 238, 242
Harpham, Geoffrey Galt, 20, 24–5, 27,
    28, 29
hastiness in *The Tale of Melibee*, 97–8,
    100–3, 111
Hector (*Troilus and Criseyde*), 235–6
Helen, 236, 240
Henrietta Maria of France (Queen), 214,
    215
Henry VI, 85
Henry VIII, 198
Heroides (Ovid), 222
Hilton, Walter, 125
Historical Thesaurus of English, 74, 78
Hoccleve, Thomas, 42, 43, 50–1, 53–63,
    66–7, 71
homunculus, 174–5
Horbello (*The Squire's Tale* [Lane]), 194,
    206
Horologium Sapientiae (Suso), 181
hospitality, 228 n.34
The House of Fame (Chaucer), 106–7

Il Filostrato (Boccaccio), 188 n.42, 224,
    234 n.48
images
    and fear, 188–9
    of soul in flight, 37, 172–7
    ubiquity of in late medieval culture,
        172–3, 175
imperialism and philology, 23, 24
impotence, 146, 165, 166
incest, 37, 217, 218, 230–40
indexing of collections, 113
inertia, 168
Inferno (Dante), 6–7, 185
instability *see* stability/instability

intuition, speaker, 76, 77, 81
invisibility *see* visibility and invisibility
Iosaphat, St, 121 see also *Barlam and Iosaphat*

Jakobson, Roman, 5
James I, 194, 195–200, 201–4, 215
Jankyn (*Canterbury Tales*), 115
January (*The Merchant's Tale*), 181–6
John (*The Miller's Tale*), 159
John (*The Reeve's Tale*), 161
John of Damascus, 121
Johnson, Barbara, 27, 31
Journal of English and Germanic Philology, 25, 26
Justinus (*The Merchant's Tale*), 182–6

Karcevskij, Sergei, 5
Kempe, Margery, 30
Kennedy, Edward Donald, 123 n.17, 126, 127, 135
keywords in context (KWIC) and collocational analysis, 81
The Knight's Tale (Chaucer), 188

Lane, John
    background, 193
    "An Elegie vpon the Death of the high and renowned Princesse our late Soueraigne Elizabeth", 193–4
    see also *The Squire's Tale* (Lane)
language
    and enticing speech, 210
    as mattering, 3, 17, 19, 31
    and reason in *The Reeve's Tale*, 156–65
    skills in *The Reeve's Tale*, 36–7, 145, 146–54, 156, 168–9
    stability/instability of, 6–9, 16, 119
Launcelot (*Le Morte Darthur*), 117–21, 124–8, 129, 130–1, 133, 134–8
law
    and assembly terms, 83–4, 88–9
    borrowed suffixes and legal discourse, 58, 59, 72
    esement term, 158
    and treason, 194, 195–204, 210, 215
Le Morte Darthur (Malory)
    ascetic *vs.* lay Christianity in, 36, 117–21, 123–4, 126–8, 129, 131–5, 138–9
    as Christian text, 119–20, 123–4

instability of people in, 117–19, 120–1, 124–8, 130, 135, 136
instability of world in, 36, 117, 120, 124–8, 138
links with *Barlam and Iosaphat*, 117, 119, 122, 138–9
overview of, 36, 117–21
as secular text, 122–4
Lee, Sidney, 195
Legenda Aurea, 122
lexical fields
    assembly terms analysis, 78–80
    and borrowed suffixes, 42
    defined, 75
    scholarly approaches to, 75–6
lexical pairs, 12
lexical semantics
    and assembly terms, 74, 78–80
    scholarly approaches to, 74–7
Liber consolationis et consilii (Albertanus of Brescia)
    motivation for, 114–15
    organization of text, 112–13
    proverbs in, 95, 98–104, 106–8, 109–11
    as *The Tale of Melibee* source, 95, 109–11
likeness in *Troilus and Criseyde* (Chaucer), 218, 229, 237, 238, 239, 241, 242
The Linguistic Atlas of Late Medieval English, 13
linguistics
    availability of resources, 13–14
    and imaginative literature, 19–20, 31–6
    influence of philology on, 3, 20, 21, 31–6
    relationship to literary studies, 3, 4, 20, 32, 33
    as separate from philology, 21, 32–3
lists, 106
literary studies
    and connotation, 75
    influence of philology on, 3, 20, 21, 26–7, 31–6
    linguistics and imaginative literature, 19–20, 31–6
    as separate from philology, 24
    and sociolinguistics, 3, 4, 20, 32, 33
Livre de Melibée et de Dame Prudence (Renaud de Louens), 95, 100–5, 111, 112 n.55, 115 n.64
Lollards, 85, 90

INDEX 251

Lydgate, John, 42, 43, 50–1, 53–64, 66, 70, 71

machine learning, 81
magic
    and James I, 198–200, 209
    The Squire's Tale (Lane), 37, 194, 200, 201, 206, 207–8, 209–10, 213
Mahoney, Dhira, 123, 129
Malory, Thomas see *Le Morte Darthur* (Malory)
Malyne (*The Reeve's Tale*), 151–2, 162–4
Man of Law (*Canterbury Tales*), 159
The Man of Law (Chaucer), 159, 168
Mann, Jill, 11, 106 n.34, 234 n.48, 235 n.49
Marcus, Sharon, 20, 28
Marcus Tullius Cicero, 108–10, 111, 116
marriage
    in *Barlam and Iosaphat*, 133
    and borrowed suffixes, 65, 68
    in *Canterbury Tales*, 151–2, 181–5, 186
    in *Le Morte Darthur*, 134, 136
Mary I, 198
masculinity
    and obscene storytelling, 158 n.39
    and suffering in *Troilus and Criseyde*, 220 n.11
    women as weapons/tools for, 162 n.46
The Master of Game by Edward, Second Duke of York, 83
Maximus (*The Second Nun's Tale*), 173, 176–8, 186–8
McGann, Jerome, 23
Measure for Measure (Shakespeare), 204
The Merchant of Venice (Shakespeare), 122
The Merchant's Tale (Chaucer)
    and audience, 6, 16–17
    links to *The Wife of Bath's Tale*, 185–6
    and soul in flight, 37, 172, 181–6
mercy, 204, 205, 206, 212
metadiscursive commentary and assembly terms, 82
Metamorphoses (Ovid) *see* Myrrha allusion in *Troilus and Criseyde* (Chaucer)
metamorphosis, 226–7, 232
Midas story in *The Wife of Bath's Tale*, 12–13
Middle English Dictionary, 9 n.14, 13, 78–80, 82–7, 91–2

Mill, John Stuart, 75
Miller (*Canterbury Tales*)
    as antagonist in *The Reeve's Tale*, 147, 157–60, 162, 164, 166
    and class, 143–4
    see also Symkyn (miller in *The Reeve's Tale*)
misreading
    and soul in flight, 183
    and women, 12–13
Modern Philology, 25
The Monk's Tale (Chaucer), 95 n.1, 97, 114
morality
    and Chaucer's reaction to Dante, 6–8
    and economic success in *The Reeve's Tale*, 157 n.34
    see also ethics
Moten, Fred, 145 n.7, 148, 151 nn.20–1, 169 n.63
mourning, 136–7
Mukařovský, Jan, 5
multilingualism
    and borrowed suffixes, 34, 41, 42, 47–9
    and competence, 71
multiplicity and fabliaux, 153–4, 162
munus (social debt), 242 n.62
myrrh, 37, 223–4
Myrrha allusion in *Troilus and Criseyde* (Chaucer)
    and bitterness, 220–5, 226, 227–30
    and exile, 228, 230
    and incest, 37, 217, 218, 230–40
    Myrrha as neither living nor dead, 227, 233–4, 241
    overview, 37, 217–19
    tree proverbs and imagery, 9, 37, 225–9, 232
    and weeping, 220–30, 242

Nacien (*Le Morte Darthur*), 117–18, 120, 124, 125, 126, 136
nationalism and philology, 23, 26, 32
Natural Language Processing, 81
naturalization and borrowed suffixes, 42, 46–9, 60, 65, 71
neologisms and borrowed suffixes, 46
new formalism, 18
North Berwick affair, 198, 199, 200
Northern Homily Cycle, 122
Nun's Priest's Tale, 176 n.19
nyfles term, 180, 185
Nyneve (*Le Morte Darthur*), 134

Orpheus (*Metamorphoses*), 217, 227,
    233–4, 241
Oswald *see* Reeve (*The Reeve's Tale*)
overcome term, 116
overlapping terms, 75, 77
Ovid
    influence on *Canterbury Tales*, 12–13,
        108, 218
    and suffering of writing, 222
    see also Myrrha allusion in *Troilus and
        Criseyde* (Chaucer)

Palomides (*Le Morte Darthur*), 124 n.23,
    134
Pandarus (*Troilus and Criseyde*)
    and desire, 241
    and incest, 230 n.38
    proverbs and sayings, 7, 98, 220,
        225–6
    and swooning, 237
    and sympathy, 231
Pardoner (*Canterbury Tales*), 157 n.34
Parson (*The Parson's Tale*), 152, 173
The Parson's Tale (Chaucer), 97 n.6, 152
Patterson, Lee, 96
Pearl, 46, 60–1
Peasants' Revolt, 73, 90
Pelleas (*Le Morte Darthur*), 134
penance, 132–3
Perceval (*Le Morte Darthur*), 118
Petrus Alphonsus, 103
petty treason, 195
Phillips, Edward, 193 n.3, 195
philology
    and amateur critique, 19, 29–30
    definitions, 32
    and distant reading, 27
    and historicisim, 6, 7, 9–11, 13, 14, 17,
        25–6, 31
    influence on linguistics, 3, 20, 21, 31–6
    influence on literary studies, 3, 20, 21,
        26–7, 31–6
    in journal titles, 25–6
    and mattering of language, 3, 17, 31
    as methodology *vs.* discipline, 21, 23–7
    and nationalism, 23, 26, 32
    overview of Taylor's scholarship, 3–17,
        18
    as racist and imperialist, 23, 24
    resources available, 13–14
    "return" of, 20–7
    and self-critique, 17, 27

and surface reading, 4, 6, 16, 20, 21,
    27–31
as term, 3–4, 21–3, 25–6
pity in *Troilus and Criseyde* (Chaucer),
    218, 221, 228–9, 231, 240–1, 242
Placebo (*The Merchant's Tale*), 182–6
pleasure
    and pattern recognition, 31 n.38
    and reader, 19, 28, 29, 30
poetry
    Dante *vs.* Chaucer and role of poetry,
        5–6, 231 n.42
    and linguistics, 41
    and stability, 6–9
    see also rhyme
Pollock, Sheldon, 22, 23
positional placement of borrowed suffixes,
    42, 46, 60–3, 71
post-critique, 19, 27–31, 32
praecepta in florilegia, 105
Prague School, 5
Prioress (*Canterbury Tales*), 125
prisoners of war, trading in, 235–6
productivity and borrowed suffixes, 41–3,
    45–6, 51–2, 56, 69
Promptorium Parvulorum, 82
pronouns
    and female subjectivity in *Troilus and
        Criseyde*, 11–12
    and loss of localization in *The Reeve's
        Tale*, 152–3, 154, 161, 162
    plural pronouns in *Troilus and
        Criseyde*, 237
proverbs
    collections of as assemblages, 89
    as common voice, 106
    formats for, 99
    in *Liber consolationis et consilii*, 95,
        98–104, 106–8
    in *Livre de Melibée et de Dame
        Prudence*, 95, 100–5, 111
    and stability, 225, 226
    and textual space, 105, 116
    trees, 9, 37, 225–7
    in *Troilus and Criseyde*, 8, 220, 225–6
proverbs in *The Tale of Melibee*
    and ethics, 108–16
    and florilegial form, 36, 97–108, 112
    overview, 95–8
    visibility and invisibility, 96–7, 101,
        108–16

INDEX

253

prudence
- of Canace in *The Squire's Tale* (Lane), 193–4, 198, 206–14
- early modern concept of, 206–7
- and Elizabeth I, 37
- as feminine aristocratic virtue, 207, 208

Prudence (*The Tale of Melibee*)
- and anger, 208
- and assembly terms, 88–9
- proverbs and advice, 36, 97–8, 103–4, 105, 108–12, 114, 116
- and prudence as feminine virtue, 207, 208
- and *The Squire's Tale* (Lane), 37

Publilius Syrus, 100, 101–2, 104

punctual systems, 156

puns
- in *The Reeve's Tale*, 36–7, 147, 156
- in *The Shipman's Tale*, 14

purgatory, 184, 185–6

quiting, 147, 154 n.25, 157, 159, 160, 162, 164, 166

racism and philology, 23, 24

rape, 158 n.39, 162–4

rashness *see* hastiness in *The Tale of Melibee*

readerly resistance
- to authorial intention, 16
- in Chaucer's response to Dante, 7
- in *The Tale of Melibee*, 115–16
- in *Troilus and Criseyde* (Chaucer), 171

readers
- and attachment, 16
- and authority, 13
- as community, 228
- mismatch, 13
- reader pleasure, 19, 28, 29, 30
- women as misreaders in Chaucer, 12–13

reading
- affective reading, 4, 28, 29, 30
- against the grain, 6, 19, 28
- close reading, 27
- distant reading, 13–14, 27, 35
- misreading, 12–13, 183
- practices in Chaucer, 37, 172, 186, 189
- reparative reading, 19, 28, 31, 35
- slow reading, 13, 29
- and soul in flight imagery, 37, 173, 189

suspicious reading, 4, 6, 28
- and weeping, 224
- *see also* surface reading

reason see *reson* term

Reeve (*The Reeve's Tale*)
- and class, 10, 143–6
- and dialect, 143 n.2, 144
- dislike of, 143–5, 146, 155, 160
- impotence of, 146, 165, 166
- language skills, 36–7, 145, 146–54, 156, 165, 168–9
- as Northerner, 10, 143 n.2, 144
- as sacrifice or scapegoat, 146, 146 n.8, 165–9
- and winning, 155, 158, 165–6

The Reeve's Tale (Chaucer)
- class in, 10, 36–7, 143–4, 167–8
- dislike of, 165
- fight in, 152–4, 161–2
- overview, 36–7, 143–6
- quiting, 154 n.25, 157, 159, 160, 162, 164, 166
- resonance and language skills, 36–7, 145, 146–54, 156–65, 166, 168–9
- and rigidity, 155–65
- and status, 145, 151–2, 154, 155–69
- as tragedy, 36–7, 143–6, 151–2, 154, 155–69

Regement of Princes (Hoccleve), 42, 43, 50–1, 53–63, 66–7, 71

religion
- and assembly terms, 85–7, 89
- borrowed suffixes and religious discourse, 57, 59–60, 65, 71
- critique in *The Reeve's Tale*, 152

Renaud de Louens, 95, 100–5, 111

reparative reading, 19, 28, 31, 35

resistance
- and Myrrha, 227
- in *The Reeve's Tale*, 148, 150–2, 154, 156, 164, 166, 167–8
- and resonance, 148, 150, 151 n.20, 156, 164
- and skepticism in *Troilus and Criseyde*, 171
- *see also* readerly resistance

Reson and Sensuallyte (Lydgate), 42, 43, 50–1, 53–64, 66, 70, 71

reson term
- and *The Reeve's Tale*, 36–7, 146–54, 164–5
- and *The Tale of Melibee*, 104–6, 116

254   INDEX

resonance
   and assembly terms, 73, 83–4, 86–7,
      89
   and *The Reeve's Tale*, 36–7, 146–54,
      156–65, 166, 168
rhyme
   and borrowed suffixes, 34, 41, 42,
      43–4, 45–6, 60–72
   double/feminine, 44
   in Gower, 15
   rhyme royal, 60, 217
   single/masculine, 44
rhyme royal, 60, 217
Rolle, Richard, 125
Romance lexemes, 49
royal personage
   of Elizabeth I, 212–13
   of James I, 209
   as mysterious, 208
   in *The Squire's Tale* (Lane), 196, 197,
      198, 203, 207–14
   and treason, 195–200, 203, 207–14
Rubin, Gayle, 235
rubrics, 113
rugs, 14

sacrifice in *The Reeve's Tale*, 146, 165–9
Said, Edward, 29
scientific discourse and borrowed suffixes,
   59, 72
The Second Nun's Tale (Chaucer), 37, 172,
   173, 176–8, 186–8
seduction
   in *Barlam and Iosaphat*, 133–4
   in *Le Morte Darthur*, 133–4
   in *The Summoner's Tale*, 180–1
   and treason in Gunpowder Plot, 201–3
   and treason in *The Squire's Tale*
      (Lane), 200–1, 203–6, 210, 215
self-critique, 17, 27
semantic analysis
   and qualitative analysis, 82–9
   quantitative approaches to, 80–2, 89
sententiae
   and assemblages, 89
   and *The Tale of Melibee*, 98, 100–5,
      107, 111, 113–14
sentiment analysis
   and connotation context analysis, 81–2
   and intuition, 76, 77, 81
   limits of, 87
serement term, 10

sex
   in *Barlam and Iosaphat*, 133
   female sexual morality and Dante, 8
   female sexuality and Wife of Bath
      (character), 65
   in *Le Morte Darthur*, 133–4
   in *The Merchant's Tale*, 182–3, 185
Shakespeare, William, 122, 204
Ship of Faith, 132
The Shipman's Tale (Chaucer), 14
silence in *The Reeve's Tale*, 161–4
sin and instability, 117–19, 120, 125
slow reading, 13, 29
social aesthetics, 183
sociality and puns, 14
sociolinguistics
   defined, 19
   and imaginative literature in, 19–20,
      31–6
   philology's influence on, 3, 20, 21,
      31–6
   relationship to literary studies, 3, 4, 20,
      32, 33
Somme le Roi (Laurent), 182
soul in flight
   images and iconography, 37, 172–7
   in *The Merchant's Tale*, 37, 172, 181–6
   in *The Second Nun's Tale*, 37, 172, 173,
      176–8, 186–8
   in *The Summoner's Tale*, 37, 172,
      178–81
souls
   battle for, 175
   Gregory I on state of post-mortem, 177,
      178, 179
   saving souls *vs.* lives, 134, 138
South English Legendary, 122
space
   physical space in *The Reeve's Tale*,
      160–1
   and resonance, 147–50
   textual space and proverbs, 105, 116
speech
   Elizabeth I and speeches, 197 n.15,
      212–13
   enticing speech, 210
Speech to the Troops at Tillbury
   (Elizabeth I), 212–13
The Squire's Tale (Chaucer), 37, 193
The Squire's Tale (Lane)
   and magic, 37, 194, 200, 201, 206,
      207–8, 209–10, 213

INDEX

and mercy, 204, 205, 206, 212
plot, 194
reactions to, 195
royal personage in, 196, 197, 198, 203,
    207–14
and *The Tale of Melibee*, 37, 103, 193,
    194, 204, 211, 212
and treason, 37, 193, 200–1, 203–6,
    209–11, 214–15
stability/instability
    instability of people in *Le Morte
        Darthur*, 117–19, 120–1, 124–8,
        130, 136
    instability of world in *Barlam and
        Iosaphat*, 36, 117, 120–1, 124,
        126, 127, 132–3, 138
    instability of world in *Le Morte
        Darthur*, 36, 117, 120, 124–8, 138
    of language, 6–9, 16, 119
    and poetry, 6–9
    and proverbs, 225, 226
    and sin, 117–19, 120, 125
    and status in *The Reeve's Tale*, 167–8
    unstable as term, 120–1
status
    and *-age* suffix, 59, 60
    and borrowed suffixes, 71
    and community obligations in *Troilus
        and Criseyde*, 218, 219, 231
    and connotations about stigmatized
        people, 77
    and *The Reeve's Tale*, 145, 151–2, 154,
        155–69
    see also class
storytelling
    and audience, 6, 16–17
    masculinity and obscene storytelling,
        158 n.39
suffering
    and purgatory, 184
    in *Troilus and Criseyde*, 220 n.11,
        239–40
    and writing, 222–3
suffixes, borrowing of
    and analyzability, 67–9, 70, 72
    and decomposability, 34, 42, 43, 45–6,
        55–7, 70
    and discourses, 41, 43–4, 47, 52,
        57–60, 65, 71, 72
    and lexical density, 55–7, 70
    motivations for, 42–4, 63–7, 70–1
    and multilingualism and

translanguaging, 34, 41, 42, 43,
    47–9, 60, 71–2
and naturalization, 42, 46–9, 60, 65, 71
overview of, 34, 41–3
and positional occurrence, 42, 46,
    60–3, 71
and productivity, 41–3, 45–6, 51–2,
    56, 69
and salience, 42, 45, 64, 65, 67–9, 70
scholarship on, 49–51
and study methodology, 42, 51
and token counts, 42, 51–5, 69
and transparency, 42, 46, 55, 56, 57,
    69, 72
Summa logicae (William of Ockham), 75
The Summoner's Tale (Chaucer), 37, 173,
    177–81, 186
surface reading
    and affective reading, 4, 28, 29, 30
    and amateur critique, 29–30
    and authority, 13
    defined, 18–19
    as philological method, 4, 6, 16, 20,
        21, 27–31
    and sociolinguistics, 35
    vs. suspicious reading, 4, 28
Suso, Henry, 181
suspicion and assembly terms, 83–7, 90
suspicious reading, 4, 6, 28
swiving, 162–3
swooning in *Troilus and Criseyde*
    (Chaucer), 233–5, 237
Symkyn (miller in *The Reeve's Tale*),
    152–4, 155, 157, 161–2
Symkyn's wife (*Canterbury Tales*), 152,
    153
sympathy in *Troilus and Criseyde*
    (Chaucer), 218, 231–2, 235, 238
synonyms
    defined, 75
    and end rhymes with borrowed
        suffixes, 66–7

The Tale of Melibee (Chaucer)
    and agency, 74, 210–11
    and anger, 208
    and assembly terms, 73–4, 87–90
    doublets in, 14, 15, 74, 90, 97, 100
    and English lexical forms, 108–9
    and enticing speech, 210
    hastiness in, 97–8, 100–3, 111

256 INDEX

placement in *Canterbury Tales*, 95, 99, 114
and prudence as feminine aristocratic virtue, 207, 208
and *The Squire's Tale* (Lane), 37, 103, 193, 194, 204, 211, 212
structure of, 99
see also proverbs in *The Tale of Melibee*
Taylor, Karla
  on assembly terms, 73–4
  on authentication, 170–2
  on communicating unshared experience, 173
  on death and *Canterbury Tales*, 189
  on domain of poetry, 231 n.42
  on doublets, 14, 15, 74, 90, 97
  on end rhymes, 63–4
  on inertia, 168
  and language as mattering, 3, 17
  on language as tool to understand past, 119
  on *Middle English Dictionary*, 9 n.14
  on Ovid's influence on Chaucer, 218
  on Pandarus (*Troilus and Criseyde*), 241
  and philology as term, 3–4
  on proverbs, 8, 9, 225
  reading emphasis of, 171–2
  on *The Reeve's Tale*, 144
  scholarly overview of, 3–17, 18
  on social aesthetics, 183
  and sociolinguistics, 20
  and *The Tale of Melibee*, 14, 15, 74, 90, 97, 193
  on *Troilus and Criseyde*, 219, 241
  works
    Chaucer Reads 'The Divine Comedy', 4, 5, 6–9, 170–2, 225
    "Chaucer's Reticent Merchant", 16
    "Chaucer's Uncommon Voice", 10
    "Chaucer's Volumes", 12
    "Inside Out in Gower's Republic of Letters", 10
    "Language in Use", 10
    "Social Aesthetics", 14, 15, 97 n.7
tears *see* weeping
tense, 6–7, 170
textiles, 14
Thomas Aquinas, 199
tidings, 106, 107

token counts and borrowed suffixes, 42, 51–5, 69
tragedy, *The Reeve's Tale* (Chaucer) as, 36–7, 143–6, 151–2, 154, 155–69
transcendence, 170–1, 172
translanguaging and borrowed suffixes, 34, 42, 43, 47–9, 60, 71–2
translation, close, 103 n.27
transparency and borrowed suffixes, 42, 46, 55, 56, 57, 69, 72
treason
  and Gunpowder Plot, 194, 200–4
  and James I, 195–200, 201–4, 209, 215
  law, 194, 195–204, 210, 215
  petty, 195
  and royal personage, 195–200, 203, 207–14
  and seduction, 200–6, 210, 215
  and *The Squire's Tale* (Lane), 37, 193, 201–6, 209–11, 214–15
  and witchcraft, 37, 198–200
Treason Acts, 196 n.10, 198
trees proverbs and imagery
  in *Aeneid*, 9, 225, 232
  in *Troilus and Criseyde*, 9, 37, 225–30, 232, 237
Trentals, 177, 178–9, 180
The Trials of Guy Fawkes, 200–4
Troilus (*Troilus and Criseyde*)
  and death, 220, 227, 233, 234–5
  and grief, 224, 230, 233, 241
  and language, 7, 8
  and Pandarus, 217, 237
  and silence, 236–7
  swoon, 234 n.48, 237
  and tree imagery, 225–6, 230, 232
Troilus and Criseyde (Chaucer) *see under* Chaucer, Geoffrey
The True Law of Free Monarchies (James I), 196, 197
Turner, James, 23

unicorn, parable of, 129

Variae (Cassiodorus), 96 n.2
vengeance
  and James I, 200
  and *Liber consolationis et consilii*, 114–15
  and *The Reeve's Tale*, 147
  and *The Summoner's Tale*, 204

and *The Tale of Melibee*, 109–12, 114–15, 193
Vidrea (*The Squire's Tale* [Lane]), 194, 200, 205, 206, 209–10
Villiers, George, 214
Virgil see *Aeneid* (Virgil)
visibility and invisibility
    and proverbs in *The Tale of Melibee*, 96–7, 101, 108–16
    and soul in flight, 176, 177, 187
vision
    and authentication in Chaucer, 171, 173–4, 176–80, 183, 188–9
    and conversion, 186–7
    and Docking, 176
    and Gregory I, 177, 181
    and transcendence in Dante, 170–1
visualizations, data, 80
volume/custume rhyme, 12

Walker, Michelle Boulous, 29
Warner, Michael, 29–30
Warren, Michelle, 21, 22
Warren, Nancy Bradley, 11
weeping
    Barlam and Iosaphat, 133, 137, 138
    and Myrrha tale in Ovid, 220–30, 242
    and reading, 224
    in *The Squire's Tale* (Lane), 205, 207, 208, 209
    in *Troilus and Criseyde*, 217, 220–5, 226–30, 242
Wetherbee, Winthrop, 9 n.12, 230 n.38, 231
white magic
    and Barbara Napier, 199
    in *The Squire's Tale* (Lane), 37, 200, 206, 207–8, 209, 210, 213
Wife of Bath (*Canterbury Tales*)
    and female sexuality, 65
    and marriage, 186
    misreading by, 12–13
    and purgatory, 184 n.36, 185–6

The Wife of Bath's Tale (Chaucer)
    and compilation, 101 n.19, 115
    and death, 184 n.36
    and female sexuality, 65
    links with *The Merchant's Tale*, 185–6
    misreading in, 12–13
    and purgatory, 184 n.36, 185–6
William of Auvergne, 199
William of Ockham, 75
Wimsatt, James, 46, 47, 60–1, 62–3, 71
wine cask imagery, 149–51, 152
winning and Reeve, 155, 158, 165–6
Winters, Margaret, 33
witchcraft
    and James I, 198–200, 209
    The Squire's Tale (Lane), 37, 194, 196
    and treason, 37, 198–200
Witchcraft Act of 1604, 200
women
    agency of in *The Tale of Melibee*, 210–11
    and community obligations in *Troilus and Criseyde*, 11–12, 217, 218, 219
    female authority, 12–13
    female sexuality in *Canterbury Tales*, 65
    Lane's interest in women's leadership, 193–4
    as misreaders in Chaucer, 12–13
    prudence as feminine aristocratic virtue, 207, 208
    readers and literary authority, 13
    saving souls of *vs.* sinning in *Barlam and Iosaphat* and *Le Morte Darthur*, 133–4, 138
    traffic in and *Troilus and Criseyde*, 235–42
word clouds, 80
writing and suffering, 222–3
Wycliffite texts
    and assembly terms, 85–6, 90
    and borrowed suffixes, 44

TABULA GRATULATORIA

Elizabeth Allen
Stephen Barney
Candace Barrington
Stephanie L. Batkie
Andreea Boboc
Catherine Brown
Celeste Brusati
Ardis Butterfield
K.P. Clarke
Alison Cornish
Jillian Coronato
Anne Curzan
Rebecca Davis
Susanna Fein
John M. Fyler
John M. Ganim
Tony Gillum
Warren Ginsberg
Sarah Goeppner
Richard Firth Green

Kenneth Hodges
Ashby Kinch
Elon Lang
David Lavinsky
Traugott Lawler
Karla Mallette
Robert J. Meyer-Lee
Peggy McCracken
Colette Moore
Susan Nakley
Christopher Palmer
Catherine Sanok
Michael Schoenfeldt
Elizabeth Sears
R. Allen Shoaf
Melissa X. Stevens
Walter Wadiak
Claire M. Waters
R.F. Yeager